Big Business and
Industrial Conflict in
Nineteenth-Century France

Big Business and Industrial Conflict in Nineteenth-Century France

A Social History
of the Parisian Gas Company

LENARD R. BERLANSTEIN

University of California Press

BERKELEY   LOS ANGELES   OXFORD

HD
9581
F 74
C 663
1991

University of California Press
Berkeley and Los Angeles, California

University of California Press, Ltd.
Oxford, England

Library of Congress Cataloging-in-Publication Data
Berlanstein, Lenard R.
    Big business and industrial conflict in nineteenth-century France:
a social history of the Parisian Gas Company / Lenard R. Berlanstein.
        p.   cm.
    Includes bibliographical references and index.
    ISBN 0-520-07234-0 (alk. paper)
    1. Compagnie parisienne de l'éclairage et du chauffage par le gaz—
History. 2. Gas industry—France—History—19th century. 3. Big
business—France—History—19th century. I. Title.
HD9581.F74C663   1991
363.6'3'094436—dc20   90-47352
                                                                  CIP

Printed in the United States of America
9 8 7 6 5 4 3 2 1

The paper used in this publication meets the minimum requirements
of American National Standard for Information Sciences—Perma-
nence of Paper for Printed Library Materials, ANSI Z39.48–1984. ∞

Contents

Illustrations

Tables

Preface

Students of modern France will find some useful business histories to consult, but they will not find social histories of enterprises. The boundaries between business history and social history are regrettably high. Economic historians focus on the firm's structure and strategies. Labor historians, usually lacking corporate records, examine workers in a particular trade or city. Although the need to study business and labor together to understand either fully might seem self-evident, such work is rarely done. The research on my last book, *The Working People of Paris, 1871–1914*, made me acutely aware of the distortions that might arise from an inability to look at matters from inside the firm. That is why uncovering the rich corporate papers of the Compagnie parisienne de l'éclairage et du chauffage par le gaz—nearly sixteen hundred cartons in the Archives de Paris—was so satisfying. Initial concerns about the representativeness of a public utility proved unnecessary. In fact, a microstudy of the Parisian Gas Company (PGC) raises fundamental questions about the social history of French industrialization.

Founded in 1855, the PGC has to be counted among France's earliest big businesses. A cardinal reason to take an interest in the firm is that it emerged before there were fixed administrative methods or well-grounded expectations about work in a large industrial enterprise. Indeed, the PGC helped establish routines, career routes, and norms. Moreover, its personnel provides a meaningful focus on the social changes that were diffusing through industrial France. Still another reason to study the company is that its managers had to confront powerful efforts to restructure industrial relations on a national scale by the last decade of the nineteenth century. To discern in the PGC an industrializing France writ small makes quite a bit of sense.

This book delineates the emergence of three socio-occupational groups created by capitalistic development, salaried managers, white-collar employees, and industrial laborers. Only the last group has received significant attention. The wage earners at the PGC conformed to a pattern that is rapidly becoming familiar: they evolved from combative peasant-workers into a settled labor force. The implications of this evolution for the labor movement, political behavior, and industrial relations require elucidation. The moment is perhaps propitious to focus anew on industrial workers and the problem of class formation. As I write, the fruits of a generation of "the new labor history" have come under critical scrutiny. The prevailing emphasis on the shop-floor experience suddenly appears a bit passé. Labor history has taken a linguistic turn in some circles, with an analysis of culture displacing a dissection of capitalism. An investigation of the work force in the gas plants offers the opportunity to test the dominant as well as the revisionist claims about class formation.

There is a well-established historiographical context for treating wage earners. The literature on white-collar employees, however, is much thinner, and on managerial personnel it is hardly extant. In this volume I have heeded the call to study middle-class and elite groups, endeavoring to give their careers, material conditions, concerns, and collective action as much attention as social historians conventionally devote to workers. What I have discovered goes far to explain how industrial development in France reinforced, rather than disrupted, some of the most salient features of preindustrial society. At the same time, the PGC exposes the dynamics of a society that was becoming more urban and industrial. It illuminates the emergence of a powerful economic elite, the engineer-managers of large enterprises. It also portrays a new sort of petite bourgeoisie—white-collar clerks caught painfully between conformity and radicalization. The evolution of these groups was as dramatic as that of wage earners.

The PGC's personnel experienced a fundamental break around 1890. Up to then, the firm had been, in fact and in spirit, a private enterprise run on the basis of market calculations. It became far more of a de facto public service, responding to the democratizing policies of the Radical Republic (and its early manifestations in Paris) thereafter. The PGC had to assimilate the consequences of an extraordinary caesura in French sociopolitical life. There was a crisis of the liberal order between roughly 1890 and 1910, and the PGC became deeply entangled in it. The laissez-faire orthodoxies that had shaped relations between the state and society for most of the century suddenly faltered. A wide array of political forces, from moderate conservatives to Socialists, sought new sorts of connections between the public authorities and the emerging industrial society—all in the name of social peace. The PGC's dependence on a municipal concession forced it to respond to the crisis, perhaps more thoroughly than any other firm in France. Its personnel reacted, too, by organizing and by making demands that reflected nationwide currents of unrest in the era of the Dreyfus Affair. Rather quickly the PGC became for Radicals, Socialists, syndicalists, conservative reformers, and right-wing populists a preeminent "experiment" in achieving social harmony. Their reforms, however, generated intense strife as well as institutionalized solutions to discontents. The PGC thus crystalizes an important moment in the history of French industrial relations. Its salaried managers, bookkeepers, and manual laborers acted angrily in ways that expressed classwide concerns. It would not be unreasonable to draw general lessons about France's long-term industrial turbulence from their experience.

A word is in order about the organization of this book. After struggling with the project, I decided that the history of the PGC needed to be told from four quasi-independent perspectives. The Parisian public and its elected leaders took the firm as a notable example of "financial feudalism" and eventually saw it as an exploitative employer that had to be brought into line with evolving norms. To managers the PGC was a source of life-long careers and a forum for exercising the authority that their rigorous training had bestowed on them. Employees and workers put their subordination behind them and came to challenge that very authority. Reconstructing the story of the PGC chronologically proved cumbersome. In the end, I opted to relate the history four times, in a spiraling manner, from the perspective of different participants. This technique entailed some degree of repetition and forced me to be intentionally sketchy at times so as to curtail the repetitiveness. The benefits I hope to have derived are greater control over details and more opportunity for analysis.

• • •

At one point the director of the gas company, beleaguered from many sides, announced that his task was not to please people but merely to fulfill minimal contractual obligations. The statement was arrogant but rather characteristic of corporate attitudes. My standards for this study are a good deal higher. I do wish to please—and inform—all readers. I should like to convince them that this microstudy addresses important issues in meaningful ways. I have sought not to fall back on the PGC's position of being satisfied in meeting no more than minimal standards. Only the readers can judge my success.

Many friends and colleagues helped further these aspirations. I thank Louis Bergeron, Linda Clark, Cissie Fairchilds, Rachel Fuchs, Richard Kuisel, John Merriman, Philip Nord, Nicholas Papayanis, Donald Reid, and Mark Thomas for favors large and small. John Weiss and Terry Shinn provided important guidance to the sources on French engineers. Michael Miller and Oliver Zunz offered useful comments on papers drawn from this material. The staff of the Archives de Paris has my gratitude for expediting the research, as do the secretaries at the History Department of the University of Virginia for reproducing drafts so efficiently. The Center of Advanced Study at the University of Virginia provided leave time that allowed me to bring this project to fruition. The Small Grants Committee at the university covered some expenses in producing the illustrations. I thank Peter Stearns for permission to use portions of an article I published in *The Journal of Social History* and the editors at Unwin-Hyman Limited for allowing me to include material from the forthcoming *Nationalism in France*. I owe deep thanks to Jack R. Censer for reading the entire manuscript and giving much advice and encouragement.

PART ONE

THE PARISIANS' COMPANY

ONE

The Golden Age of a Corporation, 1855–1885

One gas engineer, in a rare show of wit, remarked that the eighteenth century may have been the "age of enlightenment," but the nineteenth century was shaping up to be the "age of light."[1] That engineer was commenting on one aspect of a general revolution in everyday comforts: nineteenth-century Parisians, like other urban Europeans, expected—even demanded—to be taken out of the nocturnal obscurity that had seemed inevitable for millennia. Rising standards for lighting touched the public thoroughfares and the home. Better illumination was perhaps one of the created needs that an increasingly commercialized society foisted with accelerating and unrelenting pace on innocent consumers. Nonetheless, effective street illumination became a symbol for improvements in urban civilization and a sign, for those who so wished to construe it, of ineluctable material progress. Reassuring as gas lighting may have been to the public, it also became the source of big business and political contention. Regulating the new amenity in the public interest proved difficult in a France governed by liberal notables.

The Formation of the Company

In 1855, the Compagnie parisienne de l'éclairage et du chauffage par le gaz was born and quickly developed into one of France's greatest industrial enterprises. It supplied at least half the coal gas consumed in France through the 1870s.[2] The firm was indeed an exemplar of the new indus-

1. *Le Gaz: Organe spécial des intérêts de l'industrie de l'éclairage et du chauffage par le gaz*, August 31, 1864, p. 108.
2. Archives départementales de la Seine et de la ville de Paris (henceforth cited as AP), V 8 O¹, no. 269, "Usine des Ternes."

trial capitalism that was just beginning to transform the French and European economies. Its legal form, a limited-liability corporation, was still rare in a world of family enterprises and partnerships. The salaried managers who took charge had to coordinate processes across quasi-autonomous departments and oversee the allocation of resources on a scale that was exceptional. Corporate assets of the Parisian Gas Company (PGC) grew from 55 million francs at the founding to 256 million thirty years later. Managers oversaw a factory labor force of forty-two hundred (in 1885), of which only a tiny fraction had attachments to the conventional crafts. Another new social type, the salaried white-collar employee, numbered 1,975 in 1885. By that time the PGC had become the ninth-largest enterprise and the largest manufacturing firm in France. Only transportation concerns and the Anzin mines were bigger.[3] The PGC also foreshadowed the rise of big business based on high technology. It is true that the production of coal gas was not in itself enormously sophisticated. It required only roasting coal in air-tight retorts and collecting the escaping gases.[4] Yet the necessary quality-control techniques as well as the transformation of residues into industrial chemicals fused applied science and enterprise in a particularly innovative manner.

The PGC was a private enterprise, but its operations necessarily entailed coordination with the public authorities. The precise obligations that the city of Paris imposed on gas producers and that the companies expected of the city were the subject of literally continuous negotiations, reconsiderations, and debate—often acrimonious—from the moment gaslights appeared on the streets of Paris before 1820. Here politics entered the picture. The public authority tried to safeguard the interests of both the community and consumers, and the two interests did not always coincide. At the same time, gas manufacturers, being powerful capitalists, sought the best possible deal for themselves and their investors. They had the ability to manipulate issues and confound the authorities by withholding expertise or limiting options. Conflicts of interest explain why the seemingly innocuous effort to put gaslights on the streets and into stores and homes engendered interminable and rancorous discussion.

3. Bertrand Gille, *La Sidérurgie française au XIXe siècle* (Geneva, 1968), p. 295, ranks the thirty largest firms in 1881 on the basis of capital.
4. On the early history of gas production, see Malcolm Peebles, *Evolution of the Gas Industry* (London, 1980); Trevor Williams, *A History of the British Gas Industry* (Oxford, 1981); Wolfgang Schivelbusch, *Disenchanted Night: The Industrialization of Light in the Nineteenth Century*, trans. Angela Davies (Berkeley and Los Angeles, 1988); Arthur Elton, "The Rise of the Gas Industry in England and France," in *Actes du VIe Congrès international d'histoire des sciences, Amsterdam, 1950*, 2 vols. (Paris, 1953), 2:492–504.

The formation of the PGC is shrouded in some of the mystery that surrounds most other aspects of public administration under the rule of "the Sphinx," as Emperor Louis-Napoléon was known.[5] In place of fact a legend has arisen about the creation of an imposing gas corporation as a result of the bold entrepreneurship of those paragons of Imperial capitalism, Isaac and Emile Pereire. The claim has often been made that the PGC was one of their pioneering accomplishments, along with Europe's first industrial bank.[6] Their role in the making of the PGC was in truth peripheral and even parasitic. The PGC was formed from the merger of six preexisting gas firms following the wishes of their owners and the urgings of the public authorities. A single, powerful gas firm was a solution to the difficult problem of producing and distributing an urban amenity that was quickly becoming vital for some key elements in the population.

As a new industry in the early decades of the nineteenth century, gas faithfully traced the limits of scale set by technology, financial markets, and consumer demand. These forces at first imposed a relatively modest scale on gas producers, just as they did on forge masters and on textile manufacturers. In 1852 there were six gas concerns serving Paris and four more in the suburbs (in addition to one purveyor of bottled gas).[7] Neither the firms themselves nor the principal gas plants anticipated the large concentrations of capital that the PGC would eventually entail, as the figures in table 1 suggest. A major constraint on the size was the limited demand for gas within the circumscribed areas that their distribution systems could reach. Theoretically it was possible to produce huge batches of coal gas at a centralized plant simply by multiplying the number of retorts roasting coal. But the ability to deliver the gas to faraway customers effectively and at a reasonable cost was lacking. As the distance from the source increased, enormous amounts of gas were lost through leaks in the mains, and gas pressure at the destination fluctuated so widely as to make its use impossible. Thus, gas production became dispersed in modest-sized plants

---

5. On the lack of public sources for the history of Paris under the Second Empire, see Anthony Sutcliffe, *The Autumn of Central Paris: The Defeat of Town Planning, 1850–1970* (Montreal, 1971), pp. 335–336.
6. Rondo Cameron, "The Crédit mobilier and the Economic Development of Europe," *Journal of Political Economy* 61 (1953), 464; Theodore Zeldin, *France, 1848–1945*, 2 vols. (Oxford, 1973–1977), 1:82; David Harvey, *Consciousness and the Urban Experience* (Oxford, 1985), p. 80; Alain Plessis, *De la Fête impériale au mur des fédérés* (Paris, 1979), p. 104.
7. On the pre-merger gas situation, see *Journal de l'éclairage au gaz* (1852–1855); Henri Besnard, *L'Industrie du gaz à Paris depuis ses origines* (Paris, 1942), chaps. 1–2; Frederick Colyer, *Gas Works: Their Arrangement, Construction, Plant, and Machinery* (London, 1884), chaps. 1–4.

Table 1. Assets of Merging Gas Companies and
Principal Gas Plants, 1855

	Value (francs)
Firm/Principal owner	
Compagnie anglaise/L. Margueritte	13,628,000
Compagnie française/Th. Brunton	10,824,000
Compagnie parisienne/V. Dubochet	5,739,000
Compagnie Lacarrière/F. Lacarrière	4,494,000
Compagnie Belleville/R. Payn	3,294,000
Compagnie de l'Ouest/Ch. Gosselin	2,021,000
Gas plants	
Ternes and Trudaine	472,849
Vaugirard	545,198
Poissonnière	464,182
La Tour	235,835
Ivry	353,208
Belleville	139,428
Passy	79,291

Source: AP, V 8 O[1], no. 723, deliberations of December 26, 1855,
and October 30, 1856.

in the midst of populous neighborhoods. No one firm was up to the task
of serving the city as a whole. The Compagnie française, for example,
served the present-day third and fourth arrondissements from a factory
on the rue du Faubourg Poissonnière.[8]

The dynamism of nineteenth-century capitalism quickly expanded
these limits. Improvements in the manufacturing of gas pipes and joints
and the development of mechanical means for regulating pressure permitted the concentration of production. Moreover, the experience of the railroad companies paved the way for the accumulation of ever-greater
amounts of capital through the sale of bonds, which tapped the savings of
cautious and modest investors.[9] By the 1840s there was no longer any
reason one large firm could not control the Parisian gas industry. That
situation seemed all the more desirable since it was obvious that the industry was still in its infancy and would call for rare technological and

8. AP, V 8 O[1], no. 24, "Canalisation: Extraits des rapports et délibérations, 1834 à
1855"; Préfecture de la Seine, *Pièces diverses relatives à l'éstablissement des conduites pour l'éclairage au gaz dans Paris* (Paris, 1846).
9. AP, V 8 O[1], no. 25, "Canalisation"; Charles Freedeman, *Joint-Stock Enterprises
in France, 1807–1867* (Chapel Hill, N.C., 1979), p. 83.

entrepreneurial talent to handle the vast investments that would soon be necessary.[10]

Another impetus for merger came from the municipal authorities, who increasingly insisted on uniformity of marketing arrangements from the various producers. The introduction of gas services had immediately raised in Paris, as it did in all other large cities, the thorny problem of regulation in a liberal era. Private lighting had heretofore been a matter of individuals buying oil lamps or candles, but gas required sinking mains under streets, spurring concern for public safety. The authorities gradually (and reluctantly) arrived at viewing gas as a "natural monopoly" and then sought means to protect customers and derive financial benefits for the city. By 1822, when gas was still a novelty, the prefect had already given the companies exclusive rights to particular sectors of the city (though there were disputes over precise boundaries) and soon imposed the obligation to serve streets with a minimal demand. The city was not yet ready to set uniform gas rates, and there was as yet no set of uniform contractual obligations for gas producers. These would come with the agreement of 1846, which made gas into a regulated industry.[11]

With this agreement Paris established once and for all the practice of granting to a utility a monopoly for a fixed number of years. Later, some public figures would express their regret over the failure to follow the British example of creating perpetual utility companies, but the municipality would return repeatedly to a concession with limited duration. Most politicians agreed that this arrangement was in keeping with French custom.[12] The charter of 1846 gave the six gas companies a concession lasting seventeen years. Before this charter was in effect, prices for gas had varied from one firm to another, reaching as high as sixty centimes per cubic meter, but averaged forty-eight centimes. In the 1846 agreement, the companies undertook to charge forty-seven centimes and to reduce the price by a centime a year until the rate of forty centimes was attained. The firms would sell gas to the city for street lighting at the putative at-cost rate of twenty-four centimes. Furthermore, they agreed to pay certain duties and to sell the gas mains to the city at a low price when the concession ended as compensation for their monopoly.[13] With

10. The companies were eager to merge partly to prevent competition and stop customers on border streets from bargaining for lower rates. See AP, V 8 O¹, no. 751, "Affaire Deschamps."
11. Besnard, *Gaz à Paris*, chap. 2.
12. *Procès-verbaux des délibérations du Conseil municipal de Paris* (henceforth cited as *Conseil municipal*), March 8, 1881.
13. Besnard, *Gaz à Paris*, chap. 2. Note that gas was sold mainly by the hour, not by volume, at this time.

the several firms at last adhering to a single set of regulations, the stage was set for a merger of the firms, which was triggered by an unforeseen economic perturbation.

The charter of 1846 was sealed just as the Parisian economy was shaken by the most serious crisis of the century followed by the uncertainties of political revolution. Gas consumption fell (according to one source by as much as 25 percent), and owners felt the heavy burdens of amortizing the capital for so short a concession. In February 1850 they petitioned the prefect to revise the gas charter on the basis of unification and a longer concession.

A new agreement was hammered out and approved by the administration with what appeared in retrospect to be record speed. The city and the companies were ready to accept in 1852 another eighteen-year concession, with the cost of gas being reduced in stages to thirty-five centimes per cubic meter. The "revolution of 1852," with the simultaneous recovery of economic confidence and the imposition of the steady, guiding hand of a Bonaparte, undoubtedly quickened the negotiations. It brought the producers to settle for a shorter concession than they might have wished in the hope of benefiting from the sudden commercial upturn. The unusual concord between the industrialists and the municipal authorities proved futile, however, for the Council of State rejected the agreement on the grounds that it could be made more favorable to private consumers. This action opened a final round of negotiations, which centered on the price of gas, a matter that would continue to trouble the Parisian gas industry throughout the rest of the century.[14]

A great deal of ink flowed from the companies, outside experts, and public officials about manufacturing costs. Estimates were generally in the range of twenty to twenty-five centimes per cubic meter, but one went as low as three centimes.[15] The industrialists offered, and the city accepted, a rate of thirty-three centimes for private consumers; but once again the Imperial administration upset the accord. Louis-Napoléon had appointed a commission to examine the matter, and its finding was that prices could be lower. Showing foresight for which he never received credit, the emperor insisted on the consumer's interests, and negotiations were on the

14. Ibid., chaps. 2–3; *Journal de l'éclairage au gaz* (1854–1855).

15. Compagnies de l'éclairage par le gaz de la ville de Paris, *Rapports et délibérations de la commission municipale: Mémoires et documents divers*, 3 vols. (Paris, 1855–1856); A. Chevalier, *Observations sur le projet de traité pour l'éclairage au gaz de la ville de Paris* (Paris, 1854); Mary et Combes, *Rapport sur le prix de revient du mètre cube du gaz de l'éclairage tel qu'il résulte des livres de commerce des compagnies anglaises, françaises, et parisiennes* (Paris, 1854); Pelouze, *Rapport de la sous-commission du gaz: 19 août et 2 septembre 1853* (Paris, n.d.).

verge of collapse. It was at this crucial moment that the Pereire brothers entered the picture and "created" the PGC.

The Pereires did not contribute bold entrepreneurship but simply facilitated concessions from all sides. Some thirty-seven years after the fact, a municipal councilman depicted their role as a matter of bribing the proper authorities. His claim was corroborated by one of the firm's stockholders, who revealed in a private letter that the Pereires dispensed three million francs to get the project off the ground.[16] There is of course no means to probe the allegations. One way or another the Pereires managed to include themselves in what would prove to be an excellent investment. Under their guidance the emperor, the companies, and the city agreed to a fifty-year concession, the longest ever considered, with gas for thirty centimes for private consumers. The Pereires joined the pioneer industrialists of the coal gas industry as founders of the PGC and provided fifteen million of the fifty-five million francs of capital. That was an investment the financiers would never have to regret.

The provisions of the contract, which took effect on January 1, 1856, provided the framework in which the PGC operated until its demise at the end of the concession.[17] In addition to fixing the cost of gas once and for all at thirty centimes for private consumers, it gave the city a price of fifteen centimes for public lighting. The new company was obligated to lay gas mains under a street when a minimal level of demand existed. There were provisions specifying the quality of gas that had to be maintained and the supply of coal the company had to keep in stock to ensure against shortages. The city also negotiated certain financial benefits for itself. The PGC was obligated to pay a two-centime duty on every cubic meter sold. At the end of the concession the city was entitled to the distribution system below the thoroughfares without owing any compensation. Most important, Paris gained the right to half the profits of the PGC after 1872, calculated after a deduction of 8.4 million francs for reserves and debt service. That stipulation made the city a partner in a profitable private enterprise.

The charter of 1855 eventually proved to be a source of political embarrassment for the Imperial government. Critics, especially republican ones, characterized it as a sellout to the interests of "financial feudalism," as an

16. Conseil municipal de Paris, *Rapports et documents: 1892*, no. 14, "Rapport . . . par F. Sauton," pp. 30–31; AP, V 8 O¹, no. 616, Graverand to director, April 12, 1880; Maurice Charany, "Le Gaz à Paris," *La Revue socialiste* 36 (1902): 425.
17. For published copies of the charters, see Préfecture de la Seine, *Service public et particulier de l'éclairage et du chauffage par le gaz dans la ville de Paris* (Paris, 1883). Besnard, *Gaz à Paris*, chap. 3, covers the details of the charter of 1855.

alienation of the public interest to selfish monopolists. Under the Third Republic municipal councilmen endlessly discussed the failings of the charter. However, a more balanced assessment is in order. The essential objection made against the gas agreement—that the contract allowed the PGC to charge far too much for gas and thereby reap fabulous, unearned profits—needs qualification. First, the agreement did result in a substantial and immediate reduction in gas rates. If there had been no new charter, consumers would have paid forty centimes or more for another seven years. Aldermen had been under pressure from consumer groups to effect this reduction, and many gas users were probably more interested in immediate costs than the long-term consequences of the concession.[18] Moreover, fixing the rate at thirty centimes happened before the PGC had substantially reduced the cost of production—as it would do in the decade after the charter was signed. Thirty centimes might have seemed indefensibly high in 1865, but not in 1855. Finally, municipal councilmen chose to pursue the interest of the city over that of individual consumers in this agreement. Had they not procured so many financial advantages for Paris, they might have lowered the gas rate for customers. In effect, the public officials decided to impose a hidden tax of sorts on gas users. Given the social profile of consumers—a matter I shall soon explore—this was one of the more progressive taxes levied by the city. Where the Imperial authorities were at fault was in neglecting to create the means to reduce prices in anticipation of falling production costs. They might have been more mindful of the fact that gas companies of London produced handsome returns while selling gas for 15.5 centimes. Yet the agreement did not merit all the opprobrium it received for the rest of the century.[19]

In fact, the revision of the charter worked out in 1861 deserves far more censure, for the opportunity to rectify problems was utterly wasted. The context for the renegotiations was the annexation of the Parisian suburbs. It was already evident that production costs were falling dramatically and that a reduction of the gas rates was in order. Moreover, the city had the leverage to force the PGC into concessions. The company wanted the right to supply gas to the new districts of the enlarged capital, destined for spectacular development. The city might have threatened to award the lucrative gas contract to a new firm. Yet the authorities did not strike a worthy

18. *Journal de l'éclairage au gaz*, 1854, no. 7 (October 20): 98–99.
19. Placing the agreement in a larger context, one could argue that the state proved no more capable of extracting concessions from the new railroad companies. See Kimon Doukas, *The French Railroad and the State* (New York, 1945), pp. 34–43; Jeanne Gaillard, "Notes sur l'opposition au monopole des compagnies de chemin de fer entre 1850 et 1860," *Révolution de 1848* 44 (December 1950).

bargain. Indeed, they not only left the defective provisions of the 1855 charter intact, but they also allowed gas executives to impose expensive burdens on the city. The municipal government wound up subsidizing the PGC's lucrative expansion into the annexed areas by guaranteeing a 10 percent return on capital expenditures, paying seventeen francs for each meter of gas main laid there and contributing 0.14 centimes for each cubic meter of gas sold. The ostensible reason for the generosity to the rich gas company was to compensate for the putative risks of the venture. Reasonable observers might have concluded that the negotiators greatly exaggerated those risks. Furthermore, the revision of 1861 finalized another expensive mistake, the city's sharing the firm's amortization costs. Parisian negotiators should have insisted, as several councilmen had since 1855, that the company alone bear that expense. The city's capitulation brought it a concession not worth having, the right to half of the corporate assets when the charter ended in 1906. This was not a wise arrangement for the city because the PGC now had an incentive to allow its plant and equipment to deteriorate as the charter neared its end.[20] In fact, when a new firm took over gas production in 1907, the management decided that several of the PGC's factories were essentially worthless. The successor company had to undertake more than a hundred million francs of immediate capital improvements.[21] Not only did Paris receive little for supporting amortization costs; it paid the cost twice—once when the PGC charged the expenditure to the operating budget and again when the company deducted 8.4 million francs before sharing profits. The courts eventually put a stop to the double payment, but not until Paris had sacrificed millions of francs.[22] Perhaps the authorities who accepted the revised charter were only taking their cue from the state, which had agreed to an excessively generous settlement with the railroad companies a year earlier to encourage development at any price.[23] Nonetheless, the charter of 1861 was indefensible. It represented, at best, a dereliction of duty on the part of Baron Georges-Eugène Haussmann and his staff or, at worst, an instance of corruption. Compared with prior bargaining, this charter signaled an

20. *Rapport présenté par le Conseil d'administration de la Compagnie parisienne du gaz à l'Assemblée générale* (henceforth cited as *Rapport*), September 14, 1860, pp. 3–13; Besnard, *Gaz à Paris*, chap. 3.
21. AP, V 8 O¹, no. 1643, "Société du gaz de Paris," deliberations of June 7, 1910.
22. *Rapport*, March 28, 1899, p. 41.
23. Doukas, *French Railroad and the State*, pp. 34–35. The railroad agreement of 1859 had many of the same features as the PGC's new charter, including public aid for new construction and sharing in the profits after 1872. See also M. Blanchard, "The Railroad Policy of the Second Empire," in *Essays in European Economic History, 1789–1914*, ed. François Crouzet et al. (New York, 1969), pp. 98–111.

alarming decline in the ability of the Imperial administration to defend the public interest.

One more opportunity to modify the gas contract arose in 1870; but at that point the city had little to offer the PGC in exchange for renouncing its most lucrative privileges. As a result of the newest round of bargaining, Paris advanced the onset of profit sharing by two years. In return, the PGC raised the amount of profits exempted from sharing by four million francs. The 1870 charter also put an end to public subsidies for operations in the annexed zone, but not before the PGC had rushed to lay gas lines ahead of need so that the municipality would share the cost.[24] Though this contract marked a return to a higher level of public responsibility than in 1861, Paris still remained unable to wring real benefits from the PGC. The negotiators unwisely treated impending armed conflict with Otto von Bismarck as a remote possibility. The Franco-Prussian War, ruining gas sales, deprived the treasury of the early shared profits it had paid dearly to receive.

Once the 1870 charter was signed, relations between the city and the company were finalized—much to the regret of aldermen in subsequent decades. Despite a excess of venom on the part of consumers and efforts at negotiations from both sides, no successful new agreement emerged. The provisions laid down in 1855 allowed the PGC to become a very large and rich enterprise even as it presented the firm with serious public-relations problems.

The Sociology of Gas Consumption

The changes in lighting technology during the nineteenth century, from candle to electricity, easily lent themselves to a discourse of progress. Observers found it congenial to tout the triumph of civilization over darkness, using light as a metaphor for material advancement. Behind the hackneyed pronouncements of optimism was one of the many revolutions of everyday life that was so much a part of the nineteenth century. Parisians of varied social categories gradually discovered, each at their own pace, that more and better illumination was a pleasing luxury and, eventually, a necessity. Even before access to that luxury had descended down the social hierarchy, gas production had become big business. What happened to gas consumption was paradigmatic for the evolution of a consumer society in nineteenth-century France.

The growth of a consumer economy in France was a particularly com-

24. *Rapport*, March 29, 1867, p. 16; September 23, 1869, pp. 1–20.

plex and even paradoxical affair. On the one hand, French enterpreneurs were leaders in developing modern commercial institutions, like department stores. Michael Miller is surely correct to observe that the flourishing of mass retail outlets presupposed a bourgeoisie that was open to consumer innovations and willing to define social status in terms of purchasable commodities.[25] On the other hand, it is a commonplace of French economic history that manufacturers failed to find a mass market for products and instead pursued a strategy of high quality and low volume. Not only were the urban and rural masses excluded from the consumer economy until the twentieth century by the lack of disposable income; those who had comfortable livelihoods seemed to resist the "civilization of gadgets." Many visitors from Victorian Britain expressed surprise at the lack of home comforts among prosperous Parisians.[26] An analysis of gas use does nothing to dispel the incomplete and selective features of nineteenth-century French consumerism. But such an analysis may reveal some of the mechanisms that guided the uneven expansion of the consumer market.

Contemporary perceptions of gas use were so misleading as to undermine confidence in the value of qualitative evidence. The Paris Chamber of Commerce announced that gas lighting was "general" already in 1848. Two engineers writing a few years later argued that gas could "now be considered among the necessities of social life" and would soon become so even for the working classes. Their observation echoed the assurances the PGC's management passed along to stockholders, that the use of gas had "become like air and water."[27] These appreciations lend credence to one historian's claim—quite erroneous, as it turns out—that one in five Parisians lit their homes with gas by the end of the Second Empire.[28] These commentators were not mistaken to find an exceptional acceleration in the demand for better lighting, but they exaggerated the extent to which gas served the newly manifested need.

There can be no question that Parisians easily accommodated them-

25. Michael Miller, *The Bon Marché: Bourgeois Culture and the Department Store, 1896–1920* (Princeton, 1981), pp. 237–240.
26. Donald J. Olsen, *The City as a Work of Art: London, Paris, Vienna* (New Haven, 1986), pp. 37, 119, 122; Zeldin, *France,* 2:612–627.
27. Chambre de commerce de Paris, *Statistique de l'industrie à Paris pour les années 1847–1848* (Paris, 1851), p. 125; Exposition universelle internationale de 1878, *Rapports du jury international. Groupe III. Les Procédés et les appareils de chauffage et d'éclairage par M. Barlet* (Paris, 1881), p. 46; J. Gatliff and P. Pers, *De l'éclairage au gaz dans les maisons particulières* (Paris, 1855), p. 2.
28. Louis Girard, *La Deuxième République et le Second Empire, 1848–1870* (Paris, 1981), p. 199.

selves to higher standards of illumination and embraced innovations that provided more lighting. Progressive administrators who sought to improve public lighting in the face of an initially indifferent population eventually found Parisians pressuring them for still better lighting. A technical improvement in the burners of street lamps nearly tripled the amount of light they produced and won the applause of the public in the 1860s. The appearance of electrical lamps reproduced the cycle of skepticism followed by acceptance. The early experiments provoked derision from the press, and some editors wondered if the intense illumination would not blind people. It was not long, however, before local politicians had to include among their campaign promises the provision of electrical lights in the neighborhoods they represented. The organizers of the Universal Exposition of 1900 recognized that standards of lighting had become categorically higher than they had been just a decade earlier and took pains to endow their project properly. The Champ de Mars during the 1900 celebration had nearly five times the lighting power as in 1889. Of course, improvements had a self-defeating quality, for success in meeting current expectations produced still higher ones.[29]

The growing sensitivity to illumination on the streets found a counterpart inside the home. The first mark of rising standards was the widening use of oil lamps in the late eighteenth century. They moved beyond workshops and the homes of the rich into modest households when the Swiss inventor Aimé Argand dramatically improved their effectiveness by increasing the draw of air reaching the flame in 1786. Numerous innovations, simplifications, and price reductions followed. The "art of lighting," to use the term of one of the earliest engineers working in the field, was now a matter of evolving technology. Architects welcomed the cheapening of plate-glass production and incorporated larger and more numerous windows into their plans. The Bibliothèque Sainte-Geneviève, the first library in France to remain open at night, was built in 1843 and pointed in the direction that household amenities could take.[30] The demand for illumination accelerated vastly in the second half of the century along with

29. *Le Gaz*, no. 9 (June 15, 1861): 104; AP, V 8 O¹, no. 270, director to prefect, June 4, 1857; Gatliff and Pers, *De l'éclairage*, p. 8; Eugène Defrance, *Histoire de l'éclairage des rues de Paris* (Paris, 1904), pp. 107–121; J. Laverchère, "Eclairage intensif par le gaz des parcs et des jardins du Champ-de-Mars et du Trocadéro," *Le Génie civil* 37 (1900): 27. For campaign posters promising electrical lighting, see Archives de la Préfecture de police (henceforth cited as Préfecture), B/a 695.
30. E. Paul Bérard, *L'Economie domestique de l'éclairage* (Paris, 1867), pp. 6–28; E. Péclet, *Traité de l'éclairage* (Paris, 1827). On the Bibliothèque Sainte-Geneviève, see David Pinkney, *Decisive Years in France, 1840–1847* (Princeton, 1986), pp. 105–109.

the means to satisfy it. The engineer Philippe Delahaye measured the per capita consumption of lighting in Paris from the three principle sources, gas, kerosene, and electricity; he found a forty-five-fold increase between 1855 and 1889.[31] Clearly the PGC came into existence just as daily life in France was entering into a dependence on combustible energy sources.[32]

The public's receptivity to improved means of illumination (and of heating as well) provided a most favorable business climate for the PGC. The firm grew vigorously. The first thirty years saw total gas consumption in Paris and its suburbs rise sevenfold, from 40 million to 286 million cubic meters (see appendix, fig. A1). Gas use doubled during the decade of the 1860s and again during the 1870s. The PGC began its concession with a mere thirty-five thousand customers inherited from the former firms. Initially the clientele was necessarily limited because gas lines reached only the first floors of buildings. A potential user on an upper floor would have had to pay for long and expensive connector pipes from the gas main in the street to the dwelling, and few wanted to bear the expense. The PGC resolved this limitation by installing mounted gas mains (*conduites montantes*) in the stairwells of buildings. With this innovation customers had only to rent or buy connecting pipes (*branchements*) from the hallway to their lodgings. The company began installing such mounted mains in March 1860, and a vast potential market opened. Another restraint on private consumption disappeared soon after the PGC began operating. Its predecessors had offered gas only during the night, the hours that street lamps were lit. This restriction meant that industrial use of gas or heating with gas in the home was not possible. The PGC began day service on September 1, 1856; within three years it had as day customers 163 restaurants, 233 bakeries, 63 hotels, and more than a thousand cafés.[33] Partly as a result of these measures, the PGC was able to expand far beyond the clientele it had inherited to 190,000 customers in 1885 (see appendix, fig. A2).

Rising standards of lighting and more useful arrangements for residents did not necessarily produce a mass market for the PGC, however.

31. *L'Abaissement du prix du gaz à Paris* (Paris, 1890), p. 21.
32. David Landes notes a sixfold increase in world consumption of commercial energy sources between 1860 and 1900. See his *Unbound Prometheus: Technological Change and Industrial Development in Western Europe from 1750 to the Present* (Cambridge, 1969), p. 98. See also Fred Cottrell, *Energy and Society: The Relation between Energy, Social Change, and Economic Development* (New York, 1955), for the concepts of low-energy and high-energy societies. Nineteenth-century Europe was clearly in transition from one to the other.
33. AP, V 8 O¹, no. 724, deliberations of March 22, 1860; no. 765, "Répartition des abonnés faisant usage du gaz pendant le jour (février 1860)."

The clientele of the original gas firms had consisted primarily of commercial establishments on the first floors of buildings; even in the 1880s as the era of electricity was dawning, the PGC still relied heavily on those users. The president of the company affirmed in 1880 that a majority of subscribers (74,400 out of 135,500) were industrial or commercial enterprises.[34] Of course, each of the business customers was likely to use far more gas than an average residential user. Between 1855 and 1885, supplying gas to residents was an appendage to the main business of lighting commercial and industrial establishments.

The PGC could not have been founded at a better moment to grow and prosper by bringing gas to Parisian businesses. The capital was about to undergo two decades of dramatic changes that would enlarge and enrich this clientele. Since gas was the energy source of choice in terms of efficiency, convenience, and novelty, commercial firms adopted it as a matter of course. In the modern Paris that emerged under Baron Haussmann, urban renovations accompanied and accentuated the commercial transformation of the capital. Luxurious apartment buildings appeared along Haussmann's attractive boulevards, especially in the western quarters, and central Paris lost residents but was filled during the day by salespeople, clerks, business agents, and wholesalers. A new shopping district arose to the north and west of the *grands boulevards* to supplement the older one around the Palais Royal and along the rue de Richelieu (second arrondissement). It was no wonder that the portion of the capital's working population earning a living from commerce rose from 12 to 30 percent during the golden age of the PGC.[35]

The commercial vocation of Paris was favored by two great transformations, the booming world economy of the 1850s and the railroad revolution. Paris became the center of a vast export trade as the well-off in Britain, the Americas, and elsewhere purchased its handicrafts. French exports rose fivefold between 1846 and 1875, and a quarter of the manufactured goods sent abroad was made in Paris.[36] The railroads centralized

---

34. Frédéric Margueritte, *Observations présentées à Monsieur le Préfet de la Seine sur une pétition tendant à obtenir la réduction du prix de vente du gaz d'éclairage* (Paris, 1880), p. 20. His figures are not perfectly consistent with those in other sources, but they at least have an illustrative value.

35. David Pinkney, *Napoleon III and the Rebuilding of Paris* (Princeton, 1958); François Loyer, *Paris au XIXᵉ siècle: L'Immeuble et l'espace urbaine*, 3 vols. (Paris, n.d.); Philip Nord, *Paris Shopkeepers and the Politics of Resentment* (Princeton, 1986), chap. 3.

36. Maurice Lévy-Leboyer and François Bourguignon, *L'Economie française au XIXᵉ siécle: Analyse macro-économique* (Paris, 1985), pp. 43, 49; Roger Price, *An Economic History of Modern France, 1730–1914* (London, 1975), pp. 158–159.

commercial activities in the capital. They made tourism, retailing, and all other sorts of exchange of information and personnel increasingly feasible. Haussmannization concentrated these changes by giving the growing bourgeois population new neighborhoods, a new housing stock, and new patterns of urban life. Philip Nord has argued that department stores were products of the spatial reorganization of the city, depending as they did on massive concentrations of consumers on the boulevards. These emporiums became among the best customers of the PGC, but they provide only one example of the ways commercial expansion gave a boost to gas consumption.[37]

The British writer Philip Gilbert Hamerton claimed that his countrymen had invented the home but the French, especially the Parisians, "invented the street." His remark underscores the transformation of Paris from a city that contained pleasures to a showcase of monumentality, public pleasures, and commercialized leisure during the Second Empire.[38] Gas lighting was an essential accompaniment to the metamorphosis. The streets with the largest gas consumption in 1868 traced the core of commercial Paris—the *grands boulevards* (132,000 cubic meters), the rue de Rivoli (90,500), the rue Saint-Honoré (82,000), and the boulevard Sébastopol (77,500). The use of gas was closely associated with public display. Parisians had probably received their first indoor experience of gas lighting in cafés. Indeed, one of the earliest pubs to be served by gas took the name Café du gaz.[39] The predecessor of the department store during the first years of the nineteenth century, the commercial arcade, put the new energy source to good effect. One observer of 1817 described the passage des Panoramas in the second arrondissement as "a fairy country . . . brilliantly illuminated . . . by [gas]light reflected endlessly off windowpanes and mirrors."[40] Theaters became showcases for gas lighting, not only with their grand chandeliers, but also because stage technicians learned how to use gas for enhancing sets. The Théâtre Gymnase spent thirteen

---

37. Nord, *Shopkeepers*, pp. 132–137. On the use of gas by department stores in the 1860s, see AP, V 8 O^1, no. 751, "Etat comparatif des consommations du gaz de divers établissements particuliers (1864–1866)."
38. Olsen, *City as a Work of Art*, pp. 219–224, 231. An important study of Parisian leisure and entertainment in this period is Robert Herbert, *Impressionism: Art, Leisure, and Parisian Society* (New Haven, 1988).
39. AP, V 8 O^1, no. 753, "Comptabilité des abonnés"; Defrance, *Eclairage des rues*, p. 99.
40. Cited in Nord, *Shopkeepers*, p. 90. By no means was the gas lighting in arcades always so brilliant. Emile Zola described the Passage du Pont Neuf, lit by three gas jets, as dingy and sinister-looking. See his *Thérèse Raquin*, trans. L. W. Tancock (Baltimore, 1962), p. 1.

thousand francs on gas fixtures in 1867. The press marveled at the fact that the Grand Hôtel alone used more gas than the entire city of Orléans.[41]

The great establishments of Haussmann's boulevards were the PGC's most important customers. In 1886, just as electricity was about to coopt some of this business, the Bon Marché department store and the Grands Magasins du Louvre topped the list with more than five hundred thousand cubic meters each (table 2). Some of the celebrated cafés and famous dance halls of the city used more than a hundred thousand cubic meters. The Tivoli-Vaux-Hall paid annual bills of nearly forty thousand francs. The 128 customers consuming more than forty thousand cubic meters annually (0.07 percent of all customers) used 5 percent of all gas consumed in Paris. This clientele had enormous influence as well. Their glamour, prestige, and visibility ensured that when people thought of the City of Lights, they had gas lighting in mind. Such large customers made gas seem not only efficient but also progressive. They set the style for a myriad of smaller stores, offices, and pubs.

The lighting needs of commercial Paris easily surpassed the industrial uses of gas, though there were important exceptions. Among the PGC's largest customers were the Sommier and Lebaudy sugar refineries. Brewers and liquor distillers also took advantage of gas as an easily regulated source of heat. Some of the largest printers used gas motors to drive their presses and ranked with department stores as customers. On the whole, however, gas had not entered directly into production processes, and manufacturers used it mainly for lighting.[42] Gas engineers had hoped to sell their product to foundries, but the Société industrielle des métaux of Saint-Denis was the only large one to use it. The largest jewelry manufacturer in Paris, Savard, was only a modest consumer; its craftsmen did not use coal gas to fuel their burners. The imposing Cail machine company, which employed more than two thousand workers, used much less gas than the Café américain on the boulevard des Capucines. During the

---

41. *La Presse*, August 26, 1863, p. 3; AP, V 8 O¹, no. 672, deliberations of October 16, 1867. On the uses of gas in nineteenth-century theaters, see Terence Rees, *Theatre Lighting in the Age of Gas* (London, 1978).

42. Gas did have an impact on daily work patterns, and the introduction of gas lighting raised labor protests here and there. I have not found examples of protest in Paris, but see Pierre Cayez, *Métiers jacquards et hauts fourneaux: Aux origines de l'industrie lyonnaise* (Lyon, 1978), p. 295; Elinor Accampo, *Industrialization, Family Life, and Class Relations: Saint Chamond, 1815–1914* (Berkeley and Los Angeles, 1989), p. 82; and Harvey, *Urban Experience*, p. 7, citing the remarks of Friedrich Engels on Manchester.

Table 2. The Twenty Largest Gas Customers
in 1886

Firm	Annual consumption (cubic meters)
1. Grands Magasins du Louvre	533,457
2. Bon Marché (department store)	505,624
3. Hôtel Continental	351,149
4. Grand Hotel	324,702
5. Théâtre Eden	303,128
6. Raffinerie Lebaudy (sugar)	283,857
7. Bazar de l'Hôtel de Ville	268,768
8. Belle Jardinière (department store)	255,431
9. Raffinerie Sommier (sugar)	252,044
10. Christofle (silversmiths)	199,043
11. Grande Imprimerie Nouvelle	187,537
12. Imprimerie Dupont	182,894
13. Folies Bergères	161,627
14. Société industrielle des métaux	159,021
15. Café Américain	135,502
16. Grand Café	109,828
17. Théâtre Odéon	107,280
18. Théâtre Gymnase	106,033
19. Tivoli-Vaux-Hall (ballroom)	95,030
20. Cail (machinery)	81,073

Source: AP, V 8 O¹, no. 707, "Consommation de divers établissements."

golden era of gas, display, spectacle, and simple illumination were its principal applications.

Gas use was nearly universal among commercial and industrial firms. Approximately four-fifths of the ninety-three thousand workshops and stores in Paris of 1880 used gas.[43] In view of this massive success and of the familiar terms on which Parisians lived with gas outside their homes, it is surprising how rarely they used gas inside their residences. Reliance on less efficient and less elaborate forms of energy was not a simple matter of affordability. The Parisian bourgeoisie was almost as hesitant as the common people about putting gas fixtures into its homes. The use of gas thus raises interesting questions about preferences, habits, and innovations among French consumers.

The statistics on domestic consumption at the beginning of the electri-

43. Margueritte, *Observations*, p. 20.

Claude Monet's painting of a Parisian apartment—luxurious but lacking gas-lights. *Un coin d'appartement,* 1875; courtesy Musée d'Orsay.

cal era, in 1889, comment ironically on the PGC's frequent assurances that gas had become a necessity of life. Only 15 percent of all residences were adjacent to mounted mains and therefore were potential gas users. The policies of the PGC presented one reason for the limited availability of gas, but a discussion of marketing practices can and should be postponed until

Table 3. Residential Gas Use in Paris, 1888

Arrondissement	No. Residences	No. Adjacent to Mounted Main	No. Using Gas	% Using Gas
First	23,012	6,616	2,243	9.8
Second	24,927	8,304	3,083	12.4
Third	31,809	9,240	3,053	9.6
Fourth	32,098	4,168	1,239	3.9
Fifth	24,910	3,904	1,095	3.1
Sixth	31,139	4,776	1,374	4.4
Seventh	26,100	3,880	1,051	4.0
Eighth	23,279	9,558	5,525	23.7
Ninth	41,525	15,688	6,241	15.0
Tenth	53,152	12,798	3,955	7.4
Eleventh	67,599	9,204	1,945	2.9
Twelfth	31,177	1,504	301	1.0
Thirteenth	26,291	355	70	0.3
Fourteenth	27,082	580	140	0.6
Fifteenth	28,472	389	75	0.3
Sixteenth	16,012	2,640	919	5.7
Seventeenth	41,499	5,160	1,374	3.3
Eighteenth	53,931	1,863	350	0.7
Nineteenth	34,439	651	153	0.4
Twentieth	36,499	432	47	0.1
Total	684,952	101,710	34,235	5.0

Source: AP, V 8 O¹, no. 30, "Statistique des maisons de Paris au point de vue de la consommation du gaz."

a later point. The matter that concerns us at present is that most households that had the option of lighting with gas did not do so. In the city as a whole, only a third of the apartments near mounted mains used gas. The range was from 58 percent in the wealthy eighth arrondissement to 8 percent in the poor twentieth. No more than 5 percent of all Parisian residences were customers of the PGC. Far from being a necessity of life, domestic gas was a curiosity (see table 3).

Evidently the use of gas had not become a class phenomenon, dividing the bourgeoisie from the urban masses. To be sure, there were wealthy people who could not have done without gas. The elegant town house of the duc de Montesquieu on the quai d'Orsay had fifty gas jets (*becs de gaz*) in 1860. The largest domestic consumer, as might be expected, was Baron James de Rothschild, whose palace on the rue Saint-Florentin used forty-six thousand cubic meters a year, almost as much as the Elysée-

Montmartre Theater. At the other extreme, Parisians of modest means hardly ever lit with gas. Less than 1 percent of the households paying less than five hundred francs in annual rent—below the threshold of bourgeois residences—were customers of the PGC.[44] In their pattern of gas use Parisians between these two extremes more often resembled the poor than they did the Rothschilds. Most of the apartments with access to mounted mains rented for at least eight hundred francs a year and as such were among the costliest 10 percent of Parisian residences.[45] Yet only one in three affluent renters used gas. Fewer than a thousand apartments out of sixteen thousand in the sixteenth arrondissement lit with gas. Clearly, gas at the end of its golden age had not even become a daily luxury in which the well-off indulged.

It is a commonplace that French consumers, like businessmen, were slow to accept changes. Scholars have often stressed deeply rooted cultural values and distinctive collective attitudes in accounting for their preferences. Alain Corbin, for example, explains the backwardness of French hygienic practices relative to the British in terms of unconscious predispositions regarding the body. He concludes that income and degree of urbanization were less decisive factors.[46] It is tempting to apply his approach to gas use, especially given the stereotype about French consumers being indifferent to and undemanding about domestic amenities. The French bourgeoisie supposedly spent money on food, clothes, and leisure but not on making the home comfortable.[47] Before adopting this explanation for gas consumption, it would be well to take a broader view. A full consideration of the material conditions attending gas use reduces, if not eliminates, the autonomous role of cultural values in shaping consumer behavior.

The high rates for gas in Paris played a role in limiting its use. The press screamed about this subject at times, and any Parisian who read a newspaper regularly could learn that residents of Berlin, Brussels, and

---

44. AP, V 8 O¹, no. 707, "Consommation de divers établissements"; no. 24, "Transformation de l'éclairage dans Paris (14 novembre 1892)"; no. 724, deliberations of April 12, 1860.
45. P. Simon, *Statistique de l'habitation à Paris* (Paris, 1891), p. 14, for data on the distribution of rent levels in 1890.
46. Alain Corbin, *Le Miasme et la jonquille: L'Odorat et l'imaginaire social* (Paris, 1982), p. 202.
47. The basic statement on the problematical nature of French consumerism is to be found in Maurice Halbwachs, *La Classe ouvrière et les niveaux de vie* (Paris, 1912). See also Rosalind H. Williams, *Dream Worlds: Mass Consumption in Late Nineteenth-Century France* (Berkeley and Los Angeles, 1982); Zeldin, *France*, 2:612–627; Olsen, *City as a Work of Art*, pp. 119–122.

Amsterdam paid only twenty centimes. Londoners paid half the rate of Paris; per capita consumption in London was about twice as high.[48] Noteworthy as the high cost of gas in Paris was, however, the rate alone was not the determining factor. Engineers had no trouble demonstrating quantitatively that even at thirty centimes gas provided more efficient lighting than kerosene, candles, or its other immediate competitors. It would not have been a great burden on bourgeois residents to light with gas as long as they used it prudently. A hundred hours of gas lighting would have cost them only three francs for the fuel.[49] In fact, the PGC was able to expand the domestic use of gas dramatically in the last decade of the nineteenth century even when the price remained at thirty centimes.[50]

Many Parisians refrained from using gas at home because it had certain disadvantages. Corbin has demonstrated an escalating sensitivity among French people of the nineteenth century to foul odors and an ever-stronger desire for fresh, circulating air.[51] Such sensibilities discouraged gas use. The public was well aware that gas lighting made rooms stuffy and emitted more heat than competing sources of lighting. One engineer established that gas produced almost twice the carbon dioxide that kerosene did and warned of headaches, nausea, and even slow intoxication. The residues of gas combustion faded fabrics, discolored ceilings, and marked walls.[52] Even the employees who worked in the PGC's headquarters complained about stuffy offices and irregular light.[53] Gas also produced a sulfurous odor that annoyed sensitive souls like Hippolyte Taine

---

48. For gas rates in various French and European cities see *Rapport*, March 29, 1881, p. 92; Margueritte, *Observations*, p. 30; A. Guéguen, *Etude comparative des méthodes d'exploitation des services de gaz* (Paris, 1902). For data on per capita consumption in various cities, see *Compte rendu des travaux de la commission nommée le 4 février 1885 en exécution de l'article 48 du traité . . . entre la ville de Paris et la Compagnie parisienne de l'éclairage et du chauffage par le gaz. Procès-verbaux* (Paris, 1886), p. 91; AP, V 8 O¹, no. 1677, "Etudes générales de l'éclairage étranger, 1898–1901"; no. 1070, "Notes pour servir à l'établissement des budgets."

49. Bérard, *Economie domestique*, p. 45. On the relative efficiency of gas lighting, see E. Jourdan, *Renseignements pratiques à l'usage des consommateurs de gaz* (Le Mans, 1868), pp. 10–14, and Philippe Delahaye, *L'Eclairage dans la ville et dans la maison* (Paris, n.d.), pp. 147–159, 268.

50. See chapter 2.

51. Corbin, *Miasme et la jonquille*, chap. 5.

52. Jean Escard, *Le Problème de l'éclairage à l'usine et à l'atelier* (Paris, 1910), pp. 38–40; Michel Chevalier, *Observations sur les mines de Mons et sur les autres mines de charbon qui approvisionnent Paris* (Paris, n.d.), p. 88; William Suggs, *The Domestic Uses of Coal Gas, as Applied to Lighting, Cooking, and Heating* (London, 1884), pp. 8–18, 157.

53. *Le Journal du gaz. Organe officiel de la chambre syndicale des travailleurs du gaz*, no. 76 (February 5, 1896), p. 3.

even in the street. That odor in fact was the source of a popular medical myth that identified gas plants as a refuge from cholera epidemics. One editor caricatured the PGC as a sinister figure surrounded by clouds of soot, sulfuric acid, and carbonic acid.[54] These emanations made potential customers hesitate before installing gas in their homes.

The hesitations were all the more serious in that gas was costly and inconvenient to install.[55] Customers had to pay for connector pipes from the main to their apartments, for interior pipes, and for fixtures. They also had to rent (or buy) a meter and certain cutoff nozzles on the mains. These charges amounted to thirty-six francs a year, nearly as much as a modest consumer would spend on the gas itself.[56] There were also fees for preparing the inspection papers and a monthly exaction for upkeep of the gas line. In addition, the PGC required a security deposit, which seemed to annoy potential customers. Even Baron de Rothschild and an English lord asked to be exempted from the requirement. Estimates placed the cost of initiating gas service between sixty and eighty francs.[57]

Making the installation expenses especially burdensome was the transiency of Parisian tenants, who might have used gas if they had found it previously installed in their new lodgings. The speculative construction of the Second Empire, which helped to renew the bourgeois housing stock, did give the PGC some support in this area. The Pereires' novel building enterprise, the Société immobilière, put gas fixtures in all its apartments along the new boulevard du Prince-Eugène (now the boulevard Voltaire). The industrialist Cail did the same for the sizable residential complex he developed in the tenth arrondissement. There were even isolated efforts to bring new, gas-lit apartments to the better class of wage earner. Despite these promising initiatives most tenants were unlikely to find gas fixtures ready for them to use as they took up new lodgings. Mounted mains went primarily into new apartment buildings and hardly touched the older stock of housing. Even in most new, luxurious buildings there was gas only in the hallways, not in individual apartments.[58] Landlords lacked

---

54. Girard, *Deuxième République*, p. 328; *Le Gaz*, no. 3 (April 30, 1866): 101; AP, V 8 O¹, no. 1294, press clippings.
55. The customer's responsibilities in installing gas are described in Emile Durand, *Guide de l'abonné au gaz d'éclairage* (Paris, 1858).
56. AP, V 8 O¹, no. 615, "Exonération des frais accessoires."
57. Ibid., no. 669, deliberations of September 20, 1862; no. 767, report of February 8, 1873; Margueritte, *Observations*, p. 6; Durand, *Guide de l'abonné*, pp. 35–113.
58. César Daly, *L'Architecture privée au XIXᵉ siècle. Nouvelles maisons de Paris et des environs*, 3 vols. (Paris, 1870), 1:224–225; AP, V 8 O¹, no. 725, deliberations of February 11, 1864; no. 726, deliberations of October 31, 1867; nos. 28–29,

pressure to bear the expense of installing gas fixtures. The rental market favored owners until the mid-1880s, and they easily leased unimproved properties.

Even if landlords or tenants decided to pay for the installation, they were likely to find the experience frustrating. The delays and errors arising from renting the meter, obtaining the obligatory certification from the prefecture, and completing the paperwork were so notorious that the *Daily Telegraph* of London satirized the situation in 1868. The PGC's engineers were certain that the prefect's rigor and slowness in inspecting the work seriously discouraged the operation.[59] Madame Jacquemart, a publican in Belleville, learned the labyrinthine ways of gas regulation in 1869. She had become a customer, installing the proper pipes and renting a meter without realizing that the gas mains on her street did not yet reach her building. The company had been trying to extend the mains, but the prefect had withheld authorization for more than a year. When at last the company was able to do the work and supply Jacquemart's cafe, the payment bureau ordered a cutoff of the service because the owner had not paid rent on her (unused) meter.[60] Not even the Parisian correspondent to the *Daily Telegraph* had imagined that such complications could arise, but they did.

Residents might have persevered through the difficulties and spent what they had to for installation if indeed gas was as convenient and necessary as its proponents asserted. However, gas did not have many applications and did not always accord with bourgeois life-styles. Lighting was the only use most Parisians envisioned for gas until the last years of the century. The PGC had originally hoped to develop gas heating but abandoned the idea in 1857 for lack of satisfactory stoves. Existing heaters spread disturbing odors and emitted hydrochloric acid. Moreover, gas heating was not economical. The company chose to develop coke, one of its by-products, as a source of heat and did not take gas heating seriously again until the 1890s.[61] The use of gas for cooking also proved to be some-

---

"Conduites montantes"; Michel Lescure, *Les Sociétés immobilières en France au XIXᵉ siècle* (Paris, 1980), p. 45.
59. *Le Gaz*, no. 5 (June 31, 1868): 70; Exposition universelle de 1878, *Rapports*, p. 46. British gas experts argued that public inspection improved the quality of work done on French installations. See Suggs, *Domestic Uses*, p. 49.
60. AP, V 8 O¹, no. 766, report of Lependry to director, April 18, 1869.
61. Ibid., no. 752, "Chauffage"; no. 1257, "Chauffage au gaz." When the company installed gas heaters in its appliance showroom, it took care to hide the meter from the public so as to avoid drawing attention to the cost. The PGC itself heated its offices with coke, not gas.

what of a dead end during the PGC's golden era. Gas engineers argued for the economy and convenience of gas cooking, but many customers did not like the taste of meats prepared through gas grilling. Interest in culinary uses of gas was so low that special cookbooks did not appear until the end of the century. Domestic servants slowed the entry of gas into the bourgeois home. Since they spent so much of their time in the kitchen, it is understandable that they would want a stove that heated the room during the winter as well as cooked the meals. One trade journal counseled mistresses to instruct their servants on the rationality and progress embodied in gas cooking, but maids had their own logic.[62]

When the PGC finally began to be concerned about the failure of its product to penetrate the residential market in the late 1880s, management probed the ways gas might serve the bourgeoisie. A consultant drew attention to the large Parisian *classe moyenne*, those paying five hundred to fifteen hundred francs in rent, who had so far been resistant to gas. The reason, he believed, was that these families spent most of their time in the dining room, which was rarely served by gas fixtures. When landlords had bothered to add gas lighting at all, they almost always put it in one room, the salon. Moreover, gas chandeliers (*lustres*) attractive enough for the dining room were uncommon and expensive. The consultant concluded that gas failed to enhance family life for these thousands of residents, so the tenants ignored it.[63]

Faced with all these problems, Parisians had a reasonable alternative to gas. Kerosene lamps arrived in France in the 1860s and immediately hampered the PGC from developing a domestic clientele. Per capita consumption of kerosene increased fivefold in Paris between 1872 and 1889. This source of illumination did not require expensive or cumbersome installation. Cheap and even attractive lamps quickly came to the market. They could be carried from room to room. Taken solely as a source of illumination, gas could not easily compete with kerosene. There is little wonder why the PGC was repeatedly accused of conspiring to keep duties on that fuel very high.[64]

Thus there is no reason to assume that French consumer preferences were guided primarily by an unconscious scorn for the novel or an indif-

62. Gas was best for quick cooking—omelets, a slice of ham, or an entrecote. Bourgeois cuisine entailed slow cooking over wood fires. See Zeldin, *France*, 2:750–751; Suggs, *Domestic Uses*, p. 126.
63. AP, V 8 O^1, no. 30, report of August 25, 1894.
64. Philippe Delahaye, *L'Industrie du pétrole à l'Exposition de 1889* (Paris, 1889), pp. 9–70; *Conseil municipal*, deliberations of November 7, 1892; *L'Echo du Gaz. Organe de l'Union syndicale des employés de la Compagnie parisienne du gaz*, no. 87 (November 1, 1900): 2.

ference to household conveniences. The Second Empire architect César Daly was justified in contradicting the shibboleth that the Parisian bourgeoisie was hopelessly infected with aristocratic preoccupation for public display. He asserted that domestic design in his day was "more concerned with hygiene and comfort than with ornament" and that rising standards of comfort provided the guiding principle for architects.[65] Well-off Parisians who shunned gas were responding to its concrete problems and limitations. They saw and appreciated gas in their stores, offices, and shops but had no strong urge to countenance the expense and inconvenience of bringing it into their homes. Hence the PGC benefited from rising standards of lighting mainly to the extent that commercial establishments implemented them. Nonetheless, there was a potentially large domestic market for gas since Parisians were open to new amenities that enhanced their lives at a reasonable cost. The PGC would discover and exploit this market when its older clientele seemed about to abandon gas.

The Profits of a Privileged Firm

The bookkeepers of the PGC were probably unconcerned that the source of the copious revenues they recorded was the business firm rather than the residential customer. From the clerks' vantage point their employer was faring remarkably well. The company never had an unprofitable year (see appendix, fig. A3). Indeed, it reached a new plateau of profitability every year except one (1877) between its founding and 1882. Profits rose nearly 175 percent during the 1860s as the company benefited from the annexation of the suburbs and from the commercial development of Paris. Returns rose another 65 percent during the 1870s. Top management spoke occasionally, in hushed tones, about the risks of capital, but supplying gas to the stores and offices of the city was in reality a golden opportunity.

The prosperity of the PGC may be measured in several ways. In terms of the portion of annual receipts, gross profits were enormous; they averaged 42.6 percent during the first thirty years of the firm's existence. Likewise, operating ratios (gross profits as a percentage of expenditures) underscore the success of the enterprise, averaging 72.7 percent (see appendix, fig. A4).[66] Perhaps a more refined measure, taking account of the relative yield of the investment, would be the return on immobilized capital (figure 1). Whereas government bonds yielded 4–5 percent and the

---

65. Daly, *Architecture privée*, 1:14.
66. Neither of these figures takes account of the revenues shared with the city of Paris after 1872.

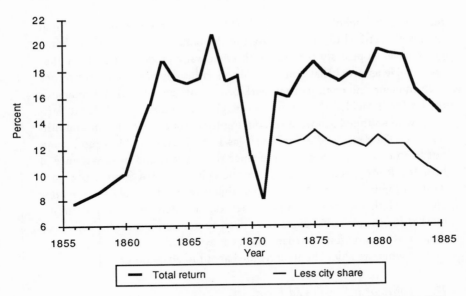

Fig. 1.   Return on capital, 1855–1885 (in percent). From AP, V 8 O¹, no. 907, *Rapports présentés par le Conseil d'administration à l'Assemblée générale, 1856–1905.*

average income from a real estate portfolio was 7–8 percent, the PGC returned an average of 17 percent during the 1860s.[67] After 1872, when the company began to share (with large sums set aside for reserves) profits with the city, the problem of calculating yields becomes more complicated. Should payments to the city be considered as part of the profits or as an expenditure? Technically, of course, the PGC was sharing its profits with Paris. Yet from the stockholder's perspective the payment was a cost of doing business, an expense no less inevitable than money spent on raw materials. Even if the city's share is deducted from gross profits, the PGC's returns on immobilized capital were still quite high, averaging 12.5 percent between 1872 and 1882. One franc of capital produced twelve centimes of profit for the PGC, whereas the Gas Lighting and Coke Company of London derived just eight centimes.[68] Only the most risky real estate venture in Paris could have been so remunerative.

Since the PGC was a limited-liability corporation, one of the handful in France before the liberalizing laws of 1863 and 1867, the stockholders

---

67. See Adeline Daumard, *Maisons de Paris et propriétaires parisiens au XIXᵉ siècle, 1809–1880* (Paris, 1965), p. 228, on profits from real estate investments.
68. AP, V 8 O¹, no. 709, report of Audouin to director, March 31, 1882.

were the chief beneficiaries of the business success. The capital of the firm originally consisted of 110,000 shares, each with a nominal value of five hundred francs. In 1860 the company raised another twenty-nine million francs in equity; but the corporate charter placed limits on the number of shares it could issue, so that was the last time ownership was further dispersed. The company subsequently covered its considerable investment needs through the sale of bonds. By 1897 the PGC had 257 million francs of debt. Although reinvestment of profits was the rule among most French firms, the PGC never tapped that source of capital.[69] Indeed, in the early years, when the firm was encumbered with the need to build productive capacity rapidly, it secured a short-term loan of four million francs from the Crédit mobilier to pay current dividends. The shareholders expected regular returns and grumbled when investment seemed to cut into their income.[70]

The identity of the PGC shareholders is destined to remain obscure, for the firm's archives do not contain a file on them. The only source is the proceedings of the annual general assemblies, which listed the stockholders who chose to attend.[71] These documents sustain the impression that ownership was rather heavily concentrated in the hands of a Parisian elite. For 1858, 380 stockholders possessed at least forty-three thousand shares, 40 percent of the outstanding equity. The owners of the merging gas firms still held the largest block of shares: the Dubochet brothers (former owners of the Compagnie parisienne) had 4,580 shares, Louis Margueritte (former owner of the Compagnie anglaise) 2,350 shares, Isaac Pereire 1,500 shares. Among the large stockholders were many titled people and well-known business figures, including members of the Haute Banque (the financial elite of France), Warburg, Mallet, Hentsch, Delessert, and Seillière. Ownership was still concentrated at the end of the golden age. In 1889, 1,047 people held 81 percent of the shares. A comparison of the lists from 1858 and 1889 shows impressive continuity. Families apparently held the PGC's stock over the long run for the sake of the returns. The duchesse de Galliera (1,154 shares), the comte de Grammont (607 shares), and the princesse de Broglie (1,037 shares) all prospered from doing so.

A detailed study of the acts of succession (inheritance tax declarations) for the fourth and fifth arrondissements in 1875 provides some insight

69. Claude Fohlen, "Entrepreneurship and Management in France in the Nineteenth Century," in *The Cambridge Economic History of Europe* (Cambridge, 1978), 7(1): 348–373.
70. *Rapport*, April 10, 1857, p. 10; May 16, 1865; AP, V 8 O¹, no. 724, deliberations of September 2, 1861.
71. AP, V 8 O¹, nos. 908–1001.

into the identity of smaller owners who may not have attended the general assemblies.[72] The findings reinforce the impression of concentrated ownership. Of the 835 estates worth at least five hundred francs declared in these primarily bourgeois districts, eighty-two contained some wealth in the form of stocks. Only six of these held the equity of the PGC; in five of the cases the stocks belonged to women without occupations, and the last case involved a rentier. The average value of their estates was just under sixty thousand francs; each person held an average of seven shares. The portrait is a classical one of small rentiers, who invested in the PGC for the same reason they bought railroad stocks and bonds, to obtain a secure income and long-term capital appreciation.[73]

The PGC did not disappoint either Madame la princesse de Broglie or the small rentier. Dividends, declared every year without exception, rose as high as 165 francs in 1882 and were not below 120 francs after 1875 (see appendix, fig. A5). This represented a return of more than 9 percent on the market value of a share. Those who retained their holdings, as many of the large owners appear to have done, realized considerable capital appreciation (see appendix, fig. A6). The market value of shares rose 54 percent between the beginning of 1862 and the end of 1869 and another 40 percent between 1872 and 1882. Nor were there many sharp drops to frighten the stockholders.[74] The narrow circle of investors in the PGC did very well as a result of their persistence.

The key to profitability was of course the high price of gas that the charter allowed the PGC to charge for fifty years. Regardless of whether thirty centimes was a reasonable rate in 1855, production costs fell by almost a third within the first ten years of operation. The PGC earned around twenty centimes on every cubic meter of gas sold. The company even made about five centimes per cubic meter on the fuel sold for street lighting, which was supposed to be "at cost."[75] Contributing to the handsome state of the PGC's balance sheet were impressive profits from the marketing of the by-products of coal distillation. The coke that remained in retorts after gas had escaped found wide use in Parisian households for heating. The firm was also fortunate to come into existence just as organic chemicals became essential to industry. Precisely at the moment the artificial dyestuffs industry was taking off, the PGC was one of the world's

72. AP, $D^1 Q^7$, nos. 11374–11380.
73. Charles-Albert Michalet, *Les Placements des épargnants français de 1815 à nos jours* (Paris, 1968), pp. 157–179.
74. The PGC did experience difficulties raising loans during the financial troubles of 1857–1858. See AP, V 8 O^1, no. 723, deliberations of May 1, 1858.
75. Ibid., no. 748, report of November 6, 1856.

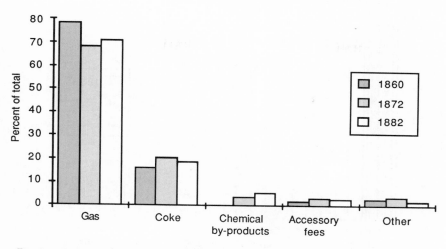

Fig. 2. Sources of Revenue for Selected Years (in percent). From AP, V 8 O¹, no. 907, *Rapports présentés par le Conseil d'administration à l'Assemblée générale, 1856–1905.*

largest suppliers of the essential raw materials, the residues of coal roasting. Naphthalene, aniline, alizarin, benzol, and naphthas all found important industrial uses. Since they were relatively scarce in the 1870s and early 1880s, the price that the PGC received for these former waste products was quite advantageous.[76] Revenues from by-products grew so substantially between 1860 and 1872 that the income derived from gas sales declined from four-fifths to two-thirds of the total (see figure 2).

With such assured profits, managers of the PGC might have chosen to overlook wasteful expenditures, but in fact they were extremely conscious of costs. Producing gas and by-products became markedly less expensive in the 1860s as engineers made some basic changes in the organization of labor and in operating procedures (see chapter 4). Their greatest challenge in reducing costs was to save on fuel and coal. Wages accounted for only a small part of operating expenses, but roughly half went to purchase coal, the basic raw material. In the earliest days of the firm there was discussion of acquiring a mine, but nothing came of it.[77] The company took other measures to reduce expenses. Its chief procurement officer received pay based on his success at arranging favorable contracts, and there were several agents on the scene at the developing coal fields of northern France.

76. Ibid., no. 721, "Instructions de Monsieur Regnault."
77. Ibid., no. 723, deliberations of October 17, 1855.

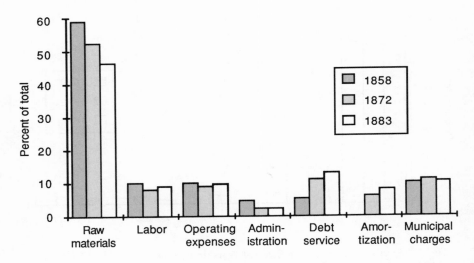

Fig. 3. Distribution of Expenditures for Selected Years (in percent). From AP, V 8 O¹, no. 907, *Rapports présentés par le Conseil d'administration à l'Assemblée générale, 1856–1905.*

The PGC could also take comfort in the fact that when coal prices rose, the company could recoup the loss by charging more for coke. And it did not necessarily have to reduce the coke rates when coal prices fell.

To save money on the roasting of coal was an obsession for production managers. They tinkered endlessly with the mix of fuels, substituting different grades of coal and burning by-products as market conditions dictated. They were even willing to risk angering the touchy stokers, whose hard job was made still more burdensome by constant changes in fuels. The search for the perfect furnace was another constant of managerial activity in the PGC, leading to basic innovations for the gas industry in France. The energetic management seemed rather oblivious to the fact that high gas rates ensured handsome profits regardless of the production costs.[78]

An expenditure the PGC could not control was the amortization of outstanding stocks and bonds. As a corporation with a limited life, these expenses necessarily burgeoned. By the 1880s they already accounted for a tenth of total expenditures—as much as labor—and would continue to put pressure on profit levels (see figure 3). Amortization costs were ex-

78. *Rapport*, March 25, 1869, p. 13.

penses of a distinct sort, however, because they went partly to the owners of the company.[79] Moreover, the PGC's negotiators had contrived to have the city pay far more than its share of the expense. The assets Paris would receive in 1906 would never compensate for the contribution it made to amortization costs. Thus stockholders had no real reason to complain about the rising portion of the budget devoted to this expense.

With the example of the PGC in mind, most owner-managers might well have concluded that their legendary secrecy about their firm's accounts was fully justified. The profits of the PGC became an issue of public discussion—indeed, scandal. "Excessive" was among the mildest terms the left-wing press applied to the returns of the PGC. Even financial journals came to regard the firm's accounts in an ironic light. The *Guide financier* noted in 1880 that "the public might believe that certain institutions are created to satisfy the needs of the people . . . and that a return of 25 to 30 percent ought to suffice to remunerate capital and risk. The public is profoundly mistaken. It is the public that is made for enterprises [like the PGC]; the interests of its shareholders are supreme."[80] Many Parisians were convinced that gas rates were unjustifiably high and produced outrageous returns for the PGC. Just how exceptional were the accounts of the PGC? The question is difficult to answer because comparative figures are rare and often problematical to use. The isolated cases historians have treated suggest that the gas company earned unusually high profits but was not entirely unique. A few firms, like the Crédit lyonnais and the Mines de la Grand' Combe, met or exceeded the financial success of the PGC, but only in their most profitable years (see figure 4). The public reacted so negatively to the profits of the PGC not only because of their consistently high level but also because they seemed unearned. The directors of the Forges d'Alais or Grand' Combe could declare that their investors undertook heavy risks and competed in an open market. The director of the PGC tried to advance a similar defense, but the public did not accept it. Parisians saw the corporation earning copious returns yearly in the safe business of supplying gas at inflated rates. They saw political manipulation, not entrepreneurship, as the source of its prosperity. Much of the public responded to the PGC as a symbol of privilege and venality—ultimately an insult to the ideals of the Republic.

---

79. When a share was amortized, the holder received an *action de jouissance* bearing 5 percent interest and entitling the holder to a share of the profits when they were above 5 percent.
80. *Guide financier*, January 27, 1880.

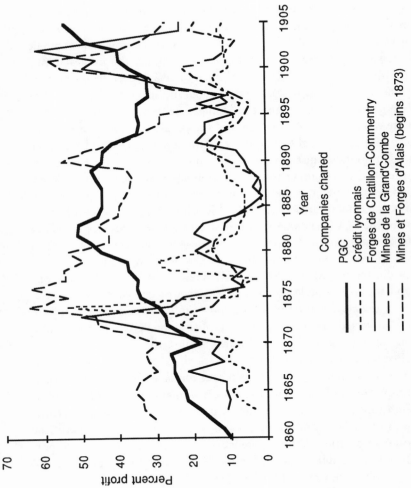

Fig. 4. Profitability of the PGC Compared to That of Other Firms (gross profits as percentage of share capital). From AP, V 8 O¹, no. 907; Jean Bouvier et al., *Le Mouvement du profit en France au XIXe siècle* (Paris, 1965), pp. 407–453.

A "State within the State"

The PGC tried to take advantage of its role as a private firm entrusted with an important public service. On the one hand, any attempt to curb its plans—say, to build a factory in a controversial locale—met with vocal claims that the restriction interfered dangerously with the firm's efforts to fulfill its public trust. On the other hand, officials who tried to regulate internal operations received a curt reminder of the private nature of the firm. The PGC was generally quite successful in mastering its fate through the 1880s. The parties with grievances against the firm could not find the means for redress. With good reason one writer referred to the PGC as a "state within the state."[81]

Efforts to cheat the gas company, hold it accountable for damages, or prosecute it met with notable failure during its golden age. Dishonest customers soon developed a repertoire of schemes to fool or bypass their meters, but in the end they were usually detected. And the company was ruthless in prosecuting cheaters. It even sued the estate of a customer who had committed suicide rather than submit to the embarrassment of a trial.[82] Users who intended to pay their bills but merely wished to circumvent the straitjacket of rules were also frustrated. Thus tenants' attempts to avoid installation costs by sharing gas from their landlords' conduits were firmly undermined. The company forced customers to switch from hourly rates to metering without having any official right to do so. It freely invaded users' premises to search for fraud with the tacit approval of the prefect.[83] Management could conceptualize relations with customers only in terms of their submission to the firm's regulations, and by and large they obtained that end.

Before the threat of electricity the PGC did not actively work to improve street lighting. The firm did not even have a well-equipped laboratory in which to test new lighting technology until after 1890. At best, it cooperated with the initiatives of municipal lighting engineers. The public, stirred by ever-rising needs, was not satisfied for long. By interna-

81. Félix Moutet, *Souvenirs de l'Exposition universelle de Paris (1878)* (Paris, 1879), p. 88.
82. AP, V 8 O[1], no. 669, deliberations of November 12, 1862; July 8, 1863; no. 92, report of October 26, 1859 (fol. 165); no. 877, entry of December 26, 1859. An anonymous customer mailed a payment of a hundred francs for gas that he or she had stolen twenty years earlier. See no. 676, deliberations of April 1, 1874.
83. Ibid., no. 274, "Correspondance avec les ingénieurs du service municipal." The prefect protested the PGC forcing its customers to switch from hourly rates to meter rates. See no. 270, report of August 3, 1857.

tional standards the City of Lights was not particularly well lit.[84] In 1867 the search for better illumination led to the first serious alternative to coal gas, oxygenated gas (*gaz oxygène*). The potential competitor jolted the PGC's shareholders so much that a special meeting of the board of directors had to be held. The new fuel did provide brilliant illumination but entailed the great expense of double mains, one for gas and one for oxygen. The entrepreneur behind the venture complained bitterly that the PGC and the city engineers conspired to suppress the alternative and never gave it a fair chance. The PGC took advantage of the charter of 1870 to insert a provision that removed any chance for the competitor to get a foothold in Paris.[85] With that challenge behind it, management returned to its aloofness regarding street lighting. Only with the early electrical experiments on the place de l'Opéra in 1878–1879 did the city have the leverage to demand better illumination. The search for improvements that the company soon undertook on the rue du 4-Septembre was an implicit admission that Parisians had a right to expect better lighting. Ultimately the PGC was fortunate that the municipal council did nothing to hasten the era of electrical lighting. The city slowed the pace of advance for electricity by insisting on experiments even when lighting was well past the testing stage and by debating the concession endlessly. The aldermen's beneficence toward the PGC was partly the unintended result of administrative inertia and partly the result of the city's dependence on revenues from gas sales. Whether there were more sinister motives is impossible to establish.[86]

Incidents of gas fires and explosions provided another, sometimes tragic, context for the public to attack the PGC. A conflagration at the Opéra Comique forced the prefect to order theater owners to adopt electricity in 1887. The most destructive of many explosions occurred on the rue François-Miron in central Paris in July 1882. Nine people were killed and sixty injured. As happened so often, the PGC escaped blame for the disaster. The examiners' report found no one at fault. A leaking water pipe had loosened the earth beneath the gas main, and vibrations from surface

84. Ibid., no. 1064, "Rapport sur les conditions de l'éclairage public (1879)"; Auguste Lévy, *Communication faite au nom de la Compagnie parisienne du gaz par M. Auguste Lévy* (Paris, 1900), pp. 3–4.

85. AP, V 8 O¹, no. 726, deliberations of October 24, 1867; no. 1642, Tessié de Motay to Alphand, January 30, 1872; *Rapport*, September 23, 1869, p. 15.

86. AP, V 8 O¹, no. 728, deliberations of January 13, 1879; no. 24, "Eclairage électrique à Berlin et à Paris (1890)"; Conseil municipal de Paris, *Note historique sur le régime de l'électricité à Paris (1878–1904)* (Paris, 1906).

traffic had caused the main to crack. Perhaps the excellence of the company's inspection operations and its success at supervising labor go far to explain why the PGC was rarely found culpable for loss of life or property. Also at work were the vigor of the defense the company always mounted and the courts' preference for finding individuals at fault.[87]

The gas company even had its own way with customers and the authorities during the period of revolutionary insurgency following the Franco-Prussian War. With coal supplies dwindling and impossible to replenish, the company ceased providing gas to private customers in November 1870. Yet management continued to charge for the rental and upkeep of meters, connector pipes, and valves. After receiving complaints, "often violent ones," from customers, the company yielded on the rental of meters five months later but insisted on collecting the maintenance fee for the connector pipes and valves. Management did suffer a moment of anguish at the hands of the Communards, but the crisis passed quickly. In late April 1871 the head of the Sûreté générale came to search for hidden arms in the corporate headquarters. While he was there, he had the safe opened and seized 183,000 francs in cash. The assistant director, Emile Camus, managed to have the money returned within a few days, probably by threatening to extinguish street lights. The Communards were evidently not interested in persecuting even this rich and unpopular corporation. Still, the close call prompted the PGC to cooperate with the insurrectionary regime "in a spirit of conciliation and prudence," but the détente was purely for appearances. Management withheld millions of francs it owed the city in duties until the government of Adolphe Thiers was firmly in control. During the Bloody Week the company somehow found arms for its employees, who protected corporate property from the "insurgents."[88] The PGC survived the greatest revolutionary threat in its history with no harm except bad memories.[89]

•   •   •

87. There were 123 gas explosions producing seven fatalities between 1882 and 1886 according to corporate records. See AP, V 8 O^1, no. 1065, "Etat numérique des explosions et autres accidents produits par le gaz"; no. 685, deliberations of June 9, 23, 1887; no. 270, director to prefect, August 13, 1898. On the rue François-Miron incident, see Préfecture, B/a 144. One explosion for which the PGC did not escape responsibility took place at the Préfecture.
88. AP, V 8 O^1, no. 727, deliberations of November 24, 1870, to August 10, 1871; no. 753, report of June 16, 1871; Denys Cochin, "La Compagnie du gaz et la ville de Paris," *Revue des deux mondes*, série 9, 54 (November 15, 1882): 438.
89. Not only was the PGC successful in most of its conflicts with local government, but it also lobbied hard in Parliament and defeated the effort to create a national tax on gas. See *Rapport*, March 28, 1874, p. 41.

The only issue that had the power to crystallize inchoate public dissatisfaction into organized protest was the question of gas rates.[90] This is not to say that controversy arose from narrow economic interests alone. The vigorous struggle to lower gas prices between 1879 and 1884 deserves attention because it combined economic, ideological, and political grievances. It brought the forces of legal and administrative conservatism into conflict with militant republicanism just as the people's regime was rooting itself. Many Parisians read a good deal more into the clash than the matter of a few centimes more or less for gas.

Frustration with the cost of gas first galvanized not the politicians and administrators charged with running Paris, but the consumers themselves. The municipal councilmen, though they might respond to the discontent of their constituents, had reason to be satisfied with the PGC's profitability. The city was finally benefiting from those sizable returns. The councilmen could regard the annual share they took from the company, which went as high as fifteen million francs, as a hidden tax on enterprises and even as a progressive levy on wealthy households. The rhetoric that swirled around the gas issue never represented the city's profits in those terms, but proponents of alternate lighting technologies were quick to suspect that the municipal council protected the gas industry from new competitors for the sake of the revenues, if not for darker reasons.

The profile of gas customers ensured that the protesters would be shopkeepers, especially dry-goods merchants, grocers, restaurateurs, and publicans, organized by twenty-seven corporate associations. Their protest revealed much frustration. They knew that rates were half as high in London. The PGC's argument that the British example was misleading carried little weight, for in 1875 Bordeaux had signed a forty-year agreement that put the price of gas at twenty-two centimes per cubic meter for private use and five centimes for public lighting. One widely read journal asserted that gas cost only three centimes to produce and distribute.[91] There were many observers, including sophisticated ones, who casually believed that

90. Discontent with gas prices had produced public clamor even before the merger of the six firms. Les Compagnies d'éclairage par le gaz de Paris, *Observations sur un travail intitulé Rapport adressé à S. M. l'Empéreur sur les expériences . . . pour déterminer les conditions économiques de la fabrication du gaz de houille* (Paris, 1855), p. 72.

91. *Conseil municipal*, deliberations of January 3, 1881; Margueritte, *Observations*, pp. 19–20, 30–33. In Brussels gas cost twenty centimes and fell to ten centimes in 1890.

profits from by-products fully covered the cost of making gas, leaving most of the PGC's thirty-centime charge as pure profit. A city lighting engineer noted that "one is so thoroughly accustomed to thinking that gas costs the company nothing" that the figure he calculated, fourteen centimes, startled him.[92]

Aggravating the sense of being cheated were the merchants' problems of economic dislocations. Under prosperous conditions protest might not have emerged because retailers would have passed the cost on to their customers. The lamentations about high overhead signaled commercial difficulties of the same sort that produced recriminations against department stores. Philip Nord has argued that Haussmann's urban renewal project bifurcated the Parisian commercial community into a declining sector in the old, central city and a prospering district along the boulevards.[93] It is likely that the shopkeepers most sensitive to high gas rates were in the former sector. The timing of organized protest, which arose in 1879, derived from the business slowdown following the Universal Exposition the year before. The recession exposed the weakened position of the merchants in the old downtown. It is also possible that the approach of the first municipal election under a secure republican regime, in 1880, encouraged mobilization.

The multiple sources of tension ensured that rallies in favor of lower gas rates would be large. The police estimated the size of a gathering in September 1880 at two hundred; in February 1881, three hundred; in March, twelve hundred; and in April, five hundred. Such was the passion generated by the "gas question" that during the municipal election of 1880 only the explosive issue of secular education received more attention.[94]

The question of gas prices engaged voters because it had an ideological dimension as well as a practical one. The militants frankly recognized the PGC as an Imperial institution in a republican era, in this most republican of cities. The firm's absurdly generous charter had been imposed on the people by a narrow, self-interested elite, they contended. The protestors of the 1880s were continuing the anti-Imperial, antimonopolist discourse that had appeared just before the Franco-Prussian War and had contributed to the diffusion of republicanism among small businessmen. The

---

92. AP, V 8 O¹, no. 1626, "Proposition de M. Sauton, 4 mars 1896."
93. Nord, *Shopkeepers*, chap. 3.
94. Préfecture, B/a 890, 916; Cochin, "La Compagnie du gaz," p. 444. On the election of 1880 Cochin wrote, "Lay education and cheap gas, those were the rallying cries."

PGC, along with the railroads, the water company, and the coach company, all stood as corrupt examples of "financial feudalism."[95] Militants of the 1880s wished to republicanize the gas industry, which meant, at the very least, making it responsible to public interest. Revoking the concession and turning the service into a municipal agency appealed to some Radicals.[96] Even Opportunist republicans, respectful of property rights, found the balance sheets of the PGC hard to defend and favored some revisions in its charter. Parisians' predisposition to distrust large concentrations of capital were reinforced in this instance by palpable evidence that a monopoly was indeed violating the public interest.[97]

Municipal politicians attempted to respond to the frustrations of their constituents, but the ideological and emotional overtones complicated the practical matter of lowering rates. The councilmen had two options. They could negotiate with the PGC and, by offering new advantages, principally a longer concession, bring the firm to accept reduced prices. This solution presupposed the fundamental legitimacy of the 1855 charter. The alternative was to compel the firm to reduce rates without offering it any compensation on the grounds that thirty centimes was an illegitimate price. Negotiation was the surer route to lower rates but entailed the politically unpopular act of giving the PGC further privileges. Most aldermen ultimately found that option unacceptable.[98]

The public agitation for lower prices had brought some councilmen to commence bargaining with the PGC. Above all else, the firm coveted a charter that would prolong the life of the company beyond 1905 and was willing to lower prices in exchange. Negotiators quickly assembled an agreement for the approval of the municipal council even before that body faced the election of 1880. The project called for a reduction of rates by five centimes in exchange for a forty-year lengthening of the PGC's charter. Moreover, the city would have to guarantee profits at the current (lofty) level. The council, however, dared not bestow so many new benefits on the firm with an election approaching, and the verdict of the balloting

95. Georges Duchêne, *L'Empire industriel: Histoire critique des concessions financières et industrielles du Second Empire* (Paris, 1869). On the antimonopolist rhetoric under the empire, see Sanford Elwitt, *The Making of the Third Republic: Class and Politics in France, 1868–1884* (Baton Rouge, La., 1975), pp. 28–30, 158–165.
96. Duchêne, displaying Proudhonist influences, anticipated revolutionary syndicalism by calling for the public monopolies to be run by cooperative associations of workers. *L'Empire industriel*, p. 316.
97. The debate over the gas monopoly was by no means unique. The same clamor for reform applied to railroads. See Doukas, *French Railroad and the State*, pp. 45–59.
98. AP, V 8 O¹, no. 1626, "Rapports du Conseil municipal."

was to make this settlement, so generous to the PGC, politically impossible.[99]

The PGC approached the negotiations secure in its right to receive thirty centimes. A legitimate contract, revised several times since 1855, had guaranteed that rate. If production costs had fallen dramatically since the firm's founding, that was only because management was doing its job; the decline did not create a consumers' right to lower prices. Spokesmen for the firm argued that comparisons with London were utterly inappropriate because British firms had no limit on their longevity and thus no amortization costs. The PGC tried to shift blame for the high rates to the city. Paris received a two-centime duty on each cubic meter sold and shared profits. If the council wished to lower gas prices, it had only to renounce the city's revenues. Management saw obtaining nothing less than a franc-for-franc compensation for reducing rates as its sacred duty to shareholders. Preferably it would take the form of a longer charter, which would reduce amortization costs. The company might also require municipal subsidies for the capital expenditures that lower rates could necessitate. The officers of the PGC claimed not to comprehend the rage of their customers and were scornful of the agitation. They perceived no grounds for compromise. However desirable a settlement on the company's terms might be, the officers recognized that there would be further opportunities if talks failed at the moment.[100]

A minority of aldermen, mostly on the right, shared the view that the PGC had a legitimate claim to thirty centimes and would have to be offered attractive compensations for lower rates. Their position received powerful reinforcement from the prefect and from the chief municipal engineer in charge of the thoroughfares, Adolphe Alphand. These administrators were not touched by the ideological side of the issue. They argued for "realism" and contested the aggressiveness of Radical aldermen. The municipal engineer and the director of the PGC were colleagues of the Corps des Ponts et Chaussées and probably shared the outlook that accompanied that elite background.[101] The prefect, who led the negotiations, was clearly hoping for some face-saving concessions from the company so as to placate Radicals and allow him to point to some sacrifices on the part of

99. Ibid., "Rapport présenté par M. Martial Bernard (séance du 27 décembre 1880)."
100. Ibid., no. 707, "Observations relatives au rapport de Monsieur Cochin"; Margueritte, *Observations.*
101. *Conseil municipal*, deliberations of 1881; AP, V 8 O¹, no. 1642, "Mémoires au Conseil municipal"; no. 274, "Correspondance avec les ingénieurs du service municipal."

the corporation. Such concessions were not forthcoming. The PGC bargained with confidence in its position.

For two years representatives of the city and the PGC searched for a settlement. The company insisted on a monopoly that would last until 1945. It asked for guaranteed profits at the high levels of the early 1880s and wanted to raise the amount of profits exempted from sharing with the city by more than a million francs. In exchange, the firm would reduce rates to twenty-five centimes, either at once or in stages. Additional small reductions would be possible as profits rose. The rate for workshops with gas motors could fall to twenty centimes. These terms were unacceptable to the majority of the municipal council. In 1882 the prefect warned the PGC that a forty-year elongation of the charter was out of the question; the council might accept twenty-seven years, at most. At one point the prefect could offer only fifteen years. The problem was that aldermen did not see the company making sacrifices, and they did not believe the city should reward the PGC for its selfish comportment.[102]

The majority of aldermen was interested in recovering the rights of Parisians—in their eyes illegitimately bargained away by a corrupt Imperial administration. They hoped to force the PGC to lower its rates, for they felt under pressure from constituents to confront, not reward, the company. The aldermen believed that a five-centime reduction, for which the PGC demanded so much in return, was far too small to satisfy the electorate. The public was counting on a reduction of at least ten centimes. Moreover, Radicals were loath to lengthen the charter. Paralleling the dilemma of national politicians in their dealings with the railroads, Parisian Radicals regarded such concessions as a dangerous alienation of public sovereignty. Yet they did not seek to expand the power of the State, so they could not firmly call for municipalization of the utility either. The Radicals' position was an uneasy compromise that recognized the practicality of a limited charter but left open the possibility for another solution sometime in the future. Pressure to prolong the charter of an Imperial institution like the PGC upset the delicate balance among conflicting values the Radicals held regarding large-scale enterprise and state power. One feature of the negotiations with the PGC that deeply displeased Radicals was exposing the contradictions in their position.

The long recession into which the Parisian economy had slipped by the end of 1882 made the climate of opinion still less hospitable for a negotiated settlement. Retailers in the declining city center felt the weight of gas

102. *Conseil municipal*, deliberations of 1882; *Rapport*, March 29, 1881; March 24, 1882.

bills all the more and renewed their demands for lower rates. One aspect of the economic hardship was a weakening of the world market for Parisian luxury products as machine production and sweated operations came into their own.[103] Certain voices found in the PGC a scapegoat for the difficulties: since fuel was so expensive, Parisian artisans could not use gas motors and so could not compete against English or German manufacturers. Councilman Level argued that the PGC had imposed a great burden on the working-class family. Because gas motors were too costly, wives could not work at home; husbands and children were not well cared for. Level promised that gas at twenty centimes would permit domestic workshops to flourish and "prepare a profound transformation in women's working conditions."[104] Given the social diffusion of gas consumption at the time, his argument was implausible. Yet it does underscore the ideological, even messianic, dimensions the debate over gas rates could assume. The economic difficulties of the 1880s raised the stakes entailed in reduced rates while making negotiations more difficult.

Radical councilmen came to the strategy of compelling the PGC to reduce rates without compensation through application of article 48 of the charter. This provision had been intended to allow the city to take advantage of fundamental changes in lighting technology ("des procédés étrangers au système actuel") that might appear after 1855. The article gave Paris the right to impose the new methods on the PGC and benefit from whatever economic advantages might result. In principle, the minister of the interior was supposed to have convened a board of outside experts every five years to consider technological progress. No such body had been summoned before the controversy arose in 1879. The protesting consumer groups clamored for a commission. They hoped it would apply article 48 to the lower production costs the PGC had achieved since 1855 and rule that reduced rates were in order.[105]

The minister finally convened a commission of gas experts in 1880, but it only protected the PGC. In the first place, the commission defined its assignment precisely as the company wished—examining changes in production, not since 1855, but rather since the last agreement with the city, in 1870. Second, the experts interpreted article 48 in a literal sense. They sought to determine whether an entirely new process for making gas had developed. They explicitly dismissed mere improvements in older methods as part of their purview. The commission also denied that progress in

---

103. On the recession, see Nord, *Shopkeepers*, chap. 4.
104. *Conseil municipal*, deliberations of August 7, 1882.
105. Besnard, *Gaz à Paris*, pp. 109–116.

the treatment of by-products was a valid consideration. Thus the vast profits from coke and organic chemicals, which protestors viewed as having reduced production costs to a negligible level, were to be ignored. Having defined progress out of existence, their conclusion was inevitable. Article 48 offered no ground for reducing gas rates.[106]

Public opinion and most aldermen never accepted the validity of the commission's report. Indeed, they took it as one more sign of the corrupting influence of the PGC. It seemed self-evident that thirty centimes was an outrageous charge and that the charter must offer some source of redress if it were a valid document. The municipal council established its own expert body, which of course found that lower prices were fully justified. Aldermen adopted the report of the second commission in April 1882 and voted to use the courts to attain its recommendation. Consumer groups loudly applauded the decision. The prefect managed to postpone the legal battle and continued bargaining with the PGC, but an attractive proposal did not emerge. By 1883 the economic crisis emboldened politicians. In February councilmen proposed to repurchase the gas monopoly and municipalize the service, but this was mainly a symbolic act and a sign of frustration. The council once again called on the prefect to confront the PGC, and in late March he gave heed to the political pressure, perhaps because he wished to soften the firm's negotiating stance. The prefect decreed an immediate reduction in gas prices to twenty-five centimes.[107]

The decree was fraught with ambiguity and had a questionable legal status, but the company feared the difficulties it would stir. The prefect issued the order but hesitated to promulgate it, so it was not yet enforceable. One councilman declared that even he did not know whether he owed the company twenty-five or thirty centimes.[108] It seems likely that the prefect had meant little more than to warn the firm. Nonetheless, the minister of the interior refused the PGC's request to revoke it, and customers began to take matters into their own hands. More than fifteen hundred of them reduced their own bills on the basis of the decree.[109] The company considered cutting off their service but backed down when the

---

106. *Procès-verbaux et rapport de la commission nommée le 23 janvier 1880 en exécution de l'article 48 du traité intervenu le 7 janvier 1870 entre la ville de Paris et la Compagnie . . .* (Paris, 1880).
107. *Conseil municipal,* deliberations of February 2, 1883, and March 28, 1883; [Préfet] E. Poubelle, *Note en réponse aux observations présentées par la Compagnie parisienne du gaz à MM. les experts le 7 février 1884* (Paris, 1884).
108. *Conseil municipal,* deliberations of March 28, 1883.
109. AP, V 8 O¹, no. 730, deliberations of April 30, 1883; no. 683, deliberations of November 20, 1883, and February 26, 1884. By late 1883 customers had withheld more than 1.2 million francs.

municipal council voted to find it in violation of its charter if it did so. In the end the company asked customers to pay thirty centimes and offered to create an escrow account in case the courts found the prefect's decree valid. In the meantime the company prepared to contest the matter before the Council of State.[110]

Management had reason to look hopefully to the Council of State, for it had ruled in favor of the PGC on other matters.[111] Moreover, the prefect's decree rested on uncertain grounds at best. Only if the council wished to take republican revenge on an Imperial institution would it penalize the firm. The predisposition was unlikely. Councillors of state had far more in common with the managers in terms of background, schooling, and outlook than with Radical aldermen. In addition, the council's jurisprudence favored broadly defined property rights over public claims. Inevitably it decided that the PGC was protected from the arbitrary decree of the Parisian administration by a legitimate charter. There were no grounds for applying article 48 under the circumstances. Management was delighted with the ruling and voted the defense lawyer a bonus of fifteen thousand francs.[112]

For its part, the municipal council had no alternative but to disappoint its constituents on gas rates. Fortunately for the aldermen, the use of gas was not yet a mass phenomenon, and the matter was not a daily concern for most voters. There was no political will to reopen negotiations with the PGC and seek reductions by granting a longer charter. The majority of aldermen appeared certain that their electors wanted that compromise no more than they wished to pay thirty centimes. Even the continuation and intensification of the recession did not change such preferences. Retailers dropped the PGC as the immediate target of anger and focused more fully on department stores.[113]

Thus the PGC traversed the contentious 1880s unscathed. Its privileges now seemed unassailable. Article 48, which had worried the company enough that it had tried (unsuccessfully) to remove it from the charter of 1870, was no longer a threat. Management could feel confident that other opportunities for a prolonged charter would arise. The municipal council could not help but be aware that it would have to make concessions if it wished to benefit consumers. It had no other leverage over the PGC,

110. Ibid., no. 730, deliberations of April 30, 1883.
111. For example, in 1882 the Council of State had overridden the prefect's decision forbidding the PGC to build a coal tar plant where it wished. See ibid., no. 682, deliberations of September 1, 1882.
112. Ibid., no. 730, deliberations of July 31, 1884.
113. Nord, *Shopkeepers*, chap. 6.

which had made clear it would surrender nothing without full compensation. Managers had to be pleased with their legal position in 1885.

Though the point was easy to overlook, managers also had reason to be pleased with the very terms of the contention. At no point had protesters questioned the internal regulation of the firm. The municipal council, too, respected completely the autonomy of the PGC as a private enterprise responsible to the stockholders. That scandalous profits might have accumulated at the expense of the personnel of the firm, as well as of the customers, seems not to have occurred to anyone. Only councilman Jules Joffrin, one of the early Socialists, spoke specifically for the gas workers, and his point was simply against lengthening the charter so as to allow their exploitation to end sooner.[114] Perhaps managers might have failed to appreciate their good fortune in this regard because they could not yet even imagine that the state would intervene in the internal operation of a private firm.

In fact, the victorious 1880s had laid the groundwork for further problems. Bitterness and frustration of public opinion toward the firm had intensified. Even local politicians who had been friendly toward big business would be hard pressed to defend the PGC as reputable. The many aldermen who were uneasy with or hostile to big business would be eager to humble this corporation above all others. Moreover, managers were to find their political vulnerability all the more debilitating when the rules of the game suddenly changed after 1890. The economic liberalism that had guaranteed the PGC its autonomy regardless of pricing policies was about to weaken. Republican politicians of the next decade would seek to reorient relations between the heretofore laissez-faire state and the emerging industrial society. The PGC would be a natural candidate for inclusion in the resulting experimentation. Thus the company's celebration in 1885 was a swan song of sorts. The firm's mastery of its own fate was about to vanish.

• • •

Ultimately the history of the PGC through the 1880s reflected poorly on the ability of French political and administrative institutions to regulate an important public service in an equitable manner. The Opportunist Republic was loath to accept blame for the shortsightedness of the Second Empire, but it offered no source of redress. There is little wonder that committed Parisian republicans read press reports on the balance sheets of the PGC and concluded that the regime of the people was not working as it should. Yet if the PGC served its stockholders so well, and so much

114. *Conseil municipal*, deliberations of August 9, 1882.

better than it did the public, it was not only because of unearned privileges. Market forces conferred earned advantages that even Radical republicans had not questioned, and the firm did garner the rewards of market operations. Only when both the marketplace and the political regime placed unaccustomed restrictions on the PGC did its golden age end. That was to happen after 1885.

TWO

The Era of Adjustments, 1885–1905

Whatever the quality of the entrepreneurial skills the managers brought to the PGC during its first thirty years, the company's success was guaranteed by fortunate circumstances. Through most decades of the nineteenth century, gas was the most efficient, modern, and desirable form of lighting; new industries had an insatiable appetite for the by-products of distillation; Paris had entered a long period of almost uninterrupted commercial expansion; and the company was able to fend off all demands that societal obligations take precedence over its business calculations. It must have been utterly disorienting for management when each of these pillars of prosperity collapsed one by one during the PGC's fourth decade. Market forces and politics came to undermine the company's successful mode of operation. A struggle for customers replaced the assurance that gas consumption would grow on its own. Furthermore, political pressure for labor reform forced the PGC to modify its bottom-line calculations. The firm did adapt to the new circumstances and even managed to recreate a semblance of its former prosperity; yet its officers could not find the means to perpetuate the company beyond 1905. They had to struggle against a multifaceted crisis of the liberal order.

The New Customers

Accustomed to ever-expanding gas consumption up to the mid-1880s, the PGC suddenly began to experience sporadic declines from the level of the previous year, as happened in 1885, 1890, 1892, 1893, 1894, 1897, 1901, and 1902. Annual use of gas hardly increased during the entire decade of the 1890s (see appendix, fig. A1). Part of the problem was the sluggishness of the Parisian economy, which had suffered from a serious recession during the 1880s and did not really recover its former vitality until around 1905.[1] The pace with which new shops, stores, hotels, restaurants, offices, and agencies opened was far below that of the 1850s and 1860s. An industry-specific difficulty was the appearance of formidable competition from another energy source, electricity.

Gas engineers had disparaged the new competitor during its initial street experiments in the 1870s. They argued that electric lighting was unreliable, expensive, and uncomfortable. However, they soon came to respect the clarity of illumination, the efficiency (even though the technology was still rudimentary), and the convenience. Electrical lighting emitted no odor, less heat than gas, and no noxious residues.[2] Unfortunately for the PGC, customers noted the same attributes. In addition to convenience, electricity had in its favor the aura of novelty and progress. Gas had enjoyed these symbolic advantages decades earlier but now lost them. The PGC's officers must have been disconcerted when *Le Temps* characterized gas in 1882 as "the lighting source of the poor."[3] Such thinking was undoubtedly on the minds of owners of the Parisian department stores, cafés, and hotels as well. Those intangible qualities weighed heavily in converting the largest commercial customers. Gas ceased to be the energy source of choice.

Electricity quickly gained many of the customers that had established gas as the preferred mode of lighting. By 1890 more than fourteen thousand electric lights were burning in Parisian cafés and restaurants. More than sixteen thousand lit theaters and concert halls, and another eight thousand illuminated the merchandise of department stores. The Grands Magasins du Louvre, once the single largest consumer of gas, had been among the first emporiums to convert to the new lighting in 1878.[4] Most of the celebrated establishments that formed the apex of commercial Paris followed suit over the next decade or so. The Grand Hôtel, which had

1. See Jacques Rougerie, "Remarques sur l'histoire des salaires à Paris au XIXᵉ siècle," *Le Mouvement social,* no. 63 (1968): 71–108, for an index of business activity in Paris.
2. P. Juppont, *L'Eclairage électrique dans les appartements* (Paris, 1886). Of course, the electrical industry had to improve its distribution systems before it could be an effective competitor.
3. *Le Temps,* no. 7817 (September 19, 1882): 1.
4. AP, V 8 O¹, no. 24, "Eclairage électrique à Berlin et à Paris"; no. 1257, "L'Importance de l'éclairage électrique comparé à la consommation du gaz"; no. 709, "Etat nominatif des établissements faisant usage de l'éclairage électrique (5 decembre 1881)"; no. 679, deliberations of October 11, 1878. On the spread of electricity, see Alain Beltran, "Du luxe au coeur du système: Electricité et société dans la région parisienne (1800–1939)," *Annales: Economies, sociétés, civilisations* 44 (1989): 1113–1136.

consumed 325,000 cubic meters of gas in 1886, switched entirely to electric lighting and had only five small gas heaters and three gas stoves in 1898. The PGC's second-largest customer in the 1880s, the Bon Marché department store, used almost no gas by the beginning of the twentieth century. The Café de la paix, which had once glowed with the warmth of gas lighting, had electric illumination and did not even employ gas for cooking. Among the emporiums only the Bazar de l'Hôtel de Ville remained an important gas customer.[5] Had the losses been confined to just the large establishments—the Paris of tourists—the PGC could have sustained them with equanimity. But the large firms set the trends. By 1890 smaller offices and agencies consumed almost as much electricity as theaters. In 1898 the leaders of the gas workers' union found themselves meeting in a neighborhood café lit with electricity.[6]

The psychological moment in which the gas era gave way to the age of electricity was, for many Parisians, the Universal Exposition of 1889. This was the first exposition at which gas shared the task of illumination with its younger rival, and one journalist portrayed the situation as a life-and-death struggle between the two energy sources. In fact, the exposition was more appropriately a symbol of the coexistence that could and would occur. The main fairgrounds, the Champ de Mars, was lit by electricity, while the Trocadéro heights, rising above the fairgrounds, had gas illumination. There was no doubt in the minds of most visitors that electricity was the superior lighting source. The reporter from *Le Pèlerin* recalled the "dazzling torrents of clarity on the Champ de Mars, even at night," for this was the first fair to remain open after dusk. The *Universal Illustré* declared that "electric lighting triumphed in all ways and revealed itself as the lighting of the future." According to *Le Cosmos*, "in the midst of profuse electric lighting . . . there seems to be no place for gas." The *Gazette Nationale* gave gas the hardest knock by describing the PGC's display pavilion as a sort of museum of medieval artifacts. Of course, it was just such attitudes—that electricity was the energy source of modern life—that caused the best customers to depart from the PGC. In spite of the many invidious comparisons, the company could take comfort from two significant victories at the exposition: gas motors ran the electric dynamos that illuminated the newly constructed Eiffel Tower, and even critics noted

5. Ibid., no. 270, "Etat de quelques établissements ouverts au public et employant le gaz."
6. *Le Journal du gaz. Organe officiel de la chambre syndicale des travailleurs du gaz*, no. 134 (July 5, 1898): 3.

that the new sort of gas lamps being tried out were decidedly more effective than the older ones.[7]

The PGC had relied so heavily on commercial and industrial customers that the early defections were ominous. Management had but one choice, to exploit the domestic market that had thus far escaped its grasp. The company pursued this option—belatedly, but successfully. Between 1885 and 1905 the PGC not only greatly expanded its list of customers; it also changed the social profile of its clientele.

As the PGC sought to expand into the domestic market, it was fortunate that resistance to gas consumption had not really been based on deeply rooted attitudinal and psychological inhibitions. Practical drawbacks and economic considerations had discouraged lighting with gas. The PGC could reduce some of the inconveniences, and it sought to do so when it had to. In 1887 the company reached out to the sixty-five thousand apartment dwellers, almost all in luxury buildings, whose residences were near a mounted main. Management did so by offering to install at its expense the internal pipes, a kitchen lighting fixture, and a stove.[8] In the first year of the program alone, nearly twelve thousand tenants became gas users, by far the largest annual increase in customers the PGC had ever experienced. By 1905, 137,000 new customers had accepted the offer of free installation of fixtures. In effect, the company had finally managed to conquer the bourgeois and haut-bourgeois residential market. Hardly an apartment that rented for more than five hundred francs was without gas. Such gains refuted the claims of one corporate officer that "gas is disdained by the upper classes and seekers of comforts."[9] Convenient and inexpensive access to gas brought it into the homes of the well-off.

Of course, even with the free installation program gas was still not likely to become a mass-consumption commodity. The common people did not reside in the fashionable buildings in which the PGC had installed mounted mains, nor would they willingly pay nearly as much in ancillary charges (meter rentals, rental of connector pipes, maintenance fees) as for the gas. Even employees at the gas company itself were deterred by these inhibitions on gas use: only one in twelve office clerks of the PGC was a customer of his employer in 1887.[10] With the prodding of city hall, the

---

7. AP, V 8 O¹, no. 1292, "Exposition de 1889," press clippings.
8. *Rapport*, March 29, 1888, pp. 6–12.
9. AP, V 8 O¹, no. 1292, "Rapports et notes émanant des divers services."
10. Ibid., 148, "Etat nominatif des agents abonnés de la compagnie (28 avril 1887)."

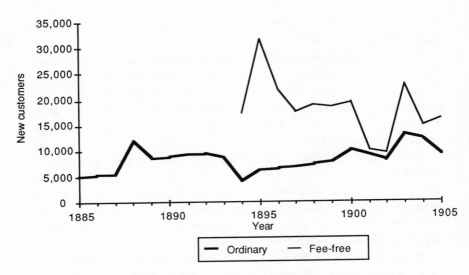

Fig. 5. Annual Number of New PGC Gas Customers, 1885–1905. From AP, V 8 O¹, no. 907, *Rapports présentés par le Conseil d'administration à l'Assemblée générale, 1856–1905.*

company took the monumental step of democratizing gas use in 1894. It created the fee-free program: residents of apartments renting for less than five hundred francs annually would not have to pay for the installation of pipes, the rental of a meter, or upkeep of equipment. Eventually the company even excused them from leaving a deposit. In exchange, the modest renters had only to accept a gas lighting fixture and a stove, both of which the company provided at its expense. The PGC decided to put mounted mains in any building in which three tenants accepted this agreement so as to make the investment profitable while diffusing the use of gas as widely as possible.[11]

There was a massive response to the fee-free program. Eighty percent of the new customers after 1894 came to the PGC as a result of the policy. Fee-free customers also accounted for 80 percent of the growth in gas consumption after 1895. In the decade between the initiation of the program and the end of the company's charter, 227,000 customers were added, as many as the PGC had had in 1889 (see figure 5). Thus the company entirely renewed its clientele in its last fifteen years.[12]

11. *Rapport*, March 29, 1893, p. 7; March 29, 1894, p. 43.
12. AP, V 8 O¹, no. 616, "Augmentation dans la consommation de l'éclairage particulier." See appendix, figure A2, for the total number of customers.

In rough terms a third of the ordinary people of Paris became gas users in these years.[13] No occupational breakdown of the new customers exists, but we can speculate that modest clerks, shopkeepers, civil servants, and salespeople formed the bulk of them. The growth of new accounts was so large that some better-off workers undoubtedly became fee-free customers as well. Whereas in 1888 barely 5 percent of residents had gas in their homes, by 1905 about two-thirds of Parisian households did. Naturally the new customers did not use gas in the same way as the former, primarily commercial ones. The average account in 1900 consumed only a third of the gas it had in the 1860s.[14] The new customers also used gas at different times of the day and for different purposes. During the PGC's first decade, daytime gas use accounted for only 10 percent of all consumption. At the expiration of the charter, however, daytime consumption reached 40 percent of total demand. Most of the increase resulted from cooking and heating. Indeed, the company had placed more than 375,000 stoves in customers' homes by 1902.[15] The general evolution, then, was from the commercial customer who lit the establishment at dusk to the small, domestic consumer who prepared meals with gas.

The democratization of gas consumption was by no means an isolated or idiosyncratic aspect of French consumerism. It occurred in the last twenty years of the century, decades that witnessed one of the most visible restructurings of popular consumerism in modern times. At that point new foods—coffee, a wide array of fruits and vegetables, dairy products—definitively entered the diet of the masses. An important feature of the new mass consumerism was the decline of the secondhand apparel market and its replacement by the ready-made clothing trade. The advent of mass gas use reflected broader trends not only in timing and direction but also in causation. As in the case of food and clothing, the change was not a simple consequence of rising disposable income. A growth of earnings was an evident prerequisite but had occurred between 1850 and 1880 without

13. I base this assertion on the fact that Paris of the 1890s had about 610,000 lodgings renting for less than five hundred francs. See P. Simon, *Statistique de l'habitation à Paris* (Paris, 1891), p. 14.
14. Dividing the volume of gas sold by the number of customers shows the average consumption per client fell from 1,703 cubic meters in 1866 to 683 in 1902. Since these figures include the gas used for public lighting, they are useful only for suggesting an order of magnitude. Another indication of the changing profile of gas use was the average gas bill. For ordinary customers it was 183 francs; for fee-free customers it was 39 francs. See AP, V 8 O¹, no. 24.
15. Ibid., no. 617, report of P. Lauriol, April 25, 1903. The reports to the stockholders provide figures on day consumption of gas.

notable changes in consumerism.[16] What permitted mass consumption was a shift in marketing methods. Just as the popular department store, with its lower markups and consumer credit, gave the common people an opportunity to buy new apparel of mediocre quality, the PGC's policies of lowering the cost of installation and distribution allowed the mass use of gas. Thus marketing innovations permitted the nineteenth-century revolution of everyday life to intensify and democratize. In the case of the gas industry the innovations helped to satisfy the ever-rising standards of lighting and convenience that had fueled the earlier prosperity of the PGC. The same forces would one day make electricity essential to domestic life.[17]

The reviving fortunes of the PGC and the gas industry in competition with electricity were primarily tied to finding a new clientele and new uses for gas. Yet there were also technical innovations that allowed gas to compete more successfully for the lighting of commercial establishments. At first the PGC had failed to find an effective response to the brilliance of electric lighting. The so-called intensive lamps that the company tried in the late 1870s were problematical in that they were so much more costly than older street lamps and required more care. The next innovation the PGC put on the Parisian thoroughfares was the hot-air intensive lamp, which recirculated the oxygen used for burning gas. The illumination was stronger, but the lights proved unsuitable for outdoor use and generated too much heat for indoors. The gas lighting industry was saved by a Viennese chemist, Carl Auer, who perfected the incandescent gas lamp, which came into wide use at the turn of the century. Whereas conventional gas lamps had produced light by igniting carbon particles, the Auer lamp burned gas for heat, which made a filament glow. Experts found that its light was nearly equal to that of an electric bulb, and it cost less.[18] The incandescent lamp complemented the growing use of gas for cooking and heating, for all the new applications required fuel that burned at a high temperature. The PGC adjusted production methods accordingly. With the Auer lamp the company was able to retain some of the large establishments that comprised its most coveted clientele. The Bazar de l'Hôtel de Ville, on the rue de Rivoli, was one department store that remained with gas lighting, using fifteen hundred incandescent lamps in 1898. The

16. Lenard R. Berlanstein, *The Working People of Paris, 1871–1914* (Baltimore, 1984), chap. 2; Maurice Lévy-Leboyer and François Bourguignon, *L'Economie française au XIXᵉ siècle* (Paris, 1985), pp. 23–42.
17. The Exposition of 1900 showed the potential for the development of electrical appliances. See AP, V 8 O¹, no. 1296, "Exposition de 1900."
18. Paul Lévy, *L'Eclairage à l'incandescence par le gaz* (Paris, 1905).

company scored a major success when the postal service chose gas over electricity, putting two thousand lamps in its headquarters and another twenty-four hundred in its neighborhood bureaus.[19] There was no question of restoring the former, unchallenged preponderance of gas lighting in the large establishments, but the Auer lamp slowed the rate of defection to electricity. The new lamp did impose one cost, however, on the gas industry: it was vastly more efficient than the older types of lighting and used much less gas. One engineer claimed that the Auer bulb consumed one-seventh the gas for the same amount of illumination. Understandably, gas companies welcomed the Auer lamp with some reservations.[20] Its principal benefit was to preserve customers, not to boost gas consumption.

A final change that augured well for the use of gas in Paris was a reduction in rates. The city and the company finally worked out an arrangement that brought the price of a cubic meter down to twenty centimes in 1903. The reduction could only encourage petit bourgeois consumers to add more gas jets or burn the ones they had longer. Gas at twenty centimes might also have encouraged them to replace their wood or coke stoves with gas ones.[21] It is interesting to note that immediately after the price reduction took effect, the rate at which bourgeois residents (those who did not qualify for the fee-free offer) became customers also picked up decisively. Between 1888, when the free installation program first reached out seriously for the bourgeois clientele, and 1902 the PGC added an average of 8,250 customers yearly. Between 1903 and 1905 it averaged 11,460 new customers a year. Once gas became a mass commodity, the PGC learned that lower rates were an essential response to competition.

It is true that in the 1880s gas lost markets as well as the symbolic advantage of representing progress and modernity. Yet there is a proper irony in calling the 1890s the dawn of the electrical era. During these very years gas finally became a household commodity, which it never had been in Paris during its golden age. The gas industry had experienced a fundamental transformation and found a place for itself beside its young competitor. In the course of adapting, the PGC extended the nineteenth-century revolution of everyday life to the masses. There were inevitable political implications in the change. The pressures weighing on a public service that served an elite were bound to be different from those on one

---

19. AP, V 8 O¹, no. 690, deliberations of August 25, 1894; no. 270.
20. René Champy, *Nouvelle encyclopédie pratique du bâtiment et de l'habitation*, vol. 11, *Eclairage public et privé* (Paris, n.d.), pp. 39–40; Lévy, *L'Eclairage*, p. 25.
21. When the Eiffel Tower opened, its restaurants resisted using gas stoves because the fuel was so expensive. See AP, V 8 O¹, no. 1292, report of Lefebvre to director, March 11, 1889.

serving the multitude. Demands for reform had a much greater reso-
nance, for politicians had to recognize that their constituents were now
gas users. Indeed, political pressures came to require as many adjustments
from the PGC as did market forces. Having saved the bottom line by facil-
itating the democratization of the clientele, the PGC's managers found
they also had to yield some of their autonomy in administering the personnel.

The Pursuit of Social Peace

Not even a decade elapsed between the first heated round of negotiations
over the disposition of the Parisian gas concession and the next round. Yet
a century might have passed, so different were the dominant issues and
outcomes. Though there were plenty of echoes of the debates that had
taken place in the 1880s, the questions that mattered most after 1890 were
far more comprehensive and transforming. They entailed nothing less
than making the PGC a model employer and public utility, guided less by
market forces than by political and ideological considerations. The discussions about the future of the company constituted a small but telling sign
that a new era in French sociopolitical life had opened in the 1890s. The
fate of the PGC became entangled with the gropings of politicians and
reformers to deal with an emerging mass industrial society. Management's
quest for a renewed charter and its partial dependence on the political
winds blowing in the mercurial capital placed the PGC on the forefront of
the shift. Indeed, it is arguable that no other French enterprise had to
adapt more fully to the faltering of the state's economic liberalism during
the 1890s. [22]

The appearance on the Parisian cultural scene of writers who refused to
look upon society as a collection of individuals and who exalted the nation
or the race is familiar to historians as a sign of the emerging crisis of the
liberal order as the nineteenth century drew to a close. [23] Less well known
was the commitment of many political leaders, ranging from the nonsocialist left to the moderate right, to achieving social peace by adjusting
policies that had heretofore been dictated by orthodox economic liberalism. Market forces no longer seemed relevant to the problems of the day.
The perceived threat of collectivism reinforced the pressure to take a new
direction. Within the context of such a crisis, Parisian municipal council-

22. For a sustained, masterful discussion of France's economic liberalism, see Richard Kuisel, *Capitalism and the State in Modern France* (Cambridge, 1981).
23. Zeev Sternhell, *La Droite révolutionnaire: Les Origines françaises du fascisme, 1885–1914* (Paris, 1978), chap. 1.

men dared to intervene in the internal operations of the PGC. Also within the context of the crisis, management accepted the need to establish labor relations and customer policy on a new basis.[24] The result was that the PGC ceased to function as a private enterprise. During the last fifteen years of the company's life, the French state seemed on the verge of founding new relations with an increasingly industrial society. The PGC became at once a model for the adaptation, a showcase for the efforts to achieve industrial peace, and a guidepost for the limits to the new initiatives.

• • •

Another round of negotiations opened by seeming much like the previous one. At the urging of thirty aldermen, the prefect renewed talks with the PGC about lower gas prices in October 1890. These aldermen came from both the right and the left, all representing districts in central Paris.[25] They were probably under pressure from shopkeeper constituents to obtain more favorable rates. Since both sides approached the talks with earlier assumptions intact, failure was inevitable. Once again the company engaged in hard bargaining; it asked for another twenty-five years in exchange for lowering its charge by five centimes. The left majority on the council, strengthened by the election earlier that year, did not approve those stipulations any more than in the 1880s. Councilmen believed that the election had given them a mandate to attack the PGC.[26] They hoped to achieve lower prices through some process, as yet obscure, that would not enhance the privileges of the despised PGC. The subcommittee examining the gas question was not even inclined to report the results of the talks to the full council.[27]

The collapse of negotiations based on older approaches opened the way for a fresh perspective as well as for an array of social considerations that had not appeared on earlier agendas. The Radical alderman Frédéric Sauton, representing the Saint-Victor quarter (fifth arrondissement), had long sought the means to reduce gas costs without lengthening the PGC's charter. He authored a plan that won the favor of the council and nearly won acceptance from the firm. Sauton looked ahead to 1906 and saw that future gas consumers could enjoy very low prices because the new gas

---

24. Judith Stone, *The Search for Social Peace: Reform Legislation in France, 1890–1914* (Albany, N.Y., 1985); Sanford Elwitt, *The Third Republic Defended: Bourgeois Reform in France, 1880–1914* (Baton Rouge, La., 1986); Herman Lebovics, *The Alliance of Iron and Wheat in the Third French Republic, 1860–1914: Origins of the New Conservatism* (Baton Rouge, La., 1988). Lebovics dates the crisis of the liberal order from the depression of the mid-1880s.
25. *Conseil municipal*, deliberations of October 26, 1892.
26. AP, V 8 O[1], no. 616, "Abaissement du prix de gaz."
27. *Conseil municipal*, deliberations of October 26, 1892.

firm, whatever it would be, would inherit without charge all the assets of the PGC. He argued that it was unreasonable to make current consumers pay for the assets so that later ones could have so favorable a situation. Sauton's ingenious proposal was to remove the cost of amortizing bonds from the PGC and place it on its successor after 1905. The savings from this arrangement, enhanced by reducing the interest on the bonds from 5 percent to 4 percent, could be used to lower gas prices. Whereas the PGC would continue to receive thirty centimes—and therefore could ask for no further concessions—customers would pay twenty-five centimes (twenty centimes for gas motors). [28]

The Sauton project provided what most alderman needed, the means to give voters lower prices without lengthening the charter. The objections raised to the plan largely concerned suspicions that the project harbored an implicit scheme to keep the PGC alive beyond 1905. An amendment incorporated into the text by royalist councilman Denys Cochin, which permitted the city to impose a longer charter on the company in 1906, strengthened that suspicion, but not enough to scuttle the project. [29] The plan also attracted the management of the PGC. Since electricity was by now a visible and feared competitor, the firm had to abandon its Olympian indifference to the customers' complaints and start competing for an enlarged clientele. It was clear that a five-centime reduction could be advantageous, all the more so because the decrease would be painless for the company. By late 1892 most aldermen rightfully believed they were on the verge of a satisfactory solution to the interminable gas question. But suddenly and unexpectedly the company raised new demands and sabotaged the project.

In December the PGC took advantage of hastily written wording in the revised charter of 1870 and made an agreement impossible. Whereas the charters of 1855 and 1861 had required the company to give the city its gas mains and distribution apparatus without charge and to have outside experts establish the value of the remaining assets, the charter of 1870 carelessly omitted these stipulations. As ratification of the Sauton proposal was in sight, the company suddenly notified the prefect that Paris would have to pay for the gas mains and accept management's evaluation of the assets, which was bound to be highly inflated. The company later withdrew the second demand but insisted that the city could not take pos-

28. Conseil municipal de Paris, *Rapports et documents, 1892,* no. 14, "Rapport . . . par F. Sauton (27 octobre 1891)"; no. 35, "Rapport . . . par Sauton (20 juin 1892)"; no. 97, "Abaissement du prix du gaz (26 juin 1892)."
29. Ibid., no. 35.

session of the plants or equipment until there was a settlement on the value and mode of reimbursement.[30] Councilmen inevitably saw the demands as insidious plotting on the part of management to take further advantage of Paris. When the prefect read the announcement to the council, cries of betrayal filled the chamber. "Here is a case of extortion!" exclaimed alderman Alphonse Humbert.[31] Never perhaps had councilmen so despised the PGC.

Why did management scuttle negotiations it had patiently pursued over several months and for the sake of which it had made (as we shall see) a number of expensive commitments? The motivations were unclear then and are still so. Aldermen assumed that the new demands, because they were unprecedented, were pretexts for hidden reasons but did not convincingly expose them. One councilman connected the failure to the death of an influential member of the board of directors, Raoul-Duval. He died in January 1892, and it is not clear why the PGC would have waited ten more months to undermine the project if that were the key to the matter.[32] Sauton himself asserted that the company had never wished to expand its productive capacity, which the lower prices would have forced it to do. This explanation falters because in 1892 the problem management faced was excess capacity.[33] It is clear that the company did want to reduce gas prices. In November it had secretly hired a publicity agent to coordinate the efforts of consumer groups in putting pressure on the council to lower gas rates.[34]

The most likely reason for the reversal of the company's position was a series of cumulative dissatisfactions. No doubt, there had always been voices warning against the project, for the PGC was in effect giving up its best bargaining chip—the promise of lower gas prices—in the campaign to achieve a longer charter. Furthermore, it was becoming increasingly clear that the value of the distribution system, which the city was supposed to receive free of charge in 1905, would be great. Between 1887 (when the free-installation program was initiated) and 1892 street mains, mounted mains, connector pipes, and stoves had cost thirty-five million francs, and the company could anticipate spending many times that

30. AP, V 8 O¹, no. 24, "Procès relatif à la canalisation."
31. *Conseil municipal*, deliberations of December 5, 1892.
32. Ibid., deliberations of January 25, 1901 (remark of Ernest Caron); AP, V 8 O¹, no. 688, deliberations of January 30, 1892.
33. The PGC had rushed into a huge expansion of plant and equipment in the early 1880s only to meet recession and stagnating gas consumption for the next decade and a half.
34. AP, V 8 O¹, no. 1257, Jules Aronssohn to director, November 23, 1892.

amount over the next thirteen years.[35] The ambiguity of the 1870 charter presented a chance to recover part of the expenses, and some executives must have found the opportunity irresistible. The final, and probably principal, reservation was the labor demands that aldermen continued to add to the Sauton project. By December the project was no longer a simple device to reduce gas prices. It had become nothing less than a blueprint for idealized industrial relations. The demands would be expensive to meet, but that was not management's only objection. The labor clauses councilmen wanted to add threatened to undermine managerial authority over personnel. Ultimately the social agenda of the municipal council came to take precedence over the practical matter of gas prices and made an agreement between the city and the company unattainable.

• • •

Councilman Sauton had negotiated during 1892 with the issue of gas prices foremost in his mind. But the gas question was already deeply embroiled in larger social issues that had not arisen earlier. The unfocused lamentation of the Socialist alderman Jules Joffrin about the company's exploitation of its personnel in 1882 erupted into a major and compelling campaign a decade later. The councils of the 1890s insisted on better treatment for workers and employees, but not just for the sake of the personnel. The nonsocialist left had grown concerned about the industrial society that was emerging in laissez-faire France. The aldermen worried that labor unrest had the potential to destroy what they valued about the Republic. Political disorders in Paris and the wave of populist, antiparliamentary agitation associated with General Georges Boulanger confirmed their anxieties and encouraged them to search for solutions. Parisian Radicals, who had long stood for the creation of a popular republic, broadened their essentially negative views of government. They were prepared to compel the private enterprise at hand, the PGC, to become a laboratory for workable industrial relations. This project entailed a veritable redefinition of the relation between the state and the laboring classes in a liberal order. Of course, the council did not undertake such an ambitious project in isolation. The personnel of the PGC, now organized with the encouragement of the aldermen of the left, naturally pressured for the experiment. Moreover, national political figures of the left, sharing the councilmen's anxieties and aspirations, seconded the Parisian initiatives. Cooperation and conciliatory gestures came even from conservatives and from business

35. As we shall see, the fee-free program eventually boosted investment in gas distribution equipment.

circles. The reorientation of labor policy at the PGC was an emblematic phenomenon of the times.[36]

Efforts in the Parisian municipal council to alter relations between the laissez-faire state and society had a very modest history before 1892.[37] Electoral and ideological considerations had encouraged some interest in labor since the council first became republican, in 1870, but that interest remained circumscribed for quite a while. Until the economic difficulties of the mid-1880s construction workers were the sole beneficiaries of the council's influence. In 1873 the council brought the building unions together with contractors' associations to set wage standards for public-works projects. It was expected that the wage agreement (called the *série de prix*) would influence pay levels throughout the industry. The agreement was revised upward several times, most notably in 1882, when wages were at their apex. What councilmen hoped to accomplish was to standardize and reinforce the current practices most favorable to the construction workers, the largest category of Parisian laborers. In doing so, they wished to ensure labor peace and please a large constituency. The still unsystematic thinking of the republican council about workers was shown by its obliviousness to labor questions during the lengthy negotiations with the PGC in the 1880s.

The depression of the 1880s and the entry of a few representatives of new working-class parties into the council decidedly heated the rhetoric heard at city hall and expanded aldermen's concern about labor but did not eliminate caution. The Socialist theorist Edouard Vaillant, who was a councilman, was resolute about transforming his ideology into concrete programs to make the city a model employer and a benefactor to Parisian laborers. He proposed compelling entrepreneurs with city contracts to accept the eight-hour workday, abide by the *série de prix*, offer workers accident insurance, and favor French labor over foreign. Vaillant and his few fellow Socialists urged upon the republican councilmen progressive programs that the majority often rejected.[38]

Most councilmen during the 1880s continued to support the wage agreement. They tried to ban subcontracting (*marchandage*), which had

---

36. Stone, *Search for Social Peace*, chap. 2. Lebovics, *Alliance of Iron and Wheat*, chap. 7, portrays even the Méline ministry (1896–1898) as a regime of "social pacification."
37. The essential source on the labor policy of the Parisian municipal council is Ville de Paris, *Les Conditions du travail dans les chantiers communaux. Recueil annoté des discussions, délibérations, et rapports du Conseil municipal de Paris* (Paris, 1896).
38. Ibid., pp. 311–607.

been technically illegal since the Second Republic. As unemployment continued to rise, the council was eager to reserve jobs for French workers and did not hesitate to insist that employers limit the non-French personnel to 10 percent. Beyond these points, however, a majority was less easy to assemble. Vaillant's proposal to ensure a full complement of benefits for the workers of the metro was soundly defeated in June 1886. The council rejected his call for the eight-hour day, though it did accept nine or ten hours. That position was not too bold because it was already the practice at many work sites. Once again aldermen were willing to do no more than encourage favorable current practices.

The depth of the council's commitment to wage earners was still open to question. It treated laborers on the sites of the 1889 Universal Exposition with the same indifference it had shown toward the gas personnel. The council failed to bestow on city workers the benefits it claimed for construction laborers. Furthermore, the reforms that the council did approve were often a matter of posturing. There were no provisions for effective machinery to enforce the resolutions. Aldermen voted as a matter of principle and left it to the prefect to apply measures that were likely to be costly or to anger influential Parisians. It is no wonder the prefect gave the ordinances low priority. Councilmen also passed favorable labor measures knowing that the powers of the city were severely limited by the central government. The Opportunist Republic, dominated by sincere but socially conservative republicans, followed earlier regimes in insisting on orthodox liberalism. The ministers of the interior regularly annulled ordinances that interfered with the free operation of the marketplace. The government did not even allow Paris to encourage progressive practices, endorse the hiring of French wage earners, or advocate the nine-hour day.[39] The circumscribed powers of local government gave aldermen of the nonsocialist left room to make cost-free statements in favor of workers without being held accountable. There is not much evidence before 1890 that the republican majority sought a more meaningful voice in labor matters.

Such acquiescence to economic orthodoxy did not survive into the 1890s any more than did free trade on the national level. The council's policies regarding the PGC marked a new stage in its concerns about labor. The elections of April 27 and May 4, 1890, had sent thirty-nine Radicals (or Radical-Socialists) and nine Socialists to the council, making for a left majority of eight.[40] The solid victory of the left was especially important

---

39. Ibid., pp. 629–1860.
40. These figures are based on political affiliations provided by Le Temps.

because the pivotal public issues were shifting. Through the 1880s the Parisian left had been guided by the ideology of "shopkeeper radicalism"—patriotic, antimonopolistic, and protective of the small producer and consumer.[41] Such a republicanism had shaped the council's sparing measures in favor of workers. The Radicalism that emerged after the election, first in Paris and then briefly in the rest of France, had a different shading. It was far more concerned with the position of labor in society. Radicals drew on their heritage of concern for the autonomy of ordinary people to challenge the autocratic control of employers over their personnel.[42] Electoral pressures made a rethinking of republican priorities all the more desirable. The depression of the 1880s had tested the alliance between wage earners and Radicals. At the end of the decade Radicals watched their working-class constituency desert them for the Boulangists and then for the Socialists. Yet big-city Radicals were not prepared at that point to abandon their traditional clientele, and they contested the Socialists' claims on the working-class vote until the new century. Speaking on the Sauton project, Radical alderman Paul Strauss declared that "the council cannot consider the interests of gas workers as a secondary matter in the presence of the rise of Socialism we have witnessed."[43] Perhaps Strauss could be so open about political motives because he genuinely believed that his party had much to offer wage earners.

The radicalism that developed after 1890 was keenly attuned to the dangers alienated and oppressed workers posed to the Republic. Radicals began to perceive the wisdom of making the public authorities into protectors of wage earners. There was an agreement—a fragile one, at least—that republican liberties had to be extended to the workplace, freeing the personnel from the arbitrary power of the employer.[44] It seemed wise to find ways for capital and labor to meet and negotiate on more equal terms, and Radicals acknowledged the necessity of strengthening trade unions for

41. Philip Nord, *Paris Shopkeepers and the Politics of Resentment* (Princeton, 1986), chap. 6.
42. On the political traditions that encouraged suspicion of employers' authority, see Anne Biroleau and Alain Cottereau, *Les Règlements d'ateliers, 1789–1936* (Paris, 1984); Donald Reid, *The Miners of Decazeville* (Cambridge, Mass., 1985), pp. 67–102.
43. AP, V 8 O¹, no. 149, "Rapport présenté par M. Patenne, au nom de la première commission sur une pétition de la Fédération du personnel de la Compagnie parisienne du gaz (8 juillet 1895)."
44. On attempts to extend republican rights to the workplace, see Donald Reid, "The Third Republic as Manager: Labor Policy in the Naval Shipyards," *International Review of Social History* 30 (1985): 183–202, and "Putting Social Reform into Practice: Labor Inspectors in France, 1892–1914," *Journal of Social History* 20 (1986): 67–87.

that purpose.[45] Parisian politicians took the reorientation so far that they eventually estranged much of their petit bourgeois constituency by neglecting its interests.[46]

In accepting industrial reform, the Parisian Radicals anticipated by just a few years the direction of their comrades in national politics. Industrial reform became the agenda of the nonsocialist left as the nineteenth century drew to a close. After 1892 the state no longer prevented the city from intervening in labor matters.[47] Indeed, when the Chamber of Deputies passed significant new reforms for railroad employees in 1897, it probably took some inspiration from the municipal council's program for the gas personnel.[48] The clearest sign among national leaders of the Radicals' new social consciousness was the Léon Bourgeois government of 1895–1896, the first all-Radical one and the first to make social progress its principle concern. Inspired by solidarist principles, Bourgeois proffered the celebrated "extended hand" to the working class with promises of legislation to alleviate some of its most bitter problems.[49] On both the local and national levels, then, Radicals admitted the bankruptcy of classical liberalism and the need for new terms in ordering an industrial society. Gas workers were among the first to grasp the extended hand and receive its largess.

Negotiations over the Sauton project arrived just at the right moment to place the PGC in the position of being a test case for new industrial relations. The left majority of the council sought to apply its reform-mindedness to the personnel of the PGC in two ways. The first was to encourage union organization for both laborers and office clerks. Although some Radicals may have been sensitive to the charge that unions only exacerbated social unrest, most were impressed by the potential role of unions to balance the bargaining power of the personnel and the em-

45. Leo Loubère, "The French Left-Wing Radicals: Their Views on Trade Unionism, 1870–1898," *International Review of Social History* 7 (1962): 203–230.

46. Nord, *Paris Shopkeepers*, chap. 8.

47. Commerce Minister Alexandre Millerand's decree of August 9, 1899, which allowed communes to set "normal and current" wages for workers on public projects, is often cited as the beginning of a new era of municipal activism in labor affairs. This case study of the gas industry makes clear that the new era opened before Millerand became France's first Socialist minister, with the state passively permitting municipal ordinances it would once have annulled.

48. *Journal officiel. Chambre. Documents*, annexe no. 2,853 (session of November 30, 1897). The legislation was advanced through the efforts of Radical Maurice Berteaux and Socialist Jean Jaurès.

49. J. E. S. Hayward, "The Official Social Philosophy of the Third Republic: Léon Bourgeois and Solidarism," *International Review of Social History* 6 (1961): 19–48. See also Richard Sanders, "The Labor Politics of the French Radical Party, 1901–1909" (Ph.D. diss., Brown University, 1971).

ployer. Once created, the unions were apt to pursue goals that the council could not always sanction. Nonetheless, relations between the municipality and the unions remained for the most part cordial.[50] The second front for recasting industrial relations was for the aldermen to insist on better pay and work conditions. Radicals accepted the need to take policies regarding pensions and minimum wages out of employers' hands and make them social rights. These demands would become a formal part of any agreement with the PGC, a new cost the company would have to accept to procure any further advantages. Both the union leaders and the left majority of the council agreed that the personnel had a right to share in the profits—still deemed enormous—of the PGC. Radical councilmen were in effect calling on the gas company to become a model of the sort of industrial enterprise in which workers could feel they had a stake. The aldermen prepared themselves morally for the task of pursuing social peace by making Paris more of a model employer than it had been up to then. The council raised wages of municipal workers and set five francs as the minimum wage in June 1892.[51]

Two seminal moments for the city's labor activism, as far as the gas company was concerned, came in May and December of 1892. In the first instance, the subcommittee considering the gas question accepted the proposal by Paul Brousse, a leading Socialist councilman, that there be no agreement with the PGC without extensive improvements in pay and work conditions.[52] Paul Strauss, representing the Rochechouart quarter (ninth arrondissement) elaborated on the proposal at the end of the year. Strauss added to the Sauton project a long list of labor reforms that the PGC would have to make. The Radical alderman called on the company to set aside 2 percent of its profits for raises, create a minimum wage of 5 francs, and accord the *série de prix* to its craft workers. He also demanded another 2 percent of profits be used to raise the salaries of office clerks so that they would earn three thousand francs after fifteen years of employment and thirty-six hundred francs after twenty-four years.[53] The proposed salaries were far in excess of current pay; moreover, the Strauss amendment implied that the company would have to grant raises mainly on the basis of seniority, a practice that managers formally rejected. These provisions echoed the demands made by the workers' and employees'

50. *Le Journal du gaz* (1892–1899) chronicles the relations between the union and the municipality.
51. AP, V 8 O¹, no. 153, "Décisions relatives au personnel de la ville de Paris."
52. Ibid., no. 149, "Historique des rapports avec la ville de Paris relatif au personnel de la Compagnie."
53. *Conseil municipal,* deliberations of December 5, 1892.

unions, but profit sharing was also inspired by solidarist thought. The amendment pointed to the means by which left Radicals hoped to reconcile laborers to capitalistic society.[54] The cosponsors of these far-reaching proposals did not include any Socialists. Instead, there were twelve Radicals and Radical-Socialists, three Republicans, and one conservative (whose seat in the ninth arrondissement was home to many gas clerks).[55] The Radicals viewed this amendment not just as an essential complement to the Sauton project but also as a model for a new order of industrial relations within a society based on private property. It was the Strauss program that probably made the PGC conclude that the demands of the council were out of control and that the Sauton project would be unworkable.

The Brousse and Strauss proposals capped more diffuse but effective efforts to aid laborers. Councilmen accorded respect and support to union officials. They let management know that the city viewed the unions as a permanent and essential part of the company. The left majority gave the accusations made by the unions against the firm the status of self-evident truths. Even when union leaders did not display a suitable gratitude for the council's help, aldermen kept their disappointment to themselves.[56] The majority of councilmen embraced the most ambitious demands of the organized personnel, the five-franc minimum wage for laborers and regular promotions based entirely on seniority for white-collar clerks. The politicians saw in these demands an opportunity to liberate workers from the arbitrary actions of their employers, and the councilmen affirmed the measures to be an essential extension of republican rights to the workplace.

• • •

The Radicals' new commitment to activism in labor relations might have run into an imposing obstacle, the refusal of employers to cooperate. But the Parisian council did not meet with thoroughgoing resistance as it bargained with the PGC. Indeed, management accepted the general goals of municipal policy, if not with good grace, then with worldly resignation. The people who ran the firm had contact with an influential group of industrialists, engineers, property owners, and conservative reformers who also avowed the need to curb market forces for the sake of preserving social peace. Sharing the anxieties of the Radicals about the viability of liberal orthodoxies, these conservatives were ready to break with laissez-

54. On general interest in profit sharing, see Bernard Mottez, *Systèmes de salaire et politiques patronales: Essai sur l'évolution des pratiques et des idéologies patronales* (Paris, 1966), pp. 78–105.
55. *Conseil municipal*, deliberations of December 5, 1892.
56. See below, chapters 6 and 8.

faire policies and extend their own hand to workers. This outstretched hand bypassed unions and the state, for the conservatives sought to soften the impact of hierarchial authority within the firm rather than open industrial relations to outside intervention. The conservative reformers looked to well-designed gestures of private paternalism by employers to reconcile wage earners to prevailing property relations.[57] They had the support of moderate republican political leaders. Thus the quest for social peace in the 1890s reached beyond the Radicals in the early 1890s, and the PGC became a laboratory for reformers of the right.

The managers of the PGC were on the cutting edge of a telling strategy shift among probusiness elites. After 1890 the directors of the PGC abandoned labor policies that had made frugality their paramount concern. They no longer assumed that they could impose on the personnel any conditions that workers, as isolated individuals, were unable to resist. Recalling in an ironic manner the political motives of councilman Paul Strauss, a manager of the PGC's factory division proclaimed that "we are much concerned today with improving the fate of workers—and with reason: for socialist utopias imported from Germany, it is time to substitute a reasonable socialism and, above all, put it into practice."[58] Of course, the manager gave a peculiar meaning to "socialism," and he fully intended to put it into practice without diminishing his control over the personnel.

The officers of the PGC were aware of the theoretical writings of bourgeois reformers like Frédéric Le Play and Emile Cheysson.[59] The new corporate policies reflected the nonmarket, paternalistic principles espoused by these authors. Yet it would be a mistake to view reforming ideas as the inspiration for the new direction labor policy took within the PGC. Measures to engender the peaceful subordination of the personnel arose suddenly out of a concrete situation, a crisis of authority within the firm. In 1890 there occurred the first successful effort at unionization, encouraged by Socialist journalists and aldermen, and coal stokers (*chauffeurs*) launched a costly strike. Within two years workers and employees had well-rooted organizations.[60] Officials of the PGC hoped to dampen enthusiasm for trade unions through meaningful, paternalistic reforms. Managers were also aware that the same measures were likely to improve relations with the moderate members of the municipal council. The dual goals

57. Elwitt, *Third Republic Defended.* Lebovics, *Alliance of Iron and Wheat,* p. 32, posits that businessmen were not so much intimidated by the strength of the revolutionary forces as discouraged by the weakness of the forces of order.
58. AP, V 8 O¹, no. 1520, "Rapport de Monsieur Euchène," p. 14.
59. On this body of thought, see Michael Brooke, *Le Play: Engineer and Social Scientist* (London, 1970).
60. See below, chapter 8, for a detailed discussion of the unions.

encouraged managers to make their reforms generous, but the ultimate concern was the preservation of managerial authority within the firm. That explains why important elements of the company's program of labor concessions were in place even before the Brousse and Strauss proposals.[61] Management's distaste for the Strauss amendment did not arise from an absolute refusal to reshape industrial relations. Rather, the company viewed the amendment as undermining the new direction it wished to impart to labor relations.

The initiation of expensive labor reforms could not have come at a worse time for the PGC from a financial perspective. It was no longer the fabulously profitable monopoly of earlier decades. In fact, profits began to decline markedly just as the city called for a revision of labor practices. Still, the company could not deny that a new era of personnel management had dawned, even if they had wished to do so. The unions and the aldermen foreclosed the possibility of continuing with the old ways. Just as the municipal council prepared for its reform agenda by raising wages of city workers, so the PGC prepared itself for the new era with a change in administration. The forceful director of the firm, Emile Camus, resigned (to enter the board of directors) in April 1892 and turned the leadership over to Stéphane Godot, an engineer with close ties to leading theorists of industrial paternalism.[62] In a France with many advocates of bourgeois reform but few practitioners, the PGC would provide a working model illustrating the promise and the limits of the approach.

By no means did management believe that a simple capitulation to the union's demands was in order, despite pressure from aldermen. The company strove to improve workers' compensation and take the edge off their grievances while reinforcing the "proper" moral ties and patterns of subordination between workers and their employer—in a way the Strauss amendment did not. Thus lamplighters, who had displayed their militancy by rallying to the union, demanded a raise from 75 to 120 francs a month but did not get it. Instead, the company doubled the supplement they received for night rounds and offered them a larger sum for handling more than their quota of street lamps. Likewise, managers rejected the navvies' request for a raise but did agree to compensate them for their overtime work. The company promised bill collectors special consideration for normal end-of-year raises but declined to depart from the policy of granting

---

61. AP, V 8 O^1, no. 148, "Salaires," provides a summary of the measures the PGC took.
62. Ibid., no. 733, deliberations of April 14, 1892. Camus retained a great deal of control over policy in his new, but less visible, post of "administrateur délégué à la Direction générale."

advances strictly on an individual basis. Management did not hesitate to expose the calculating nature of its concessions. Several work-team leaders from the coke yards had emerged as union activists, and the company attempted to recapture the loyalty of this class of supervisors by granting them pension rights.[63] Deciding on more comprehensive—and expensive—reforms required outside pressure. In April 1892 management created a retirement program for manual workers. Laborers could receive pensions of 360 to 600 francs after twenty-five years of work if the company judged them deserving. The provision honored Le Play's principle that enterprises should concern themselves with the totality of workers' lives. Yet the retirement plan owed its creation to pressure from Radical aldermen and, behind them, the union.[64]

The arrangement that came to be the centerpiece of the PGC's paternalism, a profit-sharing plan, likewise arose from calculation under the pressure of external constraints. Radical councilmen had tied progress on the Sauton projects to an allocation of 1 percent of profits for workers (the same portion the company put aside for employees' bonuses). Managers agreed to the demand, but only after linking it to negotiations over lowering the cost of renting meters. The director endorsed the plan in exchange for a smaller reduction in the meter rate. Moreover, the company intended to endow the project with disciplinary qualities by keeping the profits in a pension fund over which it retained control.[65] Many Radicals, enthusiastic about profit sharing as a sure route to social peace, accepted the offer despite its imperfections. The unions, however, complained bitterly. Officials insisted that wage earners needed 2 percent of profits (since there were roughly twice as many workers as white-collar employees) and demanded the bonuses at once, not in a distant and uncertain future. Seizing the moral high ground at the same time it solidified the favorable terms it had extracted on meter rentals, management agreed to give 2 percent of the profits as an annual bonus. Thus the PGC became a model employer almost in spite of itself and with some powerful inducements.[66]

However hesitant gas managers were to put abstract pronouncements on paternalism into practice, however much they abhorred the intrusion of "politics" into their personnel affairs, however frugal they wished to be, they recognized that a new era of industrial relations was at hand. The

63. Ibid., no. 1081, ordres de service nos. 341–373; no. 688, deliberations of January 16, 1892.
64. Ibid., no. 154, "L'Intervention de l'administration municipale"; no. 733, deliberations of November 17, 1892; Brooke, *Le Play*, p. 127.
65. AP, V 8 O¹, no. 154, Troost and Camus to president of municipal council, June 12, 1892.
66. Ibid., no. 149, "Historique des rapports."

PGC had added more than a million francs to its annual labor bill by the time the Sauton project fell apart.[67] When the negotiations terminated, the company did not cancel the raises, the pension plan, and the expensive profit-sharing bonus. Spending so much without concrete compensations must have troubled the board of directors; the praise they won from Radical journals like *Le Rappel* for being model employers probably provided little comfort.[68] To some extent the quest for social peace, under Director Godot's guidance, had taken on a life of its own. The principal impetus behind the new generosity toward labor, though, had been a fear of the unions and the hope of regaining mastery over the personnel. Godot and his supporters on the board of directors were committed to two potentially antagonistic goals, preserving full authority over labor and integrating workers into the social order through private paternalism.

Though labor reform was the most dramatic addition to the gas question after 1890, the concerns of small consumers also became a matter of negotiations. In effect, councilmen asked the PGC to adjust itself to the emerging consumer society at the same time as they took steps to pacify the industrial order. The aldermen accepted as axiomatic that the luxuries of the rich should become available to the common people. They pressured the PGC to establish the conditions that would allow the Parisian masses to cook and light with gas. In practice this amounted to saving them the cost of installing gas by lending them meters, connector pipes, and stoves. The council asked for this arrangement for renters paying less than five hundred francs a year, about 75 percent of all tenants. Certain aldermen also wished to extend the privilege to commercial tenants paying less than one thousand francs in annual rent. The company was now eager to extend the customer base and accepted the proposals, which were likely to be profitable anyway.[69] Provisions for the fee-free customers were incorporated into the Sauton project. Unlike the profit-sharing plan, the benefit for small customers did not survive the failure of the project. Apparently, the company viewed this concession more as a political bargaining chip than as a business decision, though it would have been a sound one.

The municipal councilmen, still eager to bring the benefits of gas to a wider clientele, kept on pressing their case. The PGC finally accepted the change in 1894, though it refrained from waiving installation costs for commercial tenants. The company was even able once again to use the concession to bargain hard on the rental rate of gas meters for regular

67. Ibid., "Tableau des augmentations des dépenses annuelles résultant . . . des améliorations apportées depuis 1889."
68. *Le Rappel*, March 11, 1892.
69. *Conseil municipal*, deliberations of November 9 and 23, 1892.

customers. The success of the program was immediate. The company could assert it saved small gas consumers more than forty-six million francs in ancillary fees by 1902, but it was also the case that fee-free customers improved the corporate balance sheet.[70] At the same time, the expanded clientele transformed the political context in which the gas question would be negotiated. It was now a matter that touched the masses directly, and politicians had to answer to voters who used gas. The new situation presented opportunities and complications to both aldermen and the company.

•   •   •

Between the failure of the Sauton project, at the end of 1892, and 1899, city hall and the PGC engaged in much litigation but not much negotiation over a renewed charter. Such a state of affairs offered few incentives for the company to continue offering measures in favor of the personnel. Nonetheless, leaders of the workers' and clerks' unions sent a relentless stream of demands, proposals, and complaints to Director Godot and to the municipal council. Union officials were pleased that excellent relations with councilmen compensated for the increasing distance, even coldness, Godot evinced.

The officials were not mistaken in their perception of enjoying the goodwill of the municipal council. Indeed, the political and partisan basis for the council's remarkable receptivity to the demands of the gas personnel merits consideration. Conventional modes of understanding social policies—the Socialists as the friends of workers, the Radicals as the friends of the petite bourgeoisie, and the right as friends of big business—do not do justice to the fluid situation. In this moment triumphant of labor reform, gas workers found support in unanticipated quarters. The solid commitment of Parisian Radicals to social reform, with tacit or open approval from national leaders, contrasts with the party's historical image as socially ambivalent and insensitive to the needs of wage earners. Just as Radicals were about to become France's governing party, they took the lead in defining policies to help workers. Whereas the Socialist Vaillant had once been the principal spokesman for laborers' interests at city hall, the gas workers found their most outspoken advocates among the Radicals, especially Alexandre Patenne.[71] He himself was a genuine worker, an autodidact engraver, son of a cabinetmaker and brother of a concierge. He continued his manual labor even as an alderman (representing the Charonne quarter in the twentieth arrondissement), but he never joined a

70. AP, V 8 O¹, no. 617, "Charges supportées par la Compagnie du fait des abonnements sans frais."
71. *Conseil municipal*, deliberations for 1892–1899.

workers' party. He remained a loyal Radical-Socialist and in 1896 campaigned as an ardent supporter of the reform-minded Léon Bourgeois ministry.[72]

The extreme left, by contrast, was surprisingly ineffective at leading the cause of the gas personnel. The municipal election of April 1893 put a gas worker, Alfred Brard, on the council. An "independent Socialist," he represented the Pont-de-Flandre quarter (nineteenth arrondissement), where the gas plant of La Villette was located and where many *gaziers* lived. Though he professed to carry their mandate to city hall, he was far less visible as a spokesman than was Patenne or Paul Strauss. The same was true for councilmen Pierre Morel and Félicien Paris, two Socialists who had once been clerks at the PGC.[73] The gas workers' union at its founding had proclaimed that the Socialists were its best friends, but relations with the extreme left subsequently became strained. Socialists kept insisting that municipalization was the only legitimate solution to the debate over what sort of enterprise would replace the PGC when its charter ended. Since municipalization could not be accomplished until after 1905, Socialists had to ask the gas personnel to wait patiently for dramatic improvements in pay and work conditions.[74] Such a stance precluded Socialists from initiating reforms, and leadership passed to the Radicals. The Socialist councilmen did not develop close ties with the reformist syndicalist leaders of the gas personnel, who were willing to talk even with deputies of the radical right about immediate benefits.

Radicals like Patenne and Strauss embraced the unions and their programs. Far from being mediators between capital and labor, they became advocates of the unions' positions, accepting without question their interpretations of events. Thus, Radicals could declare in 1895 that the company had still done "nothing" for the personnel, despite the reforms it had made prior to the failure of the Sauton project. They continued to endorse the five-franc minimum wage and insisted quite vehemently that white-collar employees had a right to regular rules for advancement, which would free them from the arbitrary decisions of their employers. They recognized the aggressive unions as democratic institutions that made a valid contribution to the Republic. The Radical aldermen even took a programmatic step in advance of the unions by articulating a new theme—that the gas personnel merited the same treatment as the civil servants of

72. Préfecture, B/a 1214.
73. AP, V 8 O¹, no. 159, clipping from *Bulletin municipal officiel,* November 28, 1899, pp. 3727–3728; *Les Travailleurs du gaz: Organe officiel de la chambre syndicale des travailleurs de la Compagnie du gaz,* no. 234 (April 5, 1910): 2.
74. Préfecture, B/a 1424, "1890–1893–1898."

Paris.[75] That status meant security, favorable pension rights, regulatory protections, and, sometimes, higher pay. The Radicals' pronouncements on the subject were vague and unsystematic at this point, but they did anticipate the agenda toward which union officials would strive after 1900.

It is true that Radicals on the national level were not completely united on a program to aid the gas workers. When Premier Emile Combes reviewed the proposals to give gas clerks promotions by seniority and to grant gas workers civil-servant status in 1904, he objected to the plan as excessively generous. Other Radicals in Parliament did so, too. Combes also opposed donating ten thousand francs to the victims of the gas strike of 1899, a cause that had become sacred to the left of the municipal council. Combes, so eager to alter relations between church and state, betrayed the side of fin-de-siècle Radicalism that had no true appetite for restructuring industrial relations.[76] Nonetheless, the social activism of a Patenne or a Strauss in the mid-1890s was the moving spirit of the party at the time and inspired the national leaders who intended to defeat the conservative alliance of Opportunist republicans and Catholics who had accepted the Republic.

The left majority of the council was even willing to spend public funds on its labor commitments, and the Radical-dominated state now allowed the Parisian government do so. Up to 1896 the council had expected to finance reforms from the profits of the monopolistic employer. Aldermen, however, could not impose unilateral concessions on the PGC, and management was still waiting for a payoff from its initial round of paternalism and was reluctant to yield still more. Under these circumstances the council acted on its sympathy for the personnel by voting three hundred thousand francs to be used for realizing long-standing union demands.[77] Aldermen were able to convince the company to contribute a like sum, perhaps because management was demoralized by the reformist political climate.

The allocation of six hundred thousand francs represented the most important victory of the unions since the failure of the Sauton project. The money enabled workers to receive the long-awaited five-franc minimum wage. Pensions for workers were raised by about two hundred francs a year. The workers in the distribution division received substantial pay in-

75. *Conseil municipal,* deliberations of July 13, December 30, 1895.
76. AP, V 8 O¹, no. 708, "Personnel–Conseil Municipal"; no. 708, "Personnel-Chambres."
77. *Conseil municipal,* deliberations of December 30, 1896. Paul Strauss proposed the allocation.

creases.[78] With these and still other benefits achieved, workers and clerks had little more to hope for in the immediate future, but they could look forward to the year 1906 with confidence. The municipality had repeatedly affirmed that any solution to the gas question would entail generous treatment for the personnel. This confidence presupposed the continuing domination of Parisian political life by the left, however, and that domination was suddenly interrupted.

Contrary to all precedents and most informed expectations, Paris temporarily became a city of the political right just as the twentieth century began. In the election of 1900, anti-Dreyfusard Nationalists and conservatives won a majority of seats on the council. This municipal revolution, not yet fully studied or understood, seems to have been a referendum on the Dreyfus Affair and on the Waldeck-Rousseau government, which had opened the way for a revision of Dreyfus's condemnation.[79] The breaking of the left's hold on city hall had potentially dramatic implications for the PGC and its personnel. Could the firm find more favor with aldermen of the Nationalist right than it did with Radicals and Socialists? Could workers and employees possibly hope for support from rightist aldermen? The municipal revolution of 1900 removed all the inevitabilities that had been building since 1890.

What was at stake for the PGC was evident in the election that took place in the Arsenal quarter (fourth arrondissement) in 1900. Henri Galli, a leader of the League of Patriots, opposed the incumbent, Charles Vaudet, a Republican Socialist. Vaudet's campaign placards informed voters of his "incessant struggle against all monopolies and especially that of gas, which in itself justifies your confidence." Galli's propaganda, entirely less expansive on the matter, simply promised to work for lower gas rates.[80] Management might well have taken Galli's victory over the incumbent as an auspicious sign, but the company also had reason to be circumspect. Though the social outlook of the new majority of the right was by no means uniform, it was clear that the election did not signal any sort of return to economic orthodoxy on the part of the council. The PGC could not count on, nor did the unions have to fear, a council that patently favored the interests of big business over those of labor. This was partly

---

78. AP, V 8 O¹, no. 1081, ordre de service no. 512. The PGC managed to take advantage of the allocation to increase the pay of nonunion supervisors. The municipal council had never intended its funds to be put to that use.

79. David R. Watson, "The Nationalist Movement in Paris, 1900–1906," in *The Right in France, 1890–1919,* ed. David Shapiro (Carbondale, Ill., 1962), pp. 49–84; Jean-Pierre Rioux, *Nationalisme et conservatisme: Le Ligue de la Patrie française, 1899–1904* (Paris, 1977); Nord, *Shopkeepers,* chaps. 9–10.

80. Préfecture, B/a 695, "Election de 1900."

because of the heterogeneous nature of the Nationalist group, which included none other than the friend of the gas personnel, Alexandre Patenne. He had retained his seat in a contest against collectivists by running as a "Patriot Socialist" and reaching out to the right for votes. His platform supported amnesty for the antiparliamentary agitator Paul Deroulède.[81] Patenne was not the sole Radical to adopt such a strategy. Altogether there were about twelve Patriot Socialists in the new majority. They were joined by a like number of plebian radicals of the right, members of the League of Patriots. Seven aldermen representing bourgeois quarters were affiliated with the League of the Fatherland, an organization with a conservative, rather elite membership but with a social program that did not differentiate it clearly from populist radicalism.[82] What united the majority was not just chauvinism and a disdain for the extreme left. The new majority was eager to achieve social peace, reconcile bosses and workers, and unite them in the name of the fatherland. The quest for social peace on an anticollectivist basis was also attractive to some of the conservative republicans and nonrepublican rightists who lent support to the Nationalist majority. Thus the municipal revolution of 1900 did not necessarily signal a profound break with the social policies of the council as it had existed under Léon Bourgeois.

Radicals and Socialists accused the PGC of financing the rightist victory. Even if the accusation was valid, the PGC had not bought itself mere minions.[83] Public opinion was so thoroughly hostile to the firm that no politician wished to be perceived as favoring it. Galli and the other Nationalists may not have been implacable enemies of the PGC, but they did express disapproval of monopolies and financial power created by privileged concessions. Even a rich businessman who represented the exclusive quarter of Muette (sixteenth arrondissement) professed a complete and inalterable distrust of the PGC.[84] In truth, the social ambiguities inherent in right-wing radicalism of the Dreyfus era provided opportunities that both the PGC and its personnel could use to build bridges to the new majority—if they acted prudently.

81. Ibid., B/a 1214, "Patenne." Some lists classified him as a "Radical antiministériel."
82. *Le Temps*, no. 14220 (May 15, 1900): 1; Rioux, *Nationalisme et conservatisme*, pp. 65–68; Nord, *Shopkeepers*, pp. 444–464. Rioux designates five of the new aldermen as "unclassifiable."
83. Préfecture, B/a 903, reports of March 23, 1901, February 7, 1902; *La Petite République*, March 2, 1901, p. 1.
84. *Conseil municipal*, deliberations of January 26, 1910 (remarks by Caplain). For the populist economics of other candidates, see their campaign platforms in Préfecture, B/a 695.

The police may have been correct in suspecting that the PGC offered bribes to *La Patrie française* for favorable editorials, but the right-wing journal had other reasons to defend the company. Nationalist aldermen had promised their constituents immediate reductions in gas prices, and that pledge meant negotiating with the PGC. A settlement was all the more urgent in that the petit bourgeois Nationalist voters were drawn from precisely the same milieu as the fee-free gas customers. Gas bills were no longer an abstract issue to the right-wing electorate. The PGC, well aware of the pressure on politicians, seized the opportunity. Managers secretly funded and encouraged aggressive consumer agitation in favor of lower prices at once.[85] The company also took steps to deal with the negative image the firm had. It was clear that the most palatable solution to the gas question was one that appeared to create a new firm to replace the despised PGC as soon as possible. The company produced just such an option for the Nationalist majority, which now had little reason to reject the solution.

Workers and clerks were no less capable of appealing to the Nationalists. Though purporting to be the scourge of revolutionary collectivists, the Nationalists posed as friends of French workers who respected property rights and suffered from exploitation at the hands of large capitalists. Antisocialists like Galli were pleased to show favor to the gas personnel as a means of bolstering their credentials for social radicalism and distancing themselves from clericalism. They did so even as they cut off funds to the Paris Bourse du Travail, the central institution of union life. Indeed, the closer the Nationalists edged to bestowing a favorable gas monopoly on big businessmen and financiers, the more they needed to make a show of their support for the rights of the common people. Thus Nationalist aldermen attended union meetings and affirmed their intention of helping workers achieve their goals. They railed against the PGC for crushing the strike of 1899 and refusing to rehire all the strikers. However much the rightists spoke in the abstract against *étatisme* and deplored the parasitic bureaucracy, they pursued the policy, first broached by Radicals, of making the gas personnel into civil servants.[86] In truth, the workers and clerks had no reason to fear the municipal revolution as a blow to their material

85. AP, V 8 O¹, no. 160, Constantin to director, August 24, 1899. Customer resistance did reemerge at the time. Some clients were not allowing meter readers into their homes. See no. 696, deliberations of July 19, 1900.
86. *L'Echo du Gaz: Organe de l'Union syndicale des employés de la Compagnie parisienne du gaz*, no. 96–112 (1901); Préfecture, B/a 1424, reports of October 14, 1900, January 9, 1902. The right-wing journal *L'Echo de Paris* (July 16, 1904) chided the Nationalist aldermen for spending public money on the gas personnel.

demands. Continuity with the Radical municipality was the order of the day.

The various contradictions and pressures inherent in Nationalist politics found their way into the last nearly successful solution to the gas question, the so-called Chamon project of 1901. (Georges Chamon, the principal figure behind the proposal, was an entrepreneur in the gas industry and a partner in the new Thomson-Houston Electrical Company.) The PGC would be replaced by a new firm, which in practice was likely to have many of the same board members and officers as its predecessor since large shareholders of the PGC (along with the Comptoir d'escompte) were putting up the capital.[87] The settlement would be generous to the PGC, so much so that the Socialists were outraged and even the prefect was opposed.[88] The company would receive a hundred million francs for its assets from the city and ninety million more from a group of financiers headed by Chamon. That sum was far more than it was entitled to under the provisions of its charter. The company would lower gas rates to twenty centimes but would receive full compensation for the reduction from the city until the end of 1905.[89] With the Radicals having established the principle of using taxes to support labor reforms, the Nationalists committed public funds to subsidize gas consumers. The Socialist aldermen were appalled by many of the provisions and labeled the plan the "Nationalists' Panama Scandal." They organized street meetings to oppose the project, charging that it was a disguised continuation of the PGC and a bonanza for the despised firm.[90] Not even generous personnel provisions could win the approval of the left. The project offered the employees and workers "assimilation"—that is, full integration into the corps of municipal employees, with a favorable interpretation of the benefits that were their due. In addition, the new company would devote 10 percent of its profits above a specific level to the personnel, recognize its unions, and offer an early retirement plan.[91] The Socialists' objections were in vain; the Chamon

---

87. AP, V 8 O¹, no. 1065, "Réunion tenue au Comptoir nationale d'escompte"; *Rapport,* February 22, 1902, pp. 1–7. Shareholders of the PGC would have 336,000 shares of the new firm reserved for them.

88. AP, V 8 O¹, no. 619, "Chambre des Députés."

89. Ibid.; *Rapport,* February 22, 1902. Municipal engineers estimated the value of the firm's assets at 181 million francs and were certain that the PGC's demands for 100 million francs for half the assets were excessive. See AP, V 8 O¹, no. 1626, "Etude . . . par M. Sauton (27 novembre 1901)."

90. AP, V 8 O¹, no. 616, "Projet du traité"; Maurice Charany, "Le Gaz à Paris," *La Revue socialiste* 36 (1902): 435.

91. AP, V 8 O¹, no. 618, "Personnel du gaz, rapport de M. Chautard et de M. Lajarrigue."

project satisfied too many interests. The rightist majority was eager to obtain lower rates and benefits for the personnel while seeming to rid Paris of the PGC. Critics could not even win gas union leaders to their side, for the latter were pleased to offer so many advantages to the rank and file.[92]

The dilemma was that Nationalism in Paris was out of tune with the Radical Republic, and the Chamon project required parliamentary approval. The complexion of the Chamber of Deputies at the turn of the century resembled the Parisian council of the 1890s, with Radicals and Socialists playing the dominant role. The left majority of deputies was receptive to the argument of Parisian Socialists that the project was ill advised and antirepublican. Jean Jaurès, the leader of parliamentary Socialism, brought his authority to bear against the plan. The chamber rejected the proposal at the end of 1902. However skilled the PGC had become at manipulating Parisian Nationalists, it was powerless against the Radical Republic.

Despite the ultimate failure of the Chamon project, it did finalize the special claims of gas workers and consumers to municipal support. The council soon voted to pay for gas at twenty centimes and for assimilation, both out of public funds, even in the absence of a wider settlement of the gas question. It arranged a loan of a hundred million francs (with 2.8 million budgeted for assimilation) to do so and managed to secure parliamentary approval.[93] Thus the fostering of a consumer society and of new relations between the state and industrial society advanced, but at the expense of Parisian taxpayers. In the meantime the future of the gas service remained confused. In 1903 the PGC made some final offers, their most generous yet, but could not interest the municipal council.[94] Parisian politics had shifted leftward once again, and aldermen were ready to listen to the pleas of Socialists for municipalization of the gas works. Even Nationalist aldermen supported the proposal, perhaps to distance themselves from the Chamon project and its bad odor as a sellout to the PGC. It was now the left's turn, however, to be out of step with national politics. The senate, the graveyard of most progressive legislation, rejected municipal ownership.[95]

Having exhausted all existing options for the gas concession, the mu-

92. Préfecture, B/a 1425, reports that most union leaders were favorable or neutral regarding the passage of the Chamon project.
93. AP, V 8 O¹, no. 699, deliberations of November 10, 1904; Henri Besnard, *L'Industrie du gaz à Paris depuis ses origines* (Paris, 1942), pp. 119–131.
94. AP, V 8 O¹, no. 698, deliberations of January 28, April 27, 1903.
95. Ibid., no. 619.

nicipal council had to invent a new one. It did so with the hybrid vested-interest regime (*régie intéressée*). The city would provide the capital, assume the risks, take the profits, and set the broad parameters for operation, but a private enterprise would manage the concessions under the supervision of the municipal engineers.[96] The personnel of the new regime was assimilated into the prefect's service. As for the PGC, it outlasted its fifty-year charter by two years. The prefect had to postpone its liquidation until 1907 because the new regime was not ready to function. The PGC disappeared a victim—if that is the correct term for so profitable an enterprise—of its own rapaciousness. Yet inflexible reaction had not been one of its vices. The company responded to a society that suddenly insisted on new relations between capital and labor and that expected a certain democratization of comforts. True, the corporate response had been far from spontaneous and remained rather limited; but then the men who ran the PGC had had no genuine taste for the changes they were compelled to confront. Moreover, the PGC had to accommodate the new expectations when its financial situation was no longer brilliant.

The Unstable Bottom Line

The strong, even overweening, satisfaction with which management announced annual profits to the shareholders withered in the mid-1880s. To keep the PGC's financial history in perspective, we must note that it ceased being an exceptionally profitable firm and became a moderately successful one. Many enterprises fared a good deal worse, for the PGC never had an unprofitable year. Nonetheless, the final two decades of the company's history were not at all splendid compared with past times. Signs of deterioration were many. Returns on invested capital entered a steady decline from 1883 and continued on the downward course until the new century began (figure 6). Starting in 1893, yields were back in the single digits, where they had not been since the founding years. During the 1890s profits were only two-thirds the level they had been in 1882, the apex of prosperity. The returns of the PGC, less the portion shared with Paris, were not much better than those of conventional real-estate investments. The public continued to know the PGC for its "absurd profits," but it was simply uninformed about the company's problems as its golden age passed.

The difficulties of the firm were not on the revenue side of the ledger. On the whole, income held up well. In only two years, 1894 and 1895, did

96. For the originality of this solution, see Besnard, *Gaz à Paris*, chap. 4.

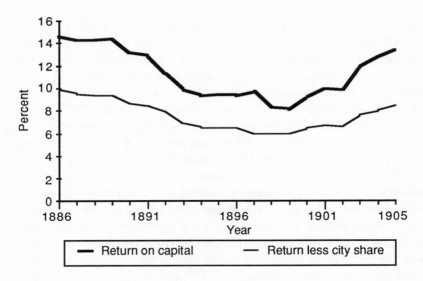

Fig. 6. Return on Capital, 1886–1905 (in Percent). From AP, V 8 O¹, no. 907, *Rapports présentés par le Conseil d'administration à l'Assemblée générale, 1856–1905.*

revenues drop below the banner year of 1882, and then only slightly (see appendix, fig. A7). What needs explanation is the cessation of the regular and sizable annual increments in income that had characterized the golden age. The stagnation of gas consumption was of course the fundamental cause, but there were contributing factors. The PGC's prosperity before the mid-1880s had been bolstered by ever-growing revenue from the sale of coke and by-products. This source of income became problematical in the era of adjustments (see appendix, fig. A8). The great advantage the PGC enjoyed by being the supplier of raw materials to the organic dye-stuffs industry faltered. Income from coal-tar and ammonia products quickly dropped by a third and stagnated thereafter. The European depression of the 1880s lowered the exceptional prices that had originally attracted the firm into the production of organic chemicals. Prices did not rebound permanently with the industrial recovery of the mid-1890s because the German chemical industry, the principle outlet for the PGC's by-products, had acquired its own supply of coal tar from the recovery ovens of the iron and steel industry.[97] Moreover, the profitable coke trade suffered, especially between 1893 and 1899. During those years the firm sold

97. L. F. Haber, *The Chemical Industry during the Nineteenth Century* (Oxford, 1958), p. 87.

less coke and at lower prices, for a variety of reasons. Coal prices tumbled as a result of overproduction, and the PGC for once was forced to pass on its savings to consumers because its monopolistic hold on the Parisian coke market had collapsed. Coal cartels from northern France, hurt by declining prices, invaded the fief of the PGC. In addition, the company itself weakened coke sales by developing gas heaters and distributing gas stoves during these years. Preferring the sale of gas to that of coke was a rational business calculation, but it meant that even the recovery of coal prices and the reconstruction of tacit understandings with the market invaders did not return revenues from coke to former levels.[98]

Another former area of growth that faltered was the income from the ancillary charges entailed in using gas—the rental of meters and connector pipes and the maintenance fees. As gas moved into mass domestic consumption, payments from these sources stagnated. Indeed, as we have seen, sacrificing this income was a prerequisite for making gas a mass-consumption commodity. It was one of the hidden costs of competing with electrical lighting.

The sluggish sources of revenue were really secondary problems. Rising expenditures that management could no longer contain were more central to the loss of a brilliant financial position. Though gas and by-product sales grew fitfully and often stagnated, the PGC found that continued heavy capital investments were necessary to adjust to a changing market (see appendix, fig. A9). The average annual capital expenditure between 1885 and 1900, 5.5 million francs, was only 20 percent below the general average of 6.8 million francs. Not until after the turn of the century, when the end of the concession was more certain and in sight, did investment drop markedly. The enduring burden of overall investment masked a change in direction of capital expenditures. Spending on productive capacity reached a peak between 1881 and 1883, when managers concluded that they faced strong, continuous growth in demand for gas. It did not materialize, though the firm completed a new factory in Clichy and started to build still another in Saint-Denis (in a quarter known as Landy). The result was excessive productive potential and underutilized plant through the 1880s and 1890s.[99] The economics of mass consumerism dic-

98. AP, V 8 O^1, no. 1016, "Comptes d'exploitation par année"; no. 25, report of Brissac to director, February 16, 1897. There was also competition from anthracite, which had been unknown in Paris before 1880.
99. Rapport, March 24, 1882, p. 39. At the end of 1881 the director estimated that consumption of gas would reach 366 million cubic meters by 1886. On the basis of the optimistic forecast, the company expanded its productive capacity. In 1886, however, sales were 80 million meters short of the estimate, and the anticipated level was not reached until 1904.

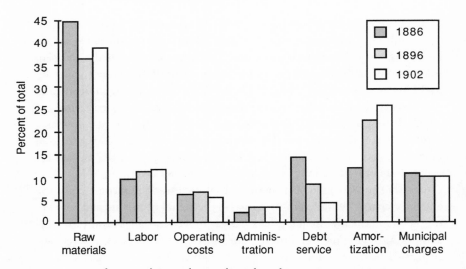

Fig. 7. Distribution of Expenditures for Selected Years (in percent). From AP, V 8 O¹, no. 907, *Rapports présentés par le Conseil d'administration à l'Assemblée générale, 1856–1905*.

tated a huge transfer of capital away from production and toward the distribution system. To reach a domestic market, the PGC needed to invest in mounted mains, stoves, and fixtures. Such expenditures jumped with the free-installation program of 1887 and even more with the fee-free program of 1894. In 1895 the company invested more than 7.3 million francs in the distribution apparatus, 40 percent more than it had spent in the benchmark year of 1882. Ultimately the firm would spend more than forty-three million francs to reach new customers. This too was a price of having lost a portion of the lighting market to its younger rival.

Another expenditure that rose ineluctably was personnel costs (figure 7). Labor had been cheap during most of the golden age, and increases in productivity easily absorbed whatever raises were granted (see chapter 4). Unit labor costs headed upward for the first time during the dramatic shortages of manpower that occurred between 1876 and 1882. A reversal of the unfavorable trend was out of the question once the politics of the "extended hand" took hold. The PGC reluctantly swallowed burdensome concessions in the 1890s.[100] Not only did laborers receive higher wages, pensions, and bonuses, but the office personnel became far more costly as well. A mass clientele of small consumers was a good deal more expensive

100. Between 1889 and 1902 annual personnel expenses rose by 6.2 million francs, according to corporate calculations. AP, V 8 O¹, no. 149, "Tableau des augmentations."

to administer than was an elite clientele of large, commercial consumers. The company was forced to increase the size of its office staff substantially as a result of the free-installation and fee-free programs. The number of clerical employees rose 61 percent between 1887 and 1900, completely out of proportion to the increase in gas consumption. Moreover, as a result of the politically motivated concessions, each employee cost the company more in salary and fringe benefits (see chapter 6).

There were also the ever-growing amortization costs of an enterprise with a limited life. Already a significant portion of the operating budget in the 1880s, these costs became still more burdensome when in 1898 the courts relieved Paris from the bad deal it had struck in 1861.[101] The city no longer had to pay its share of amortization twice. The burden of retiring outstanding debt and amortizing shares rose to nearly a third of all expenditures by 1902, almost as much as the cost of fuel and raw materials. The weight of capital charges underscores just how much of the PGC's business problems were at base political. With the company still receiving thirty centimes for every cubic meter of gas it sold, enormous revenues were guaranteed. The firm could even countenance disappointing returns from by-products. Only a longer charter, achievable through negotiation, could have reduced amortization payments.

In fact, the PGC ended its life in the midst of a surge of growth. Fueled by a recovery of revenues from gas, gross profits in its last two years reached new highs (see appendix, fig. A3). David Landes has noted that industries born of the first industrial revolution often experienced an Indian summer of growth and achievement before World War I, even as decline was in sight.[102] The gas industry sustains that interpretation. The corporate accounts show that the PGC adapted successfully to the early stages of the age of electricity. The firm developed a mass clientele that restored the earlier reality of ever-rising gas sales. Landes was nonetheless correct to characterize the recovered prosperity as an Indian summer rather than a new beginning. The company had to spend a lot more to sell the same amount of gas. Moreover, the economically unjustifiable privilege of receiving a rate of thirty centimes was about to come to an overdue end. Finally, the refuge that the PGC found in domestic consumption would soon prove every bit as porous as its former commercial market. Thus, the late achievements were temporary. The PGC expired before its long-term weaknesses were fully exposed.

101. *Rapport,* March 28, 1899, p. 41.
102. David Landes, *The Unbound Prometheus: Technological Change and Industrial Development in Western Europe from 1750 to the Present* (Cambridge, 1969), p. 260.

• • •

For all its eccentricities, the financial history of the PGC fit neatly into the general trends of French economic life of the nineteenth century. The firm, like the national economy, grew markedly while remaining within fixed structural limits and using older production methods. Its moments of exceptional growth, its stumbling phases, and its periods of recovery coincided with French business cycles.[103] It transformed itself from a "luxury" trade into a mass-production enterprise as did French industry as a whole over the long run. Though some reasons for the fit were more coincidental than substantive, the point underscores the inability of the PGC to isolate itself from wider trends despite its privileged charter and quasi-monopolistic position. The relentless and systematic search for cheaper production methods in the nineteenth century gave the company new markets and then reduced their value. Similarly, the quest for quotidian comforts, which first opened vast markets to the firm, eventually summoned a formidable competitor. That new energy source forced the PGC to adopt the entrepreneurial strategy of the twentieth century, democratizing the clientele and lowering profit margins. Then there were the cultural and political imperatives that compelled the firm to come to terms with the social consequences of industrialization. The protective charter that management had defended so vigorously shielded the PGC only to the extent that wider influences permitted. If the charter brought the PGC impressive profits before 1885, it was because market and political trends allowed that to happen. Those forces could also curtail the corporation's prosperity. The PGC's inability to transcend its economic and political context make it a useful focus for studying the social categories created by industrial development—corporate managers, white-collar employees, and factory laborers.

103. On the business cycles, see François Crouzet, "French Economic Growth in the Nineteenth Century Reconsidered," *History* 59 (1974): 167–179; François Caron, *An Economic History of Modern France*, trans. Barbara Bray (New York, 1979), chap. 1.

PART TWO

THE MANAGERS' COMPANY

THREE

The Decision Makers

Preoccupied with the governed classes, European social historians have not shown as much curiosity about the governing classes, not even about the new elite of businessmen and salaried managers emerging in the nineteenth century. Their career trajectories, responsibilities, compensations, family backgrounds, and outlooks await serious analysis.[1] The PGC, as one of France's early corporations, provides an opportunity to study salaried managers just as they came to form a distinct socioprofessional category. Corporate management was not yet a familiar activity and lacked clear-cut norms and prescriptions when the firm was founded. Only railroad companies and a few other large enterprises existed to serve as models.[2] In truth, their example was only marginally useful to decision makers at the PGC. Corporate forms and practices arose gradually within the gas company, partly through trial and error. The model of the bureaucratic state proved highly influential, too. Such were the forces molding a powerful, new economic elite.

The Administrative Hierarchy

The statutes of the PGC laid down once and for all and with Cartesian clarity the lines of authority that were supposed to direct the firm. Given

1. For one rare study of these questions, see Maurice Lévy-Leboyer, "Hierarchical Structure, Rewards, and Incentives in a Large Corporation: The Early Managerial Experience of Saint-Gobain, 1872–1912," in *Recht und Entwicklung der Grossunternehmer im 19. und frühen 20. Jahrhundert*, ed. Norbert Horn and Jürgen Kocka (Göttingen, 1979), pp. 451–472.
2. The importance of railroads in establishing patterns in corporate management is a well-known theme. See Alfred Chandler, "The Railroads: Pioneers in Modern Corporate Management," *Business History Review* 39 (1965): 16–40, and *The*

the weight of French tradition, one might expect those lines to have been highly centralized, and they were. The nature of the executive at the center, however, changed several times over the life of the firm. Furthermore, the concentration of authority proved far greater in principle than in reality, the result of both choice and circumstance. The PGC was not so inflexible as to have faced all its challenges without structural innovation. It responded to the environment with new managerial approaches and tolerated even a good deal of ambiguity about lines of authority. Of course, such flexibility did not in itself guarantee wise or appropriate decision making.

Sovereignty over the firm was vested in the stockholders, but they immediately delegated their authority to a *conseil d'administration*, or board of directors, composed of twenty elected shareholders. Meeting faithfully at least once a month for the fifty-year life of the firm, board members envisioned for themselves a supervisory role.[3] No decision would have force without their approval, but they declined to be the managers of the corporation. Instead, the very first board, led by the owners of the merging gas companies, decided on a collective executive. The board created a five-member executive committee *(comité d'exécution)* made up of rotating board members. Each member was to oversee a set of operational departments. Though the committee's name implied the passive role of carrying out the wishes of the board, the committee was actually the governing force—until the need for further change became evident.[4]

The owners of the new gas firm quickly found a collective executive too cumbersome. The first year of business brought vast new opportunities, the beginning of daytime consumption, shortages, confusion, and the need to plan for expansion. An executive committee composed of part-time managers preoccupied by interests outside the firm could not deal seriously with pressing matters. Besides, they received compensation for their tasks essentially as stockholders, through dividends. The need for a full-time chief executive who would receive ample compensation for his services to the gas company alone was manifest. In November 1856 Louis Margueritte, an owner of one of the merging firms and an influential board member, proposed the creation of the office of director. The incum-

Visible Hand: The Managerial Revolution in American Business (Cambridge, Mass., 1977). A few of the PGC's early executives had worked for railroads, but it is doubtful whether that experience was formative.

3. The deliberations of the board are in AP, V 8 O¹, nos. 723–737.

4. Ibid., no. 723, deliberations of January 11, 1856. The records of the executive committee are in nos. 665–700.

bent would provide leadership and implement all the decisions approved by the board and executive committee. These two bodies would continue to meet (in the case of the committee, as often as once a week), with the director presiding. He would also have the power to choose the committee members.[5] Thus the office became the central one in the firm even though the director was not absolute master. As the PGC grew larger and more complicated and as board members grew more distant from the gas industry, the director assumed the role of the company's animating force. On matters of potential controversy it is likely that the director was careful to consult with influential board members and build a consensus in the executive committee. In any case, minutes of the committee meetings show virtually automatic confirmation of the director's proposals.

With the appointment of a director before the first year of operation was over, the PGC would seem to have joined the ranks of the new breed of firm, still rare in France and Europe, run by a salaried manager rather than by the owner.[6] Yet this was not quite the case, at least for a while. The board of directors offered the post of director to Margueritte, but he turned it down. Another board member, Vincent Dubochet, took the position. He, like the board's first choice, had been an owner of one of the pre-merger gas companies and a founder of the PGC. Both were among the largest stockholders. Whether the board fully intended the choice to set a precedent for future appointments is unclear, but the selection of Dubochet as director was only half a step away from the owner-manager. Accentuating the incomplete transition to a new form of management was the board's failure to establish a salary for the new director until a year after his appointment.[7] The definitive move to a salaried director came with Dubochet's retirement in 1858, when the board entrusted the fate of the firm to an officer of the prestigious Corps des Ponts et Chaussées (Corps of Bridges and Roads). An annual salary of twenty thousand francs, supplemented by a generous profit-sharing bonus, was established immediately.[8] The chief executive in the PGC was no longer a collective entity nor an owner-founder but rather a graduate of France's most illustrious technical institutions and a member of a national administrative elite. Though salaried directors of corporations were soon to become com-

5. Ibid., no. 723, deliberations of November 20, 27, 1856.
6. For a historical survey of large corporations in Europe, see Herman Daems and Herman Van Der Wee, eds., *The Rise of Managerial Capitalism* (Louvain and The Hague, 1974), and Alfred Chandler and Herman Daems, eds., *Managerial Hierarchies: Comparative Perspectives on the Rise of the Modern Industrial Enterprise* (Cambridge, Mass., 1980).
7. AP, V 8 O¹, no. 723, deliberations of April 30, 1857.
8. Ibid., deliberations of May 1, 1858.

monplace, appointing one was not yet routine when the PGC was founded.[9] The firm had spent three years groping toward such an office as a solution to its executive needs.

The central office retained essentially this form throughout the rest of the company's history, but there were some adjustments. The post of assistant director was added in 1860 to help carry the growing burden of administration. The director's position also suffered a temporary demotion between 1892 and 1901. In an effort to deal with labor demands from city hall and with the threat of unions, the board appointed a well-known advocate of industrial reform to the directorship. It seems clear, though, that the person he replaced, Emile Camus, remained in command. Immediately upon resigning as director, Camus was named delegated board member, charged with "a superior control over all services." Camus received higher pay than the new director and was present at most of the crucial meetings.[10] The exposed political situation of the firm after 1890 apparently forced complications on the executive hierarchy but did not change it fundamentally.

The corporate statutes were inevitably hazy about the staff that would assist the director and executive committee. The principle of indivisible sovereignty discouraged a priori concern with the delegation of decision making. Nonetheless, the statutes did recognize thirteen "officers" of the firm; eight of them were to supervise bookkeeping departments, and the rest were entitled "engineer" or "assistant engineer" and were to oversee production operations.[11] What is noteworthy is how much the list diverged from the positions that really came to matter. By no means were the officers and the effective managers of the PGC the same. The company operated with a nebulous concept of management. Even as crucial a figure as the superintendent of a factory was not listed as an officer. By contrast, the statutes made provisions for such relative nonentities as "chief of correspondence" or "assistant cashier." Moreover, personnel records never distinguished clearly between mere clerks and managers. The conceptual framework organizing the personnel charts was salary level—above or be-

9. On the graduates of elite engineering schools heading important French corporations, see André Thépot, "Les Ingénieurs du Corps des Mines, le patronat, et la seconde industrialisation," in *Le Patronat de la seconde industrialisation,* ed. Maurice Lévy-Leboyer (Paris, 1979), pp. 237–246.
10. AP, V 8 O¹, no. 733, deliberations of April 14, 1892. The post of *administrateur-délégué* had always existed (indeed, it was required by law) but had not been filled until this awkward moment for the PGC. Camus did not move out of the director's residential suite within the corporate headquarters until 1898 (see no. 735, deliberations of August 25, 1898).
11. Ibid., no. 723, appendix to deliberations of December 26, 1855.

low three thousand francs a year—not level of responsibility.[12] Beginning managers were on the same salary ladder as office clerks; both started at eighteen hundred francs. The only difference was that the managers advanced faster. Even without a clear notion of what "management" could and should be, the PGC did develop an executive corps that served its needs well.

The new gas company quickly assembled a staff of twenty-three people, who were primarily responsible for ordinary operations (table 4). Seventeen of these headed technical departments or divisions and were graduates of state engineering institutes; the rest headed clerical departments. The managers below the director did not simply constitute a mechanism for passing on his orders. In fact, it is possible to apply the classic labels of top, middle, and lower management to the hierarchy—though admittedly the language is entirely anachronistic. Nineteen officers supervised directly the production and distribution of gas. Three others oversaw, evaluated, and perfected the work of those nineteen, so they might be considered middle management. The director and his immediate assistants coordinated the efforts of their subordinates and were chiefly responsible for general policy. These distinctions do need some qualification, but they hold true in a broad sense. Between the founding of the firm and the end of its golden age, the size of the managerial staff nearly doubled, with most of the growth at the lower level. There was hardly any further expansion at any level during the era of adjustment. The crisis through which the PGC passed did not spark a reconsideration of administrative organization, and the reduced pace of growth obviated the need for an expanded executive corps.

What sort of relations prevailed among the different managerial levels? The corporate statutes as well as national traditions would lead one to expect thorough centralization.[13] In theoretical terms, the director made all decisions, even trivial ones. In practice, his oversight did cover many matters of detail, with middle and lower managers merely supplying ad-

12. For examples of personnel charts, such as they existed within the PGC, see ibid., no. 153, "Cadre du personnel," and no. 162, "Assimilation." Michael Crozier, *The Bureaucratic Phenomenon* (Chicago, 1964), p. 273, writes of a "lag" in the development of French managerial functions because firms were overcentralized and managers gloried in being in control of everything. As we shall see, this stereotype does not quite hold for the PGC.

13. Octave Gelinier, *Le Secret des structures compétitives* (Paris, 1968); Crozier, *Bureaucratic Phenomenon*; Eugene Burgess, "Management in France," in *Management in the Industrial World*, ed. Frederick Harbison and Charles Myers (New York, 1959), pp. 207–231; James Laux, "Managerial Structures in France," in *The Evolution of International Management Structures*, ed. Harold Williamson (Newark, Del., 1975), pp. 95–113.

Table 4. Structure of Management at the PGC

	Number	
	1858	*1884*
Top Managers		
Director	1	1
Assistant director	0	1
Delegated administrator	0	1
Middle Managers		
Head of factory division	1	1
Assistant head of factory division	1	1
Head of gas production	0	1
Head of distribution division	1	1
Lower Management		
Factory superintendents	6	11
Assistant superintendents	1	10
Head of lighting department	1	1
Head of by-products department	1	1
Head of machinery department	0	1
Head of coal department	1	1
Head of coke department	0	1
Head of construction department	1	1
Head of meter department	1	1
Head of gas lines department	1	1
Assistant head of gas lines department	1	2
Head of accounting department	1	1
Head of workshops	1	1
Head of legal department	1	1
Secretary	1	1
Head of customer accounts department	1	1
Total	23	43

Sources: AP, V 8 O^1, no. 665 (fols. 500–514); no. 153.

vice or information. Yet centralization was not comprehensive. The outstanding characteristics of the PGC's authority structure were the dispersal of decision making and the unclear lines of power. An uneven pattern of centralization and decentralization quickly evolved. Both principle and pragmatism gave it a peculiar shapelessness that partook of none of the Cartesian clarity the statutes described.

Managers informally expanded their authority into areas that superiors left for them, and the latter did not guard all their powers with a ferocious jealousy. The director reserved for himself the most noble activities, appointing personnel, allocating rewards and sanctions, and authorizing expenditures. In these areas there was hardly any delegation of authority to relieve top management from involvement even in petty details. It hardly pays to conceive of a middle or lower management in these matters except as a transmission belt for decisions made at the top. Each December the director personally reviewed the records of every clerical worker and decided on annual bonuses and promotion.[14] Heads of departments participated in these decisions only by providing written comments about employees. The chief of the lighting department lacked the right to grant even a simple leave of absence for a clerk in his office. Usurping that power earned the engineer a formal rebuke.[15] Middle management did not select their own assistants or immediate subordinates; the decisions came from above. Only by restricting information available to a busy director or making strong recommendations could division chiefs assemble staffs of their choice.[16] The power to spend was likewise highly centralized. The director ruled on the type of hand towels that would be purchased for the bathrooms of the headquarters. Not until 1872 did factory superintendents gain the right to spend twenty francs without prior approval from above.[17]

By contrast, there soon came to be important spheres into which centralization did not extend. The director was actually quite removed from the daily operations of major departments. He appeared to know little about products and the ways they were manufactured and did not seek to learn about them. The company had no absolutely uniform wage or labor policies. By the 1860s factory superintendents had ceased reporting to the directors on a regular basis. In these circumstances centralization failed, not by default, but rather by conscious design. The director welcomed the benefits of delegated authority, at least in some spheres. Thus, when the opportunity to install telephones connecting the factories to headquarters appeared in 1879, the director vetoed the proposal on the grounds that the new device would undermine the responsibility belonging to his subordi-

14. The decisions were formalized at one of the last annual sessions of the *conseil d'administration* and of the *comité d'exécution*.
15. AP, V 8 O¹, no. 93, notification of January 9, 1869 (fol. 71).
16. This informal input may explain how division heads were able to have graduates of their own schools appointed under them.
17. AP, V 8 O¹, no. 1081, ordre de service no. 20; no. 751, "Secrétariat." Heads of departments and divisions were forbidden to correspond directly with suppliers (ordre de service no. 98). Corporate rules made them get the director's approval for all maintenance projects or for any changes on approved projects (ordre de service no. 93).

nates. Not until twenty years later did the PGC install telephone service, and then only because strike threats imposed the need for immediate communication.[18]

However amorphous the patterns of authority, they were not entirely the product of capriciousness on the part of successive directors. There was a logic, though not a consistent one. The centralization of budgetary and personnel decisions was in a sense ideological, reflecting the directors' conception of their sovereignty. Yet their aloofness from nearly all concerns at the factory level probably arose from pragmatic calculations about control over the labor force.[19] Management did not want workers at each of their plants uniting against the company, and the best way to encourage fragmentation was to treat each factory as an autonomous unit. Furthermore, the director wished to strengthen the hand of superintendents over the labor force by granting his managers the status of masters in their own houses. This mixture of principle and practical calculation generated much corporate policy.

Inevitably, the untidy dispersal of authority gave middle and lower managers considerable responsibility.[20] No document explicitly defined their duties. Their functions evolved as a result of experience, shared understandings, and personal initiative. Strategic, tactical, and operational decisions gravitated to executives at each level. All managers had to be active in four areas—daily operations, planning, financial oversight, and research. Even top management supervised or intervened in the details of daily routine. Most of the burdens fell on lower managers, however, and the PGC was probably understaffed at that level. The chief of the by-products department ran by himself an operation that involved revenues of some two million to three million francs and 250 workers.[21] Several superintendents directed plants with nearly a thousand laborers and millions of francs in equipment with the assistance of at most one other engineer.

Since the PGC never centralized planning procedures, every manager had to divert his eyes from current concerns to consider the future. The director depended on department heads to recommend areas of expansion and new markets. The systematic preplanning of new factories was a task

18. Ibid., no. 680, deliberations of October 31, 1879, and no. 695, deliberations of April 26, 1899. Superintendents sometimes disregarded formal directives from the chief executive. See, for example, no. 90, "Précautions prises au point de vue hygiènique pour la boisson des ouvriers."
19. See below, chapters 6 and 8.
20. The thousands of reports scattered through the archives of the PGC shed light on their functions. Especially rich are cartons 709–719, 746–770.
21. AP, V 8 O¹, no. 1060, "Usines-Traitement des goudrons et eaux ammonicales."

born of the industrial revolution, and it imposed a marathon of toil on the engineers. Any large capital improvement project involved corporate managers in inventing, testing, and perfecting equipment. When the PGC renovated its coal-handling machinery, nearly all new devices were designed by its engineers and constructed in its workshop.[22] Moreover, every department chief acquired a thick file of correspondence with inventors, for they continually explored innovations that could be useful to their departments and examined the more promising ones in their laboratories.

Oversight of bookkeeping was an activity managers dared not neglect. It was a duty on which top management insisted more than any other, issuing sharply worded reprimands when necessary. The factory managers filed fifty-six reports each day on expenditures. Scrutinizing the books was required because honesty was a problem within the accounting staff. When an embezzlement scheme in the factory accounting office was exposed in 1873, it hurt the reputation of a plant superintendent, for the director charged him with insufficient supervision.[23]

Apart from the duties imposed by current and future operations, managers undertook individual research and improvement projects. The engineers rarely left existing procedures as they found them; they devoted many of the workdays to tinkering with details of production. Although the PGC employed a consulting expert to oversee research (for many years Henri Regnault, a distinguished scientist and professor at the Collège de France), the endeavors lacked genuine coordination. Managers' projects were usually self-directed and not always intimately related to their immediate responsibilities at the firm. Nonetheless, the results could sometimes prove useful. The assistant chief of the factory division developed a crucial pressure-regulating device; the entire gas industry used the tables on gas flow calculated by the head of the factory division; a chief of the coke department was responsible for a new type of street lamp.[24] The

22. On the preplanning of factories, see Sidney Pollard, *The Genesis of Modern Management* (Cambridge, Mass., 1965), p. 262. J. Laverchère, *Manutention mécanique du charbon et du coke dans les usines de la Compagnie parisienne du gaz* (Paris, 1900), illustrates the work of the engineers in designing and building their own equipment.
23. AP, V 8 O¹, no. 161, "Etat des pièces . . ."; no. 675, deliberations of April 24, 1872; no. 676, deliberations of May 3, 1873, and January 17, 1874; *Rapport*, March 28, 1874, pp. 39–41.
24. *Bulletin de l'Association amicale des anciens élèves de l'Ecole Centrale* 35 (1903–1904): 232; AP, V 8 O¹, no. 677, deliberations of October 7, 1874; no. 672, deliberations of June 26, 1867; no. 1060, report of October 10, 1859; Philippe Delahaye, *L'Eclairage dans la ville et dans la maison* (Paris, n.d.), pp. 151–152; Alphonse Salanson, "Ecoulement du gaz en longues conduites," *Société technique de l'industrie du gaz en France. Neuvième congrès*, 1882, pp. 157–164.

managers' research agendas demonstrated a disinclination to specialize, which was all well and good given their multifarious duties.

The responsibilities assigned to each post and the career paths of the managers did not allow them to concentrate exclusively on a narrow set of technical matters. Engineers commonly moved from one department or division to another in the course of their careers. Eugène de Montserrat began as an assistant factory superintendent after graduating from the Ecole Centrale des Arts et Manufactures; he then became, successively, head of the secretariat, chief of the coke department, and chief of the distribution division. Plant superintendent Leroy had behind him several years in by-products production and in the machine shop. Louis Dhombres became an assistant factory superintendent after finishing the Ecole des Mines, moved to the coal-testing laboratory, and was promoted to the head of the mounted main office.[25] Even when serving in one post, these managers could not confine their purview to engineering questions. They had to deal with personnel problems and marketing matters, among others. The workday for the head of the by-products department might have included drafting a report on the proper way to clean a coal-tar filter and then a memorandum on the sale of ammonium sulfate to farmers in Picardy. The director did not hesitate to ask the chief of the distribution division for advice on legal strategies regarding a gas explosion, and the latter did not hesitate to respond. This engineer also had to make business calculations about which streets would be profitable to service.[26] The analysis of budgets or capital improvement options was an integral part of the managers' duties, as they usually lacked the staff to handle the financial questions for them. Being a part of a large-scale organization—and only a handful of French corporations were larger than the PGC—imposed only a limited degree of specialization on the managers.

Such duties left little room for leisure and obscured the distinction between free time and work. Managers did task-oriented labor, and there were no fixed hours on the job. Factory superintendents and their assistants lived at the work site and were on duty at all times. The director, the head of the factory division, and the chief construction engineer met on Saturday mornings to examine new projects. Sunday labor, at least on

25. In the absence of personnel dossiers for managers, one must follow their careers through the deliberations of the *conseil d'administration*, AP, V 8 O¹, nos. 723–737.
26. Ibid., no. 626, "Sulfate d'ammoniaque"; no. 92 (fols. 126–130); no. 828, "Accidents." The head of the secretariat wrote reports on the marketing of coke; see no. 751, report of June 18, 1858.

personal projects, may have been normal. When the owner of the Rossini Theater bestirred himself early one Sunday morning to have gas restored to his establishment, he found the chief of the lighting department at his office. The chief sent the impresario to see the director, who was also at work and assured him that both executives would be on the job all day.[27] As far as can be discerned from the incomplete records, vacations were not part of the annual calendar. Starting in the late 1880s there were some requests for a week's leave during the slow summer season, usually disguised as health-related absences, but these came from a minority of engineers. It was not only for wage earners that management conceived of hard work seven days a week, fifty-two weeks a year, as natural and inevitable.

Beyond constant application the company also demanded a rare combination of moral qualities from its executives. They had to be eager to accept new challenges and grow on the job. The self-confidence to make decisions on matters that were not susceptible to technical analysis was a basic requirement of their work, and it was a virtue they did not seem to lack. But self-confidence had to be tempered by self-effacement when necessary. The company was not especially sensitive to the egos of its executives and assumed their pride was expendable. The director once sent the assistant factory chief, Edouard Servier, to examine an electric pressure regulator that competed with his own invention. The mission was still more delicate in that his competitor had accused Servier of copying. Yet his superior found that Servier had nonetheless carried out the task with "the most perfect impartiality."[28] Clearly the company expected much from its engineer-managers, and these men, as a result of their backgrounds, expected much from themselves.

The Social Composition of Management

Through its early boards of directors the PGC grew under the casual supervision of some of France's most original and innovative entrepreneurs. Among these were the fourteen principle owners, partners, and directors of the gas firms that had fused to form the company. These pioneers of the gas industry in France had not been members of the conservative Orléanist business aristocracy that safely dominated the court and banking circles. Some were clearly outsiders who won great wealth despite, or perhaps as a consequence of, breaking rules. Jacques and Vincent Dubochet,

27. Ibid., no. 766, report of May 4, 1870; no. 1081, ordre de service no. 180.
28. Ibid., no. 1070, report of September 25, 1861.

owners of the former Parisian Gas Lighting Company, were born in Switzerland (Vevey) and were well known for their republican principles. They had participated in Carbonari conspiracies in their youth and became wealthy patrons of Léon Gambetta during the Government of Moral Order. Gambetta received financial support from the Dubochets for newspapers and campaigns, most notably during the May 16 (1877) crisis. Vincent's death in 1877 was marked by two distinctions: Leading Opportunist republicans were at his funeral, and he died one of the wealthiest men in France, with an estate worth more than thirty-five million francs.[29]

Louis Margueritte, the principle architect behind the merger forming the PGC and the owner of the largest pre-merger firm, was another outsider. Born into a family of well-off Rouennais merchants in 1790, Margueritte developed a serious interest in both industry and theater. He claimed to have written a tragedy that the Comédie-Française produced in 1824. Though he entered the gas industry the very next year, his ties to the arts did not dissolve. In fact, he married one Mademoiselle Minette, a former actress at the Vaudeville Theater. He eventually came to own huge estates outside Paris and died one of the largest landlords in the Seine-et-Oise. His fortune was rumored to be eighty million francs.[30]

Thomas Brunton, another board member and a partner to the merger, was born to English parents in 1793. His father had made a fortune by taking British methods of cotton spinning to Normandy. The Revolution ruined the business, and his father went to prison during the Terror. Brunton's status as an alien was reinforced by his habit—inexcusable to some proper-thinking Frenchmen—of calling himself an engineer even though he lacked a diploma from an appropriate French school. The Imperial administration declined to recommend Brunton for the Légion d'honneur because he did not "enjoy much consideration among industrialists."[31]

The pioneers of the gas industry were joined on the board by some of the men most responsible for the French "industrial revolution" of the Second Empire. The largest investors in the PGC were Emile and Isaac Pereire, the "best representatives of Saint-Simonian dynamism in service

29. J. P. T. Bury, *Gambetta and the Making of the Third Republic* (London, 1973), pp. 111, 307–308, 414, 441. On Dubochet's wealth, see AP, D Q⁷, nos. 12387–12389, 12396. Jean-Marie Mayeur, *Les Débuts de la IIIᵉ République* (Paris, 1979), p. 50, refers to Dubochet as the "Mécène des républicains."
30. Archives nationales, F¹² 5201. On hearsay regarding Margueritte's fortune, see Maurice Charanay, "Le Gaz à Paris," *La Revue socialiste* 36 (1902): 433.
31. Archives nationales, F¹² 5098.

of the Imperial economy," according to Guy Palmade.[32] Though the gas company was less pathbreaking and historically significant than the Pereires' Crédit mobilier, one of Europe's first industrial banks, it proved more enduring and profitable. The Pereires brought their circle of business associates and fellow investors to the PGC's board.[33] Hippolyte Biesta, the director of the Comptoir d'escompte and a collaborator of the Pereires in creating the Crédit mobilier, was on the first board. Alexandre Bixio, who served on the board from 1855 to 1865, also sat on the boards of the Crédit mobilier, the Railroad of Northern Spain, and the General Transportation Company, all Pereire projects. Emile's son-in-law, Charles Rhoné, was also a board member. These associations emphasized the ties of the PGC to the men who were shaking up the French economy during its most dynamic era and to other pillars of the new corporate capitalism.[34]

The Pereire circle continued to encompass most of the leading nationally connected entrepreneurs on the PGC's board even after the failure of the Crédit mobilier (in 1867) and the humbling of the family.[35] In spite of its size and profitability the company never succeeded in forging links to other great names of French capitalism, like Paulin Talabot, Henri Germain (of the Crédit lyonnais), Paul-Henri Schneider (of Le Creusot) or the Rothschilds. Only one representative of France's financial aristocracy, the Haute Banque, sat on its board—André Dassier.[36] As the significance of the Pereire group faded on the national scene, the PGC's board lost its entrepreneurial luminaries. In 1864 at least thirteen of the twenty board members served on the boards of other large and important corporations.

32. Guy Palmade, *French Capitalism in the Nineteenth Century*, trans. Graeme Holmes (London, 1972), p. 130.
33. On this circle, see Robert Locke, "A Method for Identifying French Corporate Businessmen," *French Historical Studies* 10 (1977): 261–292, and Jean Autin, *Les Frères Pereire* (Paris, 1984).
34. Charles-Joseph-Auguste Vitu, *Guide financier: Répertoire général des valeurs financières et industrielles* (Paris, 1864), lists the boards of directors of large firms. Note that reference works on French entrepreneurs, even important ones, hardly exist.
35. AP, V 8 O¹, no. 726, deliberations of April 2, 1868. Emile and Isaac Pereire resigned from the board in April 1868, but members of the younger generation remained.
36. Pierre Dupont-Ferrier, *Le Marché financier de Paris sous le Second Empire* (Paris, n.d.), p. 70. David Landes, *Bankers and Pashas* (Cambridge, Mass., 1958), p. 13, notes that "there was hardly a corporation of any importance [in France]— canal, railroad, or public utility—that did not feature among its founders and on its board the names of one or more of these few firms who formed . . . the Haute Banque." The PGC fit his description, but just barely and not for its entire life.

By 1878 only five of the PGC's *administrateurs* sat on other boards, and these were largely a legacy of the Pereire connections.[37]

The businessmen who replaced the Pereire group or sat alongside its remaining members were well-off Parisians, *grands bourgeois*, but not captains of industry or finance. The banker Charles Mussard had an estate worth 690,000 francs at his death; he was neither a Pereire nor a Dubochet. Jules Doazan, a stockbroker (*agent de change*), possessed just under a million francs. Athanase Loubet was an important merchant and a former president of the Parisian Chamber of Commerce, but his fortune of 1.8 million francs did not give him the stature of a department-store magnate.[38] Under the Third Republic the PGC increasingly lost its ties to other great corporate enterprises.

Instead, the PGC recruited to its board ever-larger numbers of distinguished scientists, state officials, and administrators to replace business leaders. The representation of scientific expertise became rather formidable. One of France's leading chemists, Henri Sainte-Claire Deville, joined the board in 1874.[39] Louis Troost, professor of chemistry at the Sorbonne, became president of the corporation and one of the more active board members. Eugène Pelouse, an applied chemist, came to the board after developing a widely used condenser for coal-gas production and finding new ways to use by-products.[40] There were also a member of the Institut de France and a vice president of the French Geological Society. Whereas these notables were eminently qualified to examine the firm's technical procedures, several of the men who joined them on the board had occupied important positions in state administration. The general inspector of mines, Meugy, came to the board in 1880. A former director of the postal service, Baron, served with him as did two former councillors of state. The stockholders confirmed the trend toward reduced ties with other corporations by placing on the board the retired director of the PGC and the current director.[41]

The shifting profile of the board of directors, from economic movers and shakers to administrators, mirrored the declining vigor and aggressiveness of the PGC's entrepreneurial policies (see chapter 4). Yet we

---

37. Vitu, *Guide financier*; Alphonse Courtois, *Manuel des fonds publics et des sociétés par actions* (Paris, 1878).

38. AP, D Q^7, nos. 12371, 10710, 10714, 12342.

39. Harry Paul, *The Sorcerer's Apprentice: The French Scientist's Image of German Science, 1840–1919* (Gainesville, Fla., 1972), pp. 77–78; L. F. Haber, *The Chemical Industry during the Nineteenth Century* (Oxford, 1958), p. 77.

40. Archives nationales, F^{12} 5231.

41. Appointments to the board were announced in the deliberations of the *conseil d'administration*. In most cases information available on these people was slender.

should not make too much of the parallel. There were more important reasons for the growing caution of the corporation, not the least of which was the approaching end of its charter (giving heavy, new investments less opportunity to pay off). Moreover, patterns of aggressiveness and caution in business policies were not clearly confined to a distinct phase of the firm's life, and it is far from certain that the board had more than a passive impact on decision making.[42] The changing composition of the board may well have reflected wider trends in the French economy rather than changes within the corporation. After all, Paris had ceased to be the center of commercial and financial innovation that it had been during the 1850s. Great names in business were fewer and farther between. The depression of the 1880s hit the economy of France harder and longer than those of other countries. When France resumed vigorous economic growth at the beginning of the new century, the innovative leaders were specialists, like Louis Renault, who confined their activities to one firm.[43] Such figures would not have considered the gas industry as marked for special growth in any case and might have turned to the infant electrical industry. The last boards of the PGC were well suited to the task at hand—finding a technological niche and adapting to new corporate responsibilities as a public service and as a model employer.

• • •

The central figure and animating force in the PGC was the director. After owner-entrepreneur Vincent Dubochet took the post for its first eighteen months, it went to a salaried manager. The PGC was one of the early firms to initiate a practice that was to become a distinctive mark of French capitalism. It sought its chief executive not among the subordinate officers already in the firm, nor among the heads of comparable firms, but rather in the civil service. After Dubochet the directors of the PGC were all engineers of the Corps des Ponts et Chaussées.

The corps was charged with overseeing and improving the nation's infrastructure, and its engineers were indisputably public servants of high rank. They had diplomas from France's most distinguished and exclusive school, the Ecole Polytechnique. Furthermore, the corps accepted only the *polytechniciens* who had graduated at the top of their classes. The corps in effect comprised a post-Napoleonic aristocracy. Recruited through rig-

42. Only two board members had enough of an attachment to the PGC to leave substantial legacies to its personnel. Those members were Germain Hervé, an early entrepreneur in the gas industry, and Raoul-Duval, an engineer-entrepreneur and a *polytechnicien*.
43. Maurice Lévy-Leboyer and François Bourguignon, *L'Economie française au XIXᵉ siècle: Analyse macro-économique* (Paris, 1985), pp. 78–84; Palmade, *French Capitalism*, pp. 187–216.

orously competitive examinations, the engineers who were admitted came overwhelmingly from haut-bourgeois families. The purpose of their long years of preparation and demanding careers was service to the state. Moreover, members were bound by powerful codes of collegial loyalty and personal honor. Wearing the distinctive military uniform at all times was obligatory for the engineers of the corps. The dignity of the corps was an ideal around which the members had to organize their lives. Aristocrats of the Old Regime had had to accept an occasional mésalliance; there was nothing they could have done about the waywardness of individual blue bloods. However, the engineers of the Corps des Ponts et Chaussées had to submit their marriage plans for approval to their director general.[44]

Preparation for the corps marked the engineers for life. Each officer was the product of about fifteen years of cloistering—first nine years at the lycée, then six years at the Ecole Polytechnique and the Ecole des Ponts et Chaussées. The latter two were run on a military model, and minute regulations governed the details of the students' lives. Vacations were short and infrequent; students spent little time outside the school. Hazing and deeply rooted customs inculcated a strong corporate identity.[45] At the same time, the rigors of the selection process and of the training bred a sense of elitism and authority. Contemporaries noted in the officers that emerged from this formative experience a distinctive comportment and even a distinctive way of thinking. No wonder the chief executives of the PGC always identified themselves first as "engineer of bridges and roads" and only then as director of the firm.[46]

The PGC was one of the earliest private enterprises to take engineers out of state service and place them in corporate management. The path by which these post-Napoleonic aristocrats came to accept—even welcome— the new career opportunities is worth examining. Members of the corps enjoyed great prestige; they were admired for their learning, for their expertise, and for the weighty matters they handled. There was hardly a family in France that would not have taken pride in having a member in the corps. The daily existence of an officer, however, was usually mundane. The pay was modest, barely enough to sustain bourgeois standards

44. On the corps, see F. Fichet-Poitrey, *Le Corps des Ponts et Chaussées: Du Génie civil à l'aménagement du territoire* (Paris, 1982), and A. Brunot and R. Coquand, *Le Corps des Ponts et Chaussées* (Paris, 1982).
45. Fichet-Poitrey, *Corps*, pp. 33–34; John Weiss, "Bridges and Barriers: Narrowing Access and Changing Structure in the French Engineering Profession, 1800–1850," in *Professions and the French State, 1700–1900*, ed. Gerald Geison (Philadelphia, 1984), pp. 30–40.
46. Brunot and Coquand, *Ponts et Chaussées*, p. 133. The directors turned over 5 percent of their salaries to the state for their pensions as engineers "on leave."

unless subsidized by private wealth. The engineers' duties could often be routine or at least subject to bureaucratic roadblocks. It is easy to imagine that there were discontents, and Honoré de Balzac, that preeminent interpreter of the bourgeois soul, left a memorable literary portrait of a troubled engineer in Gérard of *Le Curé du village* (based perhaps on his own brother-in-law). Gérard emerged from the Ecole Polytechnique with aspirations for a brilliant career and a yearning for *la gloire*. Instead, his career, though honorable, brought him mainly hard work, routine, and low pay. He came to dread a future consisting of "counting pavement stones for the state" and waiting for a small promotion every few years.[47] Balzac's speculations on the psychology of the state engineer were dramatic, to be sure, but not necessarily accurate. There was little evidence of a crisis of morale within the corps. Balzac surely underestimated the engineers' commitment to hierarchy, discipline, and service to the state.[48] Individual officers may have despaired, but they did so privately. Outwardly the corps projected a sustained attachment to its responsibilities and to its acquired status. Defections from state service were rare. Not until 1851 did the war minister find it necessary to issue a decree regulating permanent leaves of absence, allowing engineers to take outside positions. Even so, officers did not often take advantage of the regulation until the 1880s.[49] The lack of opportunities may have had much to do with the hesitations. The directorship of the small firms characteristic of the early industrial era was not suitable for men of their talent and standing even if the material rewards were attractive. But the emergence of large-scale enterprise—mines, railroads, machinery construction, and utilities—offered them a lucrative alternative that they might accept as appropriate. The appearance of firms like the PGC allowed this administrative elite to reach out and capture new positions entailing considerable economic power.

Dubochet's successor as director, Bridges and Roads Engineer Joseph de Gayffier, may not have married an actress—the corps would never have allowed that—but he was a trailblazer in his own way. De Gayffier was one of the early members of the corps to leave state service and take a position in private industry. In doing so, he helped create a model that

47. Ibid., pp. 138–141.
48. Terry Shinn, *L'Ecole Polytechnique, 1794–1914* (Paris, 1980), p. 181, on the mentality of the graduates of the institute. For an assessment of the bourgeois "soul" that differs substantially from Balzac's, see Theodore Zeldin, *France, 1848–1945*, 2 vols. (Oxford, 1973–1977), 1:11–130. Zeldin stresses the limited ambitions of most French bourgeois.
49. Brunot and Coquand, *Ponts et Chaussées*, p. 257; Shinn, *Ecole Polytechnique*, pp. 94, 167.

would eventually become commonplace in French large-scale industry. In 1858 he was still an exception and perhaps had something of Gérard in him. Born to a wealthy Auvergnat family in 1806, Joseph became a student at the Ecole Polytechnique and at the Ecole des Ponts et Chaussées by dint of hard work and uncommon intelligence. When he finished the rigorous training, he began the long, slow climb up the official rungs of the corps. By the age of forty he was still only a second-class engineer earning forty-five hundred francs a year and had already served in the departments of Indre, Somme, Oise, and Côtes-du-Nord. The modest pay and difficult work may have interested de Gayffier in more lucrative endeavors outside the corps. His subsequent employment showed how both the engineers and the corps would have to adapt to new career patterns.[50]

De Gayffier's first attempt to serve private enterprise went smoothly. In 1845 he left the corps briefly to be director of a public-works firm in Portugal and readily received a leave of absence for that purpose; he was back in the corps within two years. The next involvement with a private firm proved more complicated. De Gayffier asked for another leave in 1856 so that he could take a post with the Grand Central Railroad. His superiors at Bridges and Roads were reluctant to grant the request on the grounds that the position involved directing operations that had been subcontracted to another firm. The officials insisted that "the reputation of the corps requires that the position of engineers who take leaves from its ranks . . . must be perfectly defined and must present nothing untoward in the eyes of the public." Clearly the corps was trying to set lofty standards for outside employment, whereas de Gayffier sought to extend those limits. He finally worked out an acceptable definition of the post and received the authorized leave. During his employment with the railroad he earned six times as much as the corps would have paid him.[51]

The merging of the Grand Central Railroad with a larger line placed de Gayffier in a new predicament. He lost his position but was no longer willing to return to the corps. He was reprimanded for not reporting to his assigned post when the leave ended. Soon he suffered the further humiliation of being passed over for promotion to first-class engineer. He apparently spent two years in this ambiguous situation before the offer from the PGC arrived. Perhaps an exceptionally disgruntled state engineer was the only sort that private enterprise could attract at that time.

Why board members of the PGC selected de Gayffier to direct the firm

50. Archives nationales, F[14] 2233[1].
51. Ibid. See especially Conseil général des Ponts et Chaussées, deliberations of August 7, 1856.

is not clear. His assignments as an engineer had prepared him for work with railroads. He had planned canals, dredged harbors, and supervised the laying of track, but he had no experience whatsoever with the gas industry. Moreover, his reputation within the corps had its blemishes; internal reports described his character as "inconstant" and the quality of his work as "mediocre." Nonetheless, like most of his colleagues at Bridges and Roads, de Gayffier had had experience administering large projects. It is possible that de Gayffier had made important contacts when he worked with the Grand Central Railroad, for that was a Pereire undertaking.[52]

Still working out the terms by which state engineers would serve private enterprise, the directors of the corps did not approve de Gayffier's new post without some clarification. The officials were concerned that this position would associate him too closely with commercial operations, considered beneath the dignity of the corps. They had to receive assurances that de Gayffier's functions would entail the oversight of a large corporation serving a useful public purpose and that baser matters, such as purchasing coal, would be the responsibility of his subordinates. With those assurances de Gayffier was allowed to begin his thirteen-year career with the PGC (1858–1871). Though he was undoubtedly pleased to earn many times the salary of a Bridges and Roads engineer, his status in the corps did not cease to weigh on his mind. Apparently self-conscious about being only a second-class officer, he campaigned for a promotion even as he assumed the directorship of the PGC.[53]

Emile Camus succeeded de Gayffier as director in 1871 and remained at the helm of the firm for the next twenty years. The son of a prosperous notary from Charleville (Ardennes), Emile had entered the Ecole des Ponts et Chaussées after graduating fourteenth in his class from the Ecole Polytechnique. Like his predecessor, he had held several positions in private firms before his employment with the PGC, and none had been in the gas industry. In 1858 he had taken leave from the corps to head a firm that transformed more than three thousand hectares of marshland around Mont-Saint-Michel in Brittany into arable land. This demanding project won high praise for its technical accomplishments. In 1860 Camus was named assistant director of the PGC. How Camus came to the attention of the gas company is not, in this instance, a mystery: he had married a

52. Ibid., report of prefect to minister of commerce, January 3, 1855; undated *fiche* from Corps des Ponts et Chaussées.
53. Ibid., report of March 24, 1859; prefect to minister of commerce, July 30, 1860.

relative of de Gayffier in 1852 and had worked under his direction at the Grand Central Railroad in 1856.[54] In fact, the last director of the PGC, Léon Bertrand (appointed in 1901), was also a relative of Camus and de Gayffier.[55] The company was thus under the control of one "dynasty" for thirty-eight of its fifty years, showing the narrowness of the search for a chief executive officer. De Gayffier's successors also owed him gratitude for helping create the precedent of leaving the corps to serve a profit-making enterprise. Camus did not face questions from his commanders in the corps about the appropriateness of his position; he received a leave of absence as a matter of course.

Stéphane Godot, who became director in 1892 (serving until 1901), was the only one of the PGC's chief officers to have displayed any personal rebelliousness or an inclination to think critically about wider social questions. As a twenty-year-old student at the Ecole Polytechnique he committed an (unknown) offense that resulted in his expulsion. Receiving indulgence from the war minister, he was readmitted but dropped from ninth to twenty-fifth place in the class. Perhaps as a result of the chastising experience, he redoubled his efforts as a student at the Ecole des Ponts et Chaussées and graduated second.[56] The rest of his life was not a model of passive conformity, however. He became interested in the school of thought inspired by Frédéric Le Play and developed a reputation as an industrial paternalist. When the PGC faced a new era of industrial relations in the early 1890s, Camus turned the post of director over to Godot. The union leaders took the change as a conciliatory measure. He resigned in 1901, ostensibly for reasons of health, when a dialogue about industrial reform was no longer necessary.[57]

Godot's successor, Léon Bertrand, showed no such signs of rebelliousness or questioning. He was the son of a professor at the Ecole Polytechnique who was also an immortal of the Académie française. Léon obtained only enthusiastic praise from teachers and superiors: his character was "excellent," his work habits "irreproachable."[58] In a sense Bertrand marked the completion of an evolution among the PGC's leaders, from nonconforming entrepreneurs to unconventional state engineers to model officers of France's most distinguished technical corps.

Each of these engineer-directors was part of a national elite, not only

54. Archives nationales, F[14] 2185[1]; F[12] 5101.
55. I have been unable to discover the precise relation among all three engineers, but an elegant tomb in the Père-Lachaise cemetery attests to the alliance of their families.
56. Archives nationales, F[14] 11481.
57. See below, chapter 4, on Godot's relation to the gas personnel.
58. Archives nationales, F[12] 8516; F[14] 11520.

as a result of his own membership in the corps but also through family membership.[59] A generation or two earlier, their progenitors had been successful professionals. Camus's father had been a notary, Bertrand's grandfather a physician. The path of further ascent had led through the *grandes écoles* and from there to high state posts. The directors' family trees contained numerous *maîtres de requêtes* and *auditeurs* of the Council of State, judges, and professors. Relatives in banking or business were fewer. Among the last group were those who had also "parachuted" from a state corps into industry. Official documents were always able to categorize the directors' parents as well-off, but huge fortunes were rare. De Gayffier's personal estate of 632,000 francs was probably typical. Though substantial, it was not the wealth of a Dubochet or even of a board member like the banker Dassier, who died with a fortune of more than four million francs. By moving into the PGC, engineer-directors added sizable income to the prestige and power their relatives enjoyed as *hauts fonctionnaires*.[60] Perhaps the lure of lucre was not so powerful among most of their colleagues who remained in the corps, or perhaps desirable opportunities were lacking. As we have seen, the PGC kept its search for chief executives within narrow limits.

Was the Corps des Ponts et Chaussées the most appropriate source of leadership for the PGC? It is hard to identify specific qualities and training that made these engineers essential to the firm. Their education, highly abstract and oriented toward mathematics, did not ensure a technical grasp of industrial problems. The most valuable asset they possessed was the ability to deal as equals with the other graduates of the *grandes écoles* they were likely to meet in the course of doing business. As *polytechniciens*, they could address the prefect or municipal engineer as *mon camarade* and use the informal *tu*.[61] Such standing was worth something, but the deepest reason that the PGC's board turned to the corps to find its chief executive was no doubt a conventional, uncritical respect for hierarchy. State and society defined these men as the nation's administrative elite.

· · ·

A clear sign that the Ecole Polytechnique and the state's technical corps did not produce men with precisely the necessary preparation to direct gas production was that the PGC recruited the engineers in charge of opera-

59. Ezra Suleiman, *Elites in French Society* (Princeton, 1978); John Armstrong, *The European Administrative Elite* (Princeton, 1973).
60. AP, D Q⁷, 12341 (fols. 56–57); Shinn, *Ecole Polytechnique*, p. 90.
61. For an interesting illustration of the right to use informal forms of address as well as of the inevitable contacts made at the Ecole Polytechnique, see Ibid., no. 155, Fontaine to Godot, April 26, 1902.

tional departments from other schools. Heads of divisions, departments, and factories were graduates of the Ecole Centrale des Arts et Manufactures (founded in 1829) or the external classes of the Ecole des Mines.[62] Both of these institutes had assumed the task of training industrial leaders. Though they lacked the supreme prestige of the Ecole Polytechnique, they stood just beneath it. The bourgeois family that placed a son in one of these state schools had reason to be pleased. Industrialists often chose one of these alternatives over the Ecole Polytechnique for their heir if he was serious about continuing in business.[63]

The Ecole Centrale and the external classes of the Ecole des Mines, with their industrial mission, were products of the emerging factory era. So were their graduates. Just as the early directors of the PGC departed from convention by leaving state service and creating a new role for themselves at the helm of large firms, lower managers were creating their own social persona. The PGC was born at the moment when engineer-managers of industrial firms were appearing. Enrollment figures at the two schools attest to the rapid expansion of the milieu (table 5). No more than the PGC's director did the heads of departments or plants build their identity around business administration. Their professional designation was "industrial engineer," a new occupational title that came into common use around the time the PGC was founded. Earlier all who used the title "engineer" had been members of a state corps. The birth of civil or industrial engineering as an established occupational category can perhaps be dated from 1848, when the Society of Civil Engineers was founded.[64] Managers at the PGC

---

62. The term "external classes" needs explanation. Technically, the Ecole des Mines was an extension of the Polytechnique. It enrolled two sorts of students. The "student-engineers" were graduates of the Polytechnique, usually top-ranking ones. These students were destined for the Corps des Mines, which, like the Corps des Ponts et Chaussées, was a highly prestigious body of state engineers. The Ecole des Mines also admitted "external" students, men who had generally not attended the Polytechnique and had gained admission through an examination. These students were not eligible for the Corps des Mines and were being trained for industry.

63. The early history of the Ecole Centrale is well served by John Weiss, *The Making of Technological Man: The Social Origins of French Engineering Education* (Cambridge, Mass., 1982). See also Louis Guillet, *Cent ans de la vie de l'Ecole Centrale des arts et manufactures, 1829–1929* (Paris, 1929). On the Ecole des Mines, see Louis Aguillon, *L'Ecole des Mines de Paris: Notice historique* (Paris, 1889), and Gabriel Chesneau, *Notre école: Histoire de l'Ecole des Mines* (Paris, 1932). The external classes of the Ecole des Mines were not at first so exclusive nor so rigorous as classes at the Ecole Centrale but eventually became much more demanding. Not until its later years did the PGC recruit heavily from Mines.

64. Terry Shinn, "From 'Crops' to 'Profession': The Emergence and Definition of Industrial Engineering in Modern France," in *The Organization of Science and*

Table 5. Size of Graduating Classes at Schools
of Industrial Engineering

Year	Centrale	Mines (External Class)	Year	Centrale	Mines (External Class)
1835	16	3	1875	151	19
1840	31	4	1880	162	15
1845	48	11	1885	181	24
1850	67	15	1890	203	26
1855	72	18	1895	207	33
1860	116	17	1900	220	36
1865	135	25	1905	221	—
1870	174	17			

Sources: *Annuaire de l'association amicale des anciens élèves de l'Ecole Centrale des Arts et Manufactures. 1929* (Paris, 1929); *Association amicale des élèves de l'Ecole Nationale Supérieure des Mines. Annuaire. 1900–1901* (Paris, 1901).

benefited from its growing social acceptability. Already in 1856 Gustave Flaubert was able to have Charles Bovary's assertive mother entertain aspirations that her son would be either a judge or a civil engineer.

The sorts of firsts that PGC engineers could achieve were well illustrated by the career of Louis Arson, the chief of the factory division for thirty-eight years and, as such, the principal operational manager. Arson graduated from the Ecole Centrale in 1841 with the first diploma awarded in mechanical engineering. One of his early jobs was with a machine-construction firm that made the first French locomotives and the engines for the first transatlantic steamships. He was the first graduate of the Ecole Centrale to sit on its advisory board.[65] Arson and his colleagues at the PGC were members of the generation that helped establish the social persona for France's industrial managers. It was certainly not the case, however, that the first generation imagined itself without governing norms and models. Only by adapting some of the formal structures

---

Technology in France, 1808–1914, eds. Robert Fox and George Weisz (Cambridge, 1980), pp. 184–210; John Weiss, "Les Changements de structure dans la profession de l'ingénieur en France de 1800 à 1850," in *L'Ingénieur dans la société française*, ed. André Thépot (Paris, 1985), pp. 19–38.

65. Archives nationales, F¹² 5082; "Discours de Mont-Serrat," *Bulletin de l'Association amicale des anciens élèves de l'Ecole Centrale* 35 (1903–1904): 98–102. On Arson's private life and family, there is a carton of interesting documents: AP, D E¹, Fonds Lestringuez.

of the traditional professions did industrial managers gain social acceptance.[66]

The distinctive features of the French engineering profession, as it had developed under the tutelage of the state, deeply marked the careers and work culture of the PGC's managers. One manifestation was the reconstruction of the professional hierarchy within the company in the form of closed castes. As we have seen, top managers were graduates of the most exclusive schools, the Ecole Polytechnique and the Ecole des Ponts et Chaussées.[67] Middle and lower managers were recruited from the technical institutes of the next rank, the Ecole Centrale and Ecole des Mines. These graduates were excluded from top management regardless of their record of achievement on the job, but they had their own privileges. They monopolized the administration of divisions, departments, and factories. By contrast, men with diplomas from the least exalted of the engineering institutes, the Ecoles d'Arts et Métiers (*gazarts* as they were known), were relegated to modest posts. It was not that these schools failed to provide rigorous training and produce capable students; but the social level of recruitment was lower and the prestige less resounding. The officers of the PGC accepted the *gazarts* mainly for staff positions.[68] Thus the PGC allocated managerial posts on the basis of criteria external to the firm and replicated the hierarchy of the engineering profession.

Notions about the ways managers should do their work came from the engineering profession as well. Managers inevitably looked to the engineers of the state corps to define their responsibilities and work culture.[69] State engineers provided guidance on how a technically trained elite would function within a bureaucratic setting. They inspired ideals of authoritativeness, independence, and bureaucratic loyalty. The managers of the PGC, following the officers of the corps, eschewed specialization and readily delved into all aspects of administration, including nontechnical ones. Far from regarding mundane details as beneath them, they wel-

66. Robert Anderson, "Secondary Education in Mid-Nineteenth-Century France: Some Social Aspects," *Past and Present*, no. 53 (1971): 125.
67. The one exception proves the rule. Eugène de Montserrat, a graduate of the Ecole Centrale, was named assistant director in 1901. The PGC was liquidated before he could have moved up to the top post, if indeed that was a genuine possibility for him.
68. C. R. Day, "The Making of Mechanical Engineers in France: The Ecoles d'Arts et Metiers, 1803–1914," *French Historical Studies* 10 (1978): 439–460. Not all large corporations relegated the *gazarts* to minor posts. See Claude Beaud, "Les Ingénieurs du Creusot à travers quelques destins du milieu du XIXᵉ siècle au milieu du XXᵉ," in Thepot, *L'Ingénieur*, pp. 51–59.
69. On the functioning of the engineers of the corps, see Jean-Claude Thoenig, *L'Ere des technocrats: Le Cas des Ponts et Chaussées* (Paris, 1973), pp. 165–214.

comed involvement in every aspect of supervision. Yet even when they were directly involved in decision making, they posed as impersonal authorities who could evaluate a matter with detachment. The PGC's managers also emulated the state engineers by asserting a degree of independence from their immediate employer and identifying with a larger scientific community. They did so chiefly through their personal research projects, which were related only tangentially to their current position in the enterprise. The factory superintendent, Paul Biju-Duval, and the chief of gas production, Albert Euchène, published findings on the specific heat of iron and nickel. The assistant factory head, Edouard Servier, studied the chemistry of coal tar and made noteworthy empirical observations. His superior, Arson, turned out a steady stream of gadgets from his laboratory.[70] Though there was a good deal of tinkering and research in progress, it was not usually coordinated or directed by the firm toward established goals. The projects reflected the personal interests of the managers, and they considered the materials, laboratories, and personnel of the company at their disposal to pursue their work. The company accepted such independence and even expressed pride in the accomplishments of its engineers when they won scholarly recognition. The only limit it sought to place on the independence of its personnel was prohibiting paid consultation for other firms.[71]

Though there was this independent aspect to the managers' work culture, the impact of the French engineering tradition was to reinforce loyalties to the organization. Nurtured under the aegis of a powerful state while capitalism was still a weak motor of change, French engineers hardly had a chance to form an autonomous professional group with individual careers as the focus of professional life. Instead, state engineers imparted a sense of comfort with bureaucratic procedures, lifelong commitments to the organization, and ambiguity about the morality of the marketplace.[72] The acceptance of hard work and modest rewards coupled with a respect for hierarchical authority that characterized the *corps d'état* certainly influenced the managers of the PGC. Thus, entitling themselves civil engineers was not a superficial affectation: they were making a statement about their cast of mind and their expectations on the job.

By the late nineteenth century some contemporaries viewed it as a pe-

---

70. *Bulletin de l'Association amicale des anciens élèves de l'Ecole Centrale* 35 (1903–1904): 232; AP, V 8 O¹, no. 677, deliberations of October 7, 1874; no. 672, deliberations of June 26, 1867; no. 1060, report of October 10, 1859.
71. AP, V 8 O¹, no. 666, deliberations of June 26, 1858.
72. This analysis follows the thinking of sociologist Dietrich Rueschemeyer, *Power and the Division of Labor* (Stanford, 1986), pp. 122–124.

culiarity of French industry that engineers so dominated managerial posts in private enterprise. Though the monopoly of the profession was especially complete in France, the situation was not unique.[73] In any case, as France's industrial prowess retreated before that of its neighbors, the dominance of engineers became a source of regret and anticipated reform. Industrial critics denigrated the training that French engineers received. The attacks began with the fossilized education at the apex, the Ecole Polytechnique, on the grounds that its instruction was too mathematical, too theoretical, and contemptuous of the practical problems posed by industry. The PGC, like most firms, implicitly accepted such criticisms, for it drew its personnel from schools that were more specifically oriented toward the application of science. However, observers familiar with German technical training argued that the Ecole des Ponts et Chaussées, the Ecole Centrale, and the Ecole des Mines ultimately resembled the Ecole Polytechnique more than the German schools. All of the French institutes placed far too much emphasis on theoretical approaches and mathematical training; all relied heavily on lectures even though laboratory exercises were necessary for good instruction in the rising fields of organic chemistry and electricity; all led French engineers to develop general knowledge and eschew the specialization that would have been more beneficial to industry.[74] The critics made some worthy points, but they postulated for the engineers a narrow, technical role in production. The responsibilities that managers held in a firm like the PGC did not justify the sort of specialization and laboratory training that the critics desired. Indeed, the partial concentration that French technical institutes did permit often proved superfluous because the graduates' assignments were unrelated to their academic specialties. The ideal of the elite schools, theoretical training aimed at rapid assimilation of new concepts, was not as outmoded as the critics maintained.

73. Max Leclerc, *La Formation des ingénieurs à l'étranger et en France* (Paris, 1917). The dominance of engineers in France was not as unusual as Leclerc believed. See Heinz Hartmann, *Authority and Organization in German Management* (Princeton, 1959), p. 162; Jürgen Kocka, "Entrepreneurs and Managers in German Industry," *Cambridge Economic History of Europe* (Cambridge, 1978), 7(1): 492–589; Chandler, *Visible Hand,* p. 95.

74. Louis Bergeron, *Les Capitalistes en France (1780–1914)* (Paris, 1978), p. 70; Leclerc, *Formation des ingénieurs;* André Pelletan, "Les Ecoles techniques allemandes," *Revue de métallurgie* 3 (1906): 589–620; Antoine Prost, *Histoire de l'enseignement en France, 1800–1967* (Paris, 1968), p. 303. The presumed deficiencies of French engineering education have been summed up and forcefully reasserted in Robert Locke, *The End of Practical Man: Entrepreneurship and Higher Education in Germany, France, and Great Britain, 1880–1940* (Greenwich, Conn., 1984).

It is no wonder that the Ecole Centrale was proud of the versatility of its students.[75] Generalized training for careers modeled on the state engineers was what managers wanted and needed.

A more pertinent criticism came in the early twentieth century from Henri Fayol, the founder of managerial science in France and one of the most respected engineers of his day.[76] Fayol readily acknowledged the multiplicity of disciplines that managers had to master. For him, the deficiency in training arose from its exclusively technical character. Though engineers faced responsibilities for personnel, marketing, accounting, and financing, they received no formal instruction whatsoever in administration. Fayol refused to regard a capacity for mathematical reasoning as a sound basis for judgment in these areas. For decisions in these nontechnical fields the PGC followed the British model of empirical training on the job. Perhaps Fayol underestimated another quality that French technical training succeeded in imparting, a sense of confidence in handling the disparate responsibilities of business management. The engineer-managers of the PGC appeared comfortable with their multiple duties: their decisions may not have been especially keen, but they were consistent and conscientious. Such comfort with nontechnical fields may explain why the engineering profession ignored Fayol's challenge for so long.

The influence of the state institutes extended to staffing. In countries like Britain, where such institutes did not exist, filling managerial positions was a great problem. Owners refused to trust salaried executives to use their capital honestly and efficiently, so kinship and friendship played a large role in hiring.[77] The engineering schools of France provided the guarantees of probity and expertise that personal familiarity did across the Channel. The PGC relied on the recommendations of the school directors more than any other source of recruitment. Faith in the excellence of the alma mater, reassurances provided by shared experiences, and established contacts made managers draw their new colleagues from their own schools. Factory chief Arson recommended one engineer after another from the Ecole Centrale. As his influence waned and Paul Gigot, his assistant, took charge, appointments gravitated to the Ecole des Mines, Gigot's alma mater.

More than excellence of training, the engineering institutes offered the

75. Weiss, *Making of Technological Man*, p. 225.
76. *General and Industrial Management*, trans. Constance Storrs (London, 1949). Fayol first published his influential tract in 1916, but it was based on talks given before the war.
77. Pollard, *Genesis of Modern Management*, pp. 11–13.

PGC a cadre of managers with the proper attitudes and firm character. Despite minor variations in curriculum, all the institutes sought to impart an ideology of sobriety, discipline, and assiduousness. Standards of accomplishment were very high, and the schools worked the students mercilessly. Consciousness of class rank, continuously reassessed, ritualized the view of life as a constant struggle. Any student who did not embrace hard work and persistent application left the program. Those who remained developed a sense of intellectual and moral elitism. For good reason one historian of the Ecole Centrale has labeled it a "factory of the bourgeoisie."[78] Although not all graduates attained the schools' ideals, the PGC found among them a group of men with ample aptitude for science, a passion to apply it, and a commitment to the work ethic. The PGC took full advantage of the discipline inculcated at the Ecole Centrale and Ecole des Mines.

Satisfied with the elite schools and loyal to them, the PGC regarded the Third Republic's efforts to create new institutes of applied technology in the last two decades of the century with complete indifference. The company gave no support whatsoever to the creation of the Ecole de Physique et de Chimie Industrielle when it was founded in Paris in 1882 and hired only a few of its graduates for humble laboratory posts.[79] The firm did not wish to make a place for specialists and technicians lacking elite diplomas in its managerial structure.

Careers and Rewards

The privileged family background of the young men who received diplomas from the *grandes écoles* is well documented. Not only the Ecole Polytechnique and its schools of application (Mines and Ponts et Chaussées) but also the Ecole Centrale and the external classes of the Ecole des Mines were preserves of the well-to-do bourgeoisie.[80] The social antecedents of the PGC managers who were *centraux* conform to the rule. Their fathers

78. Weiss, *Making of Technological Man*, p. 234; Weiss, "Bridges and Barriers," pp. 39–41.

79. Ville de Paris, *Cinquantième anniversaire de la fondation de l'Ecole de physique et de chimie industrielle de la ville de Paris* (Paris, 1932). On another set of new technical schools, see Harry Paul, "Apollo Courts the Vulcans: The Applied Science Institutes in Nineteenth-Century French Science Faculties," in Fox and Weisz, *Organization of Science*, pp. 155–181.

80. Maurice Lévy-Leboyer, "Innovation and Business Strategies in Nineteenth- and Twentieth-Century France," in *Enterprise and Entrepreneurs in Nineteenth- and Twentieth-Century France*, ed. Edward Carter, et al. (Baltimore, 1976), p. 108; Weiss, *Making of Technological Man*, p. 205; Shinn, *Ecole Polytechnique*, pp. 101, 142.

Table 6. Family Background of Engineers from
Ecole Centrale

Fathers	All Graduates 1830–1900 (%)	Alumni at PGC	
		No.	%
High Income			
Property Owner	31.8	14	53.8
Businessman	34.6	5	19.2
Professional	12.7	6	23.2
Low Income			
Employee	10.9	1	3.8
Artisan	5.4	0	0.0
Farmer	4.6	0	0.0
Total	100	26	100

Sources: Archives de l'Ecole Centrale, Registres de promotion; Maurice Lévy-Leboyer, "Innovation and Business Strategies in Nineteenth- and Twentieth-Century France," *Enterprise and Entrepreneurs in Nineteenth- and Twentieth-Century France*, ed. Edward Carter, Robert Forster, and Joseph Moody (Baltimore, 1976), p. 108.

were businessmen (often retired), liberal professionals, and gentlemen property owners (table 6). Though not all were extremely rich by the standards of the day, many were, and others offered good connections. Albert Ellison was the son of a property owner who lived on the genteel rue Madeleine (eighth arrondissement). The head of the meter department was the offspring of a Parisian banker. The uncle of another engineer was the director the the major newspaper, *Le Siècle*. Alexandre Arson's mother left a fortune of more than 350,000 francs to her children. The only conspicuously humble manager to emerge from the Ecole Centrale was a son of an employee at the firm; the company had provided a fellowship and hired him when his studies were completed.[81] Thus, it seems that the emergence of large-scale industry diversified career patterns for the children of solidly established families but did not offer a source of advancement for the hardworking children of the common people. The question remains whether firms like the PGC gave these sons of the well-off the kinds of careers that allowed them to perpetuate their family status.

The PGC compensated its chief executive officer generously enough to have gratified Balzac's Gérard. The directors of the PGC had annual salaries of twenty thousand to twenty-five thousand francs, and profit-sharing

81. See sources for table 6. On Arson, see AP, D E¹, Fonds Lestringuez, contrat de mariage.

bonuses doubled or even tripled the compensation.[82] Camus, who presided over the firm during its acme of profitability, earned as much as eighty-two thousand francs. His average pay was just under seventy thousand francs, thirty-eight times the earnings of one of the firm's young office clerks. By contrast, when engineers of the Corps of Bridges and Roads achieved a long-awaited raise in 1906, their incomes were still modest. The state paid ordinary engineers (a position officers were likely to have after ten years of service) five thousand to seven thousand francs. The decree of 1906 gave chief engineers ten thousand to twelve thousand francs.[83] Falling profits inevitably lowered the compensation of the directors who headed the PGC during the era of adjustment, but Godot (who presided from 1892 to 1901) still averaged fifty thousand francs a year, and Bertrand earned an average of forty-six thousand francs between 1901 and 1905. Unlike the chief engineers in the esteemed state corps, the PGC's directors received incomes to which *grands notables* were accustomed.[84]

Most middle and lower managers had to accept less—usually much less. Their level of prosperity depended on whether they received profit-sharing bonuses as well. The PGC singled out six to eight middle and lower managers for the benefit. In 1880 the favored posts were the head of the factory division and his assistant, the chief of the distribution division, the engineer of the by-products department, the head of the coke service, the chief of the coal department, the senior accountant, and the head of the customer accounts office. The bonuses, ranging from twenty-five hundred to fifteen thousand francs, completed salaries comparable to those of chief engineers of the Corps of Bridges and Roads. Thus, the managers who received the bonuses were relatively well paid, though they may have had to wait a while to attain such compensation. Two different sorts of career pattern obtained (figure 8). A few managers were fortunate enough to head major departments for most or all of their careers and to benefit

82. The annual compensation offered to each director (announced in the deliberations of the *conseil d'administration*) was as follows: to de Gayffier, twenty thousand francs in salary plus an unspecified bonus based on profits; to Camus, twenty-five thousand francs in salary plus one thousand francs for each franc of dividends over twenty-five; to Godot, twenty-four thousand francs in salary plus one thousand francs for each million francs in profits; to Bertrand, twenty thousand francs in salary plus five hundred francs for each franc of dividends over twenty.

83. Brunot and Coquand, *Ponts et Chaussées*, p. 714; Weiss, "Changements de structure," p. 26–28.

84. In 1869, more than half the deputies in a National Assembly dominated by notables had incomes of more than thirty thousand francs a year. The chief officers of the PGC were in their range. See Robert McGraw, *France, 1815–1914: The Bourgeois Century* (Oxford, 1986), p. 167.

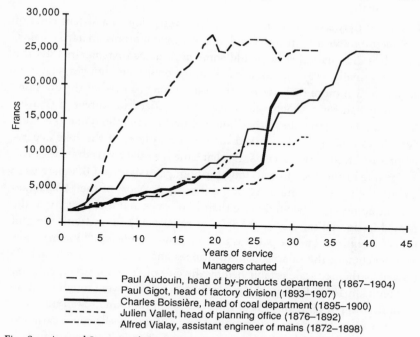

Managers charted

- - - - Paul Audouin, head of by-products department (1867–1904)
———— Paul Gigot, head of factory division (1893–1907)
▬▬▬▬ Charles Boissière, head of coal department (1895–1900)
- - - - - Julien Vallet, head of planning office (1876–1892)
– – – – Alfred Vialay, assistant engineer of mains (1872–1898)

Fig. 8. Annual Income of Managers, by Length of Career (in Francs). From AP, V 8 O¹, nos. 665–700.

from large bonuses. During Arson's long incumbency as chief of the factory division he earned a salary of fifteen thousand francs (which remained constant for thirty-eight years) and bonuses that often came to that much or more. Paul Audouin became chief of the by-products department within ten years after leaving the Ecole Centrale. In 1870, as sales to the dyestuffs industry were about soar, the director granted him a profit-sharing bonus. For twenty-five of his forty-four years with the PGC he earned at least twenty thousand francs annually and as much as twenty-six thousand francs, far more than Bridges and Roads engineers could ever hope to earn. This son of a professor at the Jardin des Plantes had no material reason to regret he had not become a state engineer.[85]

A more typical career pattern for the engineer-managers at the PGC entailed long years of moderate earnings before benefiting from high salaries and generous annual bonuses. After graduating from the Ecole des Mines, Paul Gigot began his career humbly, as a subinspector of construction at eighteen hundred francs a year. Seven years later, when his talents were recognized, he was a superintendent of the Vaugirard gas factory, but

85. On Audouin's background, see Archives nationales, Légion d'Honneur 72, dossier 38.

he earned only five thousand francs. His promotion to assistant chief of the factory division in 1868 did not bring important material gains, though it did guarantee he would some day succeed Arson. In 1883 the company finally awarded him a small annual bonus, and ten years later he began to earn more than twenty thousand francs as head of the division. The long wait for a sizable salary also characterized the career of Charles Boissière. This graduate of the Ecole Polytechnique (1863) and the Ecole des Mines (1868) slowly worked his way up to head of the coke department after twenty-seven years. At that time his salary rose dramatically.

In spite of the need to wait long for high pay, Gigot and Boissière were among the fortunate minority of gas managers. Most of their colleagues did not do nearly so well, despite their hard work and their loyalty to the firm. Managerial salaries at the PGC were probably in line with those of other large firms, but the pay was by no means munificent.[86] We may take as a benchmark the salaries paid to Bridges and Roads engineers in 1906 as well as the pay scale established by the city of Paris for its supervisory personnel in 1898. Paris paid the administrators who were roughly equivalent to lower-level managers at the PGC seven thousand to ten thousand francs a year. The city's departmental and division heads could earn sixteen thousand to eighteen thousand francs.[87] The PGC compensated its managerial personnel comparably. Their income, then, did not at all reflect the company's notorious profitability. They were paid like civil servants.

Engineers' emoluments at the PGC were slow to diverge markedly from those of the office workers (table 7). This was partly because managers began at the same modest pay as clerks, eighteen hundred francs. The salaries also reflected the humble positions in which engineers began their careers despite their elite schooling—as draftsmen, secretaries to middle managers, assistants to assistant plant superintendents—for a few years at the very least. Even Boissière, a graduate of the Ecole Polytechnique as well as the Ecole des Mines, spent three years as a draftsman with the company. When he had become chief of the coal department and was recommended for the Légion d'honneur, his file did not even mention that phase of his career. The *centralien* Théodore Bouffé began as nothing more than a chief foreman in the gas distillation plant.[88] Engineers did not usually remain at such lowly posts for more than two or three years, but the

86. For a comparison with Saint-Gobain Chemical Company, see Lévy-Leboyer, "Hierarchical Structure," p. 468; with Le Creusot, see Beaud, "Ingénieurs du Creusot," p. 54.
87. AP, V 8 O¹, no. 153, "Arrêté préfectoral concernant l'organisation du cadre du personnel supérieur des services techniques."
88. Ibid., no. 162, Pernolet to Minister of Interior, July 8, 1905; no. 678, deliberations of August 28, 1876.

Table 7. Average Annual Salaries, by Seniority
(in francs)[a]

Years of Service	Managers	Clerks
0	1,800	1,800
5	3,250	2,010
10	4,400	2,350
15	6,750	2,590
20	7,400	2,850
25	9,300	3,150

Sources: AP, V 8 O^1, no. 665–700; no. 149, report of October 22, 1900.
[a]These figures do not include annual or exceptional bonuses.

position of assistant factory superintendent—none too glorious nor re-munerative in itself—could be more enduring. Several managers were stuck as assistants for ten years or more. One graduate of the Ecole Centrale entered the PGC in 1879 and was still assistant superintendent of the Passy plant in 1902. Moreover, such unassuming starts were not usually purgatories inevitably leading to grander positions. For every Gigot, who eventually achieved a handsome compensation, there were three or four others who did not. Julien Vallet, also from the Ecole Centrale, entered the PGC a year after Gigot but did not have the same success. He retired as engineer of the construction department after thirty-one years, having attained a salary of twelve thousand francs. Still another *centralien*, Alfred Vialay, reached an income of only nine thousand francs as assistant head of the distribution division after thirty years with the PGC. Engineers of Bridges and Roads or of the city of Paris had little to envy these two; yet their situations were the typical ones. As table 8 suggests, promotions in the PGC were a slow, orderly affair at best. A few engineers never advanced out of technical-staff positions.

The gas company did not raise general salary levels significantly for managers except in compensation for heavier responsibilities. The average pay of assistant departmental and division chiefs was only 16 percent higher in 1902 (fifty-six hundred francs) than in 1858 (forty-eight hundred francs). Factory superintendents did receive significant increases (earning an average of fifty-one hundred francs in 1858 and ten thousand seven hundred francs in 1902), but in return the corporation asked more of them. Their raises reflected the burgeoning responsibilities entailed in an eightfold increase in gas production. The PGC apparently could escape having to raise salaries for its routine engineers because there was no

Table 8. Careers of Engineers, by Seniority

Level Attained	After 5 Years	After 10 Years	After 20 Years
Technical staff	9	6	5
Lower management			
Assistant factory superintendent	13	9	2
Factory superintendent	6	8	12
Assistant department head	3	5	7
Department head	1	2	5
Middle management			
Assistant division head	2	2	5
Division head	0	1	3
Totals in sample	34	33	39

Source: AP, V 8 O¹, no. 723–738.

shortage of them. The state's engineering institutes grew faster than the mediocre pace of France's industrial development required. When the company needed a machinery inspector, the head of the service could produce a list of fourteen engineers who solicited the post. The contention that France's industrial growth was slowed by a lack of technical personnel is implausible.[89] Of course, the dearth of opportunities did not necessarily reconcile executives to their modest pay. It is easy to suspect that some may have been disconcerted by the doubling of wage levels during the life of the firm while salary levels remained rather flat.[90]

Director Godot learned to his surprise and embarrassment from an irate stockholder that some factory superintendents lived well at the company's expense. The PGC gave them a house on the factory grounds, and it came with a coachman, a gardener, and a servant. Forced to justify paying for the help (about which top management had been kept ignorant, no doubt through a conspiracy of silence), production engineer Albert Euchène argued that superintendents were graduates of "les Ecoles" and therefore required such amenities.[91] Euchène may have been correct about engineers being accustomed to a genteel domesticity as a result of their family background. But most managers had to live soberly, indeed, if they existed purely on their own incomes. Prudent marriages were almost a necessity if they desired luxuries or needed to give their sons the same

89. Ibid., no. 777, report of May 21, 1872 (fol. 20); Paul, "Apollo Courts the Vulcans," p. 180.
90. See chapter 7 on wage levels and on the push for higher wages within the PGC.
91. AP, V 8 O¹, no. 162, report of Euchène, January 25, 1896.

sort of expensive schooling as they had received.[92] The head of the coke department, Emile Brissac, resided in an unpretentious apartment on the unfashionable fourth floor. His building was not even covered in the sculptured stone that denoted a luxurious residence. For all its modesty, the dwelling cost Brissac a fourth of his salary at the time. To have rented in one of the elegant edifices that lined Baron Haussmann's new boulevards might easily have cost half his earnings.[93] Careers as engineer-managers proved uncertain routes to building an estate. Factory superintendent Louis Cheron died after twenty years of employment in the PGC with a fortune of sixty-three thousand francs. Of that sum, fifty-one thousand had come from an inheritance and from a wife's dowry.[94] Only the fortunate minority of managers who attained large emoluments and profit-sharing bonuses could hope to build handsome estates. Arson had received only twelve thousand francs from his parents at his marriage but was able to give his daughter a dowry of sixty-one thousand francs.[95] Director de Gayffier died with a fortune of 632,000 francs, ten times the value of Cheron's. We can be sure that he did not earn the wealth in the Corps des Ponts et Chaussées.[96]

Not only was access to the highly paid posts limited, but most managers knew relatively early in their careers that they would never leave lower management. The PGC reflected French society at large in channeling a small core of candidates into the elite track at a young age and selecting them by criteria other than proven accomplishment on the job. Servier became assistant chief of the factory division, the chosen successor to the powerful Arson, within three years of graduating from the Ecole Centrale. His rapid elevation was not due to extraordinary promise as a student (he graduated thirty-first of 127 students) nor to the brilliance of his first years with the company. It was a matter of having the confidence of an influential member of the board of directors.[97] Similarly, Euchène became the third-ranking engineer of the factory division only three years after leaving the Ecole des Mines because Arson saw special qualities in

---

92. Shinn, *Ecole Polytechnique*, p. 52, estimates that the schooling of a serious candidate for the Polytechnique cost about five thousand francs a year. The cost of preparing for the Ecole Centrale or Ecole des Mines could not have been much less.
93. AP, D 1 P⁴ (Cadastre for 7, Cité Malesherbes). At the time Brissac was earning six thousand francs and paid fifteen hundred francs in rent.
94. Ibid., D Q⁷ 12666.
95. Ibid., D E¹, Fonds Lestringuez, contrat de mariage, Héloise Arson-Eugène Lestringuez.
96. Ibid., D Q⁷, no. 12341 (fols. 56–57).
97. "Notice nécrologique sur Edouard Servier," *Bulletin de l'Association amicale des anciens élèves de l'Ecole Centrale* 16 (1884–1885): 205–209.

him. Factory superintendents with twenty years of seniority had to watch this newcomer shoot past them. At the same time, successors to the chief executive of the PGC "parachuted" in from the Corps des Ponts et Chaussées without prior experience at the company or, for that matter, in the gas industry. In truth, there were no long, hard roads to the top at the PGC; most long, hard roads led to the middle under the best of circumstances.

It may be that engineers willingly traded off some pay and career opportunity for stable, lifelong positions within one corporate bureaucracy. In this way, too, they emulated the state engineers. Managerial careers at the gas company showed few signs of the hurly-burly of an era undergoing structural economic transformation. Seeking out new opportunities, rising and falling with the fate of recently launched enterprise, jumping from one firm to another as an attractive opening appeared—such comportment did not characterize the personnel of the PGC. Most would have been discouraged if their careers had resembled the turbulent one of a colleague, Paul Desmazes. He graduated from the Ecole Centrale in 1866 and took a position with the Charente Railroad. When ownership of the line changed, he left and became director of a glass factory. It was soon sold, however, and he became an engineer at the larger glassworks of Vierzon. He entered the PGC in 1881 but stayed for only eight years.[98] His varied career was exceptional, almost unique. Ordinarily engineers entered the PGC at an early age, and this was often their initial job in the profession. Of the fifty-one engineers whose careers we can follow, twenty-nine (57 percent) came to the company directly after graduation. The minority that did not do so spent only a short time elsewhere; the average delay between finishing school and employment with the PGC was 3.6 years. Hiring experienced managers who had proved their worth in another job was obviously not a practice in which the PGC engaged. It wanted executives who would mature entirely within the firm. Only two of the fifty-one engineers joined the PGC after ten years of work elsewhere. The PGC meant employment to be lifelong and created a training program for its recruits soon after beginning operations.[99] The company wished the new personnel to learn the ways of the firm and advance within it.

In addition to serving as the first employer, the PGC was almost as often the final employer as well. Less than a quarter of the engineers in the sample resigned their positions. Even when they did so, on average only 5.4 years after entering the PGC, the ideal of lifelong employment

98. *Bulletin de l'Association amicale des anciens élèves de l'Ecole Centrale* 32 (1900–1901): 80–81.
99. AP, V 8 O¹, no. 666, deliberations of June 11, 1859.

was being honored in the breach. The minority who departed had apparently concluded early that they could not commit themselves to the PGC, so they left in time to establish a career in another enterprise.[100]

Both the managers and the company appeared to agree on the value of career-long employment. Though the firm did not hesitate to pile responsibilities on its executives, it never fired or demoted except in rare cases of dishonesty. The directors apparently regarded an appointment that did not work out well as their fault and silently endured the consequences. The strongest sanction used to discipline managers was a discreet withholding of a bonus or a raise. Incompetence was tolerated at high levels, as demonstrated by the career of Alexandre Arson. This head of the factory division had been one of the brightest and most productive graduates of the Ecole Centrale. He had served the PGC well for many years; but as he entered his sixties, he lost touch with the latest advances in industry, and his mental powers may have diminished as well. His reports betrayed a distinct absence of clarity and loss of logical rigor. Arson's stubborn commitment to outmoded technology hurt the firm. Yet he remained in his post until his retirement in 1893. The company reduced neither his generous salary nor his large bonuses from a profit-sharing plan. When he retired after thirty-eight years, the PGC feted him and gave him a supplementary pension.[101] The response to his diminished usefulness was to shift subtly decision making to his assistant engineer. How different this practice was from that of the American steel industry of the nineteenth century, which, according to David Brody, cashiered managers when they were no longer effective.[102]

The assumption of career-long employment played a role in setting managerial salaries. Seniority was an important determinant of pay. It was not unusual for two managers with analogous posts to earn salaries that differed by as much as 30 percent if one had been with the firm much longer than the other. Engineers found their salaries rising only in small, periodical increments. This was a bureaucratic conception of pay, and it placed the focus on the long run. The engineers seemed quite comfortable

100. Among the minority of engineers who resigned their posts were those who had never intended to stay with the PGC. Their families had important interests in provincial or foreign gas firms, and they had worked for the PGC only to gain experience. Thus Dominique Favette became head of the Ottoman Gas Company, Edouard Melon director of the Lille Gas Company, and Charles Foucart owner of the Poissy Gas Company.
101. AP, V 8 O^1, no. 690, deliberations of December 27, 1893. For an example of Arson's declining grasp of his work, see no. 168, report of January 16, 1884.
102. David Brody, *Steelworkers in America: The Nonunion Era* (New York, 1960), p. 25.

with the underlying assumptions; indeed, they tried to force career-based pay on the subordinate personnel whenever possible. One immediate consequence of such an approach to compensations was to keep salaries low and slow to rise. This situation prevailed in the state bureaucracy as well.

A certain degree of paternalism accompanied the managers' lifelong careers. If one died on the job, the PGC assumed responsibility for the education of his children. It welcomed engineers' sons into the firm and, when the children were competent, delighted in having them succeed their fathers.[103] Corporate celebrations centered on long service to the firm—perhaps above all other achievements. When Superintendent Cury retired after fifty-eight years with the PGC and with one of the pre-merger gas companies, an elaborate banquet was held in his honor, and he received his full salary as a pension.[104] Thus the corporate culture of paternalism encompassed executives as well as the subordinate personnel, but with this difference: the company would always regard its workers as children needing stern guidance, whereas it insisted on initiative from its managers.

Secure careers and paternalism compensated somewhat for the modest salaries and limited horizons. So too did the responsibilities managers received, often at an early age, and the opportunities to exercise their talents. Managers could have no trouble seeing parallels with their professional models, the members of the *grands corps d'état*, and the similarities must have helped them accept their situation. Nonetheless, it is easy to imagine that some engineers had a sense of disappointment, even distress, in the face of their narrow material rewards. If so, the usual response was quiet acceptance or, occasionally, an effort to improve the situation by finding a new post. Rarely did managers draw enough attention to their discontents to make the corporation reconsider its policies. Yet one such instance occurred during the late 1870s, a booming period for the Parisian economy, when general pay levels rose substantially. The dynamic economic climate allowed and encouraged managers to seek alternatives to their modest situation within the PGC, and it was hit by a small but unprecedented flurry of resignations. Four lower-level managers left in 1879. Such circumstances brought the PGC to take its first—and only—general step to improve the pay for young engineers. That action, no

103. AP, V 8 O¹, no. 688, deliberations of June 3, 1891. When the gas main engineer suffered an untimely death, the PGC undertook to pay for the upbringing of his two children. Though the company was always prepared to give employment to the sons of one of the managers, it never guaranteed that the child would succeed his father in an important post. The PGC started sons off as assistant plant supervisors, and they would have to work their way up on their own. Most failed to do so.

104. Ibid., no. 693, deliberations of January 22, 1898.

doubt in proportion to the threat, was a measured one: the firm simply began to start recruits at tweny-four thousand francs rather than eighteen hundred francs (the pay it continued to give entering clerks).[105]

Another decision made by the director a few months later hinted at a more organized protest on the part of factory superintendents. In August 1880 the director suddenly created a series of pay steps (or "classes") for them and promised a rapid promotion of worthy individuals from one step to next. At the same time, Arson proposed giving them incentive pay.[106] The possibility that this flurry of policy reformulation was a response to collective protest by superintendents about their level of compensation must be taken seriously—though there is no direct evidence to support this speculation—for the measures mirrored precisely the ways the company answered collective demands by workers, clerks, and foremen for higher pay.[107] Moreover, the moment would have been ripe for the superintendents to take action. It was a time of soaring profits, and the company was adding workers and productive capacity as never before. Factory managers might have cited in support of their demands their growing responsibilities, inflation, and the need to maintain earnings differentials over workers, who had just received a substantial raise. In any case, nothing came of the protest, if indeed it ever materialized. The decision to initiate pay steps soon became a dead letter. Arson's proposal was ignored. Slow, discretionary advances resumed. After 1880 managers found that the time had passed to make demands on their firm. Its earnings record, brilliant up to then, soon became much less so. Plans for growth were scaled back, and gas consumption stagnated until after the turn of the century. Managers now had to contend with growing insubordination from workers and clerks. By no means were the engineers inclined to make their own discontents part of the wider challenge to authority within the firm.

The Social Role of Engineers

The superintendent of the Passy factory in 1868, Théophile Léopold, complained about his company-supplied housing. Léopold lamented that he

105. Characteristically, the PGC did not commit itself formally to the new policy. It simply put it into practice with an obvious preference for the old way.
106. AP, V 8 O^1, no. 680, deliberations of August 6, 1880; no. 716, report no. 65, "Salaire des chauffeurs." Arson's proposal called for salaries determined by a complex formula based on the yield of gas per ton of coal, the amount of coal distilled, the load per retort, and the seniority of each superintendent.
107. The foremen launched one of their two collective protests over pay at this moment. See Préfecture, B/a 176, reports of May 18, 19, 1880. See chapters 4 and 8 for responses to workers' demands for higher pay.

was forced to live in close proximity to his asistant superintendent. He resented "this cohabitation, which is so intimate for two colleagues," and affirmed that his discomfort would be "infinitely less" if he "had for a neighbor a subaltern employee, with whom no occasion for intimacy could possibly present itself." [108] The sense of caste this manager obliquely expressed gives credence to the psychological portrait that Charles Kindleberger has drawn of French managers, stressing elitism, arrogance, and the incapacity for human relations. [109] To be sure, the engineers of the PGC did uphold the formality of a bourgeois social code and were well aware of constituting an elite. Nonetheless, their acceptance of modest horizons and the loyalty they accorded an organization that demanded so much and rewarded so sparingly reveals other, more deeply rooted characteristics. Duty and hard work were the most prominent features the engineers used to represent themselves—and perhaps they did so with good reason. A useful point of departure for exploring their personalities and attitudes is the successful completion of training that exalted effort, discipline, and conformity to hierarchical rules. Whereas many bright students could not endure the strains of the scientific institutes, and many more dropped out than received degrees, the managers of the PGC had thrived in this demanding environment. All but three of forty-eight graduates of the Ecole Centrale and the Ecole des Mines had ranked in the top half of their classes; 47 percent were in the top quarter. As students, they had nearly always received favorable reports on conduct and attitude; making noise in study hall was about the worst offense any of them had committed. [110]

Ultimately, the sources are almost silent on the engineers' lives outside their managerial roles. [111] Yet the eulogy describing one former superintendent of the machinery department as "cold, feeling all the weight of the responsibilities he bore," has the ring of truth. Similarly, factory man-

---

108. AP, V 8 O¹, no. 768, "Usine Ternes," report of June 14, 1868.
109. Charles Kindleberger, "Technical Education and the French Entrepreneur," in Carter et al., *Enterprise and Entrepreneurs*, p. 25.
110. Archives de l'Ecole Centrale, registres de promotion; Archives de l'Ecole des Mines de Paris, dossiers des élèves. I was not permitted to examine the dossiers at the Ecole des Mines directly, but Madame Maisonneuve was kind enough to gather the information I solicited. I am most grateful for her assistance.
111. One reason for the silence, though undoubtedly a minor one, was the discretion of the managers about their colleagues' private lives. See, for example, AP, V 8 O¹, no. 162, Lalubié to director, January 21, 1899. Former superintendent Aubrun had an affair with the daughter of a minor employee at his plant. The current superintendent, Bodin, knew about the affair, but the director had to learn about it from the employee. Evidently, the engineers' identification with the firm did not preclude acknowledging that privacy was an absolute right.

ager Biju-Duval left a reputation for having a serious and reserved demeanor: family and music were reported to be his only refuges from work. Charles Monard of the coal department was said to be a "stranger to worldly distractions," without interests aside from his work.[112] Circumstances gave such testimony a note of verisimilitude. The engineer-managers, from wealthy families, had been raised in Paris or sent there at a young age to pursue serious study. They had resisted all the temptations of that modern Babylon and had fulfilled high parental ambitions by passing through a clearly charted course based on rigorous selection. Deferred gratification and self-control allowed them to attain the qualifications necessary for employment at the PGC. Their acceptance of the limited prospects within the corporation was an exercise of habits they had developed early in life.

Whereas several of the PGC's founders or board members had pronounced political views, managers seemed to eschew political engagement.[113] Whether their silence was the result of prudence or lack of commitment is impossible to say. Nonetheless, the managers could be mobilized to defend the industrial order they were perpetuating (and helping to transform) against challenges from the left. Their defense of the status quo derived as much or more from moral sensibilities as from class interest. The engineers, self-consciously devoted to the work ethic, thrift, deferred gratification, and hierarchical authority, imagined that workers shared none of these values. They took it as a given that among their duties was implanting their own values in their subordinates. This task was far from being a preoccupation, but it did surface when workers seemed in danger of imbibing more threatening views. So thoroughly pessimistic was the engineers' assessment of workers that it would not be hyperbolic to see the managers' perception of industrial relations as a clash of cultures, a struggle for the triumph of civilizing forces.

These moral and class concerns made managers into inveterate "social engineers." They sought opportunities to teach their inferiors thrift and

112. *Bulletin de l'Association amicale des anciens élèves de l'Ecole Centrale* 14 (1892–1893): 191; 35 (1903–1904): 230–233; 27 (1895–1896): 146.
113. One exception to this rule—and an extreme one—concerns the case of Robert Louzon. A graduate of the Ecole des Mines, he came to the PGC around the turn of the century. He sympathized with revolutionary syndicalists and even loaned Victor Griffuelhes money to pay for a headquarters for the Confédération générale du travail. It was this act that apparently caused his firing; the reformist head of the gas workers' union, Louis Lajarrigue, informed on Louzon to management. See Jean Maitron, *Dictionnaire biographique du mouvement ouvrier français*, 16 vols. (Paris, 1972), 13: 316. I am grateful to Professor Bruce Vandervort for telling me about this exceptional case.

good work habits without, in the end, having much hope they could learn the lessons. A strike or a demand for a raise set managers to planning various forms of postponed compensation. Servier argued that any wage increase granted during the 1865 labor shortage should go into a fund on which workers could draw once they were beyond the age of fifty and after having served twenty-five years with the company. Euchène, the chief of production thirty years after Servier, perpetuated the moralizing scheme. He advocated placing a raise, if there had to be one, in a pension fund.[114] The effort to impose on the labor force the career-based pay that was a part of the managers' own work culture was a major thrust of their social engineering, but not the only one. The shock of the Paris Commune impelled Arson to consider ways of preserving the social order. He arrived at the notion of creating an apprenticeship school for worthy sons of worthy workers. Having the fathers contribute two hundred francs to the tuition may not have been realistic, but Arson contended that participation would teach thrift and remind the laborer of his paternal duties. The reform was aimed at strengthening traditional sources of social cohesion, craft, and family, which Arson feared industrial development—of the very kind he directed—was undermining.[115] One engineer reasoned that even the creation of a factory commissary presented opportunities for moralization. Run by the Sisters of Charity, it would inject chaste and uplifting qualities into the plant.[116]

Contemporary social observers as well as historians frequently cast engineers in the role of mediators between industrialists and labor.[117] Their expertise, salaried status, and familiarity with the realities of production supposedly positioned them strategically to make industry more humane. The case of the PGC does nothing to sustain the claim. Its managers were unable to transcend the perceived conflict of cultures between themselves and the workers. Their paternalistic gestures, modest in any case, were enacted in response to immediate labor unrest, and the urgency to reform disappeared the moment the danger passed. Though class barriers may explain some of these limits, the legacy of the engineers' own experiences quite possibly contributed to their rigidity. Schooled (literally) in deferred gratification, they learned that life was a struggle from which even their privileged births did not preserve them. They were intent on living by the

---

114. AP, V 8 O¹, no. 148, report of June 20, 1865; no. 1520, "Mission en Angleterre du mois de mai 1893."
115. Ibid., no. 712, "Création d'institution humanitaire à l'usine Clichy."
116. Ibid., no. 717, "Avant projet: Usine du Landit."
117. Emile Cheysson, *Le Rôle social d'ingénieur* (Paris, 1897); Shinn, *Ecole Polytechnique*, p. 210; Beaud, "Ingénieurs du Creusot," p. 58.

principle that meeting obligations was its own reward. Resigned to mediocre compensation, working most of their waking hours, and living frugally, engineers could have had little sympathy for demands from below for shorter hours and higher pay. The workers' refusal to see things their way only confirmed their worst fears and reinforced their prejudices. If such stern precepts were in fact the outcome of the managers' training and career experiences, then the engineers' culture was one more reason for troubled industrial relations in France.

· · ·

A manager's angry outburst, one of the very few to have found its way into the corporate record, helps us understand what mattered deeply to this group. Paul Gigot, the chief of the factory division, penned a bitter letter to director Bertrand on the eve of retirement, asking to be relieved of his duties at once. Gigot complained of being "discouraged because the board [of directors] has not accorded me the same marks of esteem that other faithful servants have received." He noted that the PGC's president had sent Superintendent Hadamar a cordial letter at his retirement; the company had given Cury a plaque with a "very flattering" inscription; and by-products chief Audouin left the firm with a decoration "bearing witness to the esteem he enjoyed here." Gigot resentfully noted that his retirement notice, "which will remain in our archives," was a dry, formal document that did not express praise for his service.[118] Pride in a hard job done well and loyalty to a bureaucracy were important to these managers.

As the new elite of corporate managers carved out their social roles, the bureaucratic and hierarchical practices of the Napoleonic state weighed heavily on them. By contrast, the flourishing of the "new capitalism" in the mid-nineteenth century failed to create a freewheeling situation that rendered old rules obsolete. Conformist graduates of the *grandes écoles* eventually replaced the iconoclastic entrepreneurs who had founded the gas industry. The celebrated materialism and new money of the Second Empire did not produce a breakdown of standards, a loss of familiar yardsticks of achievement and expected compensation. The hierarchies established by the state engineers continued to set standards and reinforce traditional measures of achievement. The principal way the administration of the PGC diverged from public administration was in rewarding a small portion of executives with generous salaries and profit-sharing bonuses.

The managers also emulated state engineers—and decisively separated themselves from the other social groups created by industrialization—in accepting the right of their superiors to select the individuals who would

118. AP, V 8 O¹, no. 162, Gigot to director, November 16, 1905.

enjoy exceptional rewards. As we shall see in subsequent chapters, workers and white-collar employees chafed under hierarchical authority and sought to curtail it; the managers, however, accorded a legitimacy to decisions about their well-being made on high, in secret, without their input, and without reference to generalized rules. Whatever the engineers' private thoughts about the justness of the decisions touching them, they asserted and vigorously defended the right to control the personnel under their direction. At least the managers were not so hypocritical as to deny their superiors discretionary power while insisting on it for themselves. Such equity did not characterize all their stances.

FOUR

Operating the Company

The PGC represented a relatively recent departure in European economic life. Its size and complexity called for sophisticated cost controls, greater attention to marketing, the allocation of resources among distinct operating units, and strategies for dealing with a large, nontraditional labor force. This "modern enterprise" was run by salaried decision makers who proudly wore the new occupational title of industrial engineer, though they accepted for themselves many of the norms associated with the careers of high civil servants.[1] It remains to be seen whether the new type of manager imparted a distinctive direction to decisions that had to be made regarding business practices and personnel.[2]

Business Decisions

With Parisian consumers paying thirty centimes per cubic meter, good management was almost irrelevant to the profitability of the PGC. Slov-

1. For definitions of the "modern enterprise," see Roger Price, *An Economic History of Modern France, 1730–1914* (London, 1975), pp. 118, 147; Alfred Chandler, "The Railroads: Pioneers in Modern Corporate Management," *Business History Review* 39 (1965): 16–40; Alfred Chandler, *The Visible Hand: The Managerial Revolution in American Business* (Cambridge, Mass., 1977), pp. 1–3. For a general view of French business history, see Maurice Lévy-Leboyer, "The Large Corporation in Modern France," in *Managerial Hierarchies: Comparative Perspectives on the Rise of the Modern Industrial Enterprise*, ed. Alfred Chandler and Herman Daems (Cambridge, Mass., 1980), pp. 117–160.
2. Among the relatively small number of studies dealing with large French enterprises are Jean Bouvier, *Le Crédit lyonnais de 1863 à 1882*, 2 vols. (Paris, 1961); François Caron, *Histoire de l'exploitation d'un grand réseau: La Compagnie du chemin de fer du Nord 1846–1937* (Paris, 1973); Reed Geiger, *The Anzin Coal Company, 1800–1833* (Newark, Del., 1974); Pierre Guillaume, *La Compagnie des*

Table 9.   Comparative Costs of Operation, c. 1880
(in francs per thousand cubic meters of gas)

	PGC	London	Berlin	Brussels
Production costs				
Labor	25.8	14.7	19.6	16.5
Coal	89.5	66.3	87.5	31.8
Administration	7.9	8.1	12.8	13.8
Distribution	9.8	10.6	6.7	11.4
Other	1.8	2.4	6.0	20.4
Gross production costs	134.8	102.1	132.6	93.9
Less revenue from				
by-products	85.0	42.0	75.1	46.6
Net production costs	49.8	60.1	57.5	47.3

Source: AP, V 8 O¹, no. 709.

enly administration, irresponsibly generous settlements with labor, and technological backwardness would not have prevented the company from returning respectable yields. Nonetheless, the earnest and hardworking engineers who ran the firm expected better of themselves, and they gave a great deal more effort to their jobs than mere competence would have required. Balance sheets, capable of exposing waste and inefficiency when examined comparatively, show that by international standards the PGC was a well-run firm. The sense of inferiority that some French industrialists felt toward their British and German (and sometimes toward their Belgian) counterparts was unwarranted in the case of the gas industry (table 9). The PGC's above-average gross production costs were largely the result of the high price of coal—inevitable given the lack of large deposits of the right grades in France. Its net production costs, however, were enviably modest owing to substantial revenues from by-products.

The comparison invites a reevaluation of French entrepreneurship, examined from the distinctive perspective of this case study. Historians have developed some strong stereotypes about French business practices—heavily committed to the production of high-quality goods, disinclined toward mass marketing, oblivious to commercial considerations, valuing stability over growth. The term "Malthusian" inevitably arises, by which

---

mines de la Loire (1846–1854) (Paris, 1966); Robert Locke, *Les Fonderies et forges d'Alais: La Création d'une entreprise moderne* (Paris, 1978).

is meant a determination to avoid opportunities for expansion. Proponents of these views often root such behavior in the cultural predispositions of the French bourgeoisie. One grand interpretation of the Third Republic posits an implicit contract between economic elites, on the one hand, and peasants, on the other. In return for conservative economic leadership, the rural masses safeguarded society from the demands of the proletariat. In contrast to such assertions, some leading economic historians have argued that there was nothing pathological about French business practices, that on the whole, entrepreneurs responded rationally to the market situations they faced.[3]

Whereas the debate is usually framed in terms of the owner-entrepreneur, the case of the PGC reflects on decision making in a different and increasingly important milieu, that of salaried managers. The officers of the gas firm were representative of men who were soon to fill a large number of industrial posts and hold disproportionate economic power. They gained influence at a time when mass marketing emerged as a possibility and sometimes a necessity. There is reason to take special interest in the entrepreneurial spirit guiding the PGC.

It is well known that respect for entrepreneurship and for the morality of the marketplace was more deeply embedded in the social fabric of Anglo-Saxon countries than of France.[4] Nonetheless, the managers of the PGC came to their jobs armed with a set of values that helped them to be mercenary and calculating about business matters. Their earnestness about making the PGC a well-run firm displayed itself most clearly in the drive to cut expenditures. Unnecessary spending was a deeply felt affront

3. The vast literature on the subject includes David Landes, "French Entrepreneurship and Industrial Growth in the Nineteenth Century," *Journal of Economic History* 9 (1949): 45–61; François Crouzet, "French Economic Growth in the Nineteenth Century Reconsidered," *History* 59 (1974): 167–179; Claude Fohlen, "Entrepreneurship and Management in France in the Nineteenth Century," in *Cambridge Economic History of Europe* (Cambridge, 1978), 7(1): 347–381; Maurice Lévy-Leboyer, "Le Patronat français a-t-il été malthusien?" *Le Mouvement social*, no. 88 (1974): 3–49; James Laux, "Some Notes on Entrepreneurship in the Early French Automobile Industry," *French Historical Studies* 3 (1963): 129–134; Robert Aldrich, "Late Comer or Early Starter: New Views on French Economic History," *Journal of European Economic History* 16 (1987): 89–100. For an investigation of the industrial-agricultural ties, see Herman Lebovics, *The Alliance of Iron and Wheat in the Third French Republic, 1860–1914: Origins of the New Conservatism* (Baton Rouge, La., 1988).
4. For an interesting study of American businessmen's attitudes, difficult as they are to pin down, and a source of comparisons with French business leaders, see Thomas Cochran, *Railroad Leaders, 1845–1890: The Business Mind in Action* (Cambridge, Mass., 1953).

to their professionalism as engineers and to their class values. They did not relax their concern about waste simply because profit levels were so high as to excite the jealousy of the public. The minor annual expenditure of 5,026 francs for omnibus rides by agents whose jobs took them across the city created consternation on the executive committee and stern demands for strict accounting. Managers, from the director to factory superintendents, treated water as an expensive commodity that had to be husbanded. Worn-out equipment and plants with leaky roofs signified the inclination to postpone capital improvements until absolutely necessary. For the same reason, the chief clerk of the customer service department had to receive clients in a room that he claimed lacked dignity.[5] Sometimes the drive for thrift could seem counterproductive. The chief of the factory division warned that a large corporation could not be run "with the mentality of a greengrocer" and demanded larger maintenance budgets. Yet he was equally an advocate of cutting corners whenever possible.[6] Managers accepted frugality as a virtue for its own sake and as a duty to the stockholders.

Though top managers were trained in state institutes and belonged to a corps that inculcated dedication to public service, they had no difficulty transferring their loyalty from the public interest to the private firm when they accepted their posts. They displayed no impulse to apologize for the exploitative features of the corporate charter; that the concession was legal and profitable seemed to answer all objections. They even had the ability to put aside ethical niceties when the firm stood to gain. A conspicuous example of the managers' amoral approach to business dealings came during the Franco-Prussian War. The executives of the PGC did make small patriotic gestures, undoubtedly in complete sincerity. But when the government, in desperate need of horses for the army, sought to purchase them from the firm's team, managers consciously selected the oldest and weakest animals and sold them at a high price. An internal memorandum on the matter, far from expressing shame, boastfully concluded that the sale was "not at all a bad piece of business."[7] If policymakers at the PGC

---

5. The executive committee asked factory superintendents to file monthly reports on their efforts to economize: AP, V 8 O^1, no. 665, deliberations of May 23, 1857. On the economy-consciousness of managers, see no. 751, "Rapport annuel de 1869 (2 janvier 1870)"; no. 768, "Usines de Batignolles et de Saint-Denis," report of April 14, 1861; no. 668, deliberations of April 27, 1861; no. 671, deliberations of June 6, 1866. The phrase *l'esprit de l'économie* resounded continually and with reverence throughout the superintendents' reports.

6. Ibid., no. 1062, report of March 10, 1859; no. 715, "Voyage en Angleterre, année 1875."

7. Ibid., no. 753, "Inspection de la cavalerie," report of December 23, 1870.

did not behave as model entrepreneurs, it was not because they had scruples that led them to eschew maximizing profits.

The energetic pursuit of revenues and thrift brought managers to rationalize most aspects of gas production. Those steps were partly responsible for the good showing of the PGC in comparison with Europe's other major gas firms. The production methods inherited from the pre-merger operations had not been up to the highest standards of efficiency at the time. Alexandre Arson, the head of the factory division in 1856, sought to change them radically and immediately. He replaced the iron retorts used by the early companies with earthenware ones because they were less expensive and conducted heat better. In the plant on the rue de la Tour, which the PGC inherited and continued to operate for a few years, each furnace heated only one retort, a situation requiring lavish use of fuel and manpower. Once in Arson's hands, that plant quickly received new furnaces that heated five to seven retorts. Purchasing coal was the major production cost, and the pre-merger companies did not even have scales to measure how much of it they used.[8] Efficient use of coal became a preoccupation for Arson and his staff. Their initiatives in this area led to a significant innovation in the gas industry, the use of Siemens furnaces, which recirculated heated air. The PGC was the first to apply the more efficient furnace to gas production in France and realized savings of 36 percent in fuel.[9] The basic change did not fully satisfy Arson, however, and he continued his search for still less costly methods of roasting coal. After spending thirty-six thousand francs on experiments, he had not yet found the best possible equipment, but the director overruled further expenditures.[10]

The engineers managed to reduce the production cost of gas by about a third between 1857 and 1868 (figure 9). The essential breakthrough permitting the reduction entailed a new approach to distillation.[11] Previously,

---

8. Ibid., no. 665, deliberations of May 13, 1856; no. 615, report of Arson to director, February 15, 1884.
9. Ibid., no. 715, "Etude sur les résultats comparatifs de la Compagnie de 1856 à 1870 (14 décembre 1871)"; no. 712, "Fours Siemens et fours à générateur (7 avril 1891)"; no. 671, deliberations of June 11, 1864.
10. Ibid., no. 676, deliberations of May 24, 1873.
11. On the new distillation process, see ibid., no. 715, "Etude sur les résultats"; *Procès-verbaux et rapport de la commission nommée le 23 janvier 1880 en exécution de l'article 48 du traité intervenu le 7 janvier 1870 entre la ville de Paris et la Compagnie parisienne de l'éclairage et du chauffage par le gaz* (Paris, 1880), pp. 30–38. On some of the results of the new process, see AP, V 8 O[1], no. 714, report of November 7, 1874; report of June 24, 1875; no. 716, "Salaires des chauffeurs (16 mars 1880)"; no. 711, "Etude sur les réductions qu'il est possible d'introduire dans les prix de revient."

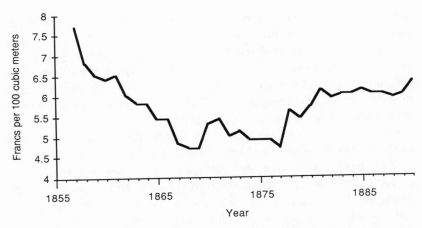

Fig. 9. Cost of Producing One Hundred Cubic Meters of Gas (in francs). From AP, V 8 O¹, nos. 718, 1016.

gas works roasted coal at relatively low temperatures, both to save fuel and to keep the lighting power of the gas high. The production staff of the PGC learned (whether through experimentation or imitation of industry leaders is not clear) that dramatic improvements in efficiency were possible by distilling at very high temperatures (1,150–1,200 degrees Centigrade).[12] Without compromising the lighting power, hot roasting raised the yield of gas from almost all grades of coal. Moreover, the larger the retort, and the more tightly packed it was, the better the results. And with larger retorts the company could save on labor and fuel. In 1855 the average retort received 60 kilograms of coal per charge; in 1869 charges had grown to 127 kilograms.[13] Arson once announced his guiding principle to be "pitilessly exploiting labor, fuel, and maintenance expenses to the complete utilization of capital."[14] He made that principle a reality during the 1860s.

Other departments could not easily replicate such success in reducing costs, but most realized significant savings. The cost of producing retorts dropped from about one hundred francs to thirty-eight francs even as they became bigger and lasted longer. The distribution division found new technologies and materials that cut the cost of laying and installing gas

12. The superintendent of the Passy plant was given a bonus of ten thousand francs for raising productivity in 1863. He may have been responsible for the use of the new method of distillation at the PGC. AP, V 8 O¹, no. 725, deliberations of March 12, 1863.
13. Ibid., no. 711, "Rapport no. 32 (8 mars 1868)."
14. Ibid., no. 716, "Salaire des chauffeurs (16 mars 1880)."

mains. Whereas being near consumers was once the central consideration in locating plants, improvements in distribution technology gave the company more freedom to use inexpensive tracts of land and allowed it to deal effectively with the greatest logistical problem, handling coal. The PGC was able to build its newer plants (eventually numbering nine) on railroad lines or near canals.[15] One of the largest expenses in increasing output was building facilities for storing gas. Production managers searched all of Europe for the best sorts of storage tanks and finally found the solution in Britain's expanding tanks, which were relatively inexpensive to build and required less land.[16] Isaac Pereire had once criticized the business sense of engineers, bemoaning their indifference to costs in the pursuit of technical perfection, but his own PGC was hardly a victim of that malady.[17]

The PGC's excellent comparative performance owed even more to raising revenues than to reducing costs. The director of the Lille Gas Company once remarked that the price of coal and the value of by-products were the keys to profitability in his industry.[18] That comment goes far to account for the advantages that the PGC held over gas producers in London or Berlin. Aside from the enviable results of receiving thirty centimes for each cubic meter of gas, the PGC obtained great profits from the derivatives of coal distillation. Indeed, management displayed its most creative handling of emerging technologies and its most masterful entrepreneurial decisions in producing and marketing by-products.[19]

The coal tar (*goudrons*) that condensed when gas cooled had been regarded as a nuisance rather than a source of revenue by most gas companies through the 1850s. The pre-merger firms of Paris sold some of the tar to distillers, who refined it for a limited number of established uses, but threw much away. The newly formed PGC continued the practice in its early days. In 1857 it had no by-products department; it subcontracted the treatment of tar to an outside firm and burned some as fuel. Yet this unwelcomed residue was about to become an essential raw material for a

15. Ibid., no. 715, "Etude sur les résultats," summarizes the improvements. See also no. 669, deliberations of April 19, 1862; no. 673, deliberations of February 3, 1869; no. 1067, "Service des usines: Briqueterie"; no. 25, report of Charles Singly to Paul Lependry, February 6, 1884; report of Servier to director, June 19, 1865.
16. Ibid., no. 715, "Voyage en Angleterre, année 1875."
17. Pereire's remarks are cited in John Armstrong, *The European Administrative Elite* (Princeton, 1973), p. 186.
18. *Compte rendu des travaux de la commission nommée par Monsieur le Ministre de l'Intérieur le 31 janvier 1890 en exécution de l'article 48 . . .* (Paris, 1890), p. 31.
19. For an overview, see the brochure prepared for the Exposition of 1878, "Produits dérivés de la houille," AP, V 8 O[1], no. 1290.

major new industry, organic dyes.[20] That industry was born about the same time as the PGC. The young gas firm took advantage of the market opportunities, at first stumbling a bit; but eventually it became an innovator and a model of efficiency.

The artificial-dye industry arose with the development of aniline purple in the mid-1850s. Aniline was a product derived from refining coal tar. Within three years numerous aniline dyes were appearing on the market. The PGC was not prepared to leap into extensive production of the chemical, though; its lack of administrative structure and its subcontracting arrangement stood in the way. Still, top management was aware of the opportunities and soon appointed Paul Audouin to head a new department and undertake the treatment of coal tar internally.[21] This was not a decision management would regret, for Audouin would make his operation exceedingly profitable through good fortune and through attention to market opportunities.

Lack of technical expertise in industrial chemistry prevented the company from rushing to profit from the enhanced value of aniline. Not until 1864 was the PGC able to market the product, and then only after some trouble. The proud graduates of France's finest technical institutes were completely dependent on temperamental British workers to show them how to manufacture aniline. The workers mounted one delaying tactic after another, and the engineers experienced problems in mastering the secrets of production on their own.[22] The incident verified the criticisms of engineering education in France, but the PGC adapted much more smoothly to a second phase of the dye industry that started with the perfection of synthetic alizarin at the end of the 1860s.

The new development in dye production required anthracene, another residue of coal distillation, and transformed it into a valuable—often exceedingly valuable—commodity. Audouin was able to lead the PGC smoothly into its production as its price soared.[23] His accomplishments were impressive enough to justify foreign manufacturers touring the

20. On the development of organic chemicals, see Paul Hohenberg, *Chemicals in Western Europe, 1850–1914: An Economic Study of Technical Change* (Chicago, 1967), and L. F. Haber, *The Chemical Industry during the Nineteenth Century* (Oxford, 1958).
21. AP, V 8 O¹, no. 723, deliberations of June 13, 1857. Before Audouin was named to head the department, a subcontractor of coal-tar distillation was named "directeur du service de l'exploitation des goudrons." The new department was soon integrated completely into the firm under Audouin's management.
22. Ibid., no. 670, deliberations of March 30, August 1, and November 26, 1864.
23. On the development of the anthracene market for the PGC, see *Procès-verbaux et rapport de la commission nommée le 23 janvier 1880*, pp. 10–14. The firm's scientific consultant, Henri Regnault, recommended caution in the face of

PGC's by-product operation. So much had the company improved its handling of organic chemicals over the false steps with aniline that the Gas Light and Coke Company of London used the Parisian plant as a model for its own.[24] The PGC produced anthracene of high-enough quality to satisfy the exacting Badische Anilin- und Soda-Fabrik, its principal customer, and continued to improve production methods. In 1875 the PGC patented its admired system for conserving heat during the distillation process.[25]

Revenues from refining coal tar contributed substantially to the gains of the stockholders and peaked just as critics were growing irate over the prosperity of the firm. The income derived from a hundred kilograms of coal tar rose from 2.3 francs in 1865 to 6.9 francs in 1880 and had been as high as eight francs in 1876, when anthracene was still a new product and especially scarce. The PGC found itself in the enviable position of having an ever-growing stock of tar as the result of increasing gas consumption, and the value of the tar appreciated rapidly. Moreover, Audouin had reduced production costs by almost a third.[26]

The ammonia water produced in purifying coal gas was another commodity that early gas companies had trouble utilizing profitably. Some sold it to alum manufacturers, but much found its way into the Seine River.[27] The newly formed PGC decided to produce ammonium sulfate and wasted little time moving into the market for chemical fertilizers, which was expanding with capitalistic agriculture. It strove to develop a loyal clientele in the heartland of commercial cultivation, the Beauce and Picardy. The sale of ammonium sulfate grew from five hundred thousand kilograms in 1869 to 2.1 million eight years later. The company could well tout its contribution to French agricultural progress. Until then, cultivators had had great difficulty procuring reliable chemicals. Fraud was rampant, and farmers had frequently renounced the use of fertilizers because of deceptions, widely fluctuating prices, or unreliable supplies. The PGC sought to encourage the use of ammonium sulfate by offering a high-quality product, keeping the price stable, and ensuring supplies to regular customers. It largely succeeded in this task, but it was also true that the

---

the new industry, but Audouin's energetic policies prevailed. See AP, V 8 O^1, no. 675, deliberations of January 31, 1872.

24. Sterling Everard, *The History of the Gas Lighting and Coke Company, 1812–1949* (London, 1949), p. 263.

25. AP, V 8 O^1, no. 677, deliberations of April 7, 1875.

26. Ibid., no. 1060, "Rapport des sous-produits, 1882"; report of February 20, 1877.

27. *Rapport*, March 23, 1871, p. 29. For early subcontracting arrangements, see AP, V 8 O^1, no. 720, "Marché avec MM. Mallet et Laming."

PGC did not resist the temptation of using its monopolistic power to charge prices not at all justified by production costs.[28]

Led by the imaginative Audouin, the PGC actively sought outlets for other by-products as well. As advances in printing machines made mass-circulation newspapers more common, the company was able to sell some residues for the manufacture of ink. The new photography industry opened an additional market for ammonium sulfate.[29] The success of the PGC in exploiting such opportunities was all the more noteworthy in that the firm did not lavish resources on Audouin's department. The by-products chief was the sole engineer, and he had to handle commercial arrangements, direct production, and oversee personnel matters. The company had one chemist, and poor pay led to frequent turnover in that post.[30] In the end, the company profited handsomely from a department it treated as marginal.

In many ways the development of coke sales challenged the commercial acumen of managers more than the chemical by-products operation did. The market for coke was small in 1855, and there were competing commodities. Parisian households had traditionally used wood for heating. Coke had had some limited uses, mainly in smelting. Expanding industrial consumption seemed at first the only viable option, for management did not anticipate residential customers. The PGC had begun with the intention of creating a vast new market for its gas as a source of heating in homes and industry. The name of the firm, the Parisian Company of Lighting and Heating by Gas, proclaimed the ambition, but it soon proved beyond its reach: within a year after the company began, it experienced difficulties in applying gas heat to domestic uses.[31] Although it did not abandon research for proper heating equipment, the company left developments dormant for another two decades. In the meantime, coke was piling up on the distillation floor faster than it could be used for fuel. Getting coke accepted into homes seemed advisable from every point of view. In 1859 the firm created a coke department, which quickly became a large and lucrative unit.

Selling coke for domestic heating engaged managers in some moder-

28. AP, V 8 O¹, no. 666, deliberations of June 5, 1858. The PGC began to sell ammonium sulfate in 1858. On commercial policies, see no. 626, "Sulfate d'ammoniaque"; no. 749, "Résultats obtenus du traitement des eaux ammonicales en 1868"; no. 1060, "Résultat du traitement des eaux ammonicales en 1871."
29. Ibid., no. 669, deliberations of January 14, 1863; no. 671, deliberations of February 25, 1865.
30. Ibid., no. 156, "Produits chimiques." On the poor pay for chemists, see no. 161, "Charles Steiner."
31. Ibid., no. 723, deliberations of November 27, 1856.

ately ambitious technological and (especially) commercial activities. When the PGC tried to encourage the use of coke in homes, the practice was so uncommon that effective heaters did not exist. The company's engineers had to work with inventors and develop their own appliances that burned coke cleanly and distributed heat as evenly as possible. Having accomplished that task, it had to persuade residents to use the apparatus. The PGC turned to demonstrations and showrooms to interest clients. It put coke stoves in conspicuous places, such as omnibus stations. It opened a showroom on a major thoroughfare, the rue du 4-Septembre. On display were a range of coke stoves, simple ones for modest clients and elegant ones that might suit the drawing rooms of well-appointed residences. By 1885 the company had sold nearly fifty-five thousand stoves on its own. The coke market was greatly expanded by the Franco-Prussian War, during which other sources of energy were hardly available at any price.[32]

Delivering the coke also had to evolve into a large-scale operation. The company at first transported coke only to its industrial customers; but in 1860 it created a domestic delivery service. It eventually employed more than two hundred carters. The wagons and uniformed deliverymen quickly became familiar sights of Parisian street life. The firm began to build its own wagons in 1867. Inevitably, the new trade that the PGC had engendered became an essential public activity. During the winter of 1879–1880 especially cold weather and snows created shortages of coke and delivery problems. The result was public panic and rioting outside the PGC's coke yards.[33]

The company was rewarded handsomely for its effective commercial ventures entailing by-products. As Table 9 makes clear, its superior performance over other European firms resulted from the sale of by-products. That trade brought in about twice as much revenue as the Brussels or London firms received. The income more than compensated for a somewhat less efficient use of labor, higher administrative costs, and the higher costs of coal. The ability of the PGC's managers to lower certain production expenses and raise revenues offers a most flattering portrait of their entrepreneurial role. However, this picture requires a broader focus. The activities analyzed so far show the engineers taking advantage of opportunities that for the most part came to them without serious risk and

32. *Le Gaz: Journal des producteurs et des consommateurs*, no. 15 (October 31, 1861): 184; *Rapport*, March 26, 1885, p. 27; March 28, 1872, p. 30. The annual reports to the stockholders provided figures on the sale of coke stoves.
33. AP, V 8 O¹, no. 667, deliberations of August 8, 1860; no. 672, deliberations of May 25, 1867; no. 768, "Usine de Belleville," reports of November 6 and December 11, 1870; *Rapport*, March 25, 1880, p. 33. Customers waited in line all night for coke during the Franco-Prussian War.

without exceptional effort. The successes did not test their will to struggle for customers and to develop markets methodically in a competitive environment. In truth, the gas managers were not entrepreneurial in this way.

The energetic defense of a monopoly over gas sold in Paris at high, fixed prices was not an exception to an otherwise competitive spirit among the PGC's managers. In fact, restricted market conditions were a model and an ideal they strove to emulate for the other products the firm sold. That managers were so often able to realize this goal says much about the compartmentalized and localized state of the French economy of the Second Empire, during which more open, national markets ostensibly emerged.

In 1857 the executive committee approved a report that called for the construction of a plant to purify ammonia water at an expense of 415,000 francs. The projected annual profits were 315,000 francs, a return of more than 75 percent—and from the very first year.[34] It is not difficult to understand why the company pursued the marketing of by-products aggressively: it was able to anticipate such profits because the residues of purification would not be sold in a competitive market. Under the direction of board member Louis Margueritte, the corporation entered into price-fixing arrangements for ammonia products. It had similar terms for marketing alkalies and pitch.[35] Engineer Audouin's strategy for selling ammonium sulfate was aimed at preserving control over prices. The PGC was the largest producer of the chemical in France, and Audouin ruled out selling any to fertilizer manufacturers, thereby cutting off competitors' supply of the essential raw material. The company effectively made fertilizer into a "luxury" commodity, sold on the basis of quality rather than price. When a firm that made alkalies from cesspool refuse threatened to enter that market, Audouin counseled lowering prices temporarily in order to drive the competitor out of business. In most instances, though, lower prices were not part of his commercial strategy, not even temporarily. Perfected equipment had brought huge increases in the yield of ammonium sulfate, from 74 liters per metric ton of coal to 106 liters. Yet the price of the chemical rose steadily from twenty-eight francs in 1867 to forty-five francs in 1875 and forty-eight francs in 1877. Thus customers did not benefit at all from the PGC's technical prowess.[36] Similarly, a cartel

34. AP, V 8 O¹, no. 665, deliberations of January 24, 1857.

35. Ibid., no. 672, deliberations of January 16, 1867; no. 1063, "Note sur la Société du charbon de Paris." Pernolet, the owner of the Société du charbon de Paris, referred to the PGC as "master of the market" for pitch and asserted that it derived a profit of 25 percent on its invested capital as such.

36. Ibid., no. 1060; no. 626, "Sulfate d'ammoniaque."

of coke producers from the department of the Nord opted to invade the PGC's "fief" by selling at lower prices, and the gas company responded with an agreement to restore the prices it traditionally charged.[37] The managers of the PGC fitted perfectly Adam Smith's description of businessmen: they were ready to pursue the invisible hand of profit—and to collude in restraint of trade whenever possible.

The efforts of the PGC to launch and develop new businesses were distinctly limited. Management eschewed patiently building markets, competing with other firms, and anticipating initial losses. The company decided to enter a venture if and when it could set high prices and extract large profits immediately. Management's aggressiveness in creating the coke trade represented the pursuit not just of profits but especially of monopolistic profits. A commission appointed by the interior minister noted, in pointedly euphemistic language, the "elevated prices at which [the PGC] has had the talent to make its coke accepted by the Parisian consumer."[38] Engineer François Hallopeau, the head of the coke department, contrasted two sorts of clientele. Manufacturers in the suburbs of Paris found the PGC's coke far too costly; if his salesmen were too aggressive, "they were shown the guard dog." But Hallopeau found urban residents to be pliant customers: "Accustomed to paying a good deal for wood or oil, they will not hesitate to pay a few francs more for coke." In fact, the company sold coke to the public at four and eventually five times the cost of production and distribution. It chose to maintain these prices rather than reduce the stock when sales were slow.[39] The company's behavior in the retort trade was little different. For a while, the PGC manufactured retorts and sold them to other gas companies, but at a markup of about 100 percent. When a smaller firm mechanized the operation and undersold the PGC, the latter quickly withdrew from the business.[40] Thus it was not at all remarkable that a newly appointed coke engineer aspired to create a monopoly over the sale of all combustible energy sources in Paris by using

37. Ibid., no. 25, reports of Brissac to director, January 7, 1887, August 13, 1888, and February 16, 1897.

38. *Compte rendu des travaux de la commission nommée le 4 février 1885 en exécution de l'article 48 du traité intervenu le 7 février 1870 entre la ville de Paris et la Compagnie parisienne d'éclairage et de chauffage par le gaz* (Paris, 1886), p. 47.

39. AP, V 8 O¹, no. 752, "Rapport sur la vente de coke (7 juillet 1866)." Lower coal prices were slow to be reflected in coke prices. See no. 752, "Chauffage," and no. 25, report of February 16, 1897.

40. Ibid., no. 1067, report of Audouin to director, March 9, 1882. The firm behaved in a similar manner regarding gas motors and meter rentals. See no. 1257, "Rapport sur la machine à gaz (22 mai 1885)"; no. 24, "Service extérieur. Renseignements divers," report of November 18, 1891.

the firm's influence over suppliers.[41] Ultimately, management regarded the exceptional level of returns from gas sales as a situation they might hope to duplicate in all other operations.

The PGC was usually able to sustain high prices and profits because markets were imperfect. In the case of coke, customers had no initial notion of what a fair price would be since the PGC practically originated the trade and accustomed the customers to high prices at once. Competition failed to whittle down prices because most potential competitors conspired with the PGC to keep prices high. The smaller merchants in the coke trade charged as much as the PGC or more. Similarly, the markup on retorts was sustainable as long as competitors took the same profits.[42] As we have seen, the PGC readily found partners in price-fixing arrangements for by-products or used its market power to drive holdouts from the scene.

The final result of such entrepreneurship was that the PGC, as a pioneer of large-scale enterprise, did little to strengthen market forces or renew business practices. The company fit into—and even reinforced—the localized, stratified, and anticompetitive features of French economic life. Although the corporation pioneered new markets, its high-price, high-profit policies condemned those markets to limited size. The PGC may have represented an aggressive sort of management, but it was aggressive in limited ways that solidified the weaknesses of national economic life.

The types of market the PGC entered or constructed had clear implications for its technological decisions. The modest size of the markets dampened pressures for innovation, with predictable results.[43] The company did not take full advantage of its breakthrough in distilling techniques; in 1905, 40 percent of the gas was still produced in ordinary furnaces rather than recuperative ones.[44] The mechanization of labor-intensive operations was also exceptionally slow. As we shall soon see, the absence of market pressures allowed the PGC to make decisions in this area almost entirely on the basis of the need to control its work force. The ministerial commissions that evaluated the corporation in 1880, 1885, and 1890 were careful not to criticize the firm for technological backwardness but still left the

41. Ibid., no. 25, report of Hallopeau to director, December 30, 1859.
42. Ibid., no. 671, deliberations of August 10 and 24, 1864; no. 672, deliberations of January 16, 1867; no. 626, report of Audouin to director, April 22, 1874; no. 1062, "Note sur la Société du charbon de Paris"; no. 1257, "Rapport sur la machine à gaz."
43. Conversely, management was most effective in promoting efficiency when it was under pressure for increased output. The rationalization of gas production occurred while immediate demand remained unfulfilled (that is, up to 1866). See ibid., no. 726, deliberations of June 14, 1866.
44. Ibid., no. 620, "Etat donnant le nombre et le type des fours de distillation . . . (19 juin 1905)." Of 6,746 retorts, 2,856 were heated by ordinary furnaces.

impression that it was exceedingly cautious and complacent. As the corporate charter neared its term, the goal of avoiding capital expenditures reinforced the caution. No wonder the new Société du gaz de Paris, which succeeded the PGC in 1907, found the assets it had inherited decidedly old-fashioned and immediately undertook an ambitious modernization program.[45]

• • •

The practices that management developed for its subsidiary products applied equally to the main business, selling gas. The director repeatedly asserted his desire to expand the clientele as much as possible, to make gas a part of daily life, "like air and water." Moreover, the corporate charter imposed on the PGC the obligation to do what was necessary to facilitate the use of gas.[46] But the director did not really mean what he said; or if he did, the policies he pursued were inappropriate. The market for gas, it will be recalled, was limited in important ways.[47] The PGC had virtually saturated the commercial sector, but the domestic market was largely untapped. By 1885, at the end of the golden era only one in six apartment houses had mounted mains; only 15 percent of apartments were adjacent to the mains; only 5 percent of households actually used gas. Such results raise questions about how the company went about marketing its principal product.

The superficial penetration of the residential clientele was generally the result of the managerial policies pursued during the golden age. The PGC treated gas much as it did by-products. It recognized a large and profitable "natural" clientele, created for the most part by beneficent forces beyond its control. These customers—commercial enterprises, in the case of gas—would pay dearly for gas, either because they had to use it or did not care about the cost. As for the potential users that might have been won over with some judicious enticements, the managers were indifferent to them. Not even the marginal profit of twenty centimes on each additional cubic meter sold interested officers in pursuing the customers who needed to be convinced. As a result, the clientele remained relatively small throughout the golden era.

Corporate policies regarding the ancillary costs entailed in using gas illustrated a cynical realism about markets—the view that some customers would employ gas at almost any price and the rest of the population was not relevant. Rather than supplying meters, connector pipes, and

45. Parisian officials were well aware that they would soon inherit antiquated and in some cases unusable plants. See Frédéric Sauton, *Etude sur la question du gaz à Paris* (Paris, 1902), p. 3.
46. *Rapport*, March 7, 1857, p. 4; March 12, 1862, p. 24; March 28, 1874, p. 6.
47. See chapter 1.

valves at nominal cost to encourage gas use, the company took a heavy profit on each. It earned a 40 percent return on the rental of the pipes connecting residences to the mains. Yields on the sale or rental of meters were between 20 and 30 percent.[48] So high were such charges that the PGC earned three to four times the income that the London or Berlin gas companies derived from their accessory charges. The Parisian firm even included a payment for the "upkeep of connector pipes" that was fictitious; the fee involved no work and was simply a supplementary cost of using gas.[49]

In addition to charging customers a steep installation fee, the PGC failed to make gas easily accessible. Mounted mains (first used in 1860) were the central means for bringing gas to residences. The firm elaborated a threefold package of incentives for lighting with gas between 1866 and 1872, but the policies did not receive enough thought or financial commitment for success. Management sought to stimulate owners of apartment buildings to install mounted mains and prepare at least three apartments for gas use (with connector pipes and fixtures) by offering a hundred francs. The payment just about covered the cost of installation, so the real encouragement was presumably the increased value of apartments with gas. Tenants in lodgings accessible to a mounted main were eligible to receive thirty francs for installing the necessary equipment. Again, that sum barely covered the cost of the work. The company also promised forty-franc incentives to gas fitters (appareilleurs) for finding tenants who would take gas and giving them the means to do so. The payment yielded a profit of about ten francs for the fitters.[50]

The marketing effort fell far short of achieving the announced goal of diffusing gas lighting broadly. Its provisions were poorly publicized. The company relied on the gas fitters to find interested landlords and tenants but failed to provide enough incentive for them to make a real effort. Managers explicitly recognized that ten francs did not excite much activity but declined to raise the bonus. In one important way the company provided the fitters with a disincentive: it had convinced them to construct mounted mains at rates below cost on the grounds that the mains would soon bring additional business from tenants who would order connector pipes and fixtures. In effect, the company had found an indirect means of

48. AP, V 8 O^1, no. 25, report of Mayniel to director, July 31, 1858; no. 1064, "Album de divers tableaux graphiques."

49. Ibid., no. 709; Pierre Mongéaud, La Question du gaz à Paris et le régime nouveau (Paris, 1908), p. 103.

50. AP, V 8 O^1, no. 671, deliberations of April 21 and June 13, 1866; Compagnie parisienne du gaz, Instruction à l'usage du personnel du service extérieur concernant la fourniture du gaz (Paris, 1879), p. 16.

pushing some of the costs of the mains on the customer again. Yet fitters failed to benefit as promised because tenants usually did not respond to the opportunity that the mounted main offered.[51] Moreover, landlords had to agree to so many provisions to receive the mains that they were confused or suspicious rather than eager.[52] Ultimately, management refused to regard the mounted-main program as an investment that could readily yield a return of 30 to 40 percent with some nurturing and careful planning. Instead, it treated the program as an expense that had to pay off at once or be cut.

Concerned about the high proportion of mains that were underutilized, managers decided to curtail the incentive program rather than pursue it with renewed vigor. In 1874 the director announced that the PGC would no longer install them simply at the request of landlords and now would favor only the buildings that were likely to be the most lucrative. Soon the company formalized the restrictions by limiting the buildings that would receive mains to those with apartments renting for at least eight hundred francs annually. The PGC thereby excluded all but the wealthiest 5 or 6 percent of Parisian tenants from gas use. In 1880 the company canceled the hundred-franc bonus to landlords; now it would install mains at its own expense, but only after the owner deposited a hundred francs, which would be returned if and when three tenants became customers.[53] Thus, the mounted-main program—the principal means for reaching residential customers—became a faithful reflection of management's cynical fatalism. The company drew the line at investments returning less than 30 percent, the yield of mains on the most luxurious buildings.[54]

The policy of withholding gas from all but the wealthiest Parisians is revealing on a number of counts. Corporate engineers calculated in 1876 that mounted mains on apartment buildings where rents were below eight hundred francs brought a 9.6 percent return on the investment.[55] That yield was of course substantial by most standards, and management's disdain underscored the inflated expectations within the firm. Furthermore, the abandonment of less wealthy tenants (not to mention the common people) announced the PGC's indifference to the marketing of gas. Profits

51. AP, V 8 O¹, no. 671, deliberations of April 21, 1866.
52. Ibid., no. 678, deliberations of February 14, 1877.
53. Ibid., no. 677, deliberations of April 14, 1875; no. 680, deliberations of December 24, 1880; no. 30, report of Forqueray to director, February 7, 1876; *Rapport*, March 23, 1875, p. 8.
54. AP, V 8 O¹, no. 30, "Statistique des conduites montantes au point de vue du prix des loyers (2 avril 1875)." For evidence that profits might have been even higher, see no. 1064, tableau no. 11.
55. Ibid., no. 30.

from the mains were "only" 9.6 percent because so few tenants saw fit to install gas fixtures, yet the company took no useful steps to make gas more attractive to the hesitant. The disappointing returns from the mounted mains were the firm's own doing. The free-installation program implemented at the end of the 1880s was an admission that earlier incentive plans had failed.

The same refusal to consider long-term growth and the maximization of profit was evident in the company's policies toward gas motors. The managers began by predicting a brilliant future for gas motors in a city with so many small workshops. Noiseless, clean, safe, and free from the requirements of police inspection, they had advantages over steam engines. The company declared its intention of supplying motors at a nominal charge in order to reap huge profits from enhanced gas consumption. Quickly, and perhaps without consciously confronting the matter, managers displaced the goal of the policy from expanding consumption to gaining immediate profits from the sale of motors. The company placed a markup of at least 20 percent on the motors it sold.[56] Once again the officers were attempting to exploit the "natural" customers who would use gas motors at any price. The trouble in this case was that the natural clientele remained tiny. The company discontinued the production of motors and bemoaned the poor performance of this operation but took no imaginative steps to build a market, which happened to be very large in capitals like Berlin.

In spite of its commercial policies, the PGC prospered. Managers were able to serve customers that needed their products regardless of cost. Otherwise, their attitude toward markets was arrogant, exploitive, and restrictive in all but rhetoric. The managers could well afford to sell gas as a "luxury" commodity during the golden age, and the brilliant corporate balance sheet raised few questions about the quality of policy-making. The passing of this era and the curtailment of a natural clientele offered a test of the managers' entrepreneurial mettle.

•   •   •

Management probably did not foresee the loss of its most lucrative gas customers and the crisis of consumption of the 1890s. If it did, it took no steps to anticipate the necessary adjustments.[57] Nonetheless, when circumstances forced the executives to act, they analyzed the options coher-

56. Ibid., no. 1257, "Machines à gaz"; no. 776, "Analyse du prix de vente des moteurs Lenoir" (fols. 88–94); no. 775, "Rapport sur la situation de l'exploitation" (fols. 476–486).
57. Ibid., no. 1062, report of Lefebvre to director, February 3, 1876. More common than underestimating the potential of electricity was ignoring the competitor.

ently and took logical steps to create a niche for gas in the era of electricity. Management's performance was not especially innovative or imaginative. It merely became open—in a conservative fashion—to reasonable options it had not considered before.

The loss of large business customers to electrical lighting renewed management's interest in gaining residential customers and in promoting gas appliances. The shifts in marketing strategy found symbolic expression in the nature of firm's participation in the universal expositions, held every decade during the second half of the century. Industrial prowess was the theme of the corporate exhibit at the Universal Exposition of 1878. Visitors were shown vials of coal tar, piles of coke, displays of gas valves, and the latest sorts of mains.[58] Probably few tourists found this showcase to be the highlight of their visit; nor did it convince them that the PGC was any closer to the way they lived their lives than was a steel mill. The motifs of the exhibit showed that the PGC was not fundamentally interested in winning customers.

The harsh decade that followed that exhibit forced the firm to reexamine its position in basic ways. The theme of the corporate pavilion at the Exposition of 1889 symbolized the direction and the extent of the reassessment. The pavilion took the form of a home furnished with all the latest gas appliances. Visitors could marvel at gas stoves, water heaters, room furnaces, and toasters. Gas motors in the kitchen scraped vegetables, rinsed bottles, and cleaned utensils. Below the domestic quarters was a restaurant with as much gas equipment as the company could invent. Despite the unkind cut by the *Gazette nationale* that the pavilion was like a museum of medieval artifacts, visitors could at least see some ways that gas would make their homes more comfortable and agreeable.[59]

The strategy for marketing gas in an age of electricity was implicit in the exhibit. The company would pursue domestic and commercial customers and do so by accentuating gas appliances as much as lighting.[60] To this end, the director charged the mechanical service department with devising and perfecting domestic appliances. Lefebvre, the engineer who headed the service, identified cooking as the most fruitful area of expansion. Not only did gas have technological advantages over electricity for that purpose, but also the strategy was recommended by deeply rooted mores. As the engineer pointed out, Frenchmen knew that it was "better

58. Ibid., nos. 1290–1291, "Exposition de 1878."
59. Ibid., no. 1292, "Exposition de 1889."
60. The PGC finally created a sophisticated lighting laboratory in 1897. Auguste Lévy, *Communication faite au nom de la Compagnie parisienne du gaz par Monsieur Auguste Lévy* (Paris, 1900), pp. 3–4.

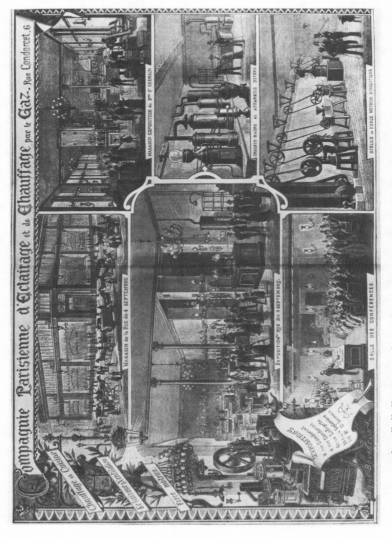

A corporate handbill illustrating the appliance showrooms. Courtesy Archives de Paris.

to eat by poor candlelight and have great food than to have brilliant light and poor food."[61] His department also perfected gas heaters and found manufacturers to produce them on a large scale. The company used its showrooms, which had specialized in coke appliances for the previous decades, to publicize and sell the ranges and furnaces. To stimulate interest in cooking with gas, the company engaged a Madame Mees to give public lessons and to write a cookbook. Between February and December 1892 nearly three thousand people attended her talks, held at the various showrooms. The company also arranged with the Dufayel department store, one of the largest in the city, to sell stoves and heaters manufactured under the corporate label in 1897.[62] The new quest for gas-powered devices sometimes brought engineers to a dead end, as well. They tinkered with gas-driven elevators, tramways, and automobiles.[63] At least these failed efforts demonstrated a determination to make gas relevant to the machine age. Such a determination had not been evident before competition from electricity intensified. The PGC also tried to recapture some of its large commercial clients, this time for the use of appliances rather than lighting. It willingly gave subsidies to well-known restaurants for the installation of stoves or grills.[64] Management may have hoped that, beyond selling more gas to cafes, it would also be familiarizing the public with meals prepared by gas.

In order for the promotion of appliances to be effective, the PGC had to find ways of convincing Parisians to install gas lines in their homes. With sixty-seven thousand apartments ready to be served by existing mounted mains, there was a large potential market close at hand but previously neglected. In 1887 the company finally took a meaningful step to build markets through a free-installation program, which lent to tenants already at mains the internal pipes, a stove, and a chandelier for the dining room. At last managers had begun to come to terms with investments designed to reap returns over the long run. Their approach to the new policy was cautious and limited, however. Nothing that the PGC did to attract residential customers was original. Gas companies in provincial cities had long lent appliances to customers; indeed, they often offered a wider range of equipment and imposed fewer restrictions. Moreover, Di-

61. AP, V 8 O¹, no. 1292, "Rapports et notes émanant des divers services."
62. Ibid., no. 1303, "Exposition culinaire"; no. 693, deliberations of November 13, 1897. The PGC maintained display spaces on the boulevard St-Germain, rue Condorcet, rue du 4-Septembre, and rue Lafayette.
63. Ibid., no. 1303, "Voitures actionnés par moteurs à gaz"; no. 691, deliberations of November 13 and 20, 1895.
64. The deliberations of the *comite d'exécution* record these agreements. See Ibid., nos. 691–694.

rector Camus at first insisted on the awkward provision that only new customers could receive free stoves; a faithful customer who had used gas prior to 1887 had to purchase a stove.[65] In spite of the success of the program in attracting new customers and expected returns of 50 percent on the investment, management was halfhearted in its commitments.

Efforts to seek a genuinely mass clientele required still more daring— almost more than management could muster. Some engineers continued to seek business exclusively among the well-off. Thus, Lefebvre, the strategist for the 1889 exposition, rejected a plan to place in the pavilion a simple restaurant serving *biftecks;* he wanted an elegant café that would attract the *grande bourgeoisie* (his term).[66] Nonetheless, the company eventually resolved to democratize gas use, provided the city would compensate it for sacrificing some of its prerogatives. One indication of management's growing acceptance of democratization was a more favorable attitude toward reduced gas rates. In 1880 the company had dismissed protest over thirty centimes as the work of outside agitators. Twelve years later, the PGC sought to organize consumer groups for the purpose of pressuring the municipal council.[67] In the Sauton project of 1892 the company agreed to gas at twenty centimes, with full compensation for the reduction, and to the fee-free program, which made gas readily available to renters paying less than five hundred francs a year (about 75 percent of all Parisian tenants). As we have seen, the agreements were not realized at once because the Sauton project fell apart; certain aldermen kept insisting on a fee-free program.[68] Faced with falling consumption in 1892, 1893, and 1894, the company finally found the courage to accept it. With that consent, gas entered petit bourgeois households.

The new mass-marketing arrangement had excellent economic justifications and a political payoff as well. Mounted mains were much more lucrative than ever before as a result of free installations and free stoves. The financial projections made by the PGC's engineers in 1892 predicted returns in the range of 30 percent on investments in mounted mains, pipes, and stoves—less than half the yield from supplying gas to regular

65. Ibid., no. 24, "Transformation de l'éclairage dans Paris (14 novembre 1892)"; no. 30, report of November 1, 1887; *Rapport*, March 28, 1888, p. 6. For the policies of provincial and foreign gas companies, see AP, V 8 O¹, no. 1002, "Note sur les moyens qu'il conviendrait d'employer à Paris pour augmenter le nombre des abonnés . . . (25 octobre 1890)."

66. AP, V 8 O¹, no. 1292, "Rapport et notes émanant des divers services."

67. Ibid., no. 1257, Jules Aronssohn to director, November 23, 1892. In 1900 the director finally admitted to stockholders that Parisians did genuinely want lower prices. See *Rapport*, March 28, 1901, p. 56.

68. AP, V 8 O¹, no. 615, "Exonération des frais accessoires."

customers but still handsome.[69] Moreover, management could anticipate valuable political benefits. Thousands of small customers complaining about expensive gas and eager for immediate relief would provide a splendid instrument for softening opposition to a renewed charter on the municipal council. The director could imagine dictating terms to the city, and the strategy almost succeeded with the Chamon project of 1901–1902 (see chapter 2).

With such advantages, it is worth asking why the PGC left the initiative for the fee-free program to the municipality and then implemented it cautiously. The few problems that managers repeatedly cited were simply not so serious as to raise grave doubts. There was the concern that regular customers might resent the special treatment modest renters were about to receive. The head of the customer accounts department worried that the program would vastly complicate the bookkeeping operations and raise the incidence of delinquent accounts—which it did to a small extent.[70] Surely these objections masked a fundamental aversion to change and risk. The PGC had every reason to expect comfortable profits from the fee-free initiative, yet the decision makers fretted over the large capital expenditures a mass market would require.[71] In the face of uncertainty, limited though the imponderables were, the status quo had its attractions. Thus leftist aldermen found themselves urging capitalists to pursue a profitable venture and even offering financial incentives for the sake of democratizing consumerism.

Characteristically, the engineers proceeded slowly, cautiously, and conservatively with mass marketing. Rather than using the program as a vehicle for embracing as many customers as possible, the PGC restricted access. The director insisted on verifying the rent levels of applicants and petitioned the prefect to check the claims against tax records. The com-

69. Ibid., no. 30, "Conduites montantes"; no. 689, deliberations of August 18, 1892. The returns on mounted mains that the engineers reported for the 1890s were much higher than those cited earlier in the chapter for the 1870s. The free-installation and fee-free programs were responsible for the larger yields. Not only did more tenants per building take gas, but their free stoves and fixtures used more of it. Thus each main generated more income.

70. Ibid., no. 24, "Renseignements concernant les recettes sur conduites montantes"; no. 90, "Tableau du personnel du bureau des recettes." The PGC might have tried to supply the common people with gas while avoiding these problems by offering prepaid meters. (The British companies had been doing so for years.) Yet the PGC never permitted this approach to mass marketing.

71. The PGC would eventually spend twenty million francs on equipment for the program. See ibid., no. 617, "Charges supportées par la Compagnie du fait des abonnements sans frais." The firm purported to have saved small consumers forty-six million francs between 1894 and 1902. The large sum attests to the burden of accessory charges.

pany even went so far as to question the qualifications of an alderman who claimed to be eligible. The PGC would not provide buildings with mounted mains until landlords put up a security deposit—a payment many no doubt refused.[72] Such hesitancy was not justified by the market testing that the company had done prior to the agreement nor by the final results. Accepting mass marketing had been the correct decision. Fee-free clients consumed 80 percent of the increase in gas sold after 1895 and restored, in the firm's last years, the high profit levels of the golden age.[73]

•   •   •

The quality of the managers' entrepreneurial decisions lacked a simple, uniform profile, so it is easier to describe what that profile was not than what it was. Clearly, the PGC's salaried executives were not Malthusian in any thoroughgoing sense. Nor were they profit maximizers (though they did not eschew huge profits). The engineers of the gas company manifested three valuable talents: they strove tirelessly to reduce costs and found appropriate techniques to do so; they exploited monopolistic opportunities successfully, especially when mass marketing was not involved; and they knew how to construct protected markets. Such talents did not lead to basic innovations in business practice; nor, if generalized, did they promise that the rise of large-scale enterprises in France would make the economy function more efficiently. The PGC's managers wished to remain aloof from market forces and largely succeeded in doing so. Even their drive for efficiency in production owed less to the pressures of the marketplace than to their sense of duty and professionalism as engineers. The strengthening of competitive pressures, such as they were by the 1890s, barely changed the quality of decision making.

The debate about whether French entrepreneurial behavior was shaped by a particular *mentalité* or was entirely a matter of rational responses to the economic environment is impossible to resolve with finality even for one isolated firm. In any case, the more important point is that the managers' cultural presuppositions weighed heavily in their business judgments. They may have displayed an immediate responsiveness to empirical realities on matters of detail, but the engineers' ideology and outlook guided policies regarding larger matters—at least until reality forced adjustments. Moreover, their professional backgrounds imposed certain predilections and expectations. Neither by training nor by vocation were

72. Ibid., no. 691, deliberations of January 9 and May 4, 1895; no. 693, deliberations of March 13, 1897; *Conseil municipal*, deliberations of December 8, 1893 (the remarks of Councilman Brousse, in particular).
73. AP, V 8 O¹, no. 617, "Augmentation dans la consommation de l'éclairage particulier."

the managers entrepreneurs. They were engineers, destined by their scholastic achievements to responsible posts. Their intellectual formation, reinforced by class values, taught them what a centime saved meant. Their training did not prepare them to take risks nor to proffer their wares to a hesitant public of consumers. The engineers leaned toward *administration;* their career expectations required stability and orderly change, if change was inevitable. The good fortune of the PGC's officers was that these requirements were consistent with handsome profits for most of the life of the firm.

Culturally shaped expectations especially influenced corporate policies regarding the labor force. In this area, however, frugality and efforts to stay aloof from market forces created results that proved visibly more problematical. Personnel management had no equivalent to gas at thirty centimes for concealing failures.

Labor Policies

Among the many responsibilities of the PGC's management was the direction of an unusually large labor force, probably the largest in Paris belonging to a single employer. The firm's policies and decisions bear attention on a number of grounds. First, the gas company had an uncommon amount of freedom to create the style of industrial relations it desired. As an early example of large-scale industry, the PGC found that patterns of behavior and expectations were not yet tightly drawn. Moreover, the company had fewer economic constraints than most firms. It operated far above the battlefield of intense competition and therefore had the ability to bestow special advantages on its work force if it chose. Liberality was all the more possible because labor was a relatively small portion of total expenses, on average 10 percent. In mining and railroads, by contrast, the wage bill was more on the order of 30 percent of expenditures.[74] Such freedom from constraint meant that the labor policy of the PGC reflected to an unusual degree the values and priorities of the managers.[75]

Industrial relations at the PGC are also of interest because they eventually had to respond to a nationwide shift in political economy. We have

---

74. Maurice Lévy-Leboyer, "Capital Investment and Economic Growth in France, 1820–1930," in *The Cambridge Economic History of Europe* (Cambridge, 1978), 8:261. For labor costs in other industries, see Jean Bouvier et al., *Le Mouvement du profit en France au XIXᵉ siècle* (Paris, 1965), p. 77.
75. On the study of labor policy from a comparative perspective, see Howard Gospel and Craig Littler, eds., *Managerial Strategies and Industrial Relations* (London, 1983); Elaine Glovka Spencer, *Management and Labor in Imperial Germany* (New Brunswick, N.J., 1984).

already seen that the company became entangled—perhaps more than any private firm in France—in a search for alternatives to market orthodoxy on the part of some conservatives and some politicians of the left. The latter sought to extend republican rights to the workplace as a matter of justice and as a strategy for integrating workers into a democratic regime. The mobilization of conservatives against collectivism and "state socialism" took several forms, including a bourgeois reform movement dedicated to reducing industrial tensions through private, paternalistic activities. The labor policies of the PGC during its last fifteen years were implicated in the search for social peace. It was not surprising that all sides regarded the firm as a test case for their respective proposals.[76]

Management, local politicians, and reformers had to develop their strategies for a large and varied labor force.[77] The wage-earning personnel at the PGC grew from about twelve hundred when the company was founded to five thousand at the end of the golden age and more than eight thousand when the charter expired. The factory laborers were distributed among seven to nine plants (depending on the moment) scattered about Paris and the suburbs.[78] In addition to the plant personnel there were lamplighters, valve greasers, plumbers, carpenters, navvies, general laborers, and still other workers. In face of such diversity it makes sense to simplify by recognizing two basic groups. The common laborers, who could learn their jobs in a matter of days or hours, comprised just less than 80 percent of the work force. More problematical for management was the other group, the stokers (*chauffeurs*), who loaded retorts with coal for distillation. The stokers' work was not skilled in the classic sense of requiring the level of dexterity and judgment acquired through long training; yet their work did demand rare attributes. Stoking called for formidable strength and endurance; most men were not up to the task of toiling in the intense heat of the furnace rooms. Scarcity gave stokers market power. If the company was not prepared for their threats, these workmen could have the firm at their mercy, at least in the short run. Managers

76. See chapter 2. One argument industrialists used against free trade was that protection would allow them to pacify workers with higher pay and shorter hours. See Lebovics, *Alliance of Iron and Wheat*, chap. 3. As we shall see, the case of the PGC raises serious doubts about the employers' sincerity.

77. Only seventeen French firms employed more than five thousand people in 1906. See Georges Dupeux, *French Society, 1789–1970*, trans. Peter Wait (London, 1976), p. 207. The PGC, with 8,000 workers, was easily in this category.

78. The plants the PGC operated during the 1860s were La Villette (nineteenth arrondissement), Ternes (seventeenth), Passy (sixteenth), Vaugirard (fifteenth), Ivry (thirteenth), Saint-Mandé (twelfth), and Belleville (twentieth). In 1905 the PGC's plants were in La Villette, Passy, Vaugirard, Ivry, Saint-Mandé, Boulogne, Alfortville, Clichy, and Landy (Saint-Denis).

preferred to think of all their laborers as "simple workers," but in practice they could not apply policies uniformly, nor could they expect uniform responses to their policies.[79]

The gas executives had only one vocabulary with which to conceptualize industrial relations, that of paternalism.[80] The notion entailed more than a strategy for imposing their interests on the personnel; it was a cultural system and a set of symbolic relationships in which managers themselves were enmeshed. The engineers had matured learning that their authority over workers was based not only on superior mental acumen but also on their responsibility for their underlings. As students in the technical institutes, they were exposed to industrial enterprises that put the principle into practice. Paul Gigot, for example, toured such plants as a twenty-one-year-old student at the Ecole des Mines. This future engineer, who would become head of the PGC's factory division in 1893, found at a zinc plant in Belgium a savings plan, a medical fund, and company housing. Gigot noted in his student journal that these initiatives were "not at all useless, when one considers the workers' complaints about their painful work, which they cannot do for many years."[81] Even as a young man, Gigot grasped the inevitable connection between paternalism, moralization of laborers, and corporate interest. There was probably not an engineer in the company who would have dissented from the proposition that employers owed workers more than their wages.

The culture of paternalism brought its own unquestioned assumptions—that poverty was inevitable for workers, that most of them were morally weak, and that intervention in their lives was effective only if performed face to face. These and other presuppositions provided a comfortable check on charitable gestures that were too ambitious. Plant superintendent Jones argued in 1865 that "any action that tended to suggest to workers that they are indispensable only spoils them."[82] The assistant factory chief seconded this opinion and argued that to grant workers' demands provided merely "a facile solution" that gave only "passing satis-

79. Chapter 7 treats manual laborers in greater detail.

80. Two important works on industrial paternalism are David Roberts, *Paternalism in Early Victorian England* (New Brunswick, N.J., 1979) and Donald Reid, "Industrial Paternalism: Discourse and Practice in Nineteenth-Century French Mining and Metallurgy," *Comparative Studies in Society and History* 27 (1985): 579–607. See also Eugene McCreary, "Social Welfare and Business: The Krupp Welfare Program, 1860–1914," *Business History Review* 42 (1968): 24–49; Joseph Melling, "Industrial Strife and Business Welfare: The Case of the South Metro Gas Company," *Business History* 21 (1979): 163–179.

81. Archives de l'Ecole des Mines, journaux de voyage, J. 1858 (194).

82. AP, V 8 O¹, no. 148, report of Superintendent Jones, April 26, 1865.

factions and soon creates new pretentions." [83] Nearly thirty years later, the new assistant chief, Albert Euchène, reaffirmed that idea, noting that workers "understand no pleasures without a drink in their hands" and that any improvement in pay benefited chiefly the pub owners. Euchène elaborated on the theme by arguing that only proper upbringing and education gave people the capacity for sobriety and providence. He found workers seriously deficient in both. Thus, the conclusion that workers had few, if any, legitimate grievances, or at least that listening to their complaints was a mistake, had a powerful hold on managers. Euchène once devoted considerable energy to "proving" with documents from the company savings plan that poorly paid workers were inclined to save more than better-paid ones. [84] That this engineer, with years of rigorous analytical training behind him, could present so flawed a study with conviction attests to his capacity for self-delusion about industrial relations. Yet he was hardly unique.

Benevolence was of course the essence of paternalism from the workers' point of view, but not from the managers'. Devoted to duty and to hard work for its own sake, the engineers conceived of their responsibility toward workers mainly in terms of ordering, guiding, and supervising them. In several corporate publications managers proclaimed their adherence to a "firm, prudent, and paternal administration." [85] A cautious moral superintendence was the essence of managerial paternalism. Though circumstances eventually forced the executives to enter into a dialogue with the labor force, not for a moment did they regard it as legitimate. Indeed, they believed that such a dialogue was fraught with dangers.

This framework for paternalistic management provided justification for the decision makers to do what they wished and ignore what they wished. There was, as well, another limit to their paternalism. The object of the managers' ultimate loyalty was not the moral ordering of society but rather the stockholders' interests. "Firm, prudent, and paternal administration" meant profits, not disinterested service to workers. Most benevolent gestures were costly, and managers could not bring themselves to spend the stockholders' money when the necessity was not self-evident. Hence their paternalistic acts arose as a response to threats and were rather transparent attempts at social control. The impetus for a broader program of reform lasted only as long as the managers felt a loss of control.

The case of the PGC frustrates scholarly efforts under way to rehabili-

83. Ibid., report of Servier, June 20, 1865.
84. Ibid., no. 1520, "Rapport de Monsieur Euchène: Mission en Angleterre du mois de mai 1893," 2: 14–16.
85. See, for example, ibid., no. 1290.

tate the reputation of the nineteenth-century *patronat*.[86] The gas managers were calculating and manipulative but not spontaneously generous—despite the enormous profits and freedom from market pressures. To convince Louis Napoleon to confer the gas concession on the new firm, its founders tried to appeal to his socialistic pretensions by promising model housing for workers. The company did in fact draw up plans when it built the enormous new plant in La Villette, then a desolate corner of Paris. When the engineers found that they could assemble a sufficiently large labor force without the housing, however, they abandoned the project entirely.[87] Plant superintendents were well aware that stokers, who worked in scorching heat and clouds of coal dust, required an adequate shower room at each plant. The head of the Saint-Mandé plant characterized his facility as "immoral, wretched." Yet top management was slow to find the funds for improvements.[88] Two of the corporation's most solidly established paternalistic institutions, the medical plan and aid to aged workers, were financed through a 1 percent withholding from the payroll. However, the company jealously guarded its control over the allocations and used the power to discipline the work force.[89] Nor were managers true to their oft-repeated word that encouraging workers to save for the future was one of their unavoidable duties. When wage earners requested a retirement plan to which they would contribute—and thus have a *right* to a pension—the director rejected the demand as unworkable. Engendering habits of thrift was managers' goal only when it reinforced their control over the personnel.[90] Indeed, after years of hoping that stokers would take their

86. Peter Stearns, *Paths to Authority: The Middle Class and the Industrial Labor Force in France, 1820–1848* (Urbana, Ill., 1978), and, much less explicitly, Michael Miller, *The Bon Marché: Bourgeois Culture and the Department Store, 1896–1920* (Princeton, 1981).

87. AP, V 8 O¹, no. 765, "Rapport sur les maisons ouvrières (2 octobre 1856)"; no. 671, deliberations of November 28, 1866; *Journal de l'éclairage au gaz*, 1853, no. 2 (June 15): 234–235.

88. AP, V 8 O¹, no. 768, "Rapports des régisseurs des usines," reports of May 24, 1868, and January 20, 1867. The Vaugirard plant did not have hot water until 1869. See no. 673, deliberations of November 3, 1869.

89. The PGC had promised to supplement the *caisse de prévoyance* with a sum equal to the 1 percent, but it ran the fund so frugally that it did not have to dip into the corporate coffers until 1890. See ibid., no. 723, deliberations of March 11, 1858; no. 149, "Caisse de prévoyance." The company created the post of "inspector of the ill" to check on those claiming sick pay. See no. 678, deliberations of September 27, 1876.

90. Ibid., no. 155, "Retraite ouvrière"; no. 148, "Procès-verbaux de la cinquième audience donnée le 10 mai 1892." Director Godot refused to allow the workers to collect for their mutual-aid society on the shop floor, but the company contributed annually to the mutual-aid society of the Anciens élèves de l'Ecole Polytechnique.

wage increases in the form of contributions to the company's pension fund (which the PGC accorded as discretionary rewards), Arson pronounced the workers' proposal a "dangerous practice."[91] To be sure, the engineer-managers were themselves hardworking, self-sacrificing, and modest in their aspirations; they asked nothing more of workers than they asked of themselves. But however true, that assertion does not alter the point that their paternalism was authoritarian and calculating rather than benevolent.

• • •

These authoritarian paternalists had to formulate specific policies under circumstances that did not always favor their stern principles. Adverse conditions prevailed especially during the first fifteen years of operation. The industrial progress of the Second Empire, accompanied by rebuilding of the capital, created peaks of prosperity that at certain moments gave labor some leverage in dealing with management. Average Parisian wage levels rose more than 20 percent during the 1860s.[92] Moreover, the PGC significantly augmented the amount of work it extracted from its laborers, particularly stokers, when it rationalized the distillation process. Such conditions generated recurrent labor unrest at the gas plants during the 1860s.

That labor was in short supply, that general wage and price levels in Paris were rising, and that the company was getting ever more work from its personnel did not bring the PGC's engineers to accept tactfully the necessity of occasional pay increases for their underlings. Instead, the managers railed against the "absurd demands" and "outrageous pretensions" of the workers—even as they calculated that a raise would not halt the decline of unit labor costs. The pay increases they finally accorded came in response to agitation, rarely in anticipation of it. Factory managers resorted to measures of "salutary intimidation" (to use the term of one superintendent) to forestall strikes and always dismissed the leaders of the movement. Even workers who eschewed strikes and politely led delegations to discuss workers' grievances could expect to be dismissed as a matter of course. Like gas consumers, the PGC's workers had to struggle for whatever improvements they were to receive.[93]

---

91. Ibid., no. 711, "Rapport no. 73: Caisse de retraite."
92. See Jacques Rougerie, "Remarques sur l'histoire des salaires à Paris au XIXᵉ siècle," *Le Mouvement social*, no. 63 (1968): 71–108, for indexes of industrial activity and wage levels.
93. AP, V 8 O¹, no. 148, report of June 28, 1865; no. 748, report of Jones to director, April 9, 1861; no. 1268, report of the superintendent of Ternes to Arson, April 26, 1867. To place such behavior in context, consult Michelle Perrot, *Work-*

Managers had difficulty adjusting to an era of rising pay levels because they regarded wages as a subject of morality and authority as well as economics. In truth, they did not want market forces to set wages any more than they wanted them to set the prices of the PGC's products. Rather than according legitimacy to the market as final arbiter of pay, managers attempted to create an internal labor market, in which laws of supply and demand yielded to their moral appreciation of what workers should earn. In exchange for relatively steady employment (in a heavily seasonal industry) and some minor fringe benefits (like the medical plan and small retirement grants), managers expected workers to leave wages to their judgment. That such an arrangement was neither attractive to workers nor realistic did not diminish the engineers' indignation when laborers rejected it. Of course, the common hands were not readily able to brush aside managers' control over them. The implication of the internal labor market for them was low pay relative to other firms offering comparable jobs.

Far from allowing labor to share in the copious corporate profits, management pursued a deliberate low-wage policy. A factory superintendent noted in 1865 that the daily 2.75 francs paid to coke haulers could attract "only the old and infirm" by the current standards in Paris. The head of the coke department explained in 1876 that wages for carters (2.75–3.75 francs a day) were far less than mere navvies could earn at most plants. Hence the company had to hire "only the rejects—weak or bad workers in all regards." The lighting engineer brought the director's attention to the plight of the greasemen when their rate of quitting tripled between 1876 and 1881. Since they had not had a raise since 1855 and did thirteen hours of responsible work a day, the engineer had to conclude that their pay might need some upgrading. The director, however, rejected the advice.[94] These examples of lower management seeming to plea for higher pay should not mislead. They agreed with their superiors on the desirability of low wages, and requests for increases came only when the inability to attract competent workers threatened to disrupt operations. Even in the early 1890s, when the company's labor practices were under public scrutiny as never before, little had changed. The assistant factory chief assembled comparative wage data in the hope of showing the municipal

---

ers on Strike: France 1871–1890, trans. Chris Turner (New Haven, 1987), pp. 249–280. The PGC was by no means aberrant.

94. AP, V 8 O¹, no. 148, report of Devillier, May 1, 1865; report of Perrin to director, December 24, 1881; no. 90, report of Hallopeau to director, January 14, 1867.

council that the PGC's laborers had no grounds for complaint. His findings demonstrated instead that the firm's pay was on a par only with disreputable industries of the *banlieue*, glue factories, animal-rendering plants, and the like. At first the engineer tried to explain away the obvious implications through strained reasoning, but eventually he buried the report.[95]

Not only did the internal labor market mean a low-wage policy, pursued to the extent circumstances allowed; it also meant unequal pay for men doing the same work. The company, for example, employed two groups of carters who delivered alkalies to industrial customers. One received a daily bonus of a franc, and the other did not. Their superior could not justify the differential in terms of work routines. Such pay differences for similar work did not embarrass management nor disturb its sense of equity. Indeed, the director refused to establish companywide standards and even encouraged factory superintendents to pay according to different scales because he wanted to engender divisions among the laborers. The executive committee would not consider a wage demand from stokers on the grounds that the workers had passed the petition from plant to plant.[96] Unequal pay was an important component of the managers' mission for moralizing workers. Whenever possible, the engineers transformed simple jobs into "careers" by introducing hierarchical pay steps achieved through seniority. Thus, coke haulers would earn 2.50, 2.75, or 3.00 francs daily depending on their years with the PGC. This "segmented labor market," as Richard Edwards calls it, was by no means the invention of the twentieth-century corporation.[97] The PGC was thoroughly wedded to it as an instrument of control and moralization. Managers justified the practice as an "encouragement to emulation." They undoubtedly viewed it as a natural extension of the career-based pay that engineers themselves had. In all probability workers were impressed mainly by its arbitrary aspects. When they finally developed a collective voice in the 1890s, they complained about being "tyrannized by twenty-five centimes."[98] Yet the general laborers could not usually resist the will of the engineers, who had scarce jobs to offer. The stokers, by contrast, had the ability to resist and did so. The director tried to impose "grades" of pay on them in 1858 but

95. Ibid., no. 148, "Renseignements sur les salaires journaliers des ouvriers pris chez différents fabricants."
96. Ibid., no. 157, report of Linote to Audouin, October 20, 1898; no. 665, deliberations of June 6, 1857; no. 148, "Etat, par usine et par profession, des salaires"; report of Gigot, December 20, 1891.
97. Richard Edwards, *Contested Terrain: The Transformation of the Workplace in the Twentieth Century* (New York, 1979). Edwards portrays the segmented labor market as a post–World War II strategy of labor control.
98. AP, V 8 O¹, no. 148, "Briqueterie et goudrons, 8 avril 1892."

had to withdraw the order within a few months.[99] The paternal authority that managers affected led them to create an internal labor market that was characterized not by a carefully considered beneficence but rather by low and inequitable wages. The managers could not imagine—nor did they care—how arbitrary their governance might have seemed at times to the labor force.

Armed with their comfortable assumptions about the futility of conceding raises, managers did not do so willingly. When the superintendent of the Vaugirard plant faced an acute shortage of stokers in 1865, he struggled to find an alternate solution. He decided to offer paid overtime work but worried that even that answer might create "unfortunate precedents." Several years later, the manager of the Passy plant railed against stokers who wanted a pay increase when he raised their work load (by having them fill larger retorts). For him, theirs remained "an incredible demand."[100] The managers' grave reservations notwithstanding, they were sometimes compelled to yield. Then they tried to meet the essentials of workers' demands, but on their own terms and with moralizing provisions attached. Such reformulations of the concessions were important to managers, for that was how they preserved the sense of paternal authority. Surrendering to strikers in 1865, the company granted not a raise but a "bonus" for regular attendance. Stokers would receive fifteen francs a month if they had no unexcused absences. Arson solemnly instructed plant superintendents that the bonuses had to be earned. Superintendent Philippot wished to go further; he favored paying bonuses only at the end of the year "to encourage a spirit of economy and moralization." He also suggested putting the extra pay in savings accounts and making stokers build a nest egg.[101] None of these ideas obtained. The harsh realities of a tight labor market militated against moralizing projects, even slender ones.

In 1876 the PGC faced another inflationary surge too powerful to ignore. The company capitulated to workers' demands and once again put a patriarchical gloss on its concession. This time the firm accompanied the raise with the creation of a voluntary savings plan (*caisse d'économie*), into which workers, it was hoped, would place their pay increases.[102] The

---

99. Ibid., no. 666, deliberations of August 3, 1858, and March 9, 1859.
100. Ibid., no. 749, report by superintendent of Passy to Arson, April 6, 1869; no. 148, report by Gigot, April 30, 1865.
101. Ibid., no. 1081, ordre de service no. 253; no. 148, report of June 25, 1865; no. 763, "Distribution des primes."
102. Ibid., no. 1081, ordre de service (July 18, 1885). Director Camus noted in this directive that he "attaches a great importance to the *caisse*" and ordered superin-

head of the factory division ordered superintendents to assemble the workers and harangue them on the benefits of putting aside their raises. At the Boulogne plant, workers listened respectfully but protested that higher costs of living would consume their gains. The plant manager, resigned to the workers' intransigence, probably did not even sense their evident resentment at the suggestion that the raise was superfluous.[103] Despite the paltry sums actually put in the savings accounts and the small number of savers involved (usually office clerks, in any case), the director reported on the plan at every stockholders meeting as if it were a fundamental component of the business. The engineers may have forced a moralizing interpretation on wage inflation, but it is likely that they spoke intelligibly only to themselves.

The PGC's decision makers had to struggle with the economic—and the moral—implications of incentive-based pay. Twice during the 1860s the managers met labor agitation with a compromise, retaining a basic rate but adding incentive pay if stokers distilled more than a specified amount of coal. They resisted a full piece-rate plan, however, and granted it only under duress.[104] Managers found incentive-based pay a problematical issue because it involved a principle they did not willingly accept: the firm might derive benefits from giving workers higher pay. Factory superintendents were united in their opposition to piece rates. They argued that they were able to extract more work from the stokers without it. Furthermore, they feared the wage bill that might result from incentive pay—even if the company was profiting from enhanced productivity. By contrast, their superior, Arson, advocated piece rates on abstract grounds, as a matter of justice and of moralization. Yet even he retreated from his support of full incentive pay when he realized that stokers' wages could reach 9.50 francs a day if productivity continued to rise at its current rate. The convoluted mixture of economic and moral calculation inherent in managers' wage policies was reflected in Arson's reasoning: "This figure is far too large to contemplate. Whatever the interest the company has in realizing such a level of labor output, it cannot reasonably consent to pay

tendents to "exercise their personal influence to encourage [*provoquer*] deposits." Camus insisted that the savings plan should receive only the savings put aside from the raise; he did not want savings from any other source. See no. 678, deliberations of October 18, 1876.

103. Ibid., no. 714, report of Hadamar to Arson, April 13, 1876.

104. Ibid., no. 715, report of December 14, 1871; no. 716, "Salaire des chauffeurs (16 mars 1880)"; no. 673, deliberations of April 21, 1869. It is useful to recall at this point that stokers' mode of pay did differ from one plant to another up to 1880.

[those wages]."[105] Arson's brand of paternalism did not allow him to rejoice in the coincidence of high wages and corporate profits. He and the rest of management clung to moral standards that denied the validity of high wages under any circumstances.[106]

Management lost its struggle to keep wages within morally permissible limits and even to keep unit labor costs down during the last great burst of Parisian prosperity of the century, between 1876 and 1882. The general inflationary spiral, the exceptional strains posed by the Universal Exposition of 1878, and the labor scarcity created in the PGC itself by the opening of a new plant in Clichy and plans for a new one in Saint-Denis defeated the engineers' efforts to restrain wages. Probably on the insistence of stokers, engineers finally accepted piece rates in 1880 (thereby preserving some semblance of moralization).[107] Still, pay began to rise faster than productivity for the first time since the creation of the PGC. By this time, as well, the corporate profits were a matter of public scandal, and it was rather convenient to point to the "exorbitant" wages earned by stokers to justify the firm's returns. Thus, a high-wage policy—for stokers, at least—arrived just as the PGC needed it politically.[108]

The dawn of the electrical era found management resigned to paying stokers quite well by the standards of the day and to devoting an ever-increasing portion of corporate expenditure to labor. The path by which they came to such a situation had no doubt frustrated workers as much as managers and convinced laborers that decisions about pay were arbitrary and capricious. In any case, the focus of industrial relations was about to shift from wage matters to the question of authority. On that subject, too, managers had to adjust their inclinations to unwelcome realities.

• • •

105. Ibid., no. 711, rapport no. 43, "Règlement du salaire de la distillation"; no. 716, "Salaire des chauffeurs (16 mars 1880)."

106. For another example of concerns that workers would earn "too much" despite rising productivity, see ibid., no. 672, deliberations of May 30, June 3, and June 6, 1868.

107. Ibid., no. 680, deliberations of March 19, 1880. The police reports noted that the workers had demanded piece rates and that management had granted that mode of pay reluctantly. See Préfecture, B/a 176, report of March 19, 1880. The assessments by the police fit the corporate documents, which stress the "change of mind" among the engineers.

108. On the jump in labor costs, see ibid., no. 1016, "Prix de revient." Having granted "exorbitant" wages to stokers, the company sought to contain costs by turning to foreign workers, who were paid less. By 1892, 40 percent of the stokers at the La Villette plant were foreign. See no. 90, "Etat numérique des ouvriers italiens"; no. 148, "Union des agents des chantiers à coke."

The managers' authoritarian paternalism was incompatible with the efforts, however modest, by politicians of the left to republicanize the workplace, to endow workers with basic rights before their employers. The PGC's decision makers took the reforms as an infringement on their rightful authority. The law of December 27, 1890, provides an example of the conflict. It was one of the few concrete benefits workers received from the Opportunist Republic. The law called for a week's pay when laborers hired for an indeterminate duration were suddenly dismissed. The PGC could not abide the legislation and refused to honor it. Several workers sued the company and won. The director beseeched the corporate attorney to find some loophole in the law, for he viewed it as a threat to the authority of the firm. "If a foreman cannot fire a worker at will without inflicting a cost on the firm," the director pleaded, "what has become of his ability to discipline?" Alas, the barrister was not able to discover convenient ways of circumventing the legislation. At one point he recommended hiring every worker with a daily written contract but conceded that the necessary paperwork would be overwhelming. In the end he could only suggest one more show of "salutary intimidation" to keep workers from exercising their newly acquired right: have foremen inform laborers that they would never be rehired if they dared to sue the company.[109]

The firm's confrontation with this piece of republican legislation was prophetic. In the same year that the law passed, the company recommenced negotiating with Paris over the fate of the gas concession. The bargaining was to place the PGC in a most uncomfortable position regarding its industrial relations. The discussions began just as the left majority of the municipal council came to a new understanding about the role of government in industrial society.[110] The city improved its workers' wages in time to demand the same from the PGC. Wages were not to be the central issue, however. The council also encouraged the creation and growth of unions among the personnel. At the very least, councilmen expected the PGC to comply with the law of 1884, which gave workers the right to unionize free of overt persecution. Many Radical aldermen also wished to see fuller cooperation between management and the unions as well as significant concessions on pay. For the foreseeable future it appeared that the PGC faced an intermediary authority between its executives and a heretofore atomized personnel.

The union posed a formidable threat to the company's authoritarian paternalism. At the same time, it presented a genuine opportunity for a

109. Ibid., no. 90, "Ouvriers renvoyés ou congédiés."
110. See chapter 2.

breakthrough culminating in cooperative industrial relations and collective bargaining—if the PGC wished to pursue that path. The workers' union formed in late 1891 showed every sign of being moderate, conciliatory, and respectful of managerial authority. The leaders initiated contacts with management by sending a humbly worded request for an audience with the director. They formally disavowed any intention of striking and described their purpose as exposing the "modifications" that workers desired. The letter ended by assuring the director that they would be pleased if the company conceded only a part of the requests.[111] That this statement accurately reflected the pacific spirit of the union is established by the fact that workers originally joined with white-collar employees in the same organization, and the clerks by no means included strikes in their arsenal of tactics. The union leaders were delighted when the recently appointed director, Godot, met with them and were encouraged by his ostensibly conciliatory approach. The director tested their goodwill by asking for secret data on the membership of the union, and the leaders gave it to him. Godot was astonished by their consummate naiveté, and the president of the Bourse du Travail (an umbrella organization of Parisian unions) had to issue a severe reprimand to the leaders for violating its rules. The union, then, was clearly not in the hands of militants or revolutionary ideologues. The inexperienced delegates even stumbled into a corporatist stance by promising to be advocates of the PGC before the municipal council in return for concessions.[112] Implicitly the leaders recognized a legitimate sphere of intervention, entailing compensations, while conceding control over the production process to management. Considering that the PGC was committed to spending more money on its personnel for political reasons, harmonious relations with the union were not out of the question.

Managers, however, never had any intention of negotiating with the union as a bona fide representative of its personnel. The union was not at all a part of the corporate program for social peace. In fact, the director's first response to the formation of a union was to consult with the legal experts about the minimum steps he could take while still adhering to the law of 1884.[113] Throughout 1892 Godot, who had his own program for

111. AP, V 8 O¹, no. 151, Chambre syndicale to director, December 3, 1891.
112. Ibid., no. 148, "Rapport sur la réunion du mercredi 11 novembre 1891"; clipping from *Le Temps*, December 31, 1891; report on union meeting of July 25, 1891; no. 150, union's executive commission to director, September 27, 1892. See below, chapter 8, for a fuller discussion of the union's orientation.
113. Ibid., no. 150, "Syndicats: Jurisprudence." The company did try to intimidate workers so they would not join the union, but the steps could not be too heavy-handed. See no. 148, "Procès-verbaux de la 4ᵉ audience donnée le 3 mars 1892."

industrial reform, feigned good intentions because he wanted union activists to bring favorable reports to the municipal council at this moment of intense negotiation over the gas monopoly. When discussions with the city collapsed at the end of the year, the director coldly informed union leaders that henceforth they could communicate with him only in writing. The pretense of collective bargaining ceased, and the municipal council became the intermediary through which the union and the company interacted. The director treated petitions from the leaders as if they came from the individuals who signed them and petitions from the union via the council as if they came from the aldermen.[114]

Faced with the unpleasant reality of industrial unrest, the PGC's managers became conservative reformers. As such, they were part of a wider movement. Pierre Sorlin has noted that "in the last decade of the century, and particularly between the municipal election of 1892 and the legislative election of 1898, the fear of socialism was a dominant characteristic of French political life."[115] Monarchists, Catholics, and conservative republicans rallied to the defense of private enterprise. The theorists of social defense called for private, paternalistic initiatives to win workers away from dangerous ideas. These leaders portrayed the workplace as a "natural" social unit, like the family. Emile Cheysson, a particularly influential spokesman because he was an engineer and a professor at the Ecole des Mines, stressed the special role his profession might play in forging social peace. Scorning "selfish" management that consulted only short-term, bottom-line interests, Cheysson counseled engineers to find ways to reconcile laborers to the industrial order through a reasonable, rational generosity.[116] He and other bourgeois reformers were responding to a moment of economic transition in French society and a crisis of the liberal order just as surely as the Radical solidarists, whose answer to the crisis was to give wage earners republican rights. The management of the PGC was well positioned to listen to the recommendations of the bourgeois reformers.

114. Ibid., no. 733, deliberations of June 8, 1893; no. 162, "Affaire Leroy." The company ultimately avoided defining the precise status of the union as a permanent institution by adopting the stance that the director was "always" prepared to listen to workers who had something to say to him. The pretense was that the workers were (or should be) unaffiliated individuals. See no. 150, "Projet de lettre, le directeur à Lajarrigue (n.d.)."

115. Pierre Sorlin, *Waldeck-Rousseau* (Paris, 1966), p. 358. Sorlin's insights have been amplified by Lebovics, *Alliance of Iron and Wheat*.

116. Emile Cheysson, *Le Rôle social de l'ingénieur* (Paris, 1897); Sanford Elwitt, *The Third Republic Defended: Bourgeois Reform in France, 1880–1914* (Baton Rouge, La., 1986).

The paternalistic rhetoric of conservative reform recommended an ordering of industrial relations in precisely the terms that the PGC's managers understood and accepted. The view that social peace depended on employers' goodwill and workers' passive acceptance of their superiors' responsible gestures inevitably made sense to them. There can be no doubt that certain executives of the company were well integrated into the reform movement. Godot was a personal friend of Cheysson.[117] The brother of the new chief of the factory division, Albert Gigot, was a founding member of the Musée social, the Comité de défense et de progrès social, and the Alliance d'hygiène sociale, all centers for disseminating reform projects.[118] Management could be expected to consider reform proposals in devising its response to the workers' challenge, such as they imagined it to be. Still, managers turned to industrial reform when they had to. No amount of admiration for theory could have made the engineers overcome their distaste for raising labor costs when they were not compelled to do so. Director Godot may have been something of an ideologue; his appointment was a display of good intentions at a crucial moment. The hard-headed Emile Camus, however, was still in charge (as "delegated board member") and could keep Cheyssonesque influences from getting out of hand. Under duress the PGC became a laboratory for social reform.

Industrial paternalists like Cheysson and Gigot had nothing to say about unions; they presumed that the proper policies would forestall their formation. Thus, the reform literature did not directly address the PGC's most immediate problem: how to make concessions to workers without strengthening the union's influence. Partly drawing on established corporate practice and partly yielding to the insistence of Radical aldermen, Godot and Camus devised a dual strategy. First, the company would woo laborers away from the union through responsible generosity, thereby winning the approval of aldermen as well. Second, the PGC would improve workers' pay without specifically yielding to any union demand. This policy, replete with risks, inaugurated nothing less than a battle between the union and the corporation for the hearts and minds of workers.

117. AP, V 8 O¹, no. 1294, Emile Cheysson to Director Godot, April 16, 1890. Cheysson addressed Godot as *mon cher ami*.
118. Sanford Elwitt, "Social Reform and Social Order in Late Nineteenth-Century France: The Musée Social and Its Friends," *French Historical Studies* 11 (1980): 443. Gigot was the author of *Les Assurances ouvrières et le socialisme d'Etat* (Paris, 1895). See also W. Tolman, *Que doit le patron à ses ouvriers en plus du salaire; suivi d'observations de MM. Levasseur, Gigot, Blondel, Delaire* (Paris, 1901). Gigot had served as *préfet de police* in Paris from 1877 to 1879 and was director of the Forges d'Alais in 1892.

The worker's union, at this point, represented mainly the various sorts of common laborers outside the distillation room—carters, coke handlers, lamplighters, greasemen, and navvies.[119] The long list of union demands contained primarily the specialized concerns of each of these groups. Underlying the detailed lists were four fundamental grievances.[120] First, the union pressed for the equalization of pay and hours among operating units and among men who did similar work. Second, it hoped to find some way to alleviate the petty tyranny inflicted on its members by foremen and other supervisors. Workers of nearly every occupational category complained about the surliness and capriciousness of their immediate supervisors. Leaders long had difficulty translating the grievances into specific demands because of their wariness about infringing on managerial prerogatives. Third, the unions asked for raises for almost all categories of laborers except the well-paid stokers. Demands were generally modest, in the range of twenty-five to fifty centimes a day. Fourth, the union representatives insisted on a minimum wage of five francs a day for all workers. The city of Paris had just passed such a provision for its laborers. According to data from the union, 1,256 of some 5,900 workers at the PGC still earned less than that figure.[121] This demand was the emotional centerpiece of collective bargaining as far as the union leadership and the rank and file were concerned. Certain aldermen also regarded the minimum wage as a test of management's seriousness about social peace.

For their part, the engineer-managers gambled that the rank and file were not attached to these positions or at least would be grateful to a firm that gave them other valuable benefits. Parsimonious as they had been before 1890, the executives were now ready to increase substantially their expenditures on labor to defeat the union and create some goodwill at the Hôtel de Ville. Their concessions intentionally differed from the union's demands, but the managers hoped they would address some of the basic discontents. Management was also perpetuating corporate tradition in disregarding the specific grievances articulated by workers, substituting their own preferences and adding moralizing elements to the concessions. Thus, laborers who asked for raises were instead given opportunities to do extra work for pay. Another alternative to a raise, pure and simple, was to increase the portion of workers in the higher "grades" on the pay scale,

---

119. Stokers had formed a union in 1890, but it had fallen apart. See below, chapter 8.
120. AP, V 8 O¹, no. 148, contains many lists of union demands.
121. Ibid., no. 626, "Etat numérique des ouvriers des usines gagnant un salaire inférieur à 5 francs." The number would have been far larger before 1890, for the company responded to the strike of that year with a general round of raises.

thereby expediting advancement.[122] The most ambitious and costly elements of the corporate program were the pension plan for manual laborers and the profit-sharing bonuses (see chapter 2). Prior to the new era of industrial relations, managers had denied that a regular retirement fund was feasible on the grounds that the manual work force was too unstable. The strategy of social defense and the struggle with the union suddenly made the reform viable. The profit-sharing plan had the attraction of moralizing workers while, presumably, keeping their minds off the five-franc minimum wage. By no means did the package of reforms represent a well-conceived plan for social defense. It was the product of a management that was on the defensive, subjected to multiple forces beyond its control and profoundly distraught by the predicament. Left to themselves, the engineers would surely have continued their frugal authoritarian paternalism.[123]

After promulgating the profit-sharing plan in November 1892, it was time for management to weigh its success in convincing workers that corporate beneficence was a surer path to improvements than union organization. Factory superintendents, ordered to study labor's response to the announced benefit, found that the union was winning the battle for support, at least in the short run. The superintendent of the Passy plant reported that half his laborers resentfully expressed their preference for the five-franc minimum wage, not the profit-sharing plan. At Landy wage earners told their boss that they would rather have five francs each day than wait all year for a 113-franc bonus. Gigot summarized the reports by arguing that the concessions had reinforced the popularity of the union. He also detected an evil cycle whereby one concession produced still more demands for others.[124] The company appeared to have blundered. The profit-sharing program was nearly three times more expensive than the minimum wage would have been but provided little satisfaction. Furthermore, the program would continue to disappoint workers because profits were not healthy in the 1890s. The bonus never attained the forty-three

---

122. Ibid., no. 1081, ordres de service nos. 340–369.
123. Recall that the company decided on the profit-sharing plan in the context of negotiations over the Sauton project. In particular, the agreement to put 1 percent (later 2 percent) of the profits aside for workers came in the context of discussions over reducing meter rental rates. The municipal council settled for a lower reduction in the rates when the company promised to bestow on workers the profit-sharing plan. See ibid., no. 154, Troost and Director Camus to president of municipal council, June 12, 1892.
124. Ibid., no. 148, "Répartition du 2 per cent," report of Gigot, June 13, 1893. The police confirmed the preference of the workers for a minimum wage. Préfecture, B/a 1424, report of November 24, 1892.

centimes a day that Godot initially promised. The supplement of thirty-eight centimes that workers received in 1893 fell to thirty-three in 1895 and to thirty in 1899.[125] Workers inevitably came to believe that they were sharing the problems, not the profits, of their firm.

Managers, unaccustomed to dealing with these sorts of issues and obviously uncomfortable in the role, miscalculated on two levels. Their long-standing disdain for what workers had on their minds led them to underestimate the emotional hold of the union's proposals.[126] More fundamentally flawed was the engineers' attempt to reduce enthusiasm for the union by granting major concessions *after* a strong organization was in place. Laborers would surely credit the union for the improvements. The corporate program of reform was not necessarily too little, but it was certainly too late.

In fact, there was not complete accord among managers on the strategies for dealing with organized labor. Aside from individual differences, there was an inevitable divergence of perspective between top and lower management. The director, fully aware of the expectatons of the public authorities and intent on prolonging the life of the firm, realized that open confrontation was dangerous. Production managers, however, in direct contact with workers and immediately threatened by the union, took a narrower view. They wished for a more aggressive policy of repression. The elderly Curry, the most senior superintendent, displayed a paranoia about organized labor from the first moment. He affirmed (in 1892) that leaders formed an "occult authority behind my back"; he asserted that they made threats with impunity; he described the union secretary as "doing whatever he wished" and treating Curry "as an equal." Biju-Duval, the manager of the Saint-Mandé plant, assumed that his duty was to "put the union delegates in their place" before they became too heady with power. The superintendents were unanimous in proclaiming that the union was the cause, not the result, of the workers' discontents and that industrial relations had been superbly harmonious before the disrupting organization emerged. Gigot, as head of the factory division, pleaded with

125. AP, V 8 O¹, no. 149, "Sommes nécessaires pour payer un salaire minimum de 5 francs"; no. 151, "Montant total des allocations de supplément de salaire"; no. 156, "Gratifications: personnel secondaire." The minimum wage would have cost about two hundred thousand francs a year to implement; the profit-sharing plan required in the range of six hundred thousand francs.
126. Rolande Trempé might explain the workers' preference in terms of how they conceptualized their wages. The minimum wage related to a view of pay as a means of subsistance. The laborers apparently did not think of their earnings as a share of the wealth they were producing. See Trempé, *Les Mineurs de Carmaux, 1848–1914*, 2 vols. (Paris, 1971), 1: 369–379.

Godot not to make any concessions on the grounds that they would only reflect well on the union. When the director discounted his advice, Gigot took the unusual step of bypassing sacred hierarchical channels, conducting an unsolicited survey of superintendents' views, and passing the results on to the director. Predictably, lower-level managers regretted the concessions and foresaw the victory of the union in the battle for workers' favor.[127] Exactly what positive steps superintendents would have had the company take was not a matter they considered. They disregarded proclamations of the municipal council in favor of workers, which so threatened hopes for a renewed charter. Perhaps they would have preferred from the start the demise of the PGC—along with their careers in the firm—to its continuance under existing circumstances. Ultimately lower managers did prove willing to sacrifice their careers to the cause of authoritarian paternalism, but in the early years of the union era top management still hoped for a less drastic solution.

· · ·

Events between the end of 1892 and 1899 seemed to vindicate the intransigence of production managers. Negotiations with the city collapsed, and membership in the union continued to grow. In the meantime, the PGC had burdened itself with much greater labor costs without having won the loyalty of its personnel. The company had to live with expensive, paternalistic policies that it would not have adopted spontaneously. It is no wonder the strategy of top management edged closer to the repressive recommendations of the production engineers.

The breakdown of bargaining with the city at the end of 1892 removed a powerful incentive for maintaining civil relations with the union. The director dropped the pretense of giving the delegates and their grievances a favorable hearing. Union leaders were forced to depend on the municipal council to communicate with the company. Throughout the mid-1890s the director continued to receive many petitions, copies of which had first been sent to the council. He would quickly dispose of the requests by explaining why they were out of the question. Labor's largest victory in the mid-1890s, the six hundred thousand francs allocated to improve wages and salaries in December 1896, arose because the city contributed half the sum and shamed the company into granting an equal amount.[128]

Having failed to win the hearts and minds of workers, top management

---

127. AP, V 8 O¹, no. 148, report of Cury, March 24, 1892; report of Gigot, December 30, 1891; report of Cury to Gigot, June 13, 1893; report of Biju-Duval to Gigot, June 13, 1893; no. 150, report of Cury to Gigot, June 5, 1893; report of Gigot to director, April 5, 1893.
128. See chapter 2.

now pursued a policy of containing the union's growth in any way that avoided open confrontation. Godot or Camus devised a strategy for ostensibly honoring the reform commitments that the company had already made while in practice undermining them. The strategy worked by taking advantage of the decentralized administration of the factory personnel and unleashing the festering antiunion sentiments of lower management and supervisors. Union leaders were to find that no one would take responsibility for blatant violations of concessions that they thought had become acquired rights.[129] Particularly frustrating to the syndicalists was the violation of promises concerning layoffs. The director had affirmed that layoffs, massive in this seasonal industry, would occur strictly according to seniority. Yet the delegates could point to case after case of open infractions.[130] The union also found itself powerless to stop other abuses—discriminatory firing practices, injustices in fining, intimidation, and demeaning gestures from supervisors. When union delegates complained to Godot, he feigned surprise and promised to look into the matter; but the complaint was lost in the hierarchical chain of command. Occasionally, Godot told the union officials that he was unable to make the superintendents obey his orders to stop the abuses; all he could do was urge the plant managers to abide by the agreements.[131]

The supervisors, for their part, excused the abuses by placing blame on foremen and other immediate supervisors. Following Godot's example, the plant managers affirmed their inability to control their underlings. Foremen too were profoundly antiunion, seeing the union as a challenge to their authority. Neither the superintendents nor the director were willing to take effective steps to curb their abuses. Indeed, management was pleased to take advantage of the foremen's hostility. The engineers did not

129. The PGC had actually used the policy earlier on the issue of foreign workers. Public pressure had forced the director to promise a reduction in the number of foreign laborers in 1885 (not long after the firm had accelerated its hiring of them). The director issued formal orders, but somehow nothing came of them. See AP, V 8 O[1], no. 1081, ordres de service, September 29, 1885, and June 23, 1892. Workers frequently accused their supervisors of favoring foreign over French wage earners.
130. Ibid., no. 150, report of Leroy to Gigot, August 11, 1893; letter of Chapelle to director, August 8, 1893; letter of Darène to director, June 14, 1894; no. 148, "Procès-verbaux de la 4e audience donnée le 3 mars 1893 aux délégués."
131. *Le Journal du gaz: Organe officiel de la chambre syndicale des travailleurs du gaz*, no. 83 (May 20, 1896): 1; no. 110 (July 5, 1897): 1; no. 112 (August 5, 1897): 1; no. 139 (September 20, 1898): 1; no. 133 (June 20, 1898): 2. The director was careful never to promise that rehiring would occur by seniority, leaving open the possibility of eliminating difficult workmen.

even pause to consider that the supervisors could be using their authority not in the company's interest but in their personal interest.[132]

The matter of decentralized authority and its abuses certainly separated the managers of the PGC from theorists of bourgeois reform. Emile Cheysson had pinpointed the foreman as a major source of industrial conflict. He argued eloquently that the foreman's arbitrary power must be curtailed and given to engineers, who, he believed, were much more capable of impartial and judicious decisions.[133] Cheysson's warnings about the abusive authority of supervisors proved to be prophetic for industrial relations within the PGC (see chapter 8). Yet gas managers did not intend to act on his recommendation. Their willingness to exploit the prejudices of foremen for the purposes of disciplining the labor force and of persecuting union members illustrated the permanent gulf that separated their authoritarian paternalism from Cheysson's conservative but humanitarian paternalism.

. . .

The sour yet stabilized relations between the company and the union were destined to deteriorate in 1898. The implicit position of lower managers, that the company might not be worth preserving if a strong union were a permanent feature of industrial relations, then gained weight among top managers. The darkening atmosphere was a result of shifts in the union's membership and goals. Up to the last year or so of the century, the union had not attracted the stokers. As long as it represented mainly the common laborers, the company could easily countenance facing it down if need be. Management's strategy was centered on public opinion and politics, not concerns about the union's power to disrupt production and force concessions.[134] This situation changed dramatically in the fall of 1898, however, when stokers began to join en masse. They brought a decided escalation of militancy; why they did so and how their joining was part of a wider revolt against industrial authority are points I shall discuss in due course. For the moment, we need to observe that the reorientation of union activity marked a dramatic heightening of tensions between labor and management.

The upsurge of militancy among the stokers engendered a renewed

132. For the problems that foremen and other immediate supervisors engendered, see chapter 8.
133. Cheysson, *Rôle social de l'ingénieur,* pp. 52–53.
134. AP, V 8 O[1], no. 148, report of Gigot, April 15, 1892. Gigot referred to the stokers as "the essential element" in determining the kind of threat the union would pose.

campaign among lower-level managers to convince the director that the moment for decisive action had arrived. They warned that instances of disobedience, disrespect, and "arrogance" were becoming commonplace in the factories. Euchène, the chief production engineer, felt compelled to call for a return to the tradition of "paternal discipline."[135] The superintendents could direct Godot's attention to prudent union leaders who for their own reasons were also alarmed. One of them spoke ominously, in February 1899, about "winds of revolution" and a "dangerous effervescence" in some production departments.[136] While Godot's concern about a situation getting out of hand grew, factory managers vowed to reassert their authority.

The seriousness of the struggle over authority as well as the desperation of the managers to reassert their domination over the labor force was demonstrated by a bizarre symbolic confrontation in November 1898. The occasion was the funeral of a foreman, Bouttier, who was reputed to have been a model of equity in his treatment of workers.[137] Union leaders wished to honor his memory by attending the last rites, offering a eulogy, and presenting a mortuary wreath. The widow gave her permission for the commemoration. The company, however, was intent on converting the funeral into a representational showdown with its adversary. Superintendent Hadamar (Bouttier's former boss) tried to get the widow to withdraw her approval for the union's presence. Having failed on that point, he intimidated her into arranging the procession so that the company's delegation (he and Euchène) would walk directly behind the bereaved family while the union members would be at the rear. Without his insistence on this protocol, Hadamar noted, "our dignity would surely have suffered." The superintendent made certain as well that the PGC's wreath preceded all others. Bouttier's last rites were, according to Hadamar's report, a brilliant triumph for the corporation over the union. His problem was to convert symbolic ascendency into reality.

Instead, Hadamar's worst fears were confirmed in March 1899, when a wildcat strike broke out at the Clichy plant, which he managed. On the urging of a foreman, Hadamar had fired two workers; the stokers, perceiving the dismissal as unjust, walked out of the plant. The production managers were unanimous in urging firm resistance, but Director Godot did not have the same freedom of action that he had had over Bouttier's

---

135. Ibid., no. 159, "Grèves de mars et août 1899."
136. *Journal du gaz*, no. 148 (February 5, 1899): 1.
137. For this revealing incident, see AP, V 8 O^1, no. 159, report of Hadamar to Euchène, November 16, 1898.

widow. A new and urgent round of negotiations with the city over the gas monopoly was at hand, and the company faced the alternatives of winning a longer charter or preparing for its liquidation. The director was not willing at this crucial moment to alienate the councilmen of the left by perpetuating labor agitation, so he admitted that mistakes had been made and rehired the wronged workers. Still worse, from the superintendents' point of view, he allowed all the strikers to return to their jobs. Lower management was appalled by the concession. After every other strike production managers had at least been able to reassert their authority by dismissing strikers. Hadamar and his colleagues predicted a general collapse of order; indeed, they declared that such a breakdown was already well advanced. Their reports described a war of nerves between management and workers.[138] Plant managers were preparing for a general strike, which they expected at any time. Apparently, they managed to convince Godot that the situation was dire, for he asked the minister of the interior to prepare for the army to intervene in case of a strike. The director sent blueprints of the factories to the prefect and requested permission to use soldiers as laborers if need be.[139] Just a few months earlier, a series of strikes against managerial authority had erupted in the Parisian machine-building industry. Now, the managers of the PGC, from top to bottom, saw themselves as key combatants in the wider struggle to reassert their prerogatives.[140]

The crisis for which engineers had been preparing came in August 1899. In a troubled and poorly organized move, stokers and some common laborers at several gas plants went on strike again. The demand for an eight-hour day at considerably reduced pay was ill conceived and divided workers more than it united them. To make matters worse, the union treasurer suddenly absconded with the strike funds and dealt a mortal blow to laborers' morale. A well-prepared management was easily able to find scabs and crush the walkout. This time the strikers were not rehired, despite intense pressure from the municipal council and from the press. The union, for the moment, lay in ruins.

Did management foment the strike and use it to crush its adversary? Journalists and politicians soon made that accusation. They did so on the grounds of a secret meeting between a manager and union leaders just prior to the walkout. The motive they attributed to the company was an

138. Ibid., "Grève, mars 1899."
139. Ibid., no. 160, Director Godot to prefect, July 4, 1899.
140. On the wider context in which the gas strike of 1899 took place, see Lenard R. Berlanstein, *The Working People of Paris, 1871–1914* (Baltimore, 1984), chap. 5.

attempt to push the city into renewing the gas monopoly.[141] The firm easily demonstrated that such evidence and reasoning were unconvincing. Yet the charge was not necessarily baseless. Journalists may have been correct, but for reasons they did not suspect. There is no conclusive evidence of the company plotting to create a strike, and one could certainly understand events without postulating such action. Nonetheless, it is entirely plausible that certain managers did consciously shape the circumstances that led to the strike and hoped it would materialize. They convinced Godot that a strike was necessary or inevitable.

Management's manipulation of the issue of the eight-hour day during the tense summer of 1899 invites suspicion of their motivations. Though the union's demand for eight hours with two charges of coal a day (instead of twelve hours with three charges) had been long-standing, leaders were not pushing the matter that summer. Other issues had come to the fore. It was the company that suddenly proposed to initiate a companywide experiment (itself an irregularity since trials had always occurred on a limited scale) with the shorter day. Moreover, the PGC offered workers a pay formula that not only reduced earnings by a third (to compensate for the lighter work load) but was complicated and sure to sow confusion. The superintendents reported that eight hours was an excellent issue with which to confound stokers, raise dissension between union leaders and members, and bring the spirit of revolt to a head.[142] Gigot, probably the architect of the strategy, noted in a report at the end of July that a strike could easily develop from the experiment because workers would not accept so large a reduction in pay. Without opposing the experiment for that reason, he predicted that there would be angry demands for an alteration in the pay scale and insisted that the company must resist with absolute firmness. Indeed, he ended the report on a note of hopeful tension: "Discipline has been destroyed in all the factories; we must *at all costs* [italics Gigot's] reestablish it. We must not hesitate. The continuation of the present situation is not possible. The occasion is excellent to return to our former authority."[143] Two days later, Godot, writing from his vacation home in Brittany, echoed Gigot's view: "We must *at all costs* [italics Godot's] finish with the indiscipline that reigns in the factories, and I find the moment opportune. . . . We can take the chance."[144] At the very moment

141. AP, V 8 O¹, no. 159, Godot to Monsieur Defrance, October 19, 1899; *Journal du gaz*, no. 162 (September 5, 1899): 1.
142. AP, V 8 O¹, no. 159, report of Gigot to director, August 2, 1899; *Journal du gaz*, no. 148 (February 5, 1899): 2.
143. AP, V 8 O¹, no. 151, "Essai de 8 heures (25 juillet 1899)."
144. Ibid., no. 160, Godot to Gigot, July 27, 1899.

these memoranda were circulating within the firm, a union leader warned that foremen were doing their best to stir up the laborers.[145] Thus the evidence establishes at the very least that executives implemented the experimental eight-hour day knowing that it could easily produce a strike and hoping that it would. The engineers were prepared to "take the chance." They apparently believed that such a strike would provide an opportunity to crush the union and return to an earlier mode of industrial relations.

Even if management did not intentionally foment the strike, their use of it to crush the union—knowing as they did the consequences—is most significant. After seven years of cold war with the organization, the engineers decided to abandon outward compliance with public opinion. They must have known that their refusal to rehire strikers put an end to any hope for a renewal of the charter in the prevailing political situation. Immediately after the strike was lost, newspapers like the *Petite République* called for rescinding the PGC's charter at once.[146] Councilmen of the left regarded the company's behavior as the final outrage in a long line of impermissible acts. Crushing the strikers negated the impact of all the financial sacrifices the firm had made up to 1899. As individuals, the engineers also sacrificed the security of their careers after 1905, no doubt a weighty concern for them. Apparently, though, the temporary recovery of industrial discipline was worth the price. There is no hint that engineers later regretted their hard line. They certainly did not soften it between the end of the strike and the disappearance of the PGC (in 1907) despite constant pressure to rehire the strikers. Seven years after the event, Euchène (now chief of the factory division of a PGC that was about to be liquidated) still described the strike in the most traumatic terms and still refused to rehire the "agitators" he had excluded from the plant in 1899.[147]

The Politics of Mechanization

Corporate policies regarding the substitution of capital for labor amplify management's perspective on industrial relations.[148] In particular, an inci-

145. *Journal du gaz*, no. 159 (July 20, 1899): 2.
146. For a sample of public opinion, see AP, V 8 O¹, no. 159, "Grèves de 1899—articles de journaux"; no. 160, *La Petite République*, August 16, 1899. On the policy of refusing to rehire strikers, see AP, V 8 O¹, no. 160, "Grèves: Août 1899." Godot even refused to receive two aldermen who wished to discuss the issue. No. 160, Lucipia to Godot, January 19, 1900.
147. Ibid., no. 150, "Affaire Plantin."
148. For a general study of capital investments in gas plants, see Derek Matthews, "The Technological Transformation of the Late Nineteenth-Century Gas Indus-

dent that occurred in 1881 reveals a great deal about how the PGC's officers made technological decisions and what sorts of results were paramount for them. Semiskilled workers in the retort-making section of the company's brickyards took advantage of the tight labor market by threatening to strike if they did not receive a raise of fifty centimes a day. Engineer Audouin castigated himself for not having installed retort-making machinery when labor agitation had surfaced three years earlier; the equipment was readily available and had been for some time. Audouin had estimated in 1878 a savings of seventeen thousand to eighteen thousand francs a year on labor, more than enough to justify the investment. This time the manager vowed not to miss the opportunity, even if the strike failed to materialize. He noted that economic considerations were only "secondary" in engendering his resolve. What made mechanization attractive was that "the use of this equipment would have the great advantage of assuring the almost absolute independence of the company over its qualified [spécial] labor." [149] Audouin's comportment in this incident suggests that the company was a laggard in adopting labor-saving technology. It also shows that economic rationality was not the central consideration. Managers turned to mechanization as a *defensive* measure to turn back challenges to its ascendancy over the personnel.

Initially, the gas industry was not heavily mechanized. Production depended on the flow of gases, not on the movement of mechanical parts. In 1878 the PGC required only eleven hundred horsepower to operate its machines. [150] As the range of new tools and devices grew, engineers kept abreast of them on an experimental basis but introduced them into the production process only belatedly and only when they believed that there was little choice. In effect, the managers made labor, not market considerations, the final arbiter of decisions on mechanization. They provide corroborative evidence for Harry Braverman's justly controversial thesis that class conflict determines the level of technology. [151]

try," *Journal of Economic History* 47 (1987): 967–980. The conclusions, based on inferences, do not specifically examine how decisions were made, nor does the author consider the ties between industrial relations and technological change.
149. AP, V 8 O¹, no. 1067, "Briqueterie de la Villette (11 juin 1881)."
150. Ibid., no. 716, report of Arson, July 15, 1877.
151. Harry Braverman, *Labor and Monopoly Capitalism: The Degradation of Work in the Twentieth Century* (New York, 1974). Braverman's provocative thesis has attracted much commentary. Among the most telling are Richard Price, "Theories of Labor Process Formation," *Journal of Social History* 18 (1984): 91–107, and Craig Littler, *The Development of the Labor Process in Capitalist Societies* (London, 1982). In spite of the objections that have been raised to the Brav-

When the ministerial commission of 1890, charged with reviewing the PGC's technological situation, characterized the company's policies as cautious but generally sound, the members did not seem to realize how antiquated were the methods for loading coal into retorts. This operation was done entirely by stokers with shovels and was a "skilled" operation. Yet gas companies all over Europe had long ago introduced a simple tool, the scoop (*cuillère*), into stoking to curtail labor shortages and the corresponding market power that hand shoveling had given to workers. Though the scoop did not eliminate the need for uncommon strength and endurance, it did make filling the retort a good deal easier. Workers who could load the scoop and empty it into a retort were far more numerous and easier to train than those who could propel coal into the retorts with a shovel. Perhaps the ministerial commission did not note the PGC's backwardness because elsewhere the scoop had become so much a part of accepted operations that the members did not even inquire about its use.[152]

Remarkably, the PGC put off introducing the scoop into its furnace rooms until 1890—no less than a quarter century after its counterpart in London. Engineers in Paris had long known about the tool and its advantages. Servier, the assistant factory chief in the 1860s, had inspected its use during a trip to London. No later than 1866, plant superintendents had experimented with it but had taken no further steps.[153] The reason for retaining shovel work, despite the recognized way it limited the labor pool, was largely, but not entirely, a matter of inertia. All things being equal (which they were not), shoveling had some production advantages over the scoop. The latter tool required some minor alterations in the arrangement of the distillation rooms; it also wore down the walls of retorts so that they had to be replaced more frequently. Moreover, a proficient stoker could pack a retort more quickly and tightly with 150 kilograms of coal instead of 135 kilograms.[154] Thus, shoveling fit into the efficient hot-roasting method somewhat better than the scoop. Ultimately, the reliance on stokers' shovels for so long reflected the PGC's distinctive operational

---

erman thesis, this study suggests that it may hold in a general sense, at least for the authoritarian paternalists I have been describing.

152. *Compte rendu des travaux de la commission nommée . . . le 31 janvier 1890,* pp. 36–148. On the use of the scoop in Britain in the 1870s, see Eric Hobsbawm, "British Gas-Workers, 1873–1914," in *Laboring Men: Studies in the History of Labor* (London, 1964), pp. 158–178.

153. AP, V 8 O¹, no. 709, report of Servier to director, May 7, 1860; no. 671, deliberations of May 9, 1866.

154. Ibid., no. 1068, report of Gigot to Arson, April 11, 1869.

situation. Since gas in Paris was expensive and the firm did not hasten to expand its clientele, demand grew steadily but not massively. This slow growth meant that the PGC had moments of labor shortage but not the chronic and desperate dearth of workers that might have made new production methods essential.[155] Furthermore, the stokers, basically seasonal migrants, had so far remained unorganized and made only wage demands. Such demands might have displeased the engineers, but they did not frighten them, especially because productivity increases often covered the raises. Management wrung its hands over a wage increase, but raises did not spur it to action. Even when unit labor costs turned upward around 1876, the company was not ready for change, though it paid a price for the inertia. In 1860 stokers' wages in London had been about a third higher than those in Paris; by 1890 the situation was reversed.[156]

Not high wages but rather the sense that management was about to lose the ability to dominate stokers finally brought an end to shoveling. In 1890 the stokers formed a union and launched a strike with a coherent set of demands. None of the stokers' earlier actions had been so well organized. The PGC, caught off guard, had to make concessions and recognize that a new era of industrial relations was at hand. This experience converted management's complacency into frenzied action: production managers achieved in a few weeks what they had not attempted in the previous twenty-five years. Scoops became a part of daily operations, and the change happened smoothly, without resistance from the stokers. Gigot, echoing Audouin nine years earlier, stated that the purpose of the change was "to assure production, not to economize."[157]

The lag between the general use of a stoking machine, the next major laborsaving innovation, and the PGC's adoption of it was considerably shorter.[158] The reason for the accelerating pace of change was the powerful

155. Pressures generated by demand probably explain why the municipal gas works of Brussels, which charged much lower rates and had made efforts to expand the clientele, was so far ahead of the PGC in mechanization. See ibid., no. 1520, "Voyage en Belgique (décembre 1892)." Engineers Euchène and Louvet noted, with some surprise, that despite the low wages paid to workers, Belgian managers were aggressive in replacing manual labor with machinery.
156. Ibid., no. 709, report of Servier to director, May 7, 1860; no. 1520, "Rapport de Monsieur Euchène: Mission en Angleterre du mois de mai 1893." The comparison is a delicate one, for patterns of stoking were rather different in the two companies, as Euchène's report makes clear. English stokers had just won the eight-hour day in 1889, but they worked more intensively than Parisian stokers.
157. Ibid., no. 148, report of Gigot, December 16, 1890.
158. There were technological advances in charging between the scoop and the mechanical charger, among them vertical and inclined retorts. They will not be discussed here because they did not play much of a role at the PGC. Arson exam-

threat of labor independence that emerged in the last decade of the century. Without yet having introduced the rudimentary scoop, the PGC's engineers had shown sporadic interest in the far more sophisticated stoking machine. This apparatus had the potential for eliminating skilled laborers entirely. The company, so hesitant in the application of innovations, was in fact at the forefront of research on a machine. By 1877 its engineers had an operational, if unperfected, stoking machine in the laboratory. The firm even took out a patent on one version.[159] Had the PGC wished to pursue its breakthrough, the apparatus would have come just in time to stave off rapidly rising labor costs.

Though outside experts spoke of labor savings of 50 percent resulting from stoking machines, managers of the PGC expressed no interest in that aspect of the innovation in their reports. They viewed the machine, as Gigot did the scoop, as a means to discipline labor. In the absence of a permanent threat to their authority, the engineers did not hasten to use the machine. In addition, they worried about the reliability and durability of the apparatus under the difficult operating conditions in the distillation rooms: burly stokers might endure the intense heat and coal dust, but mechanical parts might not. These concerns, coupled with the lack of anxiety over labor up to 1890, postponed the application of the stoking machine.[160]

Just as the strike of 1890 had promoted the use of the scoop, the strike of 1899, compelling managers to confront a breakdown of authority, decided them on mechanization at all costs. The "spirit of revolt" pushed aside their qualms about the stoking machine's reliability and seemed to leave them no choice but to rush it into use. In little more than a year after the strike, the stoking machine moved from the laboratory into the La Villette factory. The cataclysm of 1899 broke not only the managers' technological prudence but also their caution about capital expenditures. The

---

ined the innovations and sometimes even arranged for limited experiments with them but did not apply them. See ibid., no. 711, "Rapport no. 39. Examen du projet des fours à cornues verticales"; no. 1062, "Substitution des cornues verticales (janvier 1876)."

159. Ibid., no. 779, "Chargement mécanique des cornues (13 mars 1877)" (fol. 254); no. 678, deliberations of September 5, 1877. On the benefits and disadvantages of the stoking machine, see C. E. Brackenbury, *Modern Methods of Saving Labor in Gasworks* (London, 1900).

160. AP, V 8 O¹, no. 1520, "Voyage en Angleterre." Engineer Euchène was quite aware that labor costs were a good deal higher in his company than in the British ones, where stoking machines were used (1:35–43). Yet he did not show much interest in the machinery for that reason.

company spent nearly half a million francs on the mechanization of stoking in 1902 and 1903.[161]

The timing of the investment was peculiar and raises pointed questions about the motivations of management. It came when the future of the PGC was hardly assured. Management planned the capital expenditure during the negotiations over the Chamon project with the Nationalist deputies. It executed the plans as the agreement faced an uncertain, and ultimately hostile, reception before Parliament. Thus, the decision to install stoking machines must be seen as a far more precipitous and emotional move than was customary for these cautious engineers. Mechanization was, arguably, a form of revenge or at least a symbolic assertion of mastery that engineers used against the stokers. In any case, the application of laborsaving innovations at that precarious moment was hardly a business decision pure and simple.[162]

The PGC's policies of technological brinksmanship clarify the social and psychological dimensions of labor management. Apparently, the engineers found wage concessions morally painful but not intolerable. What bothered them about the workers' quest for higher pay was not so much the cost to the firm as the challenge to hierarchical authority and to their right to calculate the appropriate compensation for their subordinates. Indeed, in some ways the officers of the PGC proved less sensitive to bottom-line considerations regarding labor than their counterparts in other European capitals, as the divergent policies on the scoop demonstrate. Though Parisian engineers grudgingly accepted the need to spend more on workers, they refused to concede any degree of "independence." Perhaps authoritarian paternalists were incapable of making decisions about laborsaving machinery on economic grounds alone. They focused on power relations inherent in technologies and gave more priority to mastery over the shop floor than to extra profits.

• • •

Reinhard Bendix reminds us of the broader significance of managerial policy toward labor. He notes that it reflects "the terms on which a society undergoing industrialization will incorporate its newly recruited indus-

---

161. For a description of the charging machine that the PGC developed and eventually licensed for use abroad, see H. Laurain, "Le Chargement des cornues à gaz par le chargeur Brouwer," *Compte rendu du trentième congrès de la Société technique de l'industrie du gaz* (1903), pp. 137–150. Management also turned its attention to the mechanization of another of the stokers' functions, the extinction of coke. See AP, V 8 O¹, no. 736, deliberations of December 26, 1902.

162. The board of directors awarded hefty bonuses to the engineers who moved the stoking machinery so swiftly from the laboratory into production. AP, V 8 O¹, no. 699, deliberations of July 7, 1904.

trial workers into the social and political community of the nation."[163] That insight has disconcerting implications as far as the PGC and nineteenth-century France are concerned. Management hoped to consign its labor force to little more than complete subjugation, even though it could easily have afforded to be quite generous. The engineers resented the market forces that gave workers higher nominal wages. Though they were willing to spend more on the personnel when there were excellent political reasons for doing so, they drew the line at allowing workers to seek some control over their work. The managers, secure in their superior intellect and their own devotion to duty, could not comprehend workers' wishes to escape from their arbitrary authority. Ultimately, moral considerations—and perhaps a spirit of vindictiveness—drove labor policies at the PGC. The situation was all the more problematical in that the last decade of the century inaugurated a brief era of democratic and republican extension of rights. The balance of political forces shifted just enough to give the common people some grounds for protesting their subordination and some hope for a redress of grievances. Managers tried to come to terms with the shift, but entirely on their own grounds. Their comportment during the strike of 1899 and its aftermath illustrates the depth of their self-destructive frustration that authoritarian paternalism could not prevail under the Radical Republic. The engineers sacrificed much, including the security of their careers, to defend that principle.

In the short run that defense was costly for the engineers. By 1910, however, they might well have claimed vindication. Just as they had given up on a strategy of concessions for fear that the situation had gone too far, so too did large sections of the political elite, only a few years after the PGC disappeared. Did not the crushing of the 1899 strike foreshadow the energetic repression of labor unrest by Georges Clemenceau and Aristide Briand?[164] The managers of the PGC had always been, and remained, on the forefront of the defense of hierarchical authority.

Conclusion

The business policies of the PGC were not of one cloth. Aggressive on small matters, management was usually hesitant on core business concerns. Executives were effective at cutting costs, but the endless search for savings on fuel, for example, was more intense than the concern to cut labor costs to the bone. The managers were impressive in exploiting mo-

163. Reinhard Bendix, *Work and Authority in Industry* (Berkeley and Los Angeles, 1974), p. 441.
164. Jacques Julliard, *Clemenceau, briseur de grèves* (Paris, 1965).

nopolistic markets for by-products but fell down on doing so for gas. In the end, the decision makers were selective about the market factors to which they responded. The PGC reinforces the impression of French business as conservative, cautious, and risk-avoiding—and not just because the firm functioned with a comfortable monopoly. Management made adjustments to market forces when it had to, but it did so timidly. It treated mass marketing, even though it entailed relatively few risks and promised high returns, as a source of problems, not of opportunities.

The special value of studying the PGC resides in the opportunity to observe the direction that an emerging elite of salaried managers imparted to enterprise. The outstanding point is how little the new category of businessmen innovated in terms of style of leadership and guiding assumptions, although the elite was closer in background and inspiration to high civil servants than to the traditional *patronat*. Years of rigorous mental training did not help engineer-managers clarify their own uncertainty about market forces. On the one hand, they regarded the pursuit of self-interest as the bedrock of human motivation. That is why they made profit-sharing bonuses so important a part of the compensation package and insisted (as we shall see) on promoting subordinates on the basis of merit alone. On the other hand, they rejected the legitimacy of market forces in setting wages and commodity prices. Managers did nothing to modernize a traditional ambivalence that pervaded French society about the morality of the marketplace.[165]

The attitude of salaried managers toward corporate assets was most certainly proprietary. They easily put behind them the ethos of state service when they joined a private firm. No duty surpassed that of making money for stockholders, and they did not stop short of morally dubious activities in pursuit of the goal. Thus, the rise of a new type of business management did not create a different sort of agenda for French enterprise.

The decision makers at the PGC threw away a chance to innovate in industrial relations even though that opportunity could have been rather painless. Their objectives were those of the patriarchical industrialist, to preserve autocratic paternalism.[166] The engineers' decisions on laborsav-

---

165. It was not simply the case that management rejected market forces as the mechanism for setting the prices that the company charged. Inflation of the prices that suppliers charged the PGC engendered in managers a conspiratorial mentality. Only partially did they conceive of the economy as subject to impersonal forces. See AP, V 8 O¹, no. 845, report of Le Maire to director, February 24, 1873.

166. On traditional mill owners, see Jean Lambert-Dansette, *Origines et évolution d'une bourgeoisie: Quelques familles du patronat textile de Lille-Armentières*

ing machinery showed them to be authoritarian paternalists first and calculating businessmen second. They made a mockery of Emile Cheysson's hope that engineers could be impartial and humane experts mediating between capital and labor. No more than the dominating factory owner were the salaried managers capable of understanding the workers' situation.

In all these ways salaried managers at the PGC left business practices and hierarchical relations more or less as they found them. They administered the PGC through a distinctive cultural filter that they shared with the traditional *patronat*. Their presuppositions often proved problematical. Had management responded mechanically to impersonal market forces or simply pursued pragmatic political calculations, the history of the PGC might have been different—and longer. Their presuppositions proved equally unhelpful in dealing with another subordinate group created by economic development, the white-collar employees.

(1789–1914) (Lille, 1954); David Landes, "French Business and the Businessman: A Social and Cultural Analysis," in *Modern France*, ed. E. M. Earle (Princeton, 1951), pp. 334–353.

PART THREE

THE EMPLOYEES' COMPANY

FIVE

The Clerks at Work

Along with a cadre of managers, supervising technicians, and manual laborers, the PGC found it necessary to create a considerable body of employees. The term *employé* came into common usage in the first half of the century, forcing its way into the company of *commis* and *fonctionnaire*. Its emergence denoted the creation of another new socioeconomic category, one that the case of the PGC offers an opportunity to explore. Within the company's lifetime, white-collar workers of private firms ceased being a novelty and became a source of social concern. Reformers earnestly discussed the "employee question" at the dawn of the twentieth century.[1] The discourse denoted a rising group consciousness and a deepening sense of grievance. By no means did these developments bypass the offices of the PGC. There, as well as in many other bureaucracies, the stirring entailed evolving patterns of work, rewards, and managerial authority.

The Evolution of Clerical Work

The term *employee* brings to mind a hoard of clerks hunched over their ledgers. The gas company did have many such workers among its personnel, but the label needs to be understood in a broader sense. To be an employee was not precisely a matter of doing a specific form of work;

1. A. J. M. Artaud, *La Question de l'employé en France* (Paris, 1909); Auguste Besse, *L'Employé du commerce et de l'industrie* (Lyons, 1901); Gaston Cadoux, *Les Salaires et les conditions du travail des ouvriers et des employés des entreprises municipales de Paris* (The Hague, 1911); Ministère du commerce, Office du travail, *Seconde enquête sur le placement des employés, des ouvriers, et des domestiques* (Paris, 1901).

rather, it meant having a particular relationship to the firm. The company had a permanent commitment to its employees and would dismiss them only for serious derogation of duty. Borrowing from the language of the military, the firm gave its employees a "commission," which offered a permanent career within the firm. The chief executive of the PGC may have kept his distance from factory workers, but until circumstances rendered the practice unwieldy, he held a personal interview with each candidate for a post as an employee. The interview underscored the status of the clerk as a part of the managerial apparatus.[2] Executives usually referred to employees as "agents" of the company. The PGC expanded its commissioned personnel as fast as its manual labor force, with just under a sevenfold increase during the life of the firm (figure 10). That legendary bureaucracy, the French state, had about twenty-nine hundred employees in its ministries around the time of the Franco-Prussian War.[3] This was the corps that, according to Jules Simon, ran the nation while the deputies debated. The PGC already had half as many agents and began to surpass the ministries by the end of the century.

Bookkeepers were a significant portion of the new sort of labor force but by no means all of it. The PGC had four types of agents: the clerical workers proper, wielding pen and paper; uniformed agents, who worked outside the office; technical personnel, who evaluated and supervised equipment and capital additions; and manual laborers, whose supervisory role was thought important enough for the company to try to bind them in a special way to the firm.[4] The first group constituted about half of the commissionable employees (898 of 1,915 in 1884). They were divided into some thirty distinct units (*bureaux* or *sections*). Their official titles, displaying much variety, included accountant (*comptable*), secretary (*commis*), and especially bookkeeper (*employé à l'écriture*). Outside the offices were three large and increasingly vocal groups of uniformed, active (as opposed to sedentary) agents. The corps of meter readers (*contrôleurs de compteur*) numbered 332 by 1892. Bill collectors (*garçons de recette*) comprised a hybrid group that did not enjoy the full dignities of employee status. As the French name implies, they were generally young men, often

2. AP, V 8 O^1, no. 666, deliberations of August 17, 1858. The directive was never formally rescinded. See chapter 4 for a discussion of the director's aloofness from factory laborers.
3. Guy Thuillier, *La Vie quotidienne dans les ministères au XIXe siècle* (Paris, 1976), p. 9.
4. The corporate archives include four rather complete organizational charts of the personnel spanning the life of the firm. For 1858, AP, V 8 O^1, no. 665 (fols. 500–514); for 1884, no. 153, "Personnel"; for 1893, no. 154; for 1902, no. 162, "Assimilation."

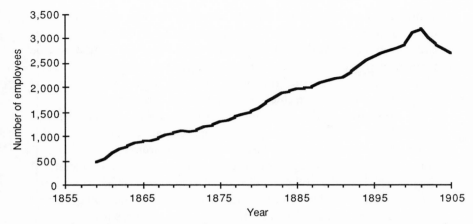

Fig. 10. Number of White-Collar Employees at the PGC. From AP, V 8 O[1], no. 1294, "Groupe de l'Economie sociale."

recruited among the office boys, who were expected to leave their jobs as they matured.[5] The responsibilities of the lighting inspectors, who numbered 184 in 1884, had many facets. Stationed in neighborhood offices (called lighting sections), they served as liaisons of first resort between the customers and the company. As such, they saw to it that customers had the proper paperwork, collected deposits, received complaints, and initiated service orders. Furthermore, they were in charge of street lighting, supervising the lamplighters and making rounds at the hour when the lights were extinguished. None of the active, uniformed agents could work bankers' hours. Their schedules essentially were task-oriented, and Sunday labor was part of the routine until they successfully prevailed on the municipal council to end it in the 1890s.[6]

The production and distribution of gas created the need for technical personnel. Men with know-how in fitting, plumbing, or construction inspected the thousands of kilometers of gas main owned by the company. They also oversaw the installation of new lines when private contractors did the actual work. The granting of employee status to factory foremen (*contre-maîtres*) was a measure calculated to induce greater loyalty. Man-

5. Ibid., no. 753, "Bureau des recettes," report of July 6, 1871. The PGC did not wish to consider the bill collectors full employees, partly because they received tips from the customers as a portion of their compensation and thus were beholden to a public beyond the firm.
6. Ibid., no. 148, "Eclairage—Personnel"; no. 153, "Revendications des contrôleurs de compteurs." A directive of 1864 ordered inspectors to keep an eye on the coke deliverymen as they made their rounds. See no. 1081, ordre de service no. 192.

agement had initially treated them as superior wage earners, but the foremen took advantage of an intense labor shortage in 1867 to demand better pay. The response of the company (fitting a pattern that should now be familiar) was to commission them and disregard the wage demand.[7] As we have seen, the PGC pursued the same strategy in 1892, when it feared the involvement of coke team chiefs in the trade union movement.

An influential model describing the degradation of clerical work was first elaborated by German social thinkers anxious about the explosive growth of the service sector in their country. They wondered whether economic change was creating a new sort of middle class or a new proletariat.[8] Their analysis of the proletarianization of employees has become a standard approach for British and American scholars.[9] The question of clerical work has received much less attention for France, perhaps because enterprises tended to be smaller and because other groups were more vocal.[10] Since fin-de-siècle France did witness the emergence of an "employee question," the proletarianization model is well worth exploring.

According to the model, a clerical career had been a path to independence before the industrial era. Like the artisan, the preindustrial clerk did a whole range of administrative activities so that he was ready either to strike out on his own, become a partner in the master's firm, or take over the family business. The expansion of large-scale organizations presumably altered the situation. A clear-cut distinction between managers and clerks arose; office work became just as subdivided as the handicrafts.[11] The employee spent his (and increasingly her) life doing one task, from which there was no escape. The job was no longer a career and certainly

7. Ibid., no. 672, deliberations of December 23, 1867; no. 767, "Proposition concernant le service des conduites montantes (1 mai 1873)"; no. 773, "Service mécanique," report of April 20, 1867; no. 780, "Personnel—Service mécanique."
8. Fritz Croner, Soziologie der Angestellten (Berlin, 1962); Jürgen Kocka, Die Angestellten in der deutschen Geschichte, 1850–1900 (Göttingen, 1981).
9. David Lockwood, The Blackcoated Worker: A Study of Class Consciousness (London, 1958); Margery Davies, Woman's Place Is at the Typewriter: Office Work and Office Workers, 1870–1920 (Philadelphia, 1982); Jürgen Kocka, White Collar Workers in America, 1890–1940 (London, 1980). For an up-to-date bibliography and nuanced discussion of the issue, see Heinz-Gerhard Haupt and Geoffrey Crossick, eds., Shopkeepers and Master Artisans in Nineteenth-Century Europe (London, 1984).
10. Historians of France have paid far more attention to salesclerks. See Michael Miller, The Bon Marché: Bourgeois Culture and the Department Store, 1896–1920 (Princeton, 1981); Theresa McBride, "A Woman's World: Department Stores and the Evolution of Women's Employment, 1870–1920," French Historical Studies 10 (1978): 664–683; Claudie Lesselier, "Employées de grands magasins à Paris avant 1914," Le Mouvement social, no. 105 (1978): 109–126.
11. On the handicrafts, see Lenard R. Berlanstein, The Working People of Paris, 1871–1914 (Baltimore, 1984), pp. 74–92.

not preparation for an independent future. Employers could easily enforce a tight discipline because they could train new people to do specialized tasks in a matter of weeks. In short, the employee had become a proletarian of the office. Of course, scholars have been careful to distinguish between objective and subjective aspects of proletarianization. The degradation of work might have led employees to support leftist internationalism, or status anxiety and the politics of resentment could have pushed them into the reactionary camp. The indeterminacy of the clerks' reaction to new work prospects makes the model all the more interesting to explore empirically, especially in view of the burgeoning of mass, extremist parties in fin-de-siècle Paris. But first we must ask to what extent the degradation of clerical work actually occurred.

The PGC may have hired a small army of employees, more than any other manufacturing firm in Paris, but that army did not, on the whole, fit the image of a vast, undifferentiated, routinized hoard of bookkeepers. The model comes closest to being accurate in the largest clerical department, customer accounts. There clerks calculated bills from figures the meter readers supplied and posted payments. The department contained 14 percent of the employees (in 1884), and they were divided into two distinct bureaus, billing (*comptes courants*) and payments (*recettes*). The routinized activities of adding figures, verifying them, completing forms, filing, and reconciling ledger sheets filled the work time of the clerks.[12] With the democratization of gas use at the end of the century, these bureaus necessarily expanded. The customer accounts department, at its largest, had just under six hundred employees, 18 percent of the tenured personnel.

No other concentration of bookkeepers was as large. The rest of the clerks worked in relatively small units: the office of the machinery department had a staff of eight, the legal department twelve, and the central factory bureau twenty-three.[13] Tasks in these units were not subdivided or specialized. Rising to the post of assistant bureau head (*sous-chef*), which usually went to the clerk with the most seniority, was not an unreasonable expectation. Even in the customer accounts department there was a sense of career hierarchy and differentiation. The clerks who headed payment sections presided over an assistant and over several bill collectors; they thought of themselves as having achieved a position of some standing in the office. Eventually they demanded tenure (*titularisation*) in their posts,

12. A detailed description of work procedures in the customer accounts department is provided in AP, V 8 O¹, no. 153, "Rapport à MM. les administrateurs."
13. The personnel documents cited in note 4 provide data on the size of clerical offices and departments.

which the company was unwilling to recognize as a fixed status.[14] Diluting the proletarianizing features of the customer accounts department even further was the practice of moving young clerks who started there into smaller offices as they matured.

Among the active agents, meter readers fit the proletarianization model, but the lighting inspectors were decidedly more difficult to classify. In general, the inspectors' work was routine, but their responsibility for certifying the proper functioning of residential fixtures required care. When a concierge was killed in an explosion in 1884, the defense of having followed proper procedure did not prevent an inspector from spending three months in prison for criminal negligence. Moreover, inspectors represented the authority of the company to the customers and were the supervisors of laborers, the lamplighters and greasemen. The uniformed agents were supposed to spy on those wage earners as they made their rounds, and a negative report could get them fired or fined.[15] As for the technical agents or foremen, they were hardly candidates for repetitive, specialized work.

Another qualification to the claim of proletarianization was the stratified structure of the employees' corps. There was a career ladder. All clerks started at fifteen hundred (later eighteen hundred) francs a year and advanced by steps of three hundred francs to thirty-three hundred francs (occasionally more). Furthermore, just over 10 percent of the employees were office heads or assistant office heads, about the same portion as in the state bureaucracy.[16] The hierarchy of clerks also included principal employees (*commis principaux*), supervisory inspectors, supervisory meter readers, chiefs of lighting sections, and other positions that stood above the common sort. Among the employees who were above the age of fifty, 32 percent (in 1884) were more than simple clerks.[17] Thus, despite its exceptional size, the PGC had not produced a consistently flattened, homogenous, and routinized personnel. Hierarchy, unspecialized assignments, and the possibility of promotion persisted. To be sure, the career trajectory no longer ended in anything like independence, but distinctions remained, and they seemed to matter to the employees.

The model of proletarianization presupposes that clerical work became ever more intense, tightly supervised, and rationalized, especially in the growing number of large firms. To what extent did big businesses like the

14. AP, V 8 O¹, no. 153, report of Dufourg to director, November 16, 1892.
15. Ibid., no. 148, "Eclairage—Personnel"; no. 828, report of Duval to director, July 30, 1884.
16. Thuillier, *Vie quotidienne*, p. 9.
17. AP, V 8 O¹, no. 153, "Personnel."

PGC create a new mode of office work that opened a dismal stage for white-collar employees? Of course, France had a less dramatic transition from the small-scale and the familial to the large bureaucratic organization than did some of its neighbors, not only because its pace of industrialization was more gradual: France had an old bureaucratic tradition based on the state. The nineteenth-century civil servant provides an important frame of reference and point of departure for evaluating clerical work at the PGC. Honoré de Balzac, along with other writers, had already made the *fonctionnaire* a stock figure characterized by stifled ambition, directionless plodding, a degree of indolence, and anxiety over status. In truth, the PGC would not have had to drive its personnel very hard to match the productivity of civil servants. A parliamentary commission of 1871 arrived at the conclusion that they accomplished no more than three to four effective hours of work a day. The standard day of seven hours, ten o'clock to five o'clock with no interruption for lunch, contained many informal breaks. Clerks ate a midday meal at their desks and did not readily countenance interruptions in it despite the absence of an official lunch hour. The work culture of civil servants was rich in subterfuges designed to avoid steady labor. The ritual of taking a smoke could keep an employee outside the office for several minutes at a time. In some ministries clerks enjoyed by custom the right to absent themselves from their desks momentarily a few times a day. Where this right was not recognized, a clerk was allowed to retrieve the hat or umbrella he had "forgotten" at the café that morning. Even when employees were at their desks, office chiefs experienced frustration when they tried to impose stringent work rules. In this panoptical age the technologies of surveillance were still primitive at the ministries. Offices grew haphazardly. Clerks worked in small, makeshift settings scattered about the ministries. Not until the Second Empire was nearing its end did ministers begin to rationalize the space within their bureaus. It is no wonder that the public had to expect a delay of two months or more before receiving a reply to a letter.[18]

Change did not take place quickly in the civil service. The penetration of laborsaving technology had to be measured in generations. Metal pens first began to replace quill pens in the 1850s, but the process was barely complete thirty years later. Just around the turn of the century the pace of technological change did accelerate as typewriters and keyboard adding machines made their appearance. With this new machinery came a decisive break, the feminization of the ministerial bureaus. Female typist-

18. Guy Thuillier, *Bureaucratie et bureaucrates en France au XIXe siècle* (Geneva, 1980), pp. 301–363, 423–562; Thuillier, *Vie quotidienne*, pp. 29–47, 70–155.

stenographers took the place of copyists, the lowest job on the promotional ladder within the ministries.[19]

The feminization of the civil service announced the impending death of an important tradition, unitary recruitment. The ministries had always required clerks to demonstrate a variety of skills. Copyists and lesser civil servants had to write neatly and do elementary numerical calculations, accomplishments that a primary-school graduate could command. At the upper levels of the office hierarchy were the *rédacteurs*, who had much more responsibility. They drafted correspondence from the chief's marginal notes and even disposed of simple matters, subject to a superior's approval. A law degree, or at least a *baccalauréat*, was necessary for this level. In the face of the diversity of needs, ministries hired only one type of clerk, one who could become a *rédacteur* and, eventually, office head. Critics of the civil service noted that unitary recruitment did not produce an invigorating climate of work. Highly educated young men were oppressed by years of waiting for an opening at a level appropriate to their training. Secondary-school and university graduates spent years doing assignments that a primary-school pupil could have handled. The critics contended that the standard thirty-year career from copyist to assistant office head was beneficial to no one, not the employee and not the minister. They called for the separate recruitment of copyists and *rédacteurs* so that better-educated youths could advance more quickly through the ranks. Of course, the plan would create dead-end careers for the copyists. Whatever the merits of the reform, it did not happen quickly. Initiatives foundered on bureaucratic inertia and loyalty to tradition. It took the female typists to break the old mold and make dead-end careers as copyists acceptable to the prevailing powers.[20]

Promotions through the *grades* (pay levels) of the civil service were a gray area in state employment. The public considered it natural and inevitable that civil servants would advance from one pay step to another on the basis of seniority. To be evaluated on the basis of service rather than performance was taken as a prerogative of the *fonctionnaire*. In fact, there was no fixed right to promotion by seniority; it was a matter of custom. When custom was observed, seniority brought the state employee only priority over younger colleagues for advancing to the next grade. Since the number of posts at each level was fixed, the employees had to wait for an opening. Office clerks would demand the right to a promotion after a predetermined number of years, but civil servants did not yet enjoy such

19. Thuillier, *Vie quotidienne*, pp. 155–210.
20. Ibid., pp. 195–225; Thuillier, *Bureaucratie*, pp. 291–294.

a prerogative.[21] Nor for that matter were there regulations on dismissals, bonuses, or pay. The minister was absolute master of his personnel, at least in principle. Over the years, the Council of State had rebuffed all efforts to limit discretionary power. Parliament considered reform from time to time but never succeeded in mustering a majority to endow civil servants with formal rights. In practice, the custom of advancements based on seniority was interrupted by exceptions based on nepotism or political considerations. Since ministers were not permanently attached to the administration, their concern about long-range efficiency was not great.[22]

To what extent did the PGC, as one of the new large-scale, private organizations, create clerical work that was clearly different from that of the state bureaucracy? As both management and clerks themselves struggled with the issue of what office work in private enterprise would be like, the situation of the *fonctionnaire* served as an influential model. Decision makers within the PGC wavered on how much they wished to borrow and depart from the model. They admitted from the start that the office personnel should have permanent careers and retirement plans, as civil servants did, but thinking about the administration of the employees on other matters shifted repeatedly.[23] The director issued regulations on fining and then renounced them as unworkable. In 1856, and again in 1859, he proposed a framework for ranking and promoting clerks along with a step system for pay (the *grades* of the civil service). They fell into disuse, however, and in 1861 the head of the distribution division offered a new plan for structuring the clerical personnel.[24] The evident confusion came to a head in 1863. Proud of its accomplishments in rationalizing manual labor, management turned to the still-untidy situation in the bureaus. The executive committee held at least six special sessions on the organization of the personnel in that year. The stated goal was "to ensure a constant assiduity among employees during work hours." One might have suspected that a meritocratic system would result, but the outcome of such unprecedented attention was yet another step system of advancement and continued ambiguity about departures from the civil-service model. The committee decreed that promotions would be attained "by seniority or

21. Jean Courcelle-Seneuil, "Du recrutement et de l'avancement des fonctionnaires," *Journal des économistes*, May 1874.
22. Thuillier, *Bureaucratie*, pp. 298–327; Guy Thuillier and Jean Tulard, *Histoire de l'administration française* (Paris, 1984), pp. 41–71.
23. On the creation of a pension plan, see *Rapport*, March 26, 1859, p. 4.
24. AP, V 8 O¹, no. 665, deliberations of March 22, 1856; no. 877, deliberations of December 2, 1859; no. 668, deliberations of May 25, 1861.

merit" after a trial period (*stage*) of two or three years.[25] Thus, even in its mood of hard-headedness, the managers of the PGC did not definitively renounce for its office workers the public servant's prerogative of being evaluated on the basis of age. Ultimately, the company labored empirically and unsystematically toward a more efficient use of its clerical labor force without having a clear conceptual framework in mind. Only when the personnel began to contest its dependent situation did management offer a reasoned and sustained defense of policies that broke with models of public administration.[26]

Managers gradually erected an apparatus of punishments and rewards, which they hoped would encourage clerks to work efficiently. The chief of the customer accounts department was a faithful advocate of careful surveillance and was allowed to employ ten agents to check the accuracy of his clerks' work. Although he found the inspectors' reports lacking in substance, he insisted that their investigations had "a great effectiveness from a moral point of view"—that is, they intimidated the clerks.[27] The director sought to make surveillance more effective by adding the sanction of fines. His table of punishments gave special weight to the offense of challenging authority. Verbal or physical attacks on superiors, or refusals to follow an order, were punishable by immediate suspension and possible dismissal. Inebriation on the job, negligence, and absences without permission brought fines of five francs for the first offense and ten for the second; the third offense resulted in suspension.[28]

Management hoped and expected that the most powerful impulse for dutiful work would come from the practice of rewarding clerks according to individual merit.[29] Disregarding the resolution of 1863 about seniority, the PGC came to promote employees up the step system of pay solely on the basis of personal performance. The director, who made all decisions on advancements, did so after consulting reports that did not even specify

25. Ibid., no. 669, deliberations of July 3 and 14, 1863; no. 670, deliberations of December 18 and 30, 1863.

26. The first official affirmation of purely meritocratic evaluations that I have found is the executive directive of May 19, 1892: ibid., no. 1081, ordre de service no. 352. This policy had been in effect for many decades before the directive, but there had been no occasion to state it explicitly.

27. Ibid., no. 90, report of Dufourg to chief of customer accounts department, January 15, 1898. In 1859 the post of *inspecteur de comptabilité* had been created, and to intimidate the employees further, his title had been upgraded to *directeur de comptabilité*. Ibid., "Procès-verbaux du conseil d'administration, 21 avril 1859."

28. Ibid., no. 148, "Règlement sur les peines encourues par les agents attachés au service des sections."

29. Ibid., no. 665, deliberations of November 8, 1856.

when the candidate had received his last raise. Management also used the retirement plan and bonuses as carrots. Gas clerks did not contribute to a pension fund, so the company proclaimed the benefits to be an earned privilege rather than a right. It also set aside 1 percent of profits for clerks' year-end bonuses. Though most clerks did receive a bonus, the director insisted that they had no inevitable right to one. Indeed, one unfortunate bookkeeper was deprived of a bonus, despite glowing reports from his superiors, because of an isolated incident of backtalk.[30] The PGC's executives hoped that performance-based rewards would raise standards of industriousness above those in the civil service. Thus office chiefs expected the staff to draft responses to customers' inquiries within a week and expedite them within two more days. Such promptness was often realized even though the ministries took two months for the same operation.[31] Nonetheless, the PGC largely failed to obtain the levels of diligence it had taken as its goal in 1863. The reasons for failure were numerous: the company's neglect to follow through on its announced sanctions, managers' tolerance for violations of rules, the imperfections in the sanctioning system, and the failure of clerks to exert themselves regardless of the penalties and rewards. In the end, evasive work practices were commonplace. The offices of the PGC were somewhat more tightly run than those of the state bureaucracy, but a basic transformation of office work had not occurred.

The bureaus of the PGC were not highly disciplined. As in the ministries, opportunities to dawdle and interrupt work were numerous—indeed, taken for granted. The smoking break was as much a detriment to continuous work at the gas company as at the ministries. The formal rules against smoking were absolute but seemingly unenforceable; that is why they were reissued every few years. Moreover, office chiefs did not manage, or did not bother, to keep their subordinates from finding reasons to leave their desks, especially in the late afternoon. A directive of 1891 noted a "great number of employees have taken to congregating in the halls and staircases before 5:00 P.M." That employees treated the official hours of work casually is clear. The order to be in the office at 9:00 A.M. sharp was reiterated as regularly as the provision against smoking.[32] The practice of signing the attendance sheet and then slipping out of the office

---

30. Ibid., no. 723, deliberations of January 2, 1857; no. 156, "Finestre, Pierre."
31. Ibid., no. 1081, ordre de service no. 80 (January 18, 1860); Thuillier, *Vie quotidienne,* pp. 81–83. A direct comparison between work in the PGC and in the ministries is not fully appropriate because the levels of authority were so much more complex in the latter.
32. AP, V 8 O¹, no. 1081, ordres de service nos. 27 (15 février 1873), 316, 327, 336, 441, 448.

for breakfast was common. The head of the payment bureau noted that the average lunch break was ten minutes longer than the mandated hour. Street peddlers entered the offices and showed their wares to clerks at their desks. Clerks scoffed at the efforts of one chief to impose a rule of silence on his personnel because no other office worked under such conditions.[33] A lighting inspector—said to be favored by his chief, a fellow Corsican—brought his children to the office, and they interfered with the work and stole office supplies. The chief did not correct the situation until the corporate director, informed in an anonymous letter, intervened.[34] If work pressures expanded beyond an acceptable limit, clerks could always absent themselves. During 1869 the thirty-three employees of the secretariat took 182 sick days and 177 excused leaves, an average of nearly eleven per agent.[35] A civil servant would probably have found the pace of work at the PGC more intense than in the state bureaucracy, but he would have recognized the subterfuges by which gas clerks imposed their own pace on their labors.

The PGC was notably unsuccessful in implementing effective means for supervising and disciplining its employees. In the early days of the firm the architecture of the offices was no more conducive to oversight than were the ministries. The creation of a new corporation from smaller gas companies did not result in the construction of new office facilities at once. Employees took up their posts in the headquarters of one of the merging firms, and expansion took place haphazardly into rented spaces in nearby buildings. Even the small secretariat had to operate from three different sites, one separated from the others by two floors. Obstacles to supervision probably provoked the decision to construct a new headquarters in 1863, a year when efficiency in the bureaus was much on the minds of decision makers. The architects of the building, designated for the rue Condorcet (ninth arrondissement), designed sizable rooms with raised, glass-enclosed offices at the ends for the chiefs. No columns or alcoves obstructed the view from that cubicle. The space made available to the billing bureau was large enough for 150 clerks to function in sight of the chief and for another hundred to work in view of the assistant chief.[36] At

---

33. Ibid., ordres de service nos. 120, 4 (30 décembre 1871), 303; no. 153, report of Dufourg to director, November 16, 1892; *L'Echo du gaz: Organe de l'Union syndicale des employés de la Compagnie parisienne du gaz*, no. 176 (August 1, 1904): 2.

34. AP, V 8 O¹, no. 162, report of inspectors of fifth section to director, May 26, 1894.

35. Ibid., no. 753, "Secrétariat. Contrôle des feuilles de présence."

36. Ibid., no. 1598, "Hôtel de la Compagnie," no. 753, "Secrétariat"; *Rapport*, March 21, 1863, p. 12; March 29, 1867, p. 24.

least the supervisors now had the technology of surveillance, and they received it about the time that ministries were taking steps to bring more order to their offices. But the PGC's headquarters proved too small for the growth that came with the customer-oriented programs of the late 1880s and 1890s. By the mid-1890s many clerks were again working beyond the view of their superiors, whose anxiety about surveillance was again on the rise.[37]

Management's sanctioning powers proved, if not empty, then at least unimposing. Soon after unveiling his table of fines, the director effectively renounced its use by stating that fines were "difficult to apply" and expressing his preference for positive sanctions.[38] The model of the civil service, which imposed fines on active agents (like letter carriers) but not on office clerks, prevailed at the PGC. The uniformed personnel, working beyond the supervision of the chief and in direct contact with customers, had to feel the weight of corporate rules, and it did. More than a fifth of the meter readers could expect to pay a fine each year.[39] Yet the bookkeeper at the PGC had no more to fear from fines than did the *fonctionnaire*. Nor did the gas company use dismissals with a heavier hand than did the state. In both cases, final warnings and ultimate warnings preceded a firing, which was often obviated through an act of indulgence. The rehiring of cashiered clerks after proper apologies and vows of good behavior was not unknown in either bureaucracy.[40]

However much gas managers came to insist on promotions solely on the basis of individual performance in the face of protests against this mode of advancement, the carrot-and-stick approach did not work nearly as well as they had hoped. This failure was partly the result of the way in which decisions on raises were made. As we have seen, the company pursued the strictest centralization in this area, with the consequence that managers most removed from a clerk's daily performance made the decision. The director had to consider hundreds of cases at a time and had only the terse reports from supervisors to guide him.[41] Employees believed—

---

37. AP, V 8 O^1, no. 90, report of January 15, 1898.
38. Ibid., no. 665, deliberations of November 8, 1856.
39. Ibid., no. 153, "Revendications des contrôleurs de compteurs." Some meter readers were made to pay (at least in part) for the gas lost in leaks they failed to detect in customers' homes. See no. 751, "Affaire Faure-Beaulieu."
40. Thuillier, *Bureaucratie*, p. 407. Leaving work without permission was a ground for dismissal at the PGC; still, three clerks at the gas-main office were caught red-handed and merely given light fines (though also stiff warnings not to repeat the offense). See AP, V 8 O^1, no. 767, report of Bruley to Lependry, June 5, 1872.
41. See chapter 4.

with some justice—that the decisions bore little relation to the degree to which they applied themselves on the job. Another reason for the failure of rewards to stimulate zeal was cultural: many employees were simply willing to forgo some of the rewards of pleasing their superiors, and accepted the penalties for not doing so, in defense of their work culture. These employees rejected for themselves the role of a proletariat of the office.

Though the PGC had trouble creating a committed and pliant office staff, the company was by no means an innovator in restructuring the work force to increase its malleability. The gas company was even less advanced than the ministries in introducing office machinery. From 1890 the civil service faced the challenge of integrating the typewriter into its work routines; the PGC virtually ignored the innovation. In 1891 the company possessed just one machine; even in 1902, out of three thousand employees, there were only two typist-stenographers.[42] The company used no keyboard adding machines even though it employed hundreds of clerks who calculated bills, added columns of figures, and verified totals. Perhaps one of the reasons for the PGC's technological conservatism as far as the office was concerned was that it retained the ideal of unitary recruitment even longer than did the ministries. The company expected any of its routine clerks in the customer accounts department to be capable of rising to subchief and therefore wanted them to be able to perform all types of work done in the bureau. As late as 1901, an executive order lumped all the employees except bill collectors into one category and subjected applicants to a uniform examination consisting of dictation, letter composition (rédaction), and numerical computations. Of course, only a small minority of the positions within the PGC required proficiency in all three areas.[43] Adherence to unitary recruitment was a sign that management thought in terms of careers, not routinized tasks.

Similarly, the PGC did not lead the way in creating a cadre of female clerks. Gas companies in Germany had discovered the cheapness and docility of female clerks in the 1880s. Even the French state had reassessed its opposition to hiring women. The postal service began to use female clerks for bureaus in large cities by the 1890s. The PGC, however, hired not one female for its office jobs in its fifty-year history. The successor gas

---

42. AP, V 8 O¹, no. 162, "Secrétariat—Personnel"; no. 688, deliberations of March 28, 1891.
43. Ibid., no. 163, ordre de service no. 669 (November 16, 1901). Even meter readers had to take this examination. See "Aux contrôleurs de compteurs," *L'Echo du gaz*, no. 176 (August 1, 1904): 3. Margery Davies, *Woman's Place*, p. 30, argues that in America new occupational titles based on functional specialization were added to the office. This did not happen at the PGC.

company apparently inherited the inhibition, for it did not even allow the labor shortages of World War I to bring females into the office. The executive council of the Société du gaz de Paris briefly considered experimenting with the departure in 1915, but nothing came of the proposal.[44] The PGC was content to deal with a male clerical force through the traditional means of cajoling and confronting.

By all available measures, the PGC did not succeed in intensifying office work notably by those traditional means. To quantify the changes in work pace, it is useful to examine the number of employees relative to the number of gas customers. That ratio, more than any other variable, determined the amount of paperwork the personnel had to handle or the number of meters they had to read. Figure 11 shows that this index of productivity rose, but quite slowly, until the mid-1880s. The ratio of clerks to customers was only 8 percent higher in 1885 than in 1860 even though the number of customers had multiplied fivefold. The company, for all its parsimony, had hired enough clerks so that the burdens of office work had not become decidedly more oppressive. Indeed, office productivity seems to have had a slump during the 1860s, which probably prompted the managers' pointed concern about the office routine in 1863. The index rose dramatically only in the last decade of the century, in response to the democratization of the clientele. Examining the ratios specifically for the billing agents, whose work was particularly sensitive to the size of the customer base, reinforces the general picture. The number of gas users per billing agent was actually lower in 1884 (900) than in 1858 (973), but it rose considerably by 1902 (1,080), after the company had succeeded in expanding the residential market.[45] Thus, this quantitative evaluation confirms the earlier qualitative assessment that the PGC did not take resolute steps to debase office tasks. A more demanding pace of work seems not to have been a policy that the firm pursued for its own sake; it was the offshoot of the quest for a wider customer base.

The escalating burdens of clerical work at the end of the century may not have cut too deeply into the clerks' relaxed routines. Employees seem to have adjusted as much by adding to their hours as by quickening their pace. Comments and complaints about overtime work began to appear after 1890. The only mention of the practice before then had been in re-

44. E. Brylinski, *L'Electricité à Paris et à Berlin* (Paris, 1898), p. 16; Susan Bachrach, "The Feminization of the French Postal Service, 1750–1914" (Ph.D. diss., University of Wisconsin, 1981); AP, V 8 O¹, no. 1634, deliberations of June 1, 1915.

45. For evidence of rising complaints about overwork in the 1890s, see AP, V 8 O¹, no. 162, "Lettres et renseignements . . . ," letter of Appelle to director (n.d.). On the steps the PGC took to attract more customers after 1886, see chapter 4.

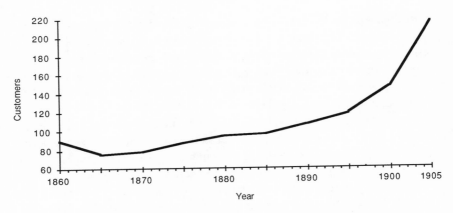

Fig. 11.   Number of Customers per Employee. From AP, V 8 O¹, nos. 153, 162, 665, 1294.

gard to special annual tasks for which the company recruited volunteers and paid bonuses.[46] Resort to overtime work suggests a white-collar labor force that refused to use every moment productively and was left to complete its work quota at a self-determined pace. Even so, it is easy to believe that the rising pressures on the job antagonized employees.

In the end, this large private corporation did not break decisively with the mode of white-collar work long found in the French civil service. Though there were nuanced differences, the employees of the PGC were not especially more disciplined than those at the ministries. The PGC failed to take effective steps to restructure the personnel in such a way as to give management more leverage. Consciously, and often unconsciously, managers accepted the work routines of civil servants as normative even when they occasionally announced an assault on lax ways. The engineers simply did not apply themselves to regimenting the clerical work force with the same resolve they accorded manual workers. In neither case were there overwhelming financial pressures to do so, but the matter was even less pressing as far as white-collar employees were concerned. The company spent only 0.2 centimes on each cubic meter of gas sold (at thirty centimes) for accounting.[47] There was no real need to rationalize; it would not have made a difference. Nor did the engineers seem to have the same moral intensity about controlling clerks as they had for the manual per-

46. Ibid., no. 153, "Rapport à MM. les administrateurs sur le fonctionnement actuel du bureau des recettes . . ." Previously, assistant office heads had had to stay late and handle unfinished work. See no. 90, report of Dufourg to Ymont, December 2, 1882.
47. Ibid., no. 1016, "Comptes d'exploitation par année."

sonnel. Haphazardly the PGC created out of its unsystematic attempts at rationalization a mixture of traditional and innovative methods that may well have redoubled the employees' resentment. Enough of the old survived to provide the gas clerks with a sense of being rooted in familiar ways. Yet the firm's halting quest for a productive work pace and especially its use of discretionary authority to reward individual performance were not part of those ways. Clerks never accepted the legitimacy of the innovations.

The employees took advantage of their superiors' ambivalence to perpetuate an evasive work culture. They rejected for themselves a professional pride that might have led to the assiduousness that engineers displayed. The lighting inspectors are a good test case for the claim. On the one hand, they were more or less typical, in terms of social and educational background, of gas clerks. On the other hand, the company gave their behavior as much scrutiny as it did any category of employee and should have fashioned a pliant corps of agents if it was going to do so at all. But it did not. Albert Arrieu, an inspector hired in 1888, incurred twenty-two fines (of three or five francs each) between then and 1892. Louis Bray received twelve punishments in as many years, including several for leaving his job to sit in a pub, one for responding angrily to a superior in the presence of other clerks, and one for neglecting to take care of a customer's request. Emile Delsol accumulated twenty fines in two years, most of them for arriving late or missing work entirely. His supervisor explained that Delsol, "living alone, could not wake up in the morning despite trying several different types of alarms." None of these records was unusual. In fact, only Delsol was ultimately fired for his poor conduct. Arrieu was promoted to secretary of his lighting section, a sedentary post that inspectors coveted, and Bray became a supervisor (*inspecteur-contrôleur*) of other inspectors.[48] Obviously, the PGC's standards were not exacting.

On average, an inspector received 1.7 fines a year. Some agents had perfect records, but they were few. Only eight in the sample of ninety-seven inspectors went three years without a punishment. By contrast, a quarter of the agents angered management enough to incur a suspension, a severe sanction that signified extreme displeasure with the clerk. The distribution of violations holds a mirror to inspectors' attitudes toward their work and to their degree of commitment to it. The picture that emerges from table 10 is of a work culture characterized by petty evasion of rules. Neglect of company business, deception, and avoidance of work

48. Ibid., nos. 164–173, "Livres du personnel."

Table 10. Abuses for Which Inspectors Were Fined

	No.	%
Neglect of duty	144	42.1
Carelessness	75	21.9
Evading work routine	40	11.7
Tardiness	39	11.4
Willful deception	17	4.9
Challenging authority	15	4.4
Failure to exercise authority	8	2.3
Drunkenness on the job	4	1.2
Total	342	99.9

Source: AP, V 8 O¹, nos. 164–173, livres du personnel.

accounted for nearly 60 percent of the fines. The average clerk in the sample was charged with one of these offenses at least once a year (with routine violations presumably going undetected). Unintended error, though not a negligible problem, was a good deal less common than willful disregard of regulations. Drinking on the job, however, was not a serious difficulty, nor was the offense that plagued Delsol. Significantly, the records on fines do not point to a cadre of employees chafing under the exercise of authority by their superiors. In fact, employees rarely challenged such authority. Likewise, inspectors rarely failed to exercise control over their own subordinates, the lamplighters and greasemen. The outlook of the inspectors was not so much *frondeur* as *fainéant*.

A reflection of the same work culture arises from the dossiers of eighty-three clerks in the payment bureau of the customer account department. Their job, being more coordinated and supervised, offered fewer opportunities for open evasion. Nonetheless, the bureau chief did not find an optimal situation. Nineteen (23 percent) of his clerks consistently ranked as "excellent" or "very good" workers. Fifteen others were "good" servants of the gas company but had room for improvement. The majority of payment clerks (59 percent) were not "good" servants in the eyes of their chief. Their problems extended from "frequent absences" to having a "violent character." Twelve percent of the office staff was in danger of being dismissed or receiving a serious sanction. As in the case of the lighting inspectors, careless work, lack of precision in executing routine tasks, and absences from one's assigned place comprised the core of the problem.[49]

49. Ibid., no. 153, "Etat des appointements alloués aux employés ayant plus de 2 ans de service."

In the face of such lackadaisical work habits, a few office heads took their revenge. They filed personnel reports that eschewed the usual bland comments and were intended to retard promotions. The chief of the customer accounts department during the 1890s, confronted with a rising work load and the displacement of clerks to desks outside a central bureau that had grown too small, tried increased surveillance. In 1895 he requested and received permission to create a "verification detachment" that would intimidate his subordinates. The chief's position was that "employees must never believe for a moment that they are lightly supervised." The formation of such a corps may well explain why his underlings hated him with a special passion.[50] More typical was the head of the by-products division, Audouin, who admitted to putting up with "disorder" in his office. Even when he arrived at the point of finding the disorder "intolerable," he still did not call for dismissing one bookkeeper who left work without permission.[51] Managers were simply not conscientious about disciplining the commissioned personnel. Such leniency, contrasting sharply with managers' vigilance regarding wage earners, encouraged clerks to develop a different sort of identity.

Filling Clerical Positions

Although the employees of the PGC rarely acknowledged that they were fortunate to have steady jobs, that was the case. Regular, lifelong office work with a promise of a pension was difficult to obtain; applicants far outnumbered openings. Even though the gas company hired an average of a hundred clerks a year owing to growth and attrition, the corporate files bulged with rejected requests for jobs. At one point the director noted receiving four applications for each appointment.[52] Why certain men were selected rather than others is impossible to say, but two criteria seemed crucial. Each employee, however humble his post, had to have a protector.[53] Usually this was a political figure—a deputy, senator, or municipal

50. Ibid., no. 90, report of Dufourg to chief of customer accounts department, January 15, 1898. As we shall see in chapter 6, this office head was the subject of continual denunciations in the union press.
51. Ibid., no. 161, dossier of François Berger, letter of Audouin to Ternet, November 5, 1878.
52. Ibid., no. 153, "Procès-verbaux de l'audience donnée le 2 novembre 1892 aux délégués . . ."
53. Even a promotional pamphlet for a commercial school noted that the diploma would take a job applicant only so far: "Recommendations play a large role." See A. Duflot, *Des Carrières ouvertes aux anciens élèves diplômés des écoles supérieures de commerce* (Paris, 1907), p. 29.

councillor. Although the protector's recommendation was typically mundane, the company was eager to avoid offending him or her since it was dependent on the goodwill of the authorities. The other feature that elicited a positive response from the PGC was having a relative currently employed by the firm. Paternalistic in outlook, the gas executives preferred to hire families rather than individuals. They considered such a policy a matter of duty and also a boost to loyalty and morale. As the office staff grew in size, management was able to recruit an ever-larger portion among the sons, nephews, and in-laws of its commissioned personnel. By 1902 at least 42 percent of the clerks in the customer accounts department had been hired with the "recommendation" of a relative already within the firm. Apparently, the PGC turned to outsiders when relatives were unavailable or notably inferior. Good contacts seemed to count for more in the hiring process than the quality of training or prior work histories.[54]

The gas clerks were disproportionately Parisian, with 48 percent of them natives of the capital. Their families of origin usually ranked above the social level of manual laborers. The majority owned income-producing property, usually a shop or land. Such was the standard background for employees of mid-nineteenth-century Paris, but nuances differentiated the gas personnel from other sorts of white-collar workers (table 11).[55] Salesclerks and railroad employees, two large Parisian groups, had slightly more plebeian origins; many had fathers who were manual workers or peasants. The personnel of financial concerns and the state had more elevated antecedents, with a relatively high portion of civil servants and rentiers. The PGC employees were very much "average" in terms of family background, fitting neatly between the two groupings. The portion of gas clerks with working-class backgrounds was somewhat inflated by the company's willingness to engage sons of its own laborers. Even with this policy it is clear that the rise of large private bureaucracies did not so much present opportunities for workers' children to leave manual labor as it allowed children of small property owners to remain above the proletariat.[56]

54. AP, V 8 O^1, no. 162, "Assimilation." One employee was hired because he was the "relative" of an office head. His schooling or prior work experience was not even mentioned in his recommendation. See no. 753, report of February 1, 1870. Another clerk was hired as the "breast cousin" of superintendent Cury—that is, they had shared the same wet nurse. See no. 161, "Renseignements sur Durray."
55. On the social origins of Parisians white-collar workers, see Berlanstein, *Working People*, pp. 30–35.
56. One of the few formal studies of social mobility in nineteenth-century France confirms these findings. William Sewell has discovered that native wage earners in Marseille experienced far less upward social mobility than did immigrants from rural backgrounds. See Sewell, *Structure and Mobility: The Men and Women of Marseille, 1820–1870* (Cambridge, 1985).

Table 11. Family Background of Parisian Employees, 1860–1880

| | Type of Employment | | | | | | | | | |
| | Gas | | Railroad | | Sales | | Bank | | State | |
Parents' Status	No.	%	No.	%	No.	%	No.	%	No.	%
Property owner	12	28.6	14	22.2	10	14.3	9	42.9	8	30.8
Shopkeeper or artisan	7	16.7	9	14.3	16	22.9	3	14.3	3	11.5
Employee	8	19.0	5	7.9	12	17.1	6	28.6	12	46.2
Cultivator	6	14.3	12	19.0	6	8.5	1	4.7	1	3.8
Wage earner	9	21.4	23	36.5	26	37.1	2	9.5	2	7.7
Total	42	100	63	99.9	70	99.9	21	100	26	100.0

Source: AP, V 4 E, marriage registers, eighteenth arrondissement, 1860–1880.

Table 12. Social Contacts of Gas Clerks,
as Suggested by Marriage
Certificates

Status	No.	%
Brides		
Manual laborer	31	65.9
Employee	7	14.9
No occupation	9	19.2
Total	47	100
Bride's Family		
Property owner	10	29.4
Shopkeeper or artisan	6	17.6
Employee	4	11.8
Cultivator	0	00.0
Wage earner	14	41.2
Total	34	100
Witnesses to Marriages		
Professional or rentier	17	14.9
Shopkeeper or artisan	32	28.1
Employee	40	35.1
Wage earner	21	18.4
Other	4	3.5
Total	114	100

Source: AP, V 4 E, marriage registers, eighteenth arrondissement, 1860–1880.

Marriage brought the PGC's employees closer to the world of manual
labor (see table 12). More than three times as many clerks wed women
who did manual labor (usually as seamstresses, cooks, or laundresses)
than wed women who did not hold jobs. Such alliances put employees in
contact with the working classes since they were twice as likely to marry
into a family headed by a wage earner as to have been born into one. The
gas employees also abandoned bourgeois niceties to the extent of cohabit-
ing with the women before marriage. Fifty-five percent of the couples declared the same address on their marriage certificates, and 18 percent le-
gitimized children on the occasion of their weddings. By contrast, patterns
of sociability, as indicated by witnesses to the marriages, drew gas employees away from wage earners and toward the *classe moyenne* and the bourgeoisie. In this manner they resembled the bank clerks more than railway
agents. Another noteworthy aspect of the gas employees' sociability was a

Table 13. Educational Background of Gas
Employees (Inspectors and
Customer Account Clerks)

Level Attained	No.	%
Primary only	40	47.6
Superior primary	21	25.0
Some secondary	16	19.0
Secondary degree	6	7.1
Some university	1	1.2
Total	84	99.9

Sources: AP, V 8 O¹, nos. 90, 164–172.

certain amount of cohesiveness among them—17 percent of the witnesses were fellow clerks at the PGC. There were grounds for a collective identity beyond the workplace.

The Parisian and petit bourgeois background of the PGC's employees was reflected in the schooling that prepared them for their posts. The company had no specific educational requirements and relied on examinations to screen candidates for competence. The clerk's parents had been willing and able to keep their sons in school beyond the legal minimum to ensure their access to such positions. Moreover, the city of Paris had furthered the parental goals by expanding the "schools of the Republic." The extant data concern lighting inspectors and the clerks of the customer accounts department, which surely overrepresent the least privileged employees and minimize scholastic achievement. Yet even in this sample the majority had more than a primary education (table 13). Though primary schooling would have made them competent to handle most tasks in the PGC, a fourth of the employees in the sample had attended one of the five superior primary schools in the capital (écoles Turgot, Colbert, Lavoisier, Arago, and Say). Created by the Guizot law of 1833, this level of schooling had atrophied for lack of a clear purpose and clientele during the July Monarchy and the Second Empire. A ministerial decree attributed to superior primary schools the mission of general education tending toward the practical but not the vocational. The republican municipal council of Paris hastened to expand them so that poor but serious primary-school students could enjoy a "legitimate" degree of upward mobility without aspiring to the distinction of secondary education. The city allowed enrollments to rise from two thousand to about thirty-five hundred during the first decade of the new republic. Councilmen, however, did not immediately see fit to eliminate the monthly tuition of eighteen francs, a considerable sum for modest households. Allowing the Ferry law to set the example, the municipality abolished tuition in 1882, but the reform came too late to benefit most clerks who entered the PGC before 1890. The superior primary schools, through which so many gas clerks passed, offered two years of training in civics (*morale*), composition, science, and drafting. A third year allowed specialization in accounting, commercial law, foreign languages, or drafting. Most superior primary students did not remain beyond one or two years; only about a third received diplomas. The employees of the PGC probably followed this pattern, but records are silent on the matter. The extra years of instruction beyond primary school, with their tuition and opportunity costs, represented a sacrifice on the parents' part and signified a certain degree of ambition.[57] One Parisian educational official affirmed, reassuringly, that superior primary-school pupils "seek to raise themselves in their own social sphere but not to leave it."[58] Whether the official was correct about the modesty of the students' aspirations and whether a post with the gas company satisfied them are questions worth considering.

Another quarter of gas employees had moved beyond the education of the masses and entered the world of the bourgeoisie by attending lycées.[59] No more than 6 percent of the general population attained this level of instruction. When Henri Le Brun or Jean-Baptiste Berre, both *bacheliers-ès-lettres*, took jobs as lighting inspectors, they probably did not feel that their station in life matched their educational attainments. Most clerks in the PGC who had passed through lycées, however, had not received the *baccalauréat*, the presumed mark of belonging to the bourgeoisie proper. The majority followed the practice of small-property-owning families in remaining at the lycée "through rhetoric." Such a background represented an investment in prestige and an effort to impress potential employers without overqualifying the students entirely for clerical work. In a few

---

57. Paul Strauss, *Paris ignoré: 550 dessins inédits* (Paris, n.d.), pp. 294–295; G. Dupont-Ferrier, *L'Enseignement public à Paris: Les Ecoles, lycées, collèges, bibliothèques* (Paris, 1913), pp. 27–30; Antoine Prost, *Histoire de l'enseignement en France, 1800–1967* (Paris, 1968), pp. 291–292.

58. Octave Gréard, *Education et instruction* (4 vols), vol. 1, *Enseignement primaire* (Paris, 1904), 309.

59. On the social composition of the student body at lycées in mid-nineteenth-century France, see Patrick Harrigan, *Mobility, Elites and Education in French Society of the Second Empire* (Waterloo, Ont., 1980).

instances families may have intended to give their sons a complete second-ary education but lacked the resources to follow through. In any case, these parents probably had in mind more genteel positions for their sons than that of uniformed gas inspector—perhaps work in the central office of the Banque de France. Yet more than a third of the gas inspectors (eleven of the thirty in the sample) had attended the lycée.

If the education of many PGC employees had encouraged them to form higher aspirations, it must also be noted that they had usually tried other lines of work and left them for one reason or another. Unlike the engineer-managers, white-collar clerks rarely had their first and only jobs with the PGC. The clerks entered the firm at an average age of twenty-seven, about seven years after they had finished their schooling or military service.[60] The list of jobs they had held before joining the company was extensive and varied—retail salesman, bank employee, bookkeeper for small busi-nesses, and so on. Service in the office of an architect or surveyor was rather common, especially for active agents, because familiarity with drafting and knowledge of construction could be a useful asset in the PGC. Most clerks had had not one but a series of positions before entering the PGC. None of them was especially secure or exalted. Henri de Paul de Lacoste left the lycée at the age of eighteen and, after a year's employment in a branch of the Crédit agricole at Agen, worked in the office of his father's spinning mill for eight years. Then he departed for Paris and served as a copyist for a series of business agents during the next two years before finally becoming a lighting inspector. Francois Le Gailliard worked for a succession of wholesale agents in Paris for two years, passed through a period of unemployment, and took jobs as a salesman in several retail stores before becoming a lighting inspector at the age of twenty-eight. Not even a *baccalauréat* assured an easy path to a respectable position. Auguste Théault held a teaching post in a private school for six years after receiving his secondary degree. Then he worked as a tutor (*répétiteur*) in three different private schools before entering the PGC. Though each of these men had some difficulty establishing himself in a career-long posi-tion, none had the misfortune of Pierre Bonnet, a lycée graduate and a former student at the Ecole des Beaux Arts. After terminating his studies, Bonnet worked in three different factories as a draftsman. Then he re-turned to his family in the Basse-Pyrénées. When he came back to Paris three years later, during the nasty economic crisis of the late 1880s, the only job he could find was as a laborer in the noisome coal-tar refinery of

60. AP, V 8 O¹, no. 149, "Retraites et secours."

the PGC. He must have been quite relieved when the construction engineer recommended him for a post in a lighting section.[61]

Thus, clerks often drifted before entering the offices of the PGC. Such itineracy had to come to an end eventually if an employee aspired to a tenured post, a pension, and fringe benefits. Large bureaucracies would not usually engage an aging clerk; the PGC had rules against hiring ones older than forty.[62] Even though the average clerk entered more than a decade before the limit applied, he usually ended his drifting then and there. Fewer than 4 percent of them resigned their posts. Since the company fired less than 1 percent of its commissioned personnel, a position with the gas firm became a permanent one for the most part.[63] The sorts of people who became gas clerks may once have aspired to something better, but as they matured, they came to realize—or were compelled to realize—that opportunities were not limitless. The superior primary schools of Paris alone graduated more than a thousand pupils a year, and about twice that many left before receiving a diploma. It was not easy to supply all these people with office careers. Moreover, though lycées enrolled a small minority of youths, half the students in provincial secondary schools were children of peasants or petit bourgeois; most of them would have to find their own way in the world.[64] Only a part of the group could expect work that measured up to its educational attainments. Thus, Jacques Meys, a student at the Ecole Turgot, was being realistic when he wrote to Engineer Audouin asking for a "modest post in one of the offices." René Delaplance, a salesman at the Bon Marché department store, also confronted the limited options of an employee when he requested work at the PGC "in order to have a more secure future."[65] At one of the first audiences that the employees' union had with top management, the delegates complained about the starting salaries for clerks. Camus's reply was blunt: the clerks were fortunate to have places in the PGC; if they could have found more lucrative posts, they would have.[66] His remarks were insensitive, but they hit

61. Ibid., nos. 164–172, "Livres du pesonnel"; no. 161, personnel dossiers.
62. Ibid., no. 666, deliberations of October 13, 1858.
63. Ibid., no. 159, "Etat des agents du personnel fixe entrés ou ayant quittés la compagnie . . ." The figures in this source probably overstate the resignations since they include certain commissioned manual workers.
64. Harrigan, *Mobility*, p. 42.
65. AP, V 8 O¹, no. 161, "Meys, William-Jacques"; no. 626, Delaplanche to director, November 8, 1892.
66. Ibid., no. 153, "Procès-verbaux de l'audience donnée le 2 novembre 1892 . . ." In 1858 a clerk was arrested for violently attacking a superintendent who had had him fired. The incident underscored the frightening prospects that a dismissed employee faced, especially if he was no longer young. See no. 723, deliberations of March 11, 1858.

on a measure of truth. And perhaps most clerks recognized it too; for even when their material situation did not please them, they usually remained with the firm.

Rewarding Clerks

Surely one of the reasons for the employees' evasive work culture was that they knew their labors would not yield genuine comforts, perhaps not even an austere but secure level of existence. The material situation of most gas clerks was chronically strained, the result of both the salary levels within the PGC and the clerks' patterns of consumption. The company did not have specific pay for each kind of work. There was a general salary scale for all nonmanual personnel. One began at fifteen hundred francs a year (eighteen hundred after 1876) and advanced by increments of three hundred francs in most instances (but occasionally less) on the basis of individual performance. The best-paid bookkeepers received thirty-three hundred francs; to earn more, an employee had to attain the post of bureau chief in a large department, which might bring four thousand or forty-five hundred francs. Even the best-paid clerks earned only a twentieth of the director's compensation, but the step system did provide, in theory, a meaningful hierarchy. A young bookkeeper receiving 125 or 150 francs a month faced an exiguous existence, especially if he had a family to support. A mature clerk, paid 250 francs a month after a career of twenty-five years, could accumulate some comforts. The question was whether the young clerk could realistically anticipate so halcyon a future. In 1892 Director Godot stated that the company's policy was to promote clerks rather rapidly to an annual salary of twenty-seven hundred francs, for that was an income on which a family could exist without making painful sacrifices.[67] In fact, his statement was an excessively optimistic interpretation of corporate policy. The white-collar pay scale was bloated at the bottom at the moment Godot addressed the issue (table 14). Seventy percent of the employees earned less than twenty-seven hundred francs. An analysis of average earnings by age (figure 12) also shows that most clerks could not hope to reach the "living salary" by the end of their careers. Perhaps Godot, under pressure from the municipal council, was obliquely promising more generous treatment of his employees, but he was not accurately describing how the PGC had heretofore operated.

The remuneration most gas employees received was more or less what Parisian craftsmen might have earned if they had been employed steadily.

67. Ibid., no. 149, "Procès-verbaux de l'audience du 16 décembre 1892 . . ."

Table 14. Distribution of Clerks' Annual
Salaries, 1891 (in francs)

Salary	No.	%
1,500	136	7.2
1,800	436	23.0
2,100	409	21.6
2,400	308	16.2
2,700	320	16.9
3,000	164	8.6
3,300	61	3.2
3,600	61	3.2
Total	1,895	99.9

Source: AP, V 8 O¹, no. 153, "Syndicat des employés commissionnés."

The PGC, in defense of its pay scale, might have pointed out that commissioned agents, unlike manual laborers, received desirable fringe benefits as
well. The firm had created a pension plan for its tenured personnel soon
after opening. It provided half of the final salary after twenty-five years of
service once a clerk has passed the age of fifty-five, and the company did
not withhold a portion of his salary to support the fund. The PGC could
and did tout the generosity of the program compared to that of other bureaucracies, but it did not grant pensions as a right and insisted on the
possibility of denying benefits to unworthy agents. The firm also ran a
medical service (supported by a 1 percent withholding), though many
clerks were unhappy with the treatment they received. One of the few
organized protests before the formation of a union involved pressure for
full sick pay instead of half pay for days missed as a result of illness. The
company formally rejected the request, but individual office heads procured the favor often for their subordinates, and clerks were far more privileged in this regard than manual workers.[68] In 1892 ten days of paid vacation became part of the clerk's annual routine. Moreover, as permanent
agents of the firm, clerks could count on corporate largess in individual
circumstances. The PGC loaned young clerks the cash needed to buy
themselves out of military service. The director even agreed to pay for the
wedding outfits of one impecunious employee and his bride.[69] There was
an annual year-end bonus as well, drawn on the 1 percent of profits set

68. Ibid., no. 157, "Procès-verbaux de la . . . caisse de prévoyance."
69. Ibid., no. 672, deliberations of March 23, 1867; no. 673, deliberations of November 3, 1869; no. 688, deliberations of May 14, 1892.

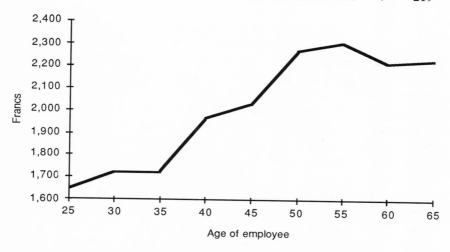

Fig. 12. Average Earnings of Employees by Age, 1892 (in francs). From AP, V 8 O¹, no. 155, "Agents commissionnés en activité au 31 décembre 1892."

aside for the purpose. The PGC was not a leader in providing fringe benefits; its programs were rarely cited as models. Yet neither was it notoriously parsimonious in this regard. Managers had to be disconcerted by the contention that benefits such as bonuses and the medical plan incited; after all, executives had hoped to instill gratitude and fidelity. The discontent had more to do with the discretionary manner in which programs were administered than with the amount committed to them. Even so, the benefits gave welcomed support to a personnel frequently pressed for cash.

On the whole, clerks struggled to maintain financial equilibrium. In 1867 Paris experienced a surge in prices and rent levels that created grave woes for the entire working population, the personnel of the PGC included. Executives determined that nearly 40 percent (375 out of 962) of their agents were "in distress" as a result of the crisis and offered temporary assistance (rather than raises).[70] The level of strain inflicted on such a group of employees with regular jobs attests to their inability to accumulate a cushion for survival in hard times. Yet this acute need was probably not the daily reality most clerks faced. Rather, their material situation was a matter of scraping by with chronic shortages of cash for small luxuries, deferring gratifications, and struggling to maintain appearances. In 1898 Albert Poiret, a meter reader earning twenty-one hundred francs

70. Ibid., no. 1286, "Employés jugés d'être en détresse." The company also gave a wage supplement during the hard times in 1858. See no. 666, deliberations of August 3, 1858. On clerks who asked for assistance from the director on an individual basis, see no. 153, "Secours une fois donné."

a year, wrote to the director about his financial plight and included an account of his expenditures for the previous months. The budget has an air of truthfulness and is worth considering. With his monthly pay of 175 francs, Poiret had these fixed expenses: rent, twenty-three francs (280 francs a year); taxes, four francs; heating and lighting, nine francs; revolving charge accounts at two department stores, ten francs; lunches at a restaurant during workdays, twenty-three francs; bread for meals, twenty-six francs; and laundering of work clothes, thirty-four francs. The high portion of income spent on restaurants and the care of clothing (13 percent and 19 percent respectively) was not unusual; similar sums appeared in budgets proposed by other clerks and by their union. In any case, these fixed expenditures left only forty-six francs a month for the purchase of family meals (other than bread) and clothing (always a major concern for office clerks) and for recreational activities. In addition, Poiret, whose wife had just given birth, had exceptional expenses totaling 123 francs arising from the pregnancy. One can see that Poiret did not have much room for maneuvering.[71]

For Poiret and most other clerks, getting by and even acquiring a few comforts required thought, planning, sacrifice, calculation, and the mobilization of available resources. Like manual workers, clerks had a household economy of makeshifts, but one in which the father's income was more certain and in which the children's earnings played less of a role.[72] The employees were not too proud to marry working women and to keep them working after the wedding. A portion of Poiret's paycheck (twenty-eight francs) went to a wet nurse, presumably because his wife was continuing working as a laundress. Company informers reported that a leader of the employees' union had a wife with a poor reputation for housekeeping in the neighborhood because she was so busy with her sewing trade.[73] Another strategic step for accumulating a living income was a second job for the employee himself. The PGC never had trouble getting clerks to do paid overtime work; in fact, the clerks in the payment bureau jealously regarded the supplementary work offered to their comrades in the billing bureau as a "privilege." But the personnel did not depend on its own firm for additional income. The case of one employee, who according to an anonymous letter worked at night for an electrical firm in Belleville and

71. Ibid., no. 150, "Affaire Poiret." So pressed for cash was one employee that he had the audacity to ask for an advance on his bonus. Ibid., "Affaire Masson."
72. I have borrowed the concept of the household economy of makeshifts from Olwen Hufton, *The Poor in Eighteenth Century France* (Oxford, 1974), and Joan Scott and Louise Tilly, *Women, Work, and Family* (New York, 1979).
73. AP, V 8 O¹, no. 148, "Lemaire."

was a translator for two German firms and an English one, was an exaggerated example of a common situation. A survey that the company tried to do on moonlighting uncovered a large number of clerks who kept the books for small firms and also those who had more exotic endeavors—a musician for the Cirque d'Hiver; two artists, several waiters, six ticket collectors at the Opéra; and a cashier at the Elysée-Montmarte dance hall. The survey was incomplete because employees were wary about providing such information. They knew that the PGC was suspicious and might take disciplinary action if they were caught working for one of the firm's suppliers, competitors, or subcontractors.[74] The letter about the ambitious clerk holding several jobs was in fact a warning to the director that he was passing secrets about coal-tar distillations to one of the German enterprises for which he translated. In general, employees tried to be discreet about their second jobs, except when complaining about how overtime tasks interfered with their moonlighting.

However much energy clerks and their wives devoted to their economy of makeshifts, it did not render the employees paragons of solvency. Indebtedness and entanglement in usury were commonplace in the office milieu. The PGC was well aware of the situation and countenanced the problems with both threats and offers of assistance. Managers feared that debts would lead clerks to dishonest or negligent behavior on the job—a worry that was not at all misplaced. Jules Le Brun, a lighting inspector who was fired for pocketing a customer's deposit (of fourteen francs), was motivated to steal by his inability to pay the rent. Having lost his gas post, Le Brun emigrated to Hanoi in search of work. The offense that finally cost Emile Delsol his post was not his chronic tardiness but rather his sneaking off to seek a loan. Humbert, a bookkeeper in the machinery department, shared that misfortune. When the engineer denied him permission to leave the office at 3:00 P.M., he departed anyway, in view of the urgency "of complementing the insufficient resources that the company's pay provides."[75]

One means of removing temptation was to force clerks with serious financial problems out of the firm. Thus, an executive order of May 1862 declared that any employee who had not removed the liens on his salary

---

74. Ibid., no. 153, "Rapport à MM. les administrateurs sur le fonctionnement actuel du bureau des recettes . . ."; no. 161, anonymous letter to director, November 9, 1889; no. 1063, "Etat des agents qui ont declaré être chargé de fonction salariée en dehors la compagnie." The union newspaper declared that most clerks secretly held second jobs.

75. Ibid., no. 162, Le Brun to director, March 4, 1893; no. 168, "Delsol"; no. 779, report of June 15, 1877 (fol. 313).

within four months would be dismissed.[76] The punitive approach was repeated in the 1870s, and certain clerks were fired.[77] Only after the employees had developed some collective power in the 1890s did the PGC adopt a slightly more helpful approach. In 1894 the company offered to advance clerks who were in arrears one month's pay, to be used exclusively for retiring their debts (under the supervision of the legal department). They would have to repay the advance in ten monthly installments. However, the offer specifically excluded employees with liens, who were once again threatened with dismissal.[78] Ultimately, only a small portion of clerks had attachments on their salaries, but the figures hardly reflected the dimensions of the debt problem.[79] Indeed, the struggle to keep creditors from notifying the firm was one more anxiety that being in arrears engendered.

The offer of salary advances was aimed at a debt problem that managers knew was all too pervasive. Clerks who avoided liens were often the victims of usurers, petty and otherwise. Resort to usurers occurred for both necessary and frivolous reasons; sometimes it is hard to distinguish between the two. One clerk described poignantly how his daughter's fatal illness and her funeral overwhelmed his resources so that he had to borrow 150 francs at 30 percent interest. Inspector Malaquin was reduced to poverty by the illness of his three children and his wife. Other sources of debt were more a matter of discretionary spending. Mignac, a clerk in the customer accounts department and a union leader, brought trouble upon himself by renting an apartment that was beyond his means. He had taken in students to share the cost, but when they left unexpectedly, he was unable to cope.[80] The records on liens show that debts to publicans and haberdashers were commonplace. Purchasing on credit was becoming an ever more important form of marketing, and retailers were eager to extend credit to employees with steady jobs.[81] Indebtedness was frequent because its roots were complex. On the one hand, employees' modest earnings placed them at risk when the inevitable emergencies arose. On the other hand, many were unwilling to live as prudently as harsh reality dictated, given that they usually earned less than the "living" salary about which Godot had spoken.[82] Debts arose from the clerks' status consciousness,

76. Ibid., no. 1081, ordre de service no. 135.
77. Ibid., no. 679, deliberations of January 21, 1879.
78. Ibid., no. 691, deliberations of November 28, 1894.
79. Ibid., no. 753, "Etat nominatif des employés frappés d'oppositions au 30 octobre 1869."
80. Ibid., no. 150, "Affaire Mignac"; "Affaire Malaquin."
81. Berlanstein, Working People, pp. 149–150.
82. Theodore Zeldin has reiterated the conventional view that peasants and clerks saved whereas wage earners spent all their disposable income. France, 1848–1945,

which readily made them small consumers. Even an employee who was a committed Socialist and a class-conscious union leader gave this portrait of his comrades: "By reason of his education, the demands of his condition require an employee to have proper and costly attire. His wife and children need more [than those of workers]. On New Year's Day a laborer can take the concierge to a bistro for a drink, and that takes care of the gratuity. An employee must hide his poverty and give the man ten francs. To be an employee is to live in poverty but appear above it." [83]

So widespread was indebtedness that the company faced a problem that went beyond the victimization of individual clerks by usurers. Loan sharking was a regular part of relations within the office and even threatened to pervert the structure of authority. In a sample of ninety-seven inspectors, two were fired for borrowing money from the lamplighters they were supposed to oversee. [84] An assistant head of the central lighting office, Chardin, was found to have lent money at usurious rates to many of his subordinates. Director Camus fired him for abuse of power in November 1876 but then decided to show indulgence, letting him escape with a warning. So established was the practice of loan sharking, however, that the chief was again making loans five months later. Camus could rid the company of Chardin, but that did not dispose of the deeper problem; a similar abuse arose in the lighting office sixteen years later. [85] Another instance of loan sharking became known to management when one clerk, Casimir Rouch, threatened to kill the chief of the accounts payable bureau. The threat was the result of Rouch's demotion, but the police investigation uncovered a loan operation that he had run within the bureau. Rouch either advanced money directly or charged a fee for putting fellow clerks in contact with usurers. Twenty to thirty agents in this office (and perhaps more in other bureaus) were said to be involved. One clerk explained that Rouch arranged a hundred-franc loan for which he would have to pay 130 francs three months later. This *affaire* revealed that loan making and influence peddling were related. A Monsieur Cuvigny lent 150 francs to Rouch and 550 francs to a meter reader to use their influence with a municipal councilman to procure a position as bill collector for him. [86] Though

---

2 vols. (Oxford, 1973–1979), 2: 1163. The reality appears not to have been so neat; Parisian employees did not spend only for necessities and emergencies.
83. *L'Echo du gaz*, no. 18 (December 16, 1897): 1.
84. AP, V 8 O¹, nos. 166–172.
85. Ibid., no. 678, deliberations of November 15, 1876; no. 162, report of chef du service extérieur to director, January 19, 1894.
86. Ibid., no. 162, "Affaire Rouch."

the customer accounts department had the lowest average pay, it was not the only center of usury. The union newspaper identified the legal office as a nest of loan sharking too.[87] In the end, managers could uncover incidents of usury but could by no means repress the practice.

The gas employees' shortage of cash was not the result of exceptionally poor pay. Management refrained from inflicting the low-wage policy for laborers on white-collar clerks. The PGC's office staff was, roughly speaking, neither better nor worse off than its peers in other large, private enterprises. At one of the few industrial firms in Paris that rivaled the PGC in size, the Cail Metallurgical Construction Company, bookkeepers generally rose to a salary of twenty-four hundred francs after ten years and then moved slowly above that level. The large department stores, Bon Marché, Printemps, and the Louvre, started clerical (not sales) personnel at a thousand francs or less but gave them yearly raises, so the average pay pulled close to that of the gas company. The Banque de France did pay more; it commissioned its personnel at two thousand francs and generally gave raises of two hundred francs every two years, up to a salary of forty-five hundred francs. The justification for higher pay was the exclusiveness of the bank's recruitment and the quest for gentlemen with *baccalauréats* in its offices.[88] Thus there were variations in the way salaries were determined, but not much variation in the actual level of pay for clerks who had the qualifications of those at the PGC. The financial difficulties that gas clerks experienced were no doubt shared by their colleagues in most other enterprises.

Since clerks' wants and needs easily surpassed their resources, raises and promotions became matters of close attention. When the municipal council took up the cause of the employees, management was eager to report an increase of 30 percent in the average salary between 1869 and 1891 (from 1,809 francs to 2,349 francs).[89] The figure was meant to place corporate policy in a favorable light but resulted from a facile analysis of pay statistics. The guiding rule to which the PGC adhered was not to grant general raises to entire categories of employees; rather, it promoted individual clerks one step at a time. There was thus an inevitable tendency for average salaries to increase as the firm and its clerical staff matured. That predictable rise was reflected in the figure the company eagerly cited. To determine whether clerks experienced better pay during the life of the

---

87. *Le Journal du gaz: Organe officiel de la chambre syndicale des travailleurs du gaz*, no. 139 (September 20, 1898): 3.
88. AP, V 8 O¹, no. 626, "Comparaisons de la situation du personnel de la Compagnie avec celle des agents de divers grands établissements de Paris."
89. Ibid., "Comparaison de la situation du personnel en 1869 et 1901."

company, it is not enough to compare average emoluments at two distinct points; one must ask whether an employee at a given age or with a given amount of seniority earned more. Considering the promotional policy of the PGC, such increased earnings could have resulted only from a faster pace of advancement up the salary hierarchy. Yet the portion of clerks promoted each year was remarkably stable—rarely surpassing 20 percent or falling below 10 percent—even during the Radical Republic.[90] Only one small qualification needs to be made to the conclusion that clerks were not receiving more pay at equal levels of seniority by the end of the century. During the late 1870s, that time of widespread and acute wage inflation, the PGC ceased starting employees at fifteen hundred francs and moved them immediately to eighteen hundred francs. The new policy hastened all newly engaged persons up the salary ladder without yielding on principle. That the change was completely unannounced and never openly acknowledged demonstrates how determined the company was to leave pay a private matter between each individual clerk and management.[91] A small part of the 30 percent increase in average salary resulted from the change, but most came from the inevitable maturing of the office staff. The individual clerk of 1890 was earning little more at a specific point in his career than his counterpart in 1865 had earned. Political pressure would be required to alter that dilemma.

Since employees received raises only with individual, step-by-step promotions, the pace of those advances was a matter of passionate concern to them. The annual decisions about advancements were, in principle, private business between the employee and management, but the results of the end-of-the-year notices were soon widely known and always created a stir among the personnel. One employee who complained about being passed over in 1899 could cite, in detail, the salary histories of six of his colleagues.[92] Where he obtained such information is unclear. The result of a promotion policy based essentially on the discretion of management was a considerable amount of inequality in pay among employees with similar seniority. The company had either to convince clerks that the decisions were just or to countenance a good deal of dissatisfaction.

In the billing bureau of 1884 there were eighteen clerks earning "living" salaries of twenty-seven hundred francs. The most recently hired employees at that level had been with the firm ten years; the most senior

---

90. Between 1871 and 1890, the portion of promoted clerks was never much above or below 15 percent. See the promotion lists in ibid., nos. 665–700.
91. The silence on the new policy may also signify management's disapproval. The officers resented having to bow to market forces (see chapter 4).
92. AP, V 8 O¹, no. 157, Aubineau to superintendent, January 2, 1899.

Table 15. Seniority Distribution at Each Salary Level, 1902

Salary (francs)											
2,100	Years of work	1	2	3	4	5	6	7	8	9	10
	No. of clerks	5	29	48	83	98	107	35	14	9	4
2,400	Years of work	4	5	6	7	8	9	10	11	12	12+
	No. of clerks	1	3	34	30	37	60	49	36	31	26
2,700	Years of work	<13	13	14	15	16	17	18	19	20	20+
	No. of clerks	34	36	43	20	27	27	32	13	13	11
3,000	Years of work	<17	17	18	19	20	21	22	23	24	24+
	No. of clerks	9	12	19	24	24	17	7	9	12	12

Source: AP, V 8 O¹, no. 149, "Assimilation."

had been with the firm thirty-four years. Among the thirty-nine meter readers paid twenty-four hundred francs in 1884, six had less than ten years of seniority, and eight had twenty or more years.[93] Such disparities were by no means exceptional. Table 15 demonstrates that they were pronounced even as late as 1902, when the company had been under intense pressure to equalize pay for more than a decade. The PGC had not made it possible for employees to count on their salaries growing steadily and predictably as they matured. The clerk not yet earning twenty-seven hundred francs after fifteen years with the firm might have been deeply troubled by his prospects.

• • •

The trade union official who described the fate of employees as "living in poverty but appearing to be above it" might have added that keeping up appearances could reinforce distress. The employees of the PGC often believed themselves to be in a precarious position. They were pressed for funds—sometimes urgently so. The hope of getting a raise or a bonus meant much to them. Their union journal opined that the end-of-the-year announcements were "more eagerly awaited than the coming of the Messiah."[94] Yet they could not anticipate regular, predictable rewards from their firm. Nor were most clerks willing to transform themselves into model employees for the sake of promotions. Management insisted on complete discretion over salary decisions and affirmed that employees must accept its decrees as equitable, the product of a careful evaluation of individual merit. The clerks had difficulty doing so and eventually found in collective organization a voice for their frustration.

93. Ibid., no. 153, "Personnel."
94. *L'Echo du gaz*, no. 18 (December 16, 1897): 1.

SIX

Employees' Grievances and Protest

"What a cantankerous group our employees have become," remarked Director Godot in 1893. "And yet, we have given them all the advantages it is reasonable to expect," he added with an easily summoned sense of indignation.[1] Godot's wistful observations raise the possibility that the model of proletarianization applied to the gas employees after all. Did the PGC's clerks, even though not clear victims of a deteriorating work regime, come to identify with the working-class left? The question assumes a special importance because the gas employees were not the only example of office workers organizing, expressing discontents, and seeking collective remedies at the turn of the century. Indeed, Godot's employees were very much on the leading edge of a broad white-collar protest movement in the decade or so before World War I. Nonetheless, we shall see that the proletarianization model distorts a complex situation.

A Sense of Grievance

A complete list of all the reforms that employees demanded during the 1890s would be extensive.[2] Each type of white-collar worker had its own specialized grievances, ones that sometimes lacked universal significance. Active agents, especially the meter readers, did not like the uniforms they had to wear; the employees said that the outfits restricted their movement and lowered their dignity.[3] Lighting inspectors resented Sunday work and

1. AP, V 8 O¹, no. 149, "Revendications du syndicat. Notes."
2. Ibid., "Revendications du personnel—employés."
3. Ibid., no. 148, ordre de service no. 390, "Personnel des contrôleurs de compteurs." The head of the lighting service thought the uniform drab and perhaps cumbersome. See no. 765, "Rapport sur les uniformes des employés du service extérieur."

argued that the company could eliminate it if there were sufficient good-will. Complaints regarding the medical service were bitter. Stories about the outrageous behavior of the company doctors were legion. A clerk's widow complained that a doctor diagnosed her husband's ailment as small-pox and never returned to administer treatment.[4] Sometimes individual personalities stirred discontent. The head of the collection bureau, Du-fourg, and the chief of the customer accounts department, Lejeune, in-spired much animosity with their overbearing manner. One union leader stated that some members joined only to spite them. The editors of the union newspaper, recognizing a theme that would draw their readers' in-terest, ran a derogatory story on at least one of the two supervisors in almost every issue.[5]

To be sure, a widespread sense of alienation arose from the petty details of daily life within the administration of the PGC. Yet these details often stood for grander principles, and the debates over small reforms did not lack references to those principles. Much research in labor history has shown that a struggle for control over the production process was a prin-cipal source of protest among manual workers.[6] To what extent were de-fensive efforts at "bureau control" behind the protest of clerks? It was more a matter of coincidence than substance that municipal politics sparked union formation about the same time that office productivity be-gan its dramatic rise.[7] On the whole, the quest for worker control played a limited role in the clerks' collective life. The meter readers, who bore the brunt of the growing customer base, specifically renounced the right to interfere with the way that the PGC organized their service.[8] The vigor of the clerks' union would be difficult to understand if defending work rou-tines was central to its purpose, for it was a resounding failure in influenc-ing the company on that point. Office productivity continued to climb at an accelerating rate throughout the life of the union (see figure 11). More-

4. Ibid., no. 780, report of May 13, 1880 (fol. 466).
5. See, for example, *Le Journal du gaz: Organe officiel de la chambre syndicale des travailleurs du gaz*, no. 31 (March 20, 1894): 3. Dufourg was "quoted" as saying that he had "no taste for parliamentary procedures" and would fire anyone who questioned his orders.
6. Joan Scott, *The Glassworkers of Carmaux* (Cambridge, Mass., 1974), and Mi-chael Hanagan, *The Logic of Solidarity: Artisans and Industrial Workers in Three French Towns, 1871–1914* (Urbana, Ill., 1980), are among many works on the pro-letarianization of skilled laborers.
7. See chapter 5 on the evolution of the work pace within the offices of the PGC.
8. *L'Echo du gaz: Organe de l'Union syndicale des employés de la Compagnie parisienne du gaz*, no. 100 (May 16, 1901): 3. The article "Service des compteurs" proclaimed that meter readers "by no means have the thought of opposing inno-vations. We consider that question outside our sphere of action."

over, the union did nothing to challenge the most comprehensive administrative reorganization in the PGC's history. Starting in 1902, management carried through the policy known as decentralization, which eliminated office posts and reassigned work in a wholesale manner, without the least input from the union. There is no evidence that union leaders tried to stop decentralization, except to protest meekly the loss of jobs.[9] The issues that leaders felt pressure to act on concerned promotions, benefits, and security. Clerks expressed deep dissatisfaction with the company's discretionary practices on rewarding and punishing. That was the dominant source of grievance. The rising pace of work was only one more reminder among others of how powerless the clerks were. Unlike certain sorts of manual workers, employees focused their collective activity on compensations rather than control.[10]

The company's handling of retirement benefits was typical of the concerns that drew clerks together in search of redress. The offer of half pay for a retiree who was at least fifty-five years old and who had served the firm for at least twenty-five years seemed generous on the surface. Yet employees resented the fact that the company refused to define the pension as a right. A consulting barrister told managers just what they wanted to hear when he affirmed that "the day that pensions become an obligation rather than a reward for service will be the day the state will have disarmed the company against its personnel."[11] To the corporate assertion that pensions should go only to individuals who had served the company well, clerks responded that a twenty-five-year career was proof in itself of sufficient conscientiousness. The worries that the PGC's policy engendered were all the more intense in that most clerks did not strive to be model employees. Their lackadaisical work culture made guaranteed pensions worth striving for.[12]

The company raised anxieties still further by reneging on its promise of retirement benefits even for worthy servants. Management craftily in-

9. *Echo du gaz*, no. 121 (April 1, 1902); no. 127 (July 1, 1902). For the company's actions, see AP, V 8 O¹, no. 679, deliberations of May 11, 1901, and April 12, 1902.
10. Some protest over the work regime did occur, but it came after the union was well established and was not a central theme among the demands. See AP, V 8 O¹, no. 149, "Modifications à apporter dans le service des sections (27 février 1893)"; no. 150, Claverie to director, December 9, 1902; no. 162, "Lettres et renseignements concernant divers agents de la compagnie."
11. Ibid., no. 152, report of Guerenet, May 12, 1898. The company solicited the consultation in response to legislative initiatives regarding pensions.
12. See chapter 5 on the employees' work culture. When a fired clerk sued the PGC (unsuccessfully) for his pension benefits, he was acting on the fears many agents must have had. See ibid., no. 694, deliberations of April 9, 1898.

tended to push the cost of pensions for clerks who retired after 1905 on its successor firm (or negotiate compensation from the city if its own charter was renewed). The many clerks hired after 1880 had a legitimate reason for feeling victimized. They could readily calculate from public documents that the PGC was putting aside only enough money to pay for employees who would complete their twenty-five years of service before 1905.[13] Efforts to find out what exactly the company intended to do about younger clerks met with frustration and failure. The director argued that since the retirement fund was financed entirely from the operating budget, clerks had no right to interfere in the company's administration of the fund. Here was a case in which corporate egoism, authoritarian paternalism, and parsimony—each a fundamental part of the fabric of management—dovetailed to infuriate a good number of employees.

The quest for security made some employees hope for the option of early retirement, perhaps after a minimum of fifteen years with, of course, a reduced pension. Some might have seen in the option a means to launch a second career or to supplement part-time work. The union's contention that employees were often "worn out" by their office tasks and needed to retire early might have seemed absurd to manual workers, but there was some sense in it. The employees' health records reported on poor vision or fatigue often enough to suggest that some would not be able to hold their jobs for twenty-five years, especially if they were in the active service. Despite the plausible case that existed for the option, the company firmly rejected early retirement.[14]

A refusal to grant employees a monthly allocation of free coke raised resentments that transcended the financial considerations involved. Clerks saw the request as a matter of equity since manual workers had long received free coke. They also considered the benefit a gesture that would help them save a bit of needed income while costing the company nothing. After all, the price the company received for gas fully covered the expense

13. A union leader affirmed that the company had informally told many recently hired clerks not to expect pensions unless the corporate charter was lengthened. See ibid., no. 149, Claverie to director, June 5, 1900.

14. Ibid., "Revendications du personnel—employés." Why the company was so firm in rejecting early retirement is unclear. As one anonymous stockholder who offered his unsolicited advice to the director pointed out, management could have used early retirement to remove inefficient clerks without being so harsh as to fire them (no. 162, letter from a "petit actionnaire" of December 19, 1898). Perhaps the PGC remained firmly opposed in recognition of its principle not to grant those reforms explicitly demanded by the union; and perhaps managers saw early retirement as a reduction of their sanctioning powers or a step toward mandatory pensions.

of purchasing coal.[15] The PGC's refusal to dispense free coke seemed to many clerks an act of mean-spiritedness and called into question the corporate pretentions to paternalism. The level of indignation was thus out of proportion to the monetary importance of the issue.

Consternation over managers' discretionary authority emerged clearly in the conflict over annual bonuses. Corporate policy on bonuses proved to entail a web of contradictions. The directors explained that all clerks who performed their jobs competently should receive a year-end bonus even as they insisted that nobody had a right to one. They also affirmed that the proper bonus was a month's pay. In 1863, however, the company began allocating 1 percent of its profits for the bonuses, which amounted to roughly two-thirds of the monthly payroll. Thus, the director was compelled either to withhold bonuses from a large number of clerks or to award less than a month's pay.[16] Not until pressure from the union and the municipal council forced the firm to confront the contradictions did corporate policy change. In 1895 the firm decided to allocate whatever sum was necessary to reward deserving employees with a month's pay. The clerks received some satisfaction, but distrust of management's ulterior motives lingered.[17]

Suspicion and accompanying resentment came to bear most forcefully on the matter of salary advancements. One office chief, violently hostile to the emerging trade organization, urged the company to reconsider its promotion policy on the grounds that this issue alone was responsible for his enemies' success. "The employees' union counts on the results of January 1 [the day raises were announced] to increase its membership," he noted.[18] An assistant office head and self-proclaimed "friend of order" was more pointed in his recommendation. "Each January 1 the union becomes stronger," he proclaimed, citing the case of a clerk who joined because he had waited seven years to advance to a salary of twenty-one hundred

15. Ibid., no. 733, deliberations of May 12, 1892; no. 149, "Fourniture du coke." Workers received four hectoliters in the winter and two in the summer. Clerks already had the right to buy coke from the PGC at a reduced rate.
16. Ibid., no. 723, deliberations of January 2, 1857; no. 725, deliberations of December 31, 1863. The surviving documents make clear that the company awarded a month's bonus to an excellent employee, not just an average one. See no. 156, "Salaires; gratifications."
17. Ibid., no. 692, deliberations of December 24, 1895. The allocation was a return to the pre-1863 policy, but it still did not ensure a bonus of a month's pay. Even in 1900 the PGC spent 460,000 francs on annual bonuses, whereas a month's pay for all employees would have cost 625,000 francs. See no. 149, "Examen des revendications générales des employés . . . (17 novembre 1900)."
18. Ibid., no. 150, letter of "un sous-chef, l'ami de l'ordre" to director, October 25, 1893.

francs, whereas a colleague had obtained that level in just three years. Significantly, the friend of order accepted the union's solution to the problem. His unsolicited advice to the director was to "make the existing inequalities disappear."[19] Even union officers admitted that their organizational activities benefited from the "promotion fever" that gripped the personnel each December.[20] It should be noted that clerks in the gas company were not alone in feeling this issue deeply. Discontents with arbitrary advancements motivated much collective protest among employees in other bureaucracies too, as we shall see shortly.

Management offered its policy on raises as a model of rationality and simple justice. It affirmed the need for modern corporations to function as meritocracies. Neither in their public pronouncements nor in their internal memorandums did managers express doubts about their ability to evaluate clerks appropriately and equitably.[21] They did not even bother to answer their many critics, who had serious questions about their methods. Those critics portrayed the PGC's promotion policies as a model of arbitrariness. They affirmed that when office chiefs were not preoccupied with advancing the careers of sons or nephews, they aided the sycophants who flattered them most. A more impersonal criticism was that meritocratic principles were invalid because there was no way to measure the quality of work. Office tasks at the PGC, asserted several union officials, were so specialized and routine that no individual initiative was possible. Therefore, to do one's job was to do it well.[22] Underlying all the objections was a pervasive resentment of decisions made on high, in secret, and without accountability, decisions that created inequalities within the status group of gas employees. The clerks and their leaders constructed an understanding of private authority that virtually excluded the possibility of equity.[23] It could be argued that clerks resented the dependency as much as the perceived inequity.

The solution that critics offered was to eliminate or at least reduce the

---

19. Ibid., letter from "un sous-chef, l'ami de l'ordre" to director, November 18, 1893.

20. *Journal du gaz,* no. 24 (December 5, 1893): 1.

21. See, for example, AP, V 8 O¹, no. 148, ordre de service no. 390. "If there are agents who have not advanced after eighteen or nineteen years of work," declared management, "they have only themselves to blame."

22. Ibid. Meter readers affirmed that "raises are accorded completely by favoritism, without taking into account work or years of service." A letter in *Le Parti ouvrier* (July 26, 1892) from the employees' union proclaimed that "some bureau chiefs make of their offices personal fiefs, where a few favorites get raises every three years, whereas others get raises only after six or seven years."

23. On the construction of meaning through exclusion, see Joan Wallach Scott, *Gender and the Politics of History* (New York, 1988), pp. 5–8.

discretionary element in advancements. The union fought for regular, predictable, periodic salary raises based on seniority. It occasionally cited with favor the example of the city of Paris, which made two-thirds of the promotions on the basis of seniority and one-third at the discretion of the office head, but quickly came to insist on a timetable for automatic advancements. Organized clerks were willing to allow the company to promote especially worthy colleagues faster, if it wished, but not slower unless there was good cause. The union proposed establishing a commission, which would include clerks, to rule on the validity of denied promotions.[24] As a comparison of the proposed timetable and the firm's practice in 1892 shows, the union was calling for both a faster pace of advancement and more secure, predictable raises:[25]

Salary (francs)	Union Proposal (years)	Corporate Practice (years)
1,800	1	4
2,100	+3	+5
2,400	+2	+5
2,700	+7	+6
3,000	+4	+3
3,300	+4	+3
3,600	+2	+6

It wanted employees to reach the "living" salary of twenty-seven hundred francs after six years, not fourteen. By its own calculations, 87 percent (1,950 of 2,252) of the agents were at least a step behind the proposed timetable, and 29 percent (656) were at least two steps behind.[26] Faster advancements were important to employees because of their tight financial circumstances. The demand for regularity in promotions also had great psychological appeal; it was a matter of dignity. If asked to choose between the two concerns, union leaders might have selected the latter as more important. Their journal proclaimed a preference for "regular advancement, however slow, to the arbitrariness of our bosses."[27]

Were the criticisms of individualistic evaluations on the part of orga-

24. AP, V 8 O¹, no. 149, Claverie to the president of the *conseil d'administration,* January 22, 1896.
25. Ibid., "Réclamations"; "Comparaison de la situation du personnel."
26. Ibid., report of November 11, 1898. Had the union made its calculations earlier, especially before 1890, the portion of agents who were behind would have been still higher.
27. *Journal du gaz,* no. 24 (December 5, 1893): 1; no. 51 (January 20, 1895): 1.

nized employees largely a matter of carping about poor treatment and resentment over having one's work judged unfavorably? It is far from certain that clerks were merely imagining abuses or raising theoretical shortcomings in the PGC's handling of promotions. In fact, there were genuine difficulties and even thoroughgoing flaws in the corporation's procedures. The company encouraged the suspicion of nepotism by assigning young clerks to work under a relative and by allowing a father's (or uncle's) good service to benefit the youth's career.[28] Moreover, the union's perception that the work routine provided employees little room to distinguish themselves was an objection to which management never responded. The most serious problem in procedure arose from the centralization of decision making. Power to promote was far removed from the officers who were in the best position to judge the relative worth of clerks, their immediate supervisors. Office chiefs wrote only terse comments about their subordinates and passed the dossier up the chain of command. Their reports may not have been effective at communicating the nuances that differentiated one clerk from another. Furthermore, the director, who actually made the decision, could not have thought carefully about most cases. Within a few days he (along with the assistant director and one or two board members) had to examine hundreds of dossiers for both raises and bonuses. The annual task topped off an already hectic schedule and came at a particularly pressured season. It is no wonder that Ernest Bican, a by-product inspector, was overlooked. He had received excellent comments from superiors for eight years but still earned eighteen hundred francs. Engineer Audouin regretted Bican's resignation in 1879 but evidently had been unable to secure him a raise.[29] A central dilemma for promotion practices within the PGC, then, was not so much a willful abandonment of impartiality by management as the use of inappropriate procedures for making meritocratic decisions. The problem was confounded by managers' failure to question the effectiveness of their work.

Union leaders did not dwell on the procedural flaws, nor did they call for decentralization. They distrusted the immediate supervisors even more than the director—faith in Godot's "good intentions" died hard.[30] Moreover, they rejected individual evaluation on principle. The most dev-

---

28. AP, V 8 O[1], no. 149, "Modifications à apporter dans le service des sections." Management actively defended the policy of having clerks serve under their relatives. See also no. 161, dossier of Charles Gosset.
29. Ibid., no. 161, dossier of Bican.
30. On the resentment of immediate superiors, see ibid., report of Simon to head of distribution service, May 30, 1893. The employees' inclination to understand discretionary decisions as a matter of favoritism rendered decentralized evaluations useless to them as a solution.

astating public exposure of the flaws in corporate practice came from the Radical alderman Alexandre Patenne. At meetings of the municipal council he did not hesitate to affirm that the gas clerks were "absolutely subjected to arbitrary will [*bon plaisir*] and favoritism." Patenne noted skeptically that "the recommendations made by departmental chiefs are subjected to the examination of higher managers, who modify them, annul some, add others. The final report arrives, thus modified, before the director, who makes it definitive without knowing the candidates who have been eliminated." Patenne concluded by asking plaintively, "What is the nature of this process if not absolute arbitrariness?"[31] If the alderman had known even more about the workings of the PGC, he might have added that the director arbitrarily dropped many recommended candidates (like Bican) to reduce expenses.

In view of these procedural problems, it is not surprising that empirical research produces more doubts about the reliability of corporate practice. A sample of personnel records from the by-products department shows that the director honored only a third of Engineer Audouin's recommendations for promotion.[32] At the same time, cases like that of Albert Arrieu raise questions about why certain employees did advance. Arrieu, a lighting inspector, had accumulated twenty-two fines between December 1888 and October 1892, yet he was still promoted to the post of secretary of his section. Henri Baudouin received eleven fines in his first two years (including ones for filing a false report and for talking back to a superior), but he was nonetheless named assistant supervisor (*inspecteur-contrôleur adjoint*). He also received raises at a faster-than-average pace. Similarly, the sixteen fines Louis Bray received between 1880 and 1891, which included two serious warnings, did not prevent him from becoming a supervisory inspector.[33] To avoid generalizing from a few examples, I have classified the inspectors' records according to the incidence of fines and compared their rates of advancement (table 16). The findings could have given little comfort to managers, who insisted on the justice of their personnel reviews.

In general, the confident assertion of authority in the firm over matters large and small, which management assumed to be an unassailable right, produced frustration among the employees. Bourgouinet, a clerk in the billing department, requested the right to wear a white (not blue) smock to protect his street clothes from dust. Shortly after both the office head

31. *Conseil municipal*, deliberations of March 26, 1896.
32. AP, V 8 O¹, no. 156.
33. Ibid., no. 172 (Arrieu); no. 168 (Baudouin); no. 166 (Bray).

Table 16. Advancements of Lighting Inspectors,
Categorized by Work Record

	Below-Average Fines		Above-Averge Fines	
Raises (francs)	No.	Average Time (yrs)	No.	Average Time (yrs)
1,800 to 2,100	21	5.3	19	5.0
2,100 to 2,400	14	6.1	17	6.2
2,400 to 2,700	11	7.1	12	6.8

Source: AP, V 8 O¹, nos. 164–173, "Livres du personnel."

and the departmental chief turned down the request, Bourgouinet, who had never been interested in the union before, was seen talking to a shop steward.[34] The PGC did have a procedure for investigating complaints, but its authoritarian features engendered more anxiety than redress. If an employee was unhappy with a supervisor's decision, the chief of the department placed the petitioner in the uncomfortable position of having to confront the superior directly, alone in the latter's office. Understandably, most plaintiffs withdrew their complaints or professed to be satisfied with the superior's explanation. The union eventually gave aggrieved clerks collective support. Delegates even pursued a matter when the victim preferred to remain anonymous. At the same time, the union provided still one more avenue for the company to intimidate its personnel. More than once, plaintiffs were placed in the position of having to declare that militants had misled them.[35]

The perception and reality of injustice in no way produced calls for a perfected means of evaluating individuals. Both union spokesmen and politicians deduced from the fact of inequities the principle that justice was impossible as long as discretionary authority continued. The solution, as far as they were concerned, was to acknowledge the employees' right to work under fixed, general, and evenly applied rules to which they had consented. That meant seniority would have to be the basis for rewards.

• • •

Even if the PGC had been able to answer the charges of the critics, its advocacy of discretionary power to punish and reward subordinates was

34. Ibid., no. 162, "Affaire Bourgouinet."
35. Ibid., "Affaire Charlot."

destined to lose the support of public opinion and of the dominant political coalitions. The debate over promotions within the gas company was one small—but illustrative—component of a broader questioning of authority. To many Frenchmen of the fin de siècle, the Republic was supposed to be the regime of equality, the one in which the little person had the same rights as the rich, a regime in which concentrations of power need not threaten *les petits*. Yet the Third Republic came into being without honoring these principles. Just as Opportunist republicans accepted monarchical and imperial institutions, they also accepted the power of employers to dispose of their personnel entirely as they saw fit. Efforts to give civil servants more regular advancements failed time and again.[36] In this context the sudden decision on the part of the Parisian municipal council to stand up for gas clerks marked a breakthrough and a sign of more to come. Radicals were poised for a new round of republican reform in the era of the Dreyfus Affair.

It was not simply that the executives of the PGC rendered arbitrary decisions; councilmen of the left now rejected on principle the subordination of employees to the discretionary power of an elite. Patenne spoke for the majority when he proclaimed it "perfectly reasonable" to insist on receiving from the PGC "a precise and inviolable regulation that any agent who does his work conscientiously can expect a salary of three thousand francs at the end of fifteen years and thirty-six hundred francs at the end of twenty-four years, so as to retire with a pension of eighteen hundred francs."[37] The Strauss amendment of 1892 had sought to make a similar provision a part of the gas company's charter. For Radicals at the end of the century, liberating humble clerks from the employers' arbitrary will was a republican obligation. For Socialists, it was an act of social justice.[38] The position of advanced republicans created an unbridgeable gulf in communication between the PGC and the municipality. Aldermen repeatedly demanded that management reveal its rules for promotion; managers repeatedly replied that the rule was advancement by merit determined through a case-by-case evaluation. Councilmen replied that that was not

36. Guy Thuillier and Jean Tulard, *Histoire de l'administration française* (Paris, 1984), pp. 46–85; Guy Thuillier, *Bureaucratie et bureaucrates en France au XIXe siècle* (Geneva, 1980), pp. 403–452.

37. *Conseil municipal,* deliberations of December 30, 1895. Patenne had proposed that the city contribute to the PGC's pension fund so that it could have a role in administering it. See AP, V 8 O¹, no. 1626, "Rapport présenté par M. Patenne sur une pétition de la Fédération du personnel ouvrier et employé . . . (8 juillet 1895)."

38. *Conseil municipal,* deliberations of December 5, 1892. Recall that almost all of the seventeen cosponsors of the amendment were Radicals.

what they meant when they asked for the rules; managers protested that there was nothing more to it. The Radical and Socialist press, following the councilmen, chided the PGC for evasiveness and lack of goodwill in refusing to disclose the regulations. The PGC retorted that a procedure based on seniority favored slackers, but the company was not able to win the battle for public opinion in Paris and, increasingly, in France.[39]

Since the left majority of the municipal council offered the employees' union unswerving support, the PGC probably hoped for more favorable treatment when the majority passed to the Nationalist right in 1900. It was disappointed. The coalition of anti-Semites, anticollectivists, anti-Dreyfusards, cultural reactionaries, and patriotic Socialists who won the election consistently found justice in the gas employees' demands for raises based on seniority. Leading right-wing aldermen like Georges Berry and Henri Galli came as honored guests to union rallies. The new majority pursued the assimilation of gas employees into the municipal personnel. Their anticapitalistic, antimonopolist rhetoric favored liberating Frenchmen from the yoke of big capital, and agitation in the PGC gave them an arena in which to demonstrate their seriousness about their principles.[40] Managers had to wait a few more years, after the Nationalist ascendancy in Paris had subsided, before the crisis of liberalism would abate.

Faced with the hostility of the left and right of the municipal council, the officers of the PGC might well have wished to believe that a strong sense of grievance was confined to a minority of Socialist clerks, who would chafe under any legitimate exercise of authority, and that most clerks appreciated their jobs and their fringe benefits. Executives could have taken comfort from the failure of the union to attract more than a small portion of their agents (before 1900 at least).[41] They were probably heartened to find antisyndicalist employees organizing and expressing their support for the firm over the union. Despite these signs that the union could be contained, it is clear that discontents were widespread even among the employees who refused to unionize. In truth, rejection of the

---

39. Ibid., no. 149, "Historique des rapports avec la ville de Paris relatif au personnel de la Compagnie."

40. Ibid., no. 1626, "Projet de résolution . . . (17 janvier 1901)"; *Echo du gaz*, no. 87 (November 1, 1900): 2; no. 92 (January 16, 1901): 1. The prolabor stance of the Nationalists would seem to support Zeev Sternhell's contention that the radical right was genuinely revolutionary. The case is not so clear-cut, however, because the Nationalists also worked toward a solution to the gas question that favored powerful financial interests. On this debate, see Paul Mazgaj, "The Origins of the French Radical Right: A Historiographical Essay," *French Historical Studies* 15 (1987): 287–315.

41. The size of the union will receive attention below.

employer's discretionary authority was not confined to a minority of left-leaning white-collar workers. Though organized groups of agents arose to oppose the "red" union and even to proclaim their contempt for clerks who "acted like workers," these very employees were deeply troubled by the PGC's personnel policies. The Corporate Association of Gas Employees, founded with help from the Nationalist aldermen, savagely attacked the union. At the same time, it made demands on the company similar to the union's. Announcing as their purpose to defend the clerks' material interests rather than attack the company, the activists of the association asked for an "elevation of salaries by regular advancement and an absolute right to early or regular retirement." [42] They insisted on seniority as the fundamental principle for raises. They too understood discretionary decisions as a matter of favoritism or capriciousness. Along with their proclaimed enemies, the leaders of the union, they called for free coke and proper endowing of the pension fund to guarantee the rights of the younger clerks. Promising to work through "loyal methods," the antiunion activists argued that the best means to defeat the union was through "voluntary concessions" from the company. [43] An undated petition from employees in the payment bureau, probably written in 1900, declared that their "dignity, love of their work, and respect for their chiefs" prevented them from ever joining the union. Indeed, the petition labeled the syndicalists *déclassés*. Nonetheless, the signatories also wanted to relay a message of discontent over corporate policies. They presented a list of "recommendations" that paralleled the standard demands of the union to a remarkable degree. They too wanted regularity of promotions, at least of the sort that municipal employees enjoyed (two-thirds by seniority), and asked for clarifications on the conditions under which bonuses might be withheld. These nonunion clerks went beyond the syndicalists in requesting changes in the work routine. Ending the prohibition on smoking and reading newspapers in the office as well as allotting more time for certain tasks were among their "respectful wishes." [44] Clearly, the questioning of management's discretionary authority had become deeply rooted among the gas clerks as a whole. Antiunion agents may have professed devotion

---

42. AP, V 8 O¹, no. 150, "Union corporative des employés du gaz."

43. Ibid., no. 149, "Projet de règlement général de l'Union corporative des employés du gaz"; Danfray to director, October 26, 1901; Lelong to director, September 12, 1901; no. 1626, "Rapport sur les revendications du personnel du gaz par René Piault (28 décembre 1901)."

44. Ibid., no. 153, "Les employés non-syndiqués du bureau des recettes à M. Godot, directeur de la Compagnie parisienne du gaz."

to the firm, but they had more in common with their unionized colleagues on the question of authority than with the engineers.[45]

• • •

The effervescence in the offices of the PGC was not an isolated phenomenon. Indeed, the gas clerks were on the cutting edge of a noteworthy protest movement—a crisis of authority—among employees in private and public bureaucracies at the turn of the century. Whereas agitation by manual laborers had been an established fact of life for quite some time, collective protest on the part of employees was for the public a new sign, either welcomed or feared, that hierarchical authority was under attack.[46] The clamor surfaced wherever white-collar workers could hope for the sympathetic intervention of the authorities, and passive discontent was undoubtedly far more widespread. One contemporary lawyer grasped the nature of the movement when he wrote about "the crisis that has emerged at the beginning of the twentieth century within the personnel of public administration."[47] As we have seen, the work conditions of civil servants had been more like those in private enterprise than they were different from them, despite commonplace assumptions to the contrary. The employees had no guaranteed rights. Ministers guarded their authority over their personnel just as jealously as did the PGC's managers. Over the years there had been various attempts to legislate the regularity of promotions, rules on dismissal, and the like for civil servants, but the efforts had always failed. The emerging opposition to the discretionary power of elites in Parisian republican politics of the 1890s was mirrored, albeit unevenly, in a renewed drive to gain rights for civil servants. Legislative initiatives for a regulatory code reappeared. The jurisprudence of the Council of State relaxed its traditional hard line in favor of absolute ministerial power. It began to instruct ministers to establish and follow regular rules. By 1909 a student of the civil service could write that "limitations on arbitrary power . . . and the observation of rules and laws—that is the

45. Unionized and nonunionized agents were able to join together to protest management's choice for assistant head of the central gas main bureau. In their petition to the director, the two groups declared themselves to be "united in a unanimous sentiment of reprobation and indignation." Thus the profound respect that nonunionized employees professed to have for their superiors and that supposedly separated them from their unionized colleagues was rather porous. See ibid., no. 150, employees of the gas main bureau to director, December 31, 1902.
46. The most complete study of white-collar trade unionism is A.-J.-M. Artaud, *La Question de l'employé en France* (Paris, 1909).
47. L. Alcindor, *Le Status des fonctionnaires* (Paris, 1909), p. 9. See also René Hugot-Derville, *Le Principe hiérarchique dans l'administration française* (Paris, 1913).

idea that triumphs today." Parliament responded to the same impulse. The 1901 Law of Association allowed civil servants to form professional organizations, though not unions. Another law, passed in August 1905, cut into ministerial prerogative to make unquestioned decisions. Clerks now had the right to view their dossiers if they were subject to a sanction. The absolute nature of hierarchical authority was increasingly hard to preserve or to justify. Even the political moderates were shifting on this issue.[48]

Public employees did not wait idly for opinion to evolve in their favor. Like the personnel of the PGC, they organized and demanded protection from the arbitrary authority of their superiors. The Law of Association inaugurated an era in which a wide range of civil servants formed a multitude of pressure groups to push for improved conditions. Chief among the concerns—an echo of the gas personnel—was uniformity in recruitment, promotions, and sanctions. Schoolteachers joined trade unions, and postal employees went beyond that measure to strike in 1899 and, more massively, in 1909. The harsh repression the government used against the *postiers* was an attempt to uphold the authority of the state in the same way that officers of the PGC strove to uphold theirs (most notably in 1899).[49] Most civil servants dared not go as far as the postal clerks. Nonetheless, Guy Thuillier is correct in seeing in the emergence of the associations "a veritable revolution, with its mass of new gestures, of complaints, of recriminations."[50] Like the PGC's personnel, public employees had come to believe that the moment was ripe to recast authority relations at work.

The weakening of employees' sense of deference, of which the agitation within the PGC was only an early part, demands broader consideration. The sociologist Michel Crozier has proposed a general framework for understanding responses to authority among the French, and his work has had a pervasive impact on the analysis of French political culture. Crozier argues that his compatriots have long had a profound cultural abhorrence of direct ("face-to-face") authority. Those subject to authority fear its discretionary use, insist that all members of a status group be treated equally,

48. Alcindor, *Status des fonctionnaires*, p. 28; Guy Thuillier, *La Vie quotidienne dans les ministères au XIXe siècle* (Paris, 1976), pp. 215–225.
49. Judith Wishnia, "French Fonctionnaires: The Development of Class Consciousness and Unionization, 1884–1926" (Ph.D. diss., State University of New York at Stony Brook, 1977); Susan Bachrach, "The Feminization of the French Postal Service, 1750–1914" (Ph.D. diss., University of Wisconsin, 1981); Max Ferré, *Histoire du mouvement syndicaliste révolutionnaire chez les instituteurs* (Paris, 1955).
50. Thuillier and Tulard, *Histoire de l'administration française*, p. 77.

and demand that as much decision making as possible be a matter of applying fixed, general rules.[51] Crozier's analysis certainly does describe the sense of grievance in the white-collar milieu at the turn of the century. But it is too broad and ahistorical to be useful for ascertaining how and why a specific protest movement arose. Was the crisis a sign of an evolving consciousness among employees? If so, what sort of consciousness was entailed? Was the crisis a defensive effort to stave off becoming a true "administrative proletariat"? A closer examination of the contention within the offices of the PGC will shed light on this complex matter.

The Organization of Protest

During the first two decades of the PGC's life, employees occasionally expressed to management their dissatisfaction over specific issues. At that point organization was rudimentary and fragile. Groups of agents, of unknown size and origin, submitted petitions through regular hierachical channels. Early on, there was a request for full sick pay. The economic troubles of 1858 generated a petition for a raise, which brought the company to offer a temporary supplement for needy clerks. In 1869 some employees asked management to emulate the paternalism of the Orléans Railroad by opening a subsidized company store.[52] The economic and political troubles that accompanied the fall of the Second Empire seemed to attach clerks more closely than ever to their firm. Some staged a demonstration against the Commune, and immediately after its fall they feted Director Camus in gratitude for having kept them out of military service.[53] The long period of quiet ended abruptly in 1891. Suddenly this

51. Michel Crozier, *The Bureaucratic Phenomenon* (Chicago, 1964). Among the works embodying Crozier's thesis are William Schonfeld, *Obedience and Revolt: French Behavior toward Authority* (Beverly Hills, Calif., 1976); Robert Gilpin, *France in the Age of the Scientific State* (Princeton, 1968); and, above all, Stanley Hoffmann, "Paradoxes of French Political Community," in *In Search of France,* ed. Stanley Hoffmann et al. (Cambridge, Mass., 1963), pp. 1–117. Crozier does not account for the attitudes toward authority except to the extent of rooting them in centuries of bureaucratic practice. One possible explanation entails the notion of sovereignty underpinning the political order. Private authority, such as managers exercised, violated the indivisible sovereignty claimed by absolute monarchs and assumed by the nation in 1789. See Michael Sonenscher, *Work and Wages: Natural Law, Politics, and the Eighteenth-Century French Trades* (Cambridge, 1989), p. 366.
52. AP, V 8 O¹, no. 666, deliberations of June 26, 1858; no. 154, petition from Monsieur Martin to director, April 30, 1869; no. 157, "Procès-verbaux de la commission administrative de la Caisse de prévoyance."
53. Ibid., no. 1801, ordre de service no. 441; no. 727, deliberations of August 10, 1871.

outwardly loyal labor force produced a persistent, demanding trade union. Its claims to being among the largest, most powerful, best-financed, and most respected organizations of white-collar employees in France were serious. The evolution of this union from a bold experiment to an established participant in industrial relations reflects noteworthy changes in the white-collar milieu.

The union had its origins in the neighborhood lighting sections in late 1891. Working well past normal hours to complete their tasks, secretaries of the sections decided to request overtime pay. When their superiors refused even to forward the petition to the director (a provocative step in this firm, which held hierarchical order sacred), the secretaries followed the lead of manual workers and began to organize.[54] With support from the municipal council, the leaders knew that the company could intimidate them and harass them in small ways, but it would not be able to fire them. According to the lighting engineer, secretaries and inspectors took the lead in recruiting office clerks for the union.[55]

Perhaps under the influence of certain councilmen, employees originally envisioned entering the same union the manual workers were in the process of founding. But that daring arrangement fell apart, much to the disappointment of some of the leading voices, after a few months. A crucial reason for the failure of a unified movement was the strenuous objection from the lamplighters to having their supervisors, the lighting inspectors, as comrades. Conciliators found no way to make the lamplighters more cordial to the "workers of the pen," whom they regarded as their oppressors. With such suspicion of the employees, the leaders of the workers' union felt compelled to seek demanding conditions for unity. Clerks would have had to agree to complete subordination. The employees' delegates could not accept such terms and struck off on their own, probably to the relief of most of their followers.[56] From the first, the organized employees chose to couch their demands in a rhetoric of reconciliation and devotion to their firm. Like most employees who dared to organize elsewhere, they probably believed that forceful but respectful negotiation could produce the gains they most desired.[57]

Thus, within the first few moments some permanent features of union life were already established—troubled relations with the workers, the

---

54. Ibid., no. 150, Cézarre to director, March 8, 1903.
55. Ibid., no. 148, "Rapport sur la réunion du syndicat des employés (23 mai 1892)."
56. Ibid., no. 148, clipping from *La Ville*, no. 24 (August 27, 1892); no. 150, clipping from *Bulletin de la Bourse du Travail*, January 29, 1893.
57. On the general orientation of employees' unions, see Lenard R. Berlanstein, *The Working People of Paris, 1871–1914* (Baltimore, 1984), pp. 188–197.

use of a language of loyalty and devotion to cover aggressive demands, and the adoption of modest means to achieve reforms that were not always so modest. The strategy began auspiciously, with Director Godot agreeing to meet with them and listen carefully. As we have seen, the company eventually responded with a series of reforms (including ten days of paid vacation a year) that the union had not specifically demanded but took as a sign of its power and as a promise of ultimate success. Intoxicated by the early achievements, the union celebrated the goodwill of the firm and looked forward to the most cordial relations. Yet management's refusal to yield on essential points, especially regarding advancements, ultimately broke the optimistic enthusiasm. Like most other organized employees, gas clerks found that firm negotiation alone had its limits. Still, employees of the PGC had an advantage most other clerks did not, the support of the municipal government. Radicals as well as Socialists accorded the union representatives respect and readily accepted their views as the authentic voice of the personnel. The strategy of the union progressively shifted from discussing presumably reasonable demands with a presumably well-intentioned employer to pressuring councilmen to pressure the company. Inevitably, the shift necessitated a change in the way the union represented its members—from devoted and dignified employees to exploited workers who deserved to share in the fabulous profits they helped their employer earn.[58] Tying itself to Parisian politics, the union was bound to shift with it—and in Paris of the Dreyfus era those shifts were not always measured ones.

In spite of the moderation they professed and the safe tactics they practiced, unionized gas employees had embarked on an audacious venture. A large and assertive organization of white-collar workers was a novelty in itself. From most of their colleagues members could expect indifference at best. Many employees regarded them as troublemakers and *déclassés* who jeopardized the dignity of the entire office staff. Bureau chiefs did not even feign the goodwill that Director Godot initially displayed. They viewed the union as a challenge to their authority and, like factory superintendents, strove to project the impression that they could not be intimidated. Supervisors saw union membership as a sign of being misled, at best, and as an act of rebellion in the case of committed syndicalists. Dufourg, head of the billing bureau, found it utterly characteristic that Casimir Rouch, the loan shark and his would-be assassin, had belonged to the union. Indeed, the police inquiry into the crime (the clerk had followed his boss

---

58. AP, V 8 O¹, no. 626, "Syndicat. Documents divers"; *Conseil municipal*, deliberations of 1892–1896.

home armed with a knife) revealed that Rouch threatened Dufourg following a demotion he had suffered because he was a union member.[59]

Who were the employees with the audacity and commitment to risk
the ire of their bosses and the ostracism of their colleagues in order to
found a union? Management estimated the size of the union at no more
than two hundred members (one in twelve employees) in 1893. It quickly
arranged for infiltrators to identify members and provide information
about internal operations. A surviving list of 110 "presumed members"
was the result of the corporate espionage. It offers the opportunity to construct a social profile of early union supporters, an enterprise that can shed
light on the origins of the crisis of authority within the offices of the
PGC.[60]

The founding members of the employees' union did not comprise a
cross section of the entire corps. Syndicalism had penetrated some bureaus, others hardly at all. The militants were drawn from the customer
accounts department, the lighting sections, and the meter service. These
were the units that had the most subdivided work, the lowest average pay,
and the least prestige.[61] The union also received some support from the
commissioned personnel closest to manual workers, the bill collectors, office boys, and gas main inspectors. Bureaus with no union members whatsoever included factory accounting, the secretariat, general accounting,
and the commercial department. An outstanding personal characteristic of
the syndicalists was their relative youth. Their average seniority (in 1893)
was 6.5 years, compared to 12.5 years for the commissioned personnel as
a whole. Only twelve of the 110 members listed had more than ten years
of service with the PGC. To a considerable extent, the militants had come
to the firm as the customer base began its unprecedented expansion in the
late 1880s. The recent recruitment explains the syndicalists' low salaries,
almost invariably twenty-four hundred francs or less. Young and poorly
paid, these union members still did not appear to have been an especially
troublesome group of employees, even though they set themselves up for
some degree of persecution. The dossier, which includes sketchy evaluations from their supervisors, cites only twenty-four of them for unusually
poor work or disrespectful attitude. Fourteen clerks were even praised for
their dutiful service, an unexpected tribute given the interest supervisors
had in blackening their reputations. Moreover, the members had advanced
up the salary scale at a normal pace. At about the same time that manage-

59. AP, V 8 O¹, no. 162, "Affaire Rouch."
60. Ibid., "Syndicat des employés." The company spy was probably one L'Hôte, an
employee in the customer accounts department. See ibid., L'Hôte to director, n.d.
61. On average salaries of each bureau, see ibid., no. 153.

ment was compiling its secret list of union members, it drew up a list of eighty-one employees who had not been promoted for seven years or more. Only three names appeared on both lists.[62]

This profile permits speculation on some social and psychological origins of the challenge to hierarchical authority. Unionization occurred among young men who wanted a better future, not among mature clerks combatting deteriorating work conditions. It is easy to believe that anxieties about the security of their pensions weighed on those who organized. They were in danger of having no pension rights after 1905 and probably resented the niggardly and evasive comportment of the firm. The profile also makes clear why early retirement would have been a major demand: union members were rarely past the age of eligibility. The composition of founding members points away from an intensifying pace of work as a precipitant of protest, for it was the senior clerks who would have been most sensitive to a deteriorating work situation. The younger clerks, and especially those in customer accounts and the lighting sections, entered the PGC when work standards were already rising. Thus, the profile suggests a unionization based on an offensive for more certainty about promotions and better pay than older clerks had known.

The employees who emerged as the leaders of the new union were rather characteristic of the rank and file. They were drawn entirely from the customer accounts department and the lighting sections. Three of the five most important leaders had been lighting inspectors. Four of them had been superior primary-school pupils.[63] Psychological qualities, more than social ones, may have marked them for leadership positions. One characteristic they definitely needed was personal courage to participate in the face-to-face meetings with Director Godot, who quickly developed the strategy of bluntness, mild provocation, and aggressiveness.[64] The syndicalists had to resist all the moral authority an engineer of Ponts et Chaussées could bring to a confrontational situation. Not many of their comrades were prepared for such a trial.

Much of the tactical success of the union was the achievement of Maurice Claverie, a former clerk in the customer accounts department who became the general secretary and, eventually, a figure of note in syndicalist

62. Ibid., no. 149, "Révélé des agents n'ayant pas été augmentés depuis sept ans au moins."
63. Ibid., no. 148, report of Saum to director, September 30, 1892.
64. The general secretary of the union once described ironically his meetings with Camus, Godot, and the president of the board, Troost: "How long and monotonous, with these cold gestures, cold words. . . . One does not know what to admire more, their icy patience or their partisanship." *Echo du gaz*, no. 101 (June 1, 1901): 1.

circles.[65] That Claverie survived in this post from the unions' founding to the demise of the PGC attests to his skills as a working-class leader. At once a dreamer and a pragmatist, he was able to adjust his analysis to new realities while retaining an essential core of beliefs. Moreover, his ideas were sufficiently variable and contained enough contradictions to permit a good deal of flexibility. Claverie devoted his talents to fostering the reformist wing of syndicalism. Rejecting the capitalistic organization of society, he did not believe that violence would lead to fundamental transformations. Like the better-known reformist syndicalists Auguste Keufer, of the printers' union, and Edouard Briat, of the precision instrument makers' union, Claverie placed his hope in a gradualistic approach to social change. "Any reform which takes a bit of capital or authority from the boss and gives it to workers," he proclaimed, "is a revolutionary act."[66] Although the rank and file were no doubt pleased with the secretary's quest for immediate gains, members were less content with another of Claverie's preoccupations, the unity of the proletariat. No gas employee was more disappointed than Claverie when clerks and manual laborers failed to form a single union. He saw only one working class, to which "workers of the pen" inevitably belonged. He resurrected projects for unification from time to time, though without much support, and chided those union members who thought only of their personal security.[67] This syndicalist had no theoretical objection to electoral activity and eagerly sought political representation for his union. Not surprisingly, he admired greatly the British Labour party. He forged good relations with the Socialist group on the municipal council and readily lent support to Socialist candidates. In fact, his enemies in the union, who eventually became numerous, often charged him with being a "socialist."

On day-to-day matters the Socialist aldermen offered political support for the union, but Claverie could not work with them on long-term goals. The Socialist group on the municipal council saw only one solution to the gas question, municipalization. Though flexible on the matter for the sake of obtaining immediate gains, Claverie had his own theoretical position, which was syndicalist—of sorts. As an alternative to municipalization, Claverie advanced a program called "gas to the gas producers" (*gaz aux gaziers*), which stipulated that the PGC be owned and run by the person-

65. Robert Brécy, *Le Mouvement syndicaliste en France, 1871–1921* (Paris, 1963), p. 143.
66. Cited in Pierre Carcanagues, *Le Mouvement syndicaliste réformiste en France* (Paris, 1912), pp. 24–36.
67. AP, V 8 O¹, no. 148, "Rapport sur la réunion du syndicat des employés du 23 mai [1892]"; no. 150, "Procès-verbaux du séance des ouvriers et employés réunies à la Bourse du Travail (11 août 1900)."

nel. This was not, however, simply the standard syndicalist blueprint for a worker-run society. Claverie argued that his plan would not entail a "shake-up of functions," for "the personnel is not only the workers but also the engineer-director, the chiefs of divisions, the factory superintendents." The principal transformation envisioned by Claverie was the replacement of a board of directors composed (he claimed) of financiers by the democratically elected representatives of the personnel—"the simple worker joining the division head or engineer, without a bit of jealousy from one or disdain from the other, . . . mind and muscle together." [68] The organic imagery and the implications of a fixed hierarchy would surely have troubled most other working-class leaders.

The obvious corporatist elements in Claverie's program were in all likelihood the product of circumstances as much as of a peculiarly eclectic mind. The union secretary had conceived of the "gas to the gas producers" project during the last two years of the century and published his thoughts in 1900, that moment of sudden change in Parisian politics. He was clearly aware of the Nationalist movement building in the capital, and he anticipated—correctly, as we shall see—that the movement would sweep along with it the gas clerks. He assessed that most employees were not sympathetic to the extreme left even if they did have grievances at the workplace. Claverie recognized the importance of giving lip service to a certain sort of hierarchy at a moment of mass populist mobilization for order and authority. His syndicalist-corporatist project was an effort to reach out to the majority of the gas clerks, who had still not entered the union and would not do so as long as it was obviously tied to collectivism and to the Dreyfusard cause. Claverie found that there were too few "workers of the pen" to achieve the sort of trade union he would have preferred, but he was willing to pay the price of ideological surrender for the sake of developing a large labor movement within the offices of the PGC. [69]

· · ·

After its initial year of organization the employees' union, its membership still rather small, settled into a period of stability and moderate accomplishment. Aside from the concessions the company voluntarily made on peripheral issues, the union was able to win some important victories. First, with the help of intense pressuring from aldermen, the PGC agreed

---

68. Maurice Claverie, "Une Expérience intéressante: Le Gaz aux gaziers," *Revue socialiste* 31 (1900): 63–67. Claverie revised his proposal seven years later and made it more purely syndicalist. See *Echo du gaz*, no. 234 (January 1, 1907): 1.
69. Préfecture, B/a 1424, report of July 1, 1903. The police quoted Claverie as proclaiming that "until a while ago, our union could justly be considered a 'red' one; but for some time now, it has turned 'yellow.'"

in 1893 to assure pensions for all clerks retiring before 1917 by depositing nearly a million francs into the fund.[70] Second, in 1896 the union persuaded the municipal council to contribute three hundred thousand francs from its share of profits to raise the pay of clerks and workers and convinced the company to contribute a like sum. Finally, the union was able to push management to alter its promotion practices, though the company never made the change a matter of official and publically announced policy. The director issued an internal memorandum in 1895 asking office heads to furnish the date of a clerk's last raise on the reports he used to make decisions on advancements. The result was that pay in the customer accounts department and lighting sections began to catch up with that in the other bureaus.[71] Managers probably thought of their discreet actions as a means to curtail the appeal of the union. At the same time, syndicalists could claim important victories.

Yet there were also frustrations for the union on fundamental issues. It could not compel the PGC to abandon discretionary procedures for promotions or to introduce early retirement options. The firm refused to yield on the matter of free coke and on numerous department-specific grievances. Likewise, the municipal council could pass resolutions in favor of the full union program, but it could not procure the demands. The management of the PGC was loath to yield any of its authority and would certainly not do so unless the city would consent to adequate compensation. Ultimately, then, the fate of the employees was tied to the gas question, the arrangement for supplying Paris with gas if and when the PGC's charter came to an end.

As long as Radicals and Socialists held a majority on the council, prospects for dramatic breakthroughs on the union program were small. The Socialist program of municipalization had no chance at this point. Moreover, the left majority was unwilling to extend the PGC's charter, a condition the company would require before granting further reforms. Maurice Claverie may have been one of the few who suspected as the end of the century approached that major initiatives were possible before 1905. Noting the anti-Dreyfusard, anti-Semitic, anti-Socialist, populist radicalism building in the volatile capital, he penned his "gas to the gas producers" project. In May 1900 the Nationalist right captured city hall and opened new problems and possibilities for the clerks' union.

70. AP, V 8 O¹, no. 734, deliberations of November 29, 1894; no. 149, "Retraite et secours."
71. Ibid., no. 1081, ordre de service no. 454 (September 23, 1895); no. 163, "Etat des augmentations accordées le 31 décembre 1902."

By no means did the mass mobilization of a rightist petite bourgeoisie bypass the employees of the PGC. Gustave Rouanet, a Socialist deputy from the Clignancourt section (eighteenth arrondissement) of Paris, where many gas clerks lived, specifically cited them as constituents of the Nationalists. Rouanet's view was that the right-wing press and plebeian demagogues had successfully appealed to powerful elements in the employees' political culture—patriotism, resentment of socialism, disdain for parliamentary democracy as practiced in the Third Republic, and hatred of Dreyfus.[72] The police, as well, believed that the Nationalists had many supporters among the gas employees.[73] Claverie soon came to acknowledge openly that the personnel he was trying to organize was not ripe for conversion to socialism. Heartened by the municipal elections of 1900, antiunion clerks formed the Corporate Association of Gas Employees. They attacked Claverie for his ties to collectivism and socialism and accused him of plotting the demise of the PGC. The association declared it would stand by the officers of the company in seeking a renewed charter— one that would guarantee the same reforms that the union sought through other means. It appeared that the trade union was on the verge of foundering on the rocks of deep political divisions in 1900.[74]

Three developments saved the union, but at the cost of ideological commitment. First, Claverie capitulated to anticollectivist employees. He severed all connections to Socialist aldermen, refusing even to support his friend and leader of the gas workers' union, Louis Lajarrigue, when the latter ran for a seat on the municipal council. Claverie backed away from all leftist solutions to the gas question. He accepted the renewal of the PGC's charter as a possible goal and even took a neutral stance on the "Nationalists' Panama Scandal," the Chamon project (see chapter 2).[75] Second, Nationalist aldermen displayed much friendliness toward Claverie's union and did nothing to encourage the rightist groups that had emerged to continue their attacks. Nationalists hoped for, and probably engineered, a fusion of the Corporate Association with the union.[76] The

72. Gustave Rouanet, "Les Elections de Paris et le parti socialiste," *Revue socialiste* 31 (1900): 716–732.

73. Préfecture, B/a 903, report of July 27, 1899.

74. AP, V 8 O¹, no. 149, "Projet de règlement général de l'Union corporative des employés du gaz." Claverie had to admit to Nationalists that he supported Socialist candidates in the municipal election of 1900, but he defended his stance by arguing that his candidates were pledged to upholding the clerks' interests. See *Echo du gaz*, no. 80 (July 16, 1900): 2.

75. Préfecture, B/a 1425, "Syndicat des employés du gaz," report of May 24, 1902; AP, V 8 O¹, no. 708, clipping from *Bulletin municipal officiel*, March 8, 1904, p. 42; *Echo du gaz*, no. 92 (January 16, 1901): 2; no. 100 (May 16, 1901): 2.

76. *Echo du gaz*, no. 87 (November 1, 1900): 1.

union leaders, for their part, found a pragmatic understanding easier to reach with the Nationalists than with the Socialist councilmen. The latter clung steadfastly to the municipialization plan, which offered no hope of immediate gains for employees. By contrast, the rightist aldermen had endless schemes for realizing the union program at once (all of them based on giving capitalists favorable terms for running the gas monopoly). It is no wonder Claverie mourned the passing of René Piault, a League of the Fatherland councilman, as "a good friend of the union."[77] The final development that transformed the union's fate was the stalemate that arose between the Nationalist municipality and left-leaning Parliament. No solution that was likely to win the approval of the city would also win the approval of the government.[78] With the gas question and the fate of the PGC bogged down in politics, employees tended to band together in a narrow pursuit of their professional interests. Collectivists and anticollectivists, Dreyfusards and anti-Dreyfusards, could agree on those interests even though they might agree on nothing else.

As a result of the Nationalist electoral victory in 1900, the union that faced the final debates over the gas question was very different from the union of the early days, despite continuity of leadership. Rapid growth was one of the differences. With only a few hundred members until the new century began, the union expanded to twelve hundred in 1903 and seventeen hundred in 1905. Two out of three employees were members as the PGC's charter neared its end.[79] A mass union developed, first, because the Nationalist politicians conferred respectability on the organization; second, once the union's acceptable status was established, employees rallied to it because they could see that negotiations over their fate had entered a crucial phase and that strong pressure was necessary to achieve their goals. The surge of new members forced Claverie to make his union into a politically neutral group that sought only pragmatic reforms. Yet even these concessions were not enough for some rightist clerks. A faction Claverie called "the Nationalists" challenged his leadership in 1903 and

77. Ibid., no. 148 (May 17, 1903): 2. The Nationalist councilman Ballière proclaimed, "I am above all a champion of the working class [la classe ouvrière]."
78. See chapter 2 on the stalement over the solution to the gas question.
79. AP, V 8 O¹, no. 162, "Rapport de Louis Lajarrigue au nom de la sous-commission du gaz sur les revendications du personnel du gaz (30 mars 1903)," p. 16; no. 150, "Procès-verbaux de la réunion du syndicat des employés, 19 janvier 1905." Of course, as far as most members were concerned, their identification with the union was not intense. The union newspaper sold no more than thirty subscriptions despite its seventeen hundred members. See Echo du gaz, no. 219 (May 16, 1906): 3.

almost won the union election. Claverie had to reconcile himself to being a leftist leader of a right-leaning trade organization.[80]

One significant continuity between the early union and the mature, mass union was that the same offices kept supplying the bulk of members, as the breakdown of the election results of 1903 clearly shows (table 17). The finding has important—and ironic—implications for the proletarianization model. It suggests that even the strongholds of early unionism had not been hotbeds of leftist activism. As more employees from customer accounts, the meter department, and the lighting sections entered the union, they brought their anticollectivist views with them. Office chiefs may have wished to believe that the clerks who gave them so many disciplinary problems, who worked so lackadaisically, were "socialists." In reality, however, they proved to be conventional petits bourgeois who resented leftist internationalism as much as their chiefs did. The clerks' chronic financial pressures and their overqualifying education had not made them define themselves as proletarians of the pen. Significantly, Claverie failed to win in the lighting sections. The union election showed that even the employees closest to proletarianized conditions by "objective" criteria refused, for the most part, to identify with workers. The gas employees joined a nonideological union with immediate goals in mind.

Thus, the gas employees' union emerged in the twentieth century as a large, powerful, influential organization courted by politicians of all stripes. The only threat it faced was a brief challenge from clerks who attempted to form a company union. That initiative, however, never received support from its natural patrons. The company preferred no union at all, yellow or red.[81] Nationalist aldermen refused to embrace it and supported Claverie's union instead. Anticollectivist employees displayed little enthusiasm for a company union; they seemed to prefer a politically neutral and independent one. Claverie's union did pay a price for enduring these tests: it was no longer ennobled by a democratic and egalitarian vision of a new social order. The union had to work with self-centered pragmatism to further the interest of its members.

However established and nonideological the union had become, it still remained committed to freeing its members from the discretionary power

80. *Echo du gaz*, no. 134 (October 15, 1902): 1. The opposition was once again charging Claverie with being a "socialist" and insisting that he be entirely neutral and concern himself only with the practical interests of the employees.
81. AP, V 8 O^1, no. 149, Danfray to director, October 26, 1901. Godot may have conspired with Claverie to make organizing difficult for the yellow union. See no. 150, Claverie to director, February 27, 1901, and ordre de service no. 652 (February 28, 1901).

Table 17. Breakdown of
Union Membership
by Office, 1903[a]

Bureau	No.	%
Lighting sections	633	40.8
Customer accounts	248	16.1
Meters	188	12.3
Gas mains	146	9.5
Workshops	81	5.2
Factory offices	75	4.9
Office boys	61	4.0
Bill collectors	58	3.8
Construction	24	1.6
Central treasury	3	0.2
Others	25	1.6
Total	1,542	100.0

Source: *Echo du gaz,* no. 168 (March 16,
1904): 2.
[a]Based on electoral participation,
these figures are approximate at best.

of superiors. The rank and file may have been anticollectivist and even antiparliamentary, but they wanted nothing to do with the meritocratic policies that the PGC professed to follow. Contention over this point probably explains why a company union never took root among the gas clerks. To this extent, the daring syndicalists of 1892 found collaborators in the conventional, petit bourgeois union members a decade later.

How was the union to achieve that goal through the pragmatic channels it chose to pursue? A consensus on the proper regime for gas employees emerged much more quickly than did a solution to the gas question as a whole. It arose in the period of Nationalist ascendancy and took the form of "assimilation," the program that would treat gas clerks as if they were employees of the city of Paris.[82] Union members had not specifically asked to become *fonctionnaires,* but the plan did address their central concerns. The presumed injustices that had arisen from the PGC's policy of discretionary advancement would be corrected at once, and future promotions would be based mainly on seniority. Retirement, including early retirement, would become a right. A host of regulations and possibilities for appeals would limit the sting of disciplinary measures. There is little won-

82. As I observed in chapter 2, Radical aldermen had broached the possibility in 1895 and 1896.

der why union members rallied to the proposal. It was also acceptable to all factions on the municipal council. By 1903 every plan for a new gas monopoly included provisions for assimilation. The program was implemented even before a successor for the PGC was found, with the city bearing the expense.[83]

Only the management of the PGC found fault with assimilation. Naturally, the executives took the plan as an insult to their authority and warned of the irregularities that would result. Still expressing absolute confidence in his discretionary evaluations, the director claimed that the very clerks who were least deserving, the ones the company had passed over for promotion, would get the largest raises as the city attempted to match seniority with salary.[84] A more practical problem also arose. Because the PGC had never accorded generous salaries to its supervisory personnel (bureau chiefs, principal clerks, supervisory inspectors, and meter readers), assimilation would produce a number of instances in which subordinates had higher pay than their superiors. In fact, the success of common employees in improving their pay through organization inspired some supervisory personnel to join the union. Since the PGC was largely powerless to guarantee their futures by that time, only respect for hierarchical authority and prejudices against unions prevented more from doing so.[85] In this era of challenges to authority the PGC's managers were all but isolated—at least until the Radical Republic lost its zeal for social reform.

Conclusion

The PGC's white-collar personnel did not suffer from capitalistic development in the same way craftsmen did. The growth of a large private enterprise transformed bureaucratic work only to a limited degree. Clerks struggled, not to reassert their control over the labor process, but rather to guarantee and improve compensations. By and large, the public official

83. AP, V 8 O¹, no. 162–163.
84. "Already the bad agents laugh at those who served the company faithfully," asserted Dufourg. Ibid., no. 163, report of Dufourg to director, July 26, 1904; "Etat nominatif des employés dont ni les aptitudes, ni les services, ni le mérite ne sont en rapport avec l'avancement dont ils sont l'objet par l'assimilation."
85. Ibid., "Service extérieur"; Laboucheux to director, n.d.; *Echo du gaz*, no. 144 (March 16, 1903): 2. In 1905 certain construction inspectors asked the director for permission to form an "Association amicale." In 1907, they formed a "Société des agents techniques de la Compagnie parisienne du gaz" and quickly informed the director of their "loyalty and deference" (see the Laboucheux letter).

who proclaimed that superior primary school pupils were content to "rise within their own sphere" proved to be correct.[86] The employees' family background, social contacts, and education tended to separate them from wage earners, and their work experience did not encourage a strong effort to overcome the class gulf. Politically, most gas clerks followed the same trajectory as Parisian shopkeepers in moving from Radicalism to Nationalism as the nineteenth century drew to a close. They did so because right-wing populists brought into Nationalism many of the themes of Radicalism.[87] Moreover, the populists convincingly portrayed themselves as champions of the work-related rights that the employees sought. In this specific instance Nationalists even delivered on their promise to help common people.

The gas clerks were unwitting participants in a wider crisis of authority within the white-collar milieu. Employees inside and outside the PGC shared a binary vision of sanctioning power that allowed for either equality or arbitrariness. Many employees of private enterprises may have wished to protest, but they were exposed to the wrath of their employers and could not expect a hand to be offered them. The unrest surfaced in the bureaucracies touched by the same political forces acting on the PGC—civil service, state-owned enterprises, the railroad companies, and the postal service. Public servants could and did call on the Radical-dominated state to give them equality of treatment. Of course, they found that the national political arena was not as amenable to populist politics as was Paris.[88]

Maurice Claverie, the union activist, found distressingly few "workers of the pen" among his comrades. A large number of employees had strong prejudices against trade unions, which they understood as a mark of the working-class status they rejected for themselves. Yet the resistance to organization crumbled when the clerks perceived a serious chance to pursue antiauthoritarian reform. Their prejudices against collectivism were more enduring. After all, the clerks' opposition to discretionary power

86. Octave Gréard, Education et instruction (4 vols), vol. 1, Enseignement primaire (Paris, 1904), p. 309.

87. Philip Nord, Paris Shopkeepers and the Politics of Resentment (Princeton, 1986), chap. 9; Arno Mayer, "The Lower Middle Class as Historical Problem," Journal of Modern History 47 (1975): 409–436.

88. On the enduring strength of economic liberalism within the Third Republic, see Richard Kuisel, Capitalism and the State in Modern France (Cambridge, 1981). On the wide but insufficient support in Parliament to give civil servants the right to unionize, see David Watson, Georges Clemenceau: A Political Biography (London, 1974), pp. 189, 206.

could find expression in idioms other than socialism, especially in turn-of-the-century Paris.

Not even within the PGC were the employees alone in denouncing important aspects of managerial authority. Manual workers did so, too, some far more aggressively than the clerks. And like the white-collar personnel, the wage earners were addressing nationwide grievances in their challenge.

PART FOUR

THE WORKERS' COMPANY

An Industrial Labor Force

Large companies like the PGC were primarily responsible for the transition from an artisanal to an industrial work force.[1] The results of the transformation require more investigation than they have yet received, since most labor studies have been concerned with craftsmen and their responses to changes at the workshop. Though historians no longer portray factory workers simply as the victims of the "dark, satanic mills"— utterly atomized, regimented, and undifferentiated—the present state of knowledge about the group is largely a matter of negative statements: industrial workers did not serve as the activists in the labor movement; they comprised a minority within the French working class; they were usually quiescent; when they did act, their protest was generally ineffective and poorly focused.[2] The industrial army that emerged at the gas plants was complex and underwent dramatic changes even in the absence of technological upheaval. Its evolution provides an opportunity to see factory workers in a more positive light.

1. For an effort to conceptualize these types of work, see Michael Hanagan, "Artisans and Skilled Workers: The Problem of Definition," *International Labor and Working-Class History*, no. 12 (November 1977): 28–31.
2. William Sewell, "Artisans, Factory Workers, and the Formation of the French Working Class, 1789–1848," in *Working Class Formation: Nineteenth-Century Patterns in Western Europe and the United States*, ed. Ira Katznelson and Aristide Zolberg (Princeton, 1986), pp. 45–70; Gérard Noiriel, *Les Ouvriers dans la société française: XIXᵉ–XXᵉ siècle* (Paris, 1986); William Reddy, *Money and Liberty in Modern Europe* (Cambridge, 1987), p. 208. Among the recent studies that will lead beyond the negative statements are William Reddy, *The Rise of Market Culture: The Textile Trade and French Society, 1750–1900* (Cambridge, 1984); Donald Reid, *The Miners of Decazeville* (Cambridge, Mass., 1986); Michael Hanagan, *Nascent Proletarians: Class Formation in Post-Revolutionary France* (Oxford, 1989).

The Stokers

One reason for the failure to come to grips with the shift from artisanal to industrial labor is the complexity of the process. Occasionally employers were able to install machines and obliterate in a single blow craft-based production methods. This seems to have happened at the bottle plant in Carmaux, brilliantly described by Joan Scott. Supine machine tenders suddenly took the place of skilled glassblowers, who had trained for fifteen years to do their jobs.[3] Such a clean break was exceptional. Indeed, employers even today have rarely succeeded in whittling down labor to a homogenized, easily replaceable body of operatives doing simple, repetitive work.[4] Nineteenth-century factory work usually involved skilled workers doing crucial operations. Sometimes these were "industrial craftsmen," who had nearly complete control over the work process. More commonly, employers were able to subdivide craft work into simpler, but still skilled, activities. They also took control of hiring and training, usually leaving supervisors with these responsibilities.[5] Some new industries had never known an artisanal phase but revolved around skilled work of the latter sort. The replacement of artisans and industrial craftsmen by skilled workers was a long and gradual process. It was surely the central development in French labor history between the Commune and World War I.[6] The stokers who produced gas for the PGC provide an example of the type of factory laborer then coming to dominate production and protest.

The PGC was born rather advanced in terms of the social evolution of the labor force. A process-centered industry, gas production did not require the fine shaping and fitting that assembling industries did. Though stokers performed the manual operations that were crucial to gas production, there was nothing intricate about their performance. Nor were there preindustrial traditions to stoking; the job arose with the nineteenth-century gas industry. Stokers did not have to adapt basic operations to particular circumstances, innovate at the job, or complete a multiplicity of

3. Joan Scott, *The Glassworkers of Carmaux* (Cambridge, Mass., 1974).
4. Patrick Fridenson, "Automobile Workers in France and Their Work, 1914–83," in *Work in France: Representations, Meaning, Organization, and Practice*, ed. Steven Kaplan and Cynthia Koepp (Ithaca, N.Y., 1986), 514–547; Roger Penn, "Skilled Manual Workers in the Labor Process, 1856–1964," in *The Degradation of Work? Skill, Deskilling, and the Labor Process*, ed. Stephen Wood (London, 1982), pp. 90–108.
5. Michael Hanagan, "Urbanization, Worker Settlement Patterns, and Social Protest in Nineteenth-Century France," in *French Cities in the Nineteenth Century*, ed. John Merriman (New York, 1981), p. 218; Lenard R. Berlanstein, *The Working People of Paris, 1871–1914* (Baltimore, 1984), pp. 92–100.
6. Reid, *Miners of Decazeville*, p. 72.

complex operations. They did the same task repeatedly and had only a small degree of autonomy, too little for the concept of craft control to be relevant. Engineers and foremen set the parameters of the tasks and modified them at will.[7] The distinguishing feature of stokers, as skilled workers, was their market power. Not many humans could perform the strenuous work of stoking in the torrid distillation rooms. And this was not the sort of work that an employer could allow to stop for very long. If pressure fell and air entered the gas mains, then the danger of catastrophic explosion was great.[8] Stokers found strategies for exploiting their market power in ways that differentiated them from common laborers and gave shape to the emerging industrial labor force.[9]

The banner of the union newspaper portrayed the stokers as barrel-chested, muscular giants, stripped to the waist and covered with coal dust and sweat. Outsiders who occasionally visited a distillation room never failed to be impressed by stokers at work. The oppressive heat, the strength required to fill a retort, the dexterity necessary for a neat job, and the physical dangers stokers abided filled visitors with admiration. The journalist Gustave Babin waxed eloquent at the sight of the PGC's stokers in action: "Athletes, for the most part, as they need to be to do such labor, these workers are superb to watch in action, in the play of reflexes they reveal. They have their special skills, their professional dexterities, which are marvelous. With great precision the stokers . . . know how to throw the shovelful of coal into a burning furnace, withdrawing their unprotected arm just as flames are about to lick it. With equally great poise they empty coke from the retort, projecting their heavy iron hooks into the incandescent tube."[10]

7. AP, V 8 O¹, no. 764, "Main-d'oeuvre de distillation (26 avril 1870)"; "Etude des modifications à introduire dans la réorganisation dans le régime du personnel ouvrier de la distillation (29 avril 1870)." These two reports by the head of the factory division are the starting points for understanding the work situation of the stokers.
8. Ibid., no. 161, report of Euchène, March 18, 1907.
9. The industry-specific skills of the stokers made their positions analogous to those of the elite of mining teams, the hewers and timbermen, as well as to puddlers in the steel industry. See Rolande Trempé, *Les Mineurs de Carmaux, 1848–1914*, 2 vols. (Paris, 1971), 1:112; Reid, *Miners of Decazeville*, pp. 72–78; Jean-Paul Courtheoux, "Privilèges et misères d'un métier sidérurgique au XIXᵉ siècle," *Revue d'histoire économique et sociale* 37 (1959): 159–189. For the argument that nineteenth-century industry created many new types of skilled workers, see Raphael Samuel, "Workshop of the World: Steam Power and Hand Technology in Mid-Victorian Britain," *History Workshop* 3 (1977): 6–72.
10. "Le Gaz d'éclairage," *L'Illustration*, no. 3084 (April 5, 1902): 251–253. Another admiring observer was Léon Duchesne, *Hygiène professionnelle: Des Ouvriers employés à la fabrication du gaz de l'éclairage* (Paris, n.d.).

A stoker firing the furnace. From *L'Illustration*, no. 3084 (April 5, 1902).

The entire operation of stoking consisted of several distinct activities, none of them easy and each with its particular physical demands and threats. First, the workmen brought several hundred kilograms of coal from the coal yard to the distillation room and pulverized it. The preparation of a hot retort for charging could be hazardous or at least noxious. Gas that had not escaped into the evacuation pipes might back up into the stokers' faces and burn or suffocate them. To prevent that, workers would open the mouth of a retort carefully and ply a glowing piece of coke so as to burn off the remaining gas. Then shoveling could commence. This op-

Stokers at work: shoveling, loading coal with a scoop, and emptying the retorts. From *L'Illustration*, no. 3084 (April 5, 1902).

eration involved propelling heavy shovelloads of coal into a retort in such a way as to fill it evenly. Obviously, practice and dexterity were needed. During the four to six hours of roasting, a special stoker, the fireman, kept the furnace filled with fuel (usually coal or coke). In the meantime, other stokers had to pay attention to the evacuation pipes. When they became clogged with condensed residues (especially naphthalenes), a stoker had to clear them—quickly—with steam. Blockage produced frequent emergencies and not a few incidents of scorched skin. When distillation ended, the job of the stokers was to clear the retorts of the coke that carbonization had produced. This operation, one Babin especially admired, was performed with a heavy iron pole that had a ring on the end. It weighed eighteen kilograms, and workers had to manipulate it in the long, hot tube in such a way as to remove the coke without unnecessarily scratching the surface of the retort. They used the pole to push the burning coke into a wagon, which they then wheeled to the yard, where it could be extinguished.[11] In the opinion of some observers, transporting the burning coke was the most hazardous activity stokers did since occasions for being burned were numerous. Reports on work accidents confirm the assessment of danger. At the PGC's largest factory, La Villette, stokers were ob-

11. AP, V 8 O¹, no. 764, "Etude des modifications."

ligated to push wagons of coke seventy meters back and forth eighteen times during each charge.[12]

Stokers also had maintenance chores that complicated the job. Firemen were responsible for the care of their furnaces and had to remove the cinders after each charge. Such upkeep had to be done faithfully, for the state of the furnace determined how hard the work was and how much stokers earned.[13] Stokers checked the retorts for fissures in the walls between charges and repaired them by spreading molten earthenware with an iron pipe. The inspection of evacuation pipes was also an important part of the maintenance activities.

Such labor was all the more difficult in that it was performed under debilitating circumstances. Temperatures in the distillation rooms rarely fell below 100 degrees Fahrenheit, and stokers were continually exposed to heat radiated from glowing surfaces. Director Camus cited the heat as the principle reason the job was beyond the capacity of most wage earners.[14] Work in the distillation rooms during the summer was reputed to be especially painful, but it did have one advantage over winter work: when stokers wheeled coke into the yard during the cold weather, the sudden change of temperature contributed to illness.

For obvious reasons the PGC needed men of rare physical endurance. Ideally, the physical giants who did stoking should also have had the dexterity for packing coke tightly.[15] In all probability the company could not insist on perfection in packing the retorts and had to settle for men who could do the work with minimal competence. One factory manager used the term "apprenticeship" to describe the training of a potential stoker. The exercise entailed setting up a retort in the courtyard and having the fledgling practice filling it with the shovel. The superintendent went on to

12. Ibid., no. 717, "Voies ferrées"; no. 151, report of Alène to director, May 11, 1897; no. 718, report no. 120, June 21, 1873. There were easier and less dangerous ways to handle the burning coke, but the company chose the method that would preserve the most value for its sale to domestic customers. For the work accident records of the La Villette plant, see AP, V bis 19 Q⁶.

13. AP, V 8 O¹, no. 764, "Etude des modifications"; no. 151, report of Euchène, November 11, 1898.

14. Compte rendu des travaux de la commission nommée par Monsieur le Ministre de l'Intérieur le 31 janvier 1890 en exécution de l'article 48 du traité entre la ville de Paris et la Compagnie parisienne de l'éclairage et du chauffage par le gaz (Paris, 1890), p. 139.

15. One superintendent wrote, "The proper or improper execution of charging determines the yield of gas from a given quantity of coal and at a given temperature." Inexperienced stokers raised the cost of production 20 percent during the strike of 1890. AP, V 8 O¹, no. 148, report of Cury to director, June 25, 1865; report of Gigot to director, October 8, 1892.

underscore the overwhelming importance of endurance by pointing out that such an apprenticeship was "as much physical as manual."[16] He no doubt meant that building stamina was crucial. The superintendents did not expect more than one in ten common laborers to be able to perform the infernal work.[17]

The harsh conditions meant that a stoker could not grow old in this line of work. The PGC's engineers professed to know hardly any who worked at the job for more than fifteen years or beyond the age of fifty.[18] Stokers inevitably spent the last third of their working lives as common laborers. If they tried to extend their careers at the furnace a year or two beyond their capacity, they paid dearly. One stoker wrote poignantly and from experience that "the last years on the job are the hardest times in a stoker's life."[19]

The evolution of stoking within the PGC illustrates how a job characterized by stable production methods could undergo profound transformation. A stoker of 1850 would have been disoriented by the work his comrade performed thirty years later. The very meaning of the stokers' work in relation to the rest of their lives had shifted over that generation. We can understand the transformation as a change from relative independence from the gas industry as a source of employment to dependence on the industry, and on the PGC in particular, for a livelihood.[20]

By any standards and under the best of circumstances the stoker's work was debilitating, yet it became far more so during the PGC's first decade of operation. The rationalization of production during the 1860s was responsible for the deterioration of conditions (see chapter 4). At that time the company became aware of the benefits of hot roasting. Raising the temperature of distillation allowed the firm to increase the number of charges per day, the size of the retorts that had to be filled, and the amount of coal in each retort while still producing gas of sufficient quality for lighting. The implementation of hot roasting caused unit labor costs to plummet and output per stoker to soar, all achieved without any mechanization whatsoever. When the PGC began operations in 1855, its factories completed only four charges in a twenty-four-hour period. Each furnace had no more than four retorts, and sometimes only one, to heat.

16. Ibid., no. 148, report of Jones, April 26, 1865.
17. Ibid., "Chantiers à coke"; "Union des agents principaux des chantiers à coke (19 novembre 1892)," p. 6.
18. Ibid., no. 151, "Etat nominatif des chauffeurs ayant été conservés tout l'été."
19. Ibid., no. 150, "Affaire Mercier."
20. I have borrowed the concept of dependency from David Brody, *Steelworkers in America: The Nonunion Era* (New York, 1960).

Those vessels were short (two meters in length) by later standards.[21] Stokers did not have an easy job, but the demands of work were far less than they would soon become. An indication of the endurable pace of labor before 1860 was that stokers did twenty-four-hour shifts, working every other day. They were able to do so because they had time to rest and sleep (on piles of coal) between the six-hour roasting periods.[22]

The rationalization of production initiated by factory chief Arson soon brought the number of charges per day up to six, one every four hours. Stokers packed 100–120 kilograms instead of 75 kilograms of coal into each retort for each charge. Thus, with hot roasting the amount of coal stokers handled per day nearly doubled between 1860 and the late 1870s and continued to increase through 1905:[23]

Year	Kg. Coal per Stoker	Year	Kg. Coal per Stoker
1860	1,460	1879	2,868
1864	2,131	1889	3,098
1867	2,526	1891	3,140
1868	2,572	1893	3,120
1877	2,874	1899	3,206
1878	2,891	1905	3,250

Maurice Lévy-Leboyer has argued that gains in productivity during the Second Empire usually resulted from intensified deployment of labor rather than from an increase in capital, and such was the case for stoking at the PGC.[24] The higher quantities of coal roasted depended entirely on the stokers' exertions.

Not only were stokers working much harder; they were doing so under increasingly adverse conditions. Hot roasting raised the heat under which stokers had to exert themselves, all the more so when Siemens furnaces were introduced. Superintendents reported temperatures of 120 degrees Fahrenheit in the distillation rooms when it was only 56 degrees outside.[25]

21. AP, V 8 O¹, no. 709, report of Servier to director, May 7, 1860.
22. Ibid., no. 148, report of Letreust, April 29, 1865.
23. Ibid., no. 763, "Tirage des cheminées (28 avril 1869)"; nos. 148, 151, 159, 163, 709, 711, 716, 768, 1520.
24. Maurice Lévy-Leboyer, "Capital Investment and Economic Growth in France, 1820–1930," in The Cambridge Economic History of Europe (Cambridge, 1978), 7 (1): 267.
25. AP, V 8 O¹, no. 675, deliberations of May 8, 1872. Another report put the temperature at 115 degrees Fahrenheit when it was 75 degrees outside. Ibid., no. 768, "Usine de Saint-Mandé," report of April 18, 1869.

Moreover, the greater number of charges per day necessitated quicker emptying of the retorts and unloading of the coke. It also made the job of clearing the retorts more difficult because the burning coke clung to the sides.[26] At the same time, maintenance chores became more troublesome and time-consuming. Hot distillation caused a much more frequent clogging of the evacuation pipes. Furnaces and retorts were also harder to keep in good repair. Rest time between the more closely spaced charges was thus severely squeezed. Indeed, some observers asserted that there was no longer any rest time.[27]

The company contrived to rearrange work patterns so as to derive all the benefits it could from hot roasting. It broke down some of the stoker's work into specialized operations. Up to the 1850s stokers, working in teams, would take turns charging, clearing, moving the coke, and firing the furnace. Each of these steps had its distinctive demands, and stokers tried to even the burdens by exchanging tasks. The company forced the stokers to specialize in one of these operations.[28] The introduction of the Siemens furnace was another way the company gained more control over production. With simple furnaces the temperature of distillation depended entirely on the firemen: they could sabotage hot roasting at will by withholding fuel from the furnaces. The Siemens furnaces, however, were not really under their control.[29] Another change in the stoker's work pattern was the abandonment of the twenty-four-hour shift. Workers could not exert themselves for so long over so many consecutive hours, and the twelve-hour shift became the rule (except in one or two plants). Workmen resented this change because the twenty-four-hour shift had allowed them to rest or take other jobs on their off days.[30]

Thus, by 1870 the work of stokers had deteriorated drastically. Indeed,

26. *Compte rendu des travaux de la commission nommée . . . le 31 janvier 1890*, p. 39. The engineers who authored this report affirmed that stokers much preferred to work with ordinary furnaces.
27. AP, V 8 O¹, no. 670, deliberations of May 25, 1864. Babin, the journalist who observed the stokers at work, remarked on the absence of a rest period. "Gaz de l'éclairage," p. 14. Even a superintendent was skeptical that stokers had much of a rest between charges. See AP, V 8 O¹, no. 160, report of superintendent of Ivry plant to Euchène, July 16, 1899.
28. AP, V 8 O¹, no. 764, "Main-d'oeuvre de distillation (26 avril 1870)"; no. 709, report of Servier to director, May 7, 1860.
29. Ibid., no. 711, report no. 43, "Règlement du salaire de la distillation"; *Compte rendu des travaux de la commission nommée le 4 février 1885 en exécution de l'article 48 du traité intervenu le 7 février 1870 entre la ville de Paris et la Compagnie parisienne de l'éclairage et du chauffage par le gaz. Procès-verbaux* (Paris, 1886), p. 189.
30. AP, V 8 O¹, no. 764, report of April 29, 1870 (fols. 18–21); no. 768, "Usine Passy," report of December 2, 1860.

it is hard to find a similar tale of deterioration in the annales of French labor history. Skilled workers were not usually passive as their work became degraded. They fought and usually drew employers to a standoff long before their work load had increased to the extent the stokers' had. Were stokers an anomalous case, or did they exemplify the helplessness of industrial workers—even skilled ones—in the face of a determined employer?

To the extent that historians have examined that industrial work force, they have concluded that the group was helpless either to resist employers' demands or to find an organizational and ideological basis for the resistance.[31] The sociologist Craig Calhoun provides a theoretical argument that purports to explain the malleability of the factory operative in contrast to the craftsman. Calhoun's formulation shifts the emphasis from resistance to adaptation.[32] He posits that skilled industrial workers, unlike artisans, were not inalterably opposed to industrial development by their very way of life. Whereas artisans had to defend the craft basis of production, skilled factory workers could use their ability to create bottlenecks at crucial steps in production to bargain with their employers. Calhoun believes that industrial workers naturally took advantage of capitalistic development to obtain improvements in their earnings and living conditions. Calhoun's model of bargaining is applicable to the stokers, who were not at all helpless before their bosses. They did use their market power to obtain immediate material gains in exchange for greater output. Such comportment, however, characterized stokers in a particular phase of their development. The model of adaptation was not relevant under all circumstances, and stokers altered their strategies as the role of work for the PCG in their lives changed. Calhoun did not see that skilled industrial workers, French ones at least, had the capacity to become more like craftsmen in their confrontations with managerial authority.

The shop floor in and of itself provides too narrow a perspective for understanding how stokers evaluated their options on the job. Their reaction to the rationalization of gas production depended, at least in part, on their way of life.[33] Stokers were one example of the sort of factory

31. Scott, *Glassworkers of Carmaux*, chap. 7; Yves Lequin, *Les Ouvriers de la région lyonnaise (1848–1914)*, 2 vols. (Lyon, 1977), 2:242–348; Michael Hanagan, *The Logic of Solidarity: Artisans and Industrial Workers in Three French Towns, 1871–1914* (Urbana, Ill., 1980).
32. Craig Calhoun, *The Question of Class Struggle* (Chicago, 1982).
33. Michael Hanagan demonstrates the importance of integrating a consideration of the workers' private lives into their work histories in "Proletarian Families and Social Protest: Production and Reproduction as Issues of Social Conflict in Nineteenth-Century France," in *Work in France*, ed. Kaplan and Koepp, pp. 418–456.

workers who did not rely on one and only one kind of labor for permanent, year-round employment. The gas industry was highly seasonal because of the limited contours of consumption: the number of stokers needed for production in July was only about 55 percent of that required in January. Stokers were very much part of a floating population that alternated between factory work and other activities, often rural employment. In 1865 the assistant chief of production, Servier, stated that "nothing attaches the stokers to the company. Our jobs are for them a *pis aller*, and they often prefer to earn less while working in the open air."[34] Three decades later the journalist Babin was still able to describe the stokers as "Bretons and Auvergnats, for the most part, who come to spend winter in the hellfires of Paris, when the earth enters its annual sleep, and who, at the first springtime sun, return to a much healthier life in the country."[35] This description, a rough approximation of reality at best, captures an important truth: stoking was only a part of the working lives of the stokers.

As members of a floating population, the stokers were by no means a special case of industrial workers. The convention of dividing social phenomena into urban and rural is often highly misleading. Yves Lequin has shown that temporary transfers of population between the countryside and the city provided a major part of industrial labor through most of the nineteenth century. "Industry founded its takeoff," Lequin writes, "on the periodic use of a circulating labor force more than on the assembling of a fixed force."[36] The phenomenon was a consequence of a pattern of rural proletarianization that was quite pronounced in France. The countryside had long known a proliferation of very small holdings, and cultivators had to supplement their incomes, often through temporary emigration and seasonal industrial activity. Rural population growth also produced underemployed village artisans, who sought seasonal work in cities. On the demand side, small and irregular markets for industrial goods made a large, permanent industrial labor force unnecessary. In the end, gas production was unexceptional in its seasonality and its use of a floating labor force. The stokers were not at all peculiar as peripatetic proletarians.

The stokers' acquiescent response to the rationalization of production until the 1880s must be understood in the context of their relative independence from the PGC. The good pay that the gas firm offered for part of

34. AP, V 8 O¹, no. 148, report of Servier, June 20, 1865.
35. "Le Gaz de l'éclairage," p. 252. On the seasonality of gas production, see Frank Popplewell, "The Gas Industry," in *Seasonal Trades*, ed. Sidney Webb and Arnold Freeman (London, 1912), pp. 148–209.
36. Lequin, *Ouvriers de la région lyonnaise*, 1:vii; Noiriel, *Ouvriers dans la société française*, pp. 44–55.

Table 18. Geographical Origins
of Stokers, 1898[a]

Region	No.	%
Auvergne	40	29.0
Brittany	27	19.6
Center[b]	15	10.9
Limousin	14	10.1
Alsace-Lorraine	12	8.7
Champagne	9	6.5
Normandy	8	5.8
Paris (city)	7	5.1
Paris (region)	6	4.3
Total	138	100.0

Sources: AP, V 8 O¹, nos. 151, 160; electoral
lists for the thirteenth, fourteenth, fifteenth,
and nineteenth arrondissements.

[a]The available sources limited the sample
to stokers at the Ivry, Vaugirard, and La Villette plants.

[b]Departments of Nièvre, Saône-et-Loire,
and Cher.

the year was an attractive option for the stokers, but it was not their only
option. Their commitment to stoking as an occupation was conditional on
being able to earn more than through other lines of work. Such was the
instrumental logic of their employment with the PGC.

The stokers were essentially rural people in background and in habits.
The earliest electoral lists for the neighborhoods they inhabited show that
the vast majority came from the provinces, usually the deep provinces
(table 18). Almost all were born in villages. They could not follow the
pattern of some industrial workers, who settled near factories and begat a
second generation of laborers *sur place*. The special "skills" stokers had,
unusual strength and endurance, could not become a family legacy; and
stokers might have wanted less demanding jobs for their children, anyway.
Thus, each generation of stokers was constantly renewed from rural
France, not from established factory communities.[37]

In the early years of the gas industry stokers seem to have organized

37. For the more common case of immigrants who eventually established a community around the factory, see Lenard R. Berlanstein, "The Formation of a Factory Labor Force: Rubber and Cable Workers in Bezons, France (1860–1914)",
Journal of Social History 15 (1981): 163–186.

their lives in a manner similar to that of the better-known "Limousins," or building workers from that province. These masons left home each year to spend the winter in Paris and rarely renounced being cultivators. Their ultimate goal was to put aside money to survive as farmers or to save up enough to round out their plots.[38] The geographical origins of the stokers tied them to the same world of proletarianized peasants. As we have seen, Babin assumed that most stokers were still peasant-workers who, even at the dawn of the twentieth century, returned to their farms each spring. That might have been true at one time, but growth and change in Paris during the Second Empire interrupted the pattern. The PGC's engineers noted agricultural labor as one alternative for stokers, but construction in Paris provided another option, probably a more important one by the 1860s. Various building activities were viable for stokers because of the seasonal patterns, the relatively high pay, and the physical requirements. Some stokers also went into the brickyards for work during the warm season. Most often the PGC expected to lose stokers to masonry, ground clearing, and foundation work.[39] Opportunities to take jobs in construction were plentiful in the Paris of Baron Haussmann.

Because stoking was not a permanent occupation but rather a part of an economy of makeshifts, often with an agrarian component, stokers acted with a great deal of independence regarding their employer. Thus, the Auvergnat Pierre Garrigoux had to be rehired eight times between July 1876 and March 1880. He had departed voluntarily seven times and was laid off only once. His leadership in the 1880 strike effort finally cost him his job with the PGC.[40] The most visible manifestation of this independence vis-à-vis the gas industry was the paradox that the PGC had a shortage of stokers during the season it needed the fewest. The difficulties in recruiting a sufficient number of stokers were greatest in July and August, when gas consumption was at its lowest point of the year. At the root of the paradox was the stokers' practice of leaving gas plants to take jobs in construction or returning to the farm, both of which were then at their peak of activity. During the moments of especially powerful demand for labor in construction, gas engineers complained that stokers left even before winter ended so as to get the best-paying jobs at building sites. There they

38. Alain Corbin, *Archaïsme et modernité en Limousin au XIXe siècle* (Paris, 1975); David Pinkney, "Migrations to Paris during the Second Empire," *Journal of Modern History* 25 (1953): 1–12; Gabriel Désert, "Aperçue sur l'industrie française du bâtiment du XIXe siècle," in *Le Bâtiment: Enquête d'histoire économique, XIVe–XIXe siècles,* ed. Jean-Pierre Bardet et al., (Paris, 1971), 35–119.
39. AP, V 8 O¹, no. 148, report of Jones, April 26, 1865; report of Gigot, April 30, 1865; report of Letreust, April 29, 1865; report of Servier, June 20, 1865.
40. Ibid., no. 150, "Affaire Garrigoux."

could earn as much, or almost as much, as in the distillation rooms while escaping the frightful physical toll of a summer near the furnaces.[41] Stokers further asserted their independence from the gas company by resisting the shift from a twenty-four-hour to a twelve-hour day. As late as 1870 a particularly acute shortage of stokers forced the PGC to offer a return to the old schedule to attract more workers.[42]

The independence signals what stokers cared about most in working for the PGC—earnings. Stokers did not constitute an occupational community rooted in a craft. They did not define their status in terms of mastery at the workplace. Distilling coal was a way of scraping together income. Alain Corbin has identified the "ferocious will to save" as the guiding rule of the Limousins, and the same point applied to the stokers.[43] The quest to maximize earnings was the focus of their working lives, and it created both areas of compromise and areas of conflict with the company. On the one hand, managers were eager to raise productivity, and the stokers were willing to accommodate, for a price. On the other hand, the engineers' moral view of wages did not honor the principle that harder work necessarily deserved greater compensation.[44] Thus, there was a large potential for conflict between management and the workers even though the latter accepted the trade-offs inherent in the logic of capitalism.

•   •   •

The reports of factory superintendents to their superiors during the 1860s place the role of labor into perspective. The managers apparently regarded neither the supply of workers nor their malleability as major concerns. Superintendents rarely noted that workers refused to increase their output or alter their routines. Even complaints about shortages of stokers were sporadic, not chronic. The manager of the Ivry plant pointed out in 1862 that the booming construction industry for the most part helped the PGC find stokers, for it attracted many hands to Paris, and they needed work in the winter. Other problems preoccupied the superintendents far more than labor: the quality of the coal, the supply of well-

41. Ibid., no. 674, deliberations of April 30, 1870; no. 148, report of Jones, June 26, 1865; report of Philippot, April 25, 1865. The stokers could have remained with the PGC, working in the courtyard, if they had been content to earn only 3.25 francs.
42. Ibid., no. 674, deliberations of April 30 and May 4, 1870. The Belleville plant ran on twenty-four-hour shifts until 1874. See no. 677, deliberations of December 12, 1874.
43. Corbin, *Archaïsme et modernité*, p. 205.
44. See chapter 4. For a theoretical perspective on consensual relations in industry, see Michael Buraway, *Manufacturing Consent: Changes in the Labor Process under Monopoly Capitalism* (Chicago, 1979), which underscores the contingent nature of workers' consent.

constructed retorts, and the state of the equipment. Labor agitation occurred from time to time, but managers would hardly have been inclined to define industrial relations in terms of a crisis, as they would in 1899.[45]

The distilling halls of the PGC were disturbed by strikes or by serious threats of strikes roughly every other year between 1859 and 1869. Peasant-workers though they may have been, the stokers had no trouble cooperating with one another and making the company aware of their discontents. In each biennial action they forced the company to give them a raise. Between the founding of the PGC, in 1855, and the Franco-Prussian War stokers had obtained a 70 percent increase in their pay. Several forces were driving their agitation. The cost of living had risen sharply in Paris, and stokers were in part safeguarding their purchasing power.[46] At the same time, stokers were demanding compensation for their greater exertion on the job. Inflation and harder work may have formed the basis for the common understanding that allowed stokers to take collective action, but they did not determine the timing or the form of the strikes. These aspects of collective protest derived from the stokers' independent status. Stokers struck when they could take advantage of their attachments to the construction industry.

The labor agitation in the PGC up to the 1880s coincided with peaks in building activity.[47] Through the nature of their strikes the stokers reminded the company of their independence from it. In "classic" strikes, workers withhold their labor and inform their employer what it would take to bring them back to the factory. The stokers instead staged a collective act of quitting and left en masse for jobs on construction sites. That is why all the strikes of the 1860s took place in the spring or summer, at the time of hiring for construction but in the dead season for gas production. Apparently, the stokers did not always specify the conditions that would keep them at the plant.[48] Such practices might appear "archaic," the action of workers who were not fully inured to the industrial process or who possessed a "preindustrial mentality"; but they were nothing of the

45. See the collection of reports from the plant superintendents, AP, V 8 O¹, no. 768; no. 148, report of Gigot, April 30, 1865.
46. On price levels in Paris, see Alain Plessis, *De la fête impériale au mur des fédérés* (Paris, 1979), p. 93.
47. On building activity in Paris, see Françoise Marnata, *Les Loyers des bourgeois de Paris, 1860–1958* (Paris, 1961), and Jacques Rougerie, "Remarques sur l'histoire des salaires à Paris au XIXᵉ siècle," *Le Mouvement social*, no. 63 (1971): 71–108.
48. For examples of early strikes, see AP, V 8 O¹, no. 148, "Grève et réclamations"; no. 1286, report of superintendent of Ternes plant to Arson, April 26, 1867.

kind.[49] The stokers' form of striking was a rational strategy arising from their position vis-à-vis the gas industry. The action might also have been designed to avoid the harsh treatment that the company reserved for strikers. Instead of firing them for making trouble, the superintendent had to convince them to remain by offering concessions.[50]

The object of collective action was not yet a complex matter of control but rather a matter of pay. The stokers were willing, perhaps eager, to labor harder provided they received higher compensation (table 19). Whether they were paid by the day or by the amount of coal distilled did not seem to make a difference to the stokers; they preferred the mode that would bring them the most income. The rationalization of gas production met with little opposition from the skilled workers because they aspired to maximize gains from lucrative work that was available for only part of the year. The raise did not even have to be proportional to the increase in exertion. When the PGC took over a gas plant near the suburb of Saint-Mandé, stokers demanded the pay level that prevailed in the company's other plants, which meant a raise of twenty-five centimes a day (6.7 percent). The new superintendent yielded to the demand only after he reorganized teams so that five men would have to do the work that six did formerly. Despite the imbalance between the raise and the increased labor extracted, no further trouble occurred. Indeed, the superintendent reported that the stokers were quite happy with the arrangement.[51]

Superintendents were often surprised by the amount of work they could extract from stokers by according a small raise. The manager of the Passy plant had not been happy about giving the stokers twenty-five centimes more per day in 1859, for it meant they were escaping the internal labor market he had aspired to construct. Nonetheless, he appraised the results of the raise with satisfaction. Not only was the superintendent able to replace the popular twenty-four-hour shift, but he was also able to introduce charges every four hours. Thus, the 7 percent raise yielded a 55 percent increase in coal distilled.[52] At the same factory nine years later, another acute labor shortage compelled the superintendent to offer the stokers a choice of work routines. They could continue at the same pay and load short (2.5 meter) retorts, requiring seventy-five kilograms of coal

49. For intriguing efforts to link the form of collective protest to workers' culture, see Reddy, *Rise of Market Culture*, chaps. 7, 10; Michelle Perrot, *Workers on Strike: France 1871–1890*, trans. Chris Turner (New Haven, 1987).

50. Organizers of collective protest were inevitably fired, if not at once, then at a convenient moment.

51. AP, V 8 O¹, no. 768, "Usine Saint-Mandé."

52. Ibid., "Usine Passy." The manager reported producing 249,000 cubic meters of gas a day in 1861 and only 160,000 in 1859.

Table 19. Average Daily Pay of Stokers
(in francs)

Year	Mode	Wage
1855	By day	3.50
1859	By day	3.75
1863	By day	5.00
1866	By day + 50 c. bonus	5.50
1869	5 f./day + 20 c. per 100 kg over 2,500 + bonus	5.95
1879	5 f./day + 20 c. per 100 kg over 2,500 + bonus	6.20
1881	3 f. per 1,000 kg + bonus	8.95
1889	3 f. per 1,000 kg + bonus	9.30
1893	3.3 f. per 1,000 kg	10.30
1899	3.3 f. per 1,000 kg	10.50

Sources: AP, V 8 O¹, nos. 148, 711, 748.

per charge, or they could load long (2.75 meter) retorts, taking a hundred kilograms of coal, and receive a raise of twenty-five centimes. The stokers chose the higher pay even though they were not going to be fully compensated for their exertion.[53] On two occasions at least, in 1865 and 1870, top production managers believed that stokers had reached the limits of human endurance and that productivity could climb no higher without basic changes in the work process.[54] Yet output per worker continued to rise without resort to mechanization, though more slowly than in the past. The incentive bonus introduced in 1869, twenty centimes per hundred kilograms of coal over twenty-five hundred kilograms distilled, apparently motivated stokers to boost output.

Though wages were the stokers' principal focus at the time, there were other issues that could unite them. Cury, the ancient superintendent of the La Villette plant, once sought to improve the lighting power of coal by treating it with heavy oils derived from coal tar. The stokers refused to abide the experience because the odor of the oil made them ill and the treated coal stuck to their shovels. Cury had to abandon the initiative.[55] Likewise, firemen occasionally resisted the endless experiments with dif-

53. Ibid., no. 749, report of superintendent of Passy plant to Arson, April 6, 1869.
54. Ibid., no. 764, "Main-d'oeuvre de distillation (26 avril 1870)"; no. 148, report of Gigot, April 30, 1865.
55. Ibid., no. 768, "Usine de La Villette," report of December 15, 1861.

ferent sorts of fuels.[56] The work routine on Sunday was another source of friction. The company attempted to make the stokers on the day shift work a full night shift too. The stokers successfully united to compel the company to accept four charges on Sunday instead of six.[57] These incidents suggest that stokers had the potential to stop or at least curtail the dramatic changes that management made in the work routine during the 1860s, but the workers did not apply their collective power to that goal.

In addition to seeking more pay, even at a high cost to themselves, the stokers held the company to a rudimentary sense of justice entailing equal pay for equal work. Rumors that stokers at another plant were earning more sparked some agitation. But the stokers were never completely successful in standardizing wages among the different plants because work routines and output differed from one to another. Furthermore, the company often succeeded in keeping them ignorant about pay levels outside their small spheres.[58] On the other hand, the stokers quickly disposed of corporate plans to impose on them the career-based pay under which unskilled workers suffered. The company tried in 1858 to create three "classes" of stokers, with twenty-five-centime differences for each step, but agitation forced management to back away from the attempt within a few months.[59]

Lacking from the stokers' repertoire of collective protests were confrontations with supervisors over unwelcome interference, insults, tests of will, and the like. The records on labor from the 1860s and 1870s, admittedly incomplete, contain no reference to such conflicts.[60] The absence is all the more noteworthy in that the stokers' increasing productivity was achieved through closer supervision, badgering, and pressuring from foremen. The number of immediate supervisors increased significantly. In 1858 there was one foreman for every thirty-seven distillation workers; in 1884 the ratio was one to twenty-three. Stokers may have resented the increased supervision but they had to deal with it as individuals, quitting or standing up for themselves. In view of the trouble that foremen would cause by the end of the century, the absence of such conflicts is telling.[61]

56. Ibid., "Usine Ternes," reports of September 16 and 23, 1860.
57. Ibid., "Usine Belleville," report of April 14, 1861; no. 717, report no. 95, Rigaud to Arson.
58. Ibid., "Usine Passy," report of April 14, 1861; no. 151, report of Arson to director, May 1, 1890.
59. Ibid., no. 666, deliberations of August 3, 1858, and March 9, 1859.
60. Ibid., no. 768; no. 148, "Réponses aux demandes concernant le personnel." Engineer Audouin reported no more than two or three suspensions a year for rebellious behavior.
61. Ibid., no. 665 (fols. 500–514); no. 153, "Personnel." On agitation against the authority of the foreman at the end of the century, see chapter 8.

The stokers clearly created consternation among management by defeating its plans for an internal labor market. Nonetheless, these physical giants proved pliant in serving the larger interests of the firm. The managers' complaints about "outrageous" demands were a sign of having been spoiled by fortunate circumstances.[62] Ultimately, engineers implicitly recognized their good fortune and showed it by tolerating wage demands without seeking to weaken labor's power through technological displacement. Over the long run, however, the firm's advantageous position was destined to disappear. It was not that stokers suddenly became "class-conscious." Rather, the conditions that kept them independent, interested primarily in higher wages, and responsive to the carrots and sticks that managers chose to wield ended during that prime transition point in Parisian social history, the economic crisis of the mid-1880s.

• • •

Historians have long recognized the quickening pace of structural change within the French labor force in the last two decades of the nineteenth century. Machinery challenged handicraft production; international competition compelled managers to reorganize and intensify work routines.[63] One further force creating a "proletariat" in France was the curtailment of temporary migrations to urban industry from the countryside. Industrial workers settled in cities.[64] The stokers participated in the last pattern of change, which entailed far more than taking up new residences. It called into question all the ways the stokers had heretofore related to their employer.

Ceasing to be rural laborers who sought winter work with the PGC was one aspect of a broader alteration in the stokers' independent status. They became *dependent* on the firm for year-round employment. No longer were they workers who put together a livelihood through varied tasks, among them stoking; they became gas workers, pure and simple. By the 1890s, 45 percent stayed in the distillation room during the summer. Most of the rest struggled for the now coveted "privilege" of having year-round work with the PGC and took jobs as common laborers in the courtyards to be on hand when stoking jobs became plentiful in the fall. Superinten-

62. For the internal labor market, see chapter 4. For a fine example of a factory manager spoiled by fortunate circumstances, see AP, V 8 O¹, no. 749, report of superintendent of Passy to Arson, April 6, 1869.

63. Jean-Marie Mayeur, *Les Débuts de la IIIᵉ République* (Paris, 1973), pp. 66–72; Michelle Perrot, "The Three Ages of Industrial Discipline in Nineteenth-Century France," in *Consciousness and Class Experience in Nineteenth-Century Europe*, ed. John Merriman (New York, 1980), pp. 149–168.

64. Lequin, *Ouvriers de la région lyonnaise*, 1:123–156; Noiriel, *Ouvriers dans la société française*, p. 83.

dents were now pleased with the number of job seekers available. Indeed, the assistant head of the factory division maintained that some of those applicants took the trouble to procure letters of recommendation from influential people.[65] The sources of this transformation into dependent workers were manifold. Some causes reached back into the deep provinces where the stokers had originated. The heavy rural exodus from Brittany, Auvergne, and Savoy, after centuries of overpopulation and temporary migration, affected the fate of the stokers. The decline of rural industry, the reconstitution of larger farms in response to more commercialized agriculture, and the broadening of peasants' cultural horizons sent thousands of rural hands to Paris and the other metropolises, where they remained permanently.[66] Like the stonemasons who began to settle in Paris some decades earlier, stokers no longer considered returning home. The demographic shifts assured a plentiful work force for the PGC, all the more so because of two crucial changes in Paris.

The local changes undermined the stokers' independence by calling into question their ties to the construction industry as an alternative to the PGC. First, the wages of stokers pulled decisively ahead of building workers by 1880 at the latest. Pay for skilled masons stagnated at around eight francs a day through the rest of the nineteenth century.[67] In the meantime, stokers had taken advantage of the PGC's critical labor shortage in 1880 to strike and win a pay rate of three francs per thousand kilograms of coal distilled. That rate assured them a daily wage of almost nine francs and eventually more. Even if stokers were willing to settle for the lower pay of construction workers, jobs would not have been easy to find. The golden era of building had passed by that time. The Parisian housing market was in recession after 1882: Paris had too many apartments, and rents stabilized until the century ended.[68] Baron Haussmann's projects had once made it possible for stokers to escape their painful work for part of the year; alternatives to stoking now became much more problematical. Stokers were likely to remain in gas production as long as the company needed them or as long as their stamina allowed. It is not surprising that when two stokers were fired in 1895 for having ruined a retort through

65. AP, V 8 O¹, no. 162, report of Euchène to director, April 10, 1906; no. 163, report of superintendent of Ivry plant to Euchène, March 23, 1902; no. 148, "Revendications. Service des usines," responses of Gigot.
66. Françoise Raison-Jourde, *La Colonie auvergnate à Paris au XIXᵉ siècle* (Paris, 1976), pp. 179–190; Maurice Agulhon et al., *Histoire de la France rurale*, vol. 3, *Apogée et crise de la civilisation paysanne, 1789–1914* (Paris, 1976), pp. 469–487.
67. Rougerie, "Remarques sur l'histoire des salaires," p. 99–100.
68. Michel Lescure, *Les Sociétés immobilières en France au XIXᵉ siècle* (Paris, 1980), p. 78.

Table 20. Stokers' Years of Work
with the PGC

Seniority	1878		1888–1889	
	No.	%	No.	%
<1	25	12.0	13	2.9
1–3	67	32.1	78	17.7
4–5	23	11.0	91	20.6
6–10	39	18.7	152	34.5
11–15	27	12.9	72	16.3
15 +	28	13.4	35	7.9
Total	209	100.1	441	99.9

Sources: AP, V 8 O¹, nos. 1290, 1293.

negligence, their immediate concern was whether the superintendent would take them back next year.[69]

The consequences of the stokers' dependency were soon visible in patterns of labor turnover (table 20). The changes after just a few years of the new conditions were quite dramatic. The portion of stokers who had remained with the PGC three years or less dropped by more than half. More stokers were staying on the job longer. The figures also attest to a reduction in purely seasonal employment. That is why the portion of stokers who lasted fifteen years was actually a good deal higher in 1878 than in 1888; men who stoked year round could not have lasted so long. Most would have been incapacitated after a decade of year-round work.

Another consequence of dependence on the PGC was an end to the paradoxical shortage of stokers during the slow season. Plant superintendents confidently reported having a surfeit of applicants during the 1890s.[70] Though stokers had once hastened to return to the countryside or snatch a good construction job when the warm weather approached, those options were no longer attractive or available. After 1880 stokers maneuvered to avoid seasonal layoffs. Indeed, the PGC's policies regarding layoffs now became a major source of grievance and frustration.

Not surprisingly, the issue surfaced first in the mid-1880s, when the stokers' dependency became manifest. The PGC had granted a large wage increase to stokers on the occasion of a strike in 1880 and then attempted

69. AP, V 8 O¹, no. 150, report of Hadamar, July 10, 1895.
70. Ibid., no. 148, report of Gigot to director, October 8, 1892. The assistant head of the factory division asserted that each factory received about forty applications a day.

to reduce its wage bill by hiring Belgians and Italians at lower pay. By 1887 more than 40 percent of the stokers at the La Villette plant, the company's largest, were foreigners.[71] French stokers complained that the foreigners were retained at the plant during the slow season whereas they were sent away and then not always rehired in the fall. Pressured by the city and by the national administration to favor French workers, the company announced a formal policy of layoffs based on seniority. The concession settled very little, however, for the PGC altered its interpretation in a mercurial manner and never clarified it in detail. Was seniority determined on a plant-by-plant basis, or was it companywide? Did a stoker who worked two full years have more or less seniority than a stoker who had returned for five consecutive winter seasons? The director allowed plant superintendents to apply the rules as they wished and to improvise. He undoubtedly did not mind that arbitrary layoff procedures sowed dissention among stokers even as they darkened relations with the company.[72]

The shift to dependency brought prominence to the distinction between stokers with the newly acquired right to work all year and those subject to layoffs. Superintendents reported that at least three years of employment with the company were necessary to establish that right, and the slow expansion of gas consumption in the 1890s must have lengthened that term. In the meantime, misunderstandings over rules were numerous, and fights among stokers, each defending his rights, broke out.[73] The solidarities promoted by common frustration with the company were partially eroded by jealousies among stokers over the issue. That these tensions could cut deep is demonstrated by the aftermath of the wildcat strike of March 1899 (see chapter 4). The company, it will be recalled, agreed to take back all strikers, but it was necessary to put them to work in plants other than the ones in which they had been employed. The stokers already at those plants protested the strikers' presence as a threat to their own layoff status. Thus, comrades-in-arms one day became squabbling job seekers the next.[74] The irony was that the March strike had been triggered by a foreman's arbitrary application of rules on layoffs. The quest for secure, year-round work had come to color relations among workers and relations between workers and the PGC in ways it could not have during the 1860s.

71. Ibid., no. 90, letter of Camus to consul general, October 1, 1887.
72. Ibid., no. 151, "Règlement à l'ancienneté pour toutes les catégories"; letter of Lajarrigue to Hadamar, November 8, 1901; Le Journal du gaz. Organe officiel de la chambre syndicale des travailleurs du gaz, no. 108 (June 5, 1897): 2.
73. AP, V 8 O¹, no. 163, report of superintendent of Ivry plant to Euchène, March 23, 1902; no. 151, letter of Lajarrigue to Hadamar, November 8, 1901.
74. Ibid., no. 159, report of Gigot, March 25, 1899.

The dependent status of stokers had not yet solidified by 1880, but already the strike of that year was different from earlier ones because of the change. The defiant stokers sent a delegation to management, not to announce a collective departure for construction sites, but rather to make specific demands regarding their situation at the PGC. Moreover, stokers were now determined to profit from their higher productivity to a greater extent than earlier. They pushed managers to accept piece-rate pay, which the engineers had been postponing for a decade.[75] Still another novel element of the stokers' strike was the nonwage grievance. To restore labor peace, the company took its first step to lighten stokers' burdens. It agreed to hire workers to carry coal from the yards to the distillation hall and to break the coal into small pieces suitable for charging. Eventually management would turn this concession to its own advantage by converting the new crew into a cadre of potential replacements for stokers, but initially it was a benefit stokers won through collective action.[76] The strike of 1880 was a relatively minor outburst—quickly settled because the company had no choice except to yield—but it did portend a reshaping of the stokers' protests.

In the end, the stokers' new status owed very little to the PGC's conscious labor policies. Management had long resisted the demand for piece rates in 1880 that eventually drove stokers' wages decisively above those in competing lines of work. The company had never offered benefits, like housing or pensions, that might have made workers cut their ties with rural life or with alternate urban jobs. Dependency came about, as we have seen, through the operation of impersonal forces. Nonetheless, the new status of labor did offer the PGC important strategic tools for dealing with its most obstreperous workers, and the company was not slow to exploit them.[77]

It would be a serious mistake to confound dependency with submissiveness. To the contrary, dependency eventually forced on stokers a new and potentially explosive set of issues that would create confrontation with the firm. The previous independent situation of stokers had reconciled their interests with the business calculations—though not the moral sensibili-

75. Ibid., no. 716, "Rapport sur les primes," no. 66, March 1880; Préfecture, B/a 176, reports of March 15–20, 1880.
76. AP, V 8 O¹, no. 151, "Communications faites à la presse parisienne"; no. 695, deliberations of June 8, 1899. It should not come as a surprise that the PGC took the step of creating a pool of potential replacements for stokers when labor tensions heightened in 1899.
77. By contrast, David Brody, *Steelworkers in America*, pp. 74–102, depicts the classic example of the United States Steel Corporation explicitly encouraging dependent status among its skilled workers.

ties—of management. Under these conditions Calhoun's model for skilled industrial workers approximated reality. But as we shall see in chapter 8, dependency brought an end to these circumstances. A brief comparison of strikes of the 1860s with those of 1890 and 1899 illustrates the changes in protest that were about to ensue. In 1890 the stokers' work stoppage won them a raise, but they still defined the outcome as a failure. In 1899 their strike demands allowed for a sharp *reduction* in pay. In effect, dependency gave stokers a set of demands that were more, not less, difficult for the company to satisfy. The stokers started to behave more like craftsmen, conscious of control over the workplace, than anyone would have heretofore imagined possible.[78]

The Common Laborers

The multifarious business activities of the PGC created a demand for general laborers to perform a wide variety of simple tasks. Unlike stoking, these jobs could be mastered quickly, and most any worker could do them. Taken together, the many sorts of common hands comprised a corps more than three times as large as the stokers. Wage earners of this kind have not had much of a presence in labor history owing to their silence. By and large they accepted the conditions offered them, either because it was the best they could hope for or because they were powerless to do otherwise. One of the noteworthy features of industrial relations within the PGC was that the common laborers acquired their own voice, for a time a clearer one than that of their comrades with market power.

With the company recognizing sixty-seven categories of unskilled workers, the diversity defies easy categorization.[79] Whatever grounds these laborers had for collective action did not derive from common work conditions. A large group of unskilled laborers was composed of coke handlers—nearly 850 of them in 1890 (table 21). These workmen took the extinguished coke from the stokers and processed it for residential use. This task involved piling the coke in large heaps, filling burlap bags with it, carrying the bags on their backs to delivery wagons, and loading the wagons. Obviously, there was nothing intricate about such work, but it was exceptionally taxing. The PGC did not begin to mechanize these op-

---

78. For confirmation of this tendency among skilled workers of modern industry, see Reid, *Miners of Decazeville*, pp. 130–139; Margot Stein, "Working to Rule: The Social Origins of a Labor Elite. Engine Drivers, 1837–1917" (Ph.D. diss., Harvard University, 1977), pp. 246, 278–292.
79. AP, V 8 O¹, no. 159, report of Bodin to Euchène, March 3, 1899.

Table 21. Common Laborers at the PGC, 1889–1890

Category	Approximate No.	Daily Pay (francs)
Distillation plants		
Coal handlers[a]	400	5.00
Purification workers	150	4.50
Courtyard workers	680	4.00
Others	60	4.50
By-products plants		
Machine operators	70	4.25
Laborers	120	3.75
Coke service		
Coke handlers	850	3.75
Carters	290	4.50
Lighting service		
Lamplighters[b]	1,050	2.40
Greasemen, waxers, repairmen[c]	275	3.75
Ditch diggers	180	3.50
Total	4,125	

Sources: AP, V 8 O¹, nos. 148, 149.

[a]These laborers were supposed to be capable of replacing stokers on a temporary basis.

[b]Lamplighters were paid 65, 70, or 75 francs a month, depending on seniority.

[c]Greasemen were paid 1,200–1,400 francs a year.

erations until the last years of the century. By the company's own estimates a coke handler carried each day 186 sacks weighing (altogether) eight thousand kilograms for a total of thirteen kilometers.[80] This toil brought the handlers a meager wage of 3.75 francs a day in 1890. The ten-hour day was often extended by the irregular arrivals and departures of the delivery carts.

Nearly three hundred coke deliverymen completed the labor force attached to this department. They formed a highly problematical service. Every year the company had a dozen or so prosecuted for theft or fraud. At one point the PGC hired undercover agents to spy on the delivery carts as they made their rounds but finally decided that the expense of such surveillance was too great and that it was easier to rely on customers' complaints to detect fraud. The record of criminality gives substance to the assertion made by the chief of the coke department that the company

80. Ibid., no. 148, "Examen des réclamations concernant le service des cokes (4 avril 1892)."

paid too poorly to attract carters of higher integrity.[81] For their part, carters had their own grievances against the firm. They bore civil and criminal responsibility for any accidents they may have caused on the crowded streets. A majority of carters affirmed their willingness to contribute two francs a month from their meager pay for a mutual insurance fund, but the company refused to help them organize one. Moreover, management forced high standards of punctuality on these workers, who were accustomed to the more casual schedules characteristic of outdoor workers. If one was five minutes late for the 5:00 A.M. call, the company assigned his wagon to another worker, and he lost a day's pay.[82]

Almost seven hundred common laborers worked in the courtyards of the distillation plants. Their jobs included unloading shipments of coal, packing by-products, and performing general maintenance chores. The company made an important distinction between the few courtyard men who could replace absent stokers and those who could not. It attempted to retain as many of the former as possible by paying them an extra fifty centimes a day.[83]

In close proximity to the courtyard workers were the two hundred or so who operated the by-products plant. Their jobs were particularly unpleasant because of the stench or fumes from the chemicals they worked with. Some had to stand all day knee deep in pools of noxious liquids. Others operated the machinery or fueled the furnaces. Eye ailments and skin rashes were common occupational hazards for these laborers. Despite these hardships, the by-products workers were among the poorest paid in the company.[84]

Another large group worked not in production but in the distribution service, as lamplighters, greasemen, waxmen, and repairmen. Because their labor was fixed, regular, and predictable, the company commissioned them after a probationary period. The thousand or so lamplighters came closest to thinking of themselves as quasi-municipal workmen: part of their pay came from a municipal subsidy (three centimes per streetlight per day), and their labor was directly related to a public service. The municipal council could alter their work routine by changing its regulations

81. Ibid., no. 90, report of Hallopeau to director, January 14, 1867. The deliberations of the comité d'exécution contain a large number of decisions to prosecute carters for theft or fraud.
82. Ibid., no. 148, "Revendications. Service des cokes (17 septembre 1892)"; report of Montserrat, December 23, 1891; report of Montserrat, April 27, 1892.
83. Ibid., no. 151, "Revendications générales—personnel ouvrier."
84. Ibid., no. 157, "Conditions du travail et d'hygiène des ouvriers des anthracènes"; "Procès-verbaux de la commission administrative de la Caisse de prévoyance," deliberations of March 11, 1864.

concerning street lighting. The PGC regarded its lamplighters as part-time laborers. It contended that the rounds of lighting, cleaning, and extinguishing the sixty-five or so assigned streetlamps required at most five hours a day. It noted that the majority of the lighters had secondary occupations, as concierges, street peddlers, shoemakers. The lighters themselves asserted that their work demanded an eight-hour day. At one point the company had a spy follow a union leader on his rounds and found that the tasks did indeed require eight hours—but only because of frequent stops in pubs or other breaks. The lamplighters, maintaining a preindustrial conception of their work routine, did not wish to define these breaks as external to the job.[85] In any case, the lighters' secondary occupations gave them some independence from the company, and they used it to be among the most turbulent of unskilled laborers.

The greasemen, waxers, and repairmen had an advantage that most wage earners would have welcomed. As "fixed workers," they were paid by the month, and their employment was permanent. Their pay was very low, however, twelve hundred to fourteen hundred francs a year. The manual workers put in thirteen-hour days, outside, painfully exposed to the elements.[86]

There were another two hundred workmen who practiced a trade—plumbers, wheelwrights, fitters, turners, and others. These laborers were not easily categorized. They were not affiliated with the Parisian crafts. Perhaps because their jobs were ancillary to the PGC's central production concerns, the tradesmen were never able to take a directing role in any protest. There was nothing about their comportment that exemplified the proud, contentious craftsmen. For the most part their fate was more closely linked to the common hands than to the stokers.[87]

In important ways the differences between stokers and common laborers was artificial, or at least superficial. Bargaining power on the job was one of the few social distinctions between stokers and common hands. The social background of the two groups could not have been more similar. Both participated in the temporary rural immigration to the capital as long as it lasted. The rural exodus from the deep provinces supplied an

85. Ibid., no. 151, report of Saum to director, June 3, 1893; reports of Saum to director, April 2, 14, and 17, 1892; "Revendications des allumeurs"; "Renseignements sur les professions des allumeurs (24 mars 1900)." In 1900, 846 of 1,028 lamplighters were reported to have second occupations.
86. Ibid., no. 148, "Syndicat. Service extérieur."
87. Mechanics who worked for the company making motors, stoves, and valves did so at piece rates under sweated conditions. They were the sort of degraded handworkers that fully trained mechanics called "small hands." See ibid., no. 151, report of Maubert, August 25, 1897.

increasing portion of both sorts of gas workers. Most stokers had roots in both camps. The company recruited them among the common hands; the stokers spent summers in the courtyards, working as general laborers. Stokers eventually returned to unskilled labor when they could no longer endure the work.[88] In a sense, stoking was not much more than a stage in the life cycle for the minority of physically qualified common laborers.

Nonetheless, the common laborers had a distinctive set of problems on the job—above all, being caught in the internal labor market that managers created for them.[89] That situation meant, as we have seen, low and uneven pay. Table 21 must be read in this context. As a result of the step system of pay, which the company imposed on them, a third to a half of each category earned twenty-five centimes less than the average pay, and a like portion earned twenty-five centimes more. Managers hoped to impart moral lessons as well as divide workers through segmented pay, and they probably achieved the second goal. In 1892 a union delegate from the coke department admitted that "young and older workers do the same job at different pay, and there results an antagonism between the two."[90] Unlike stokers, the common hands could not mount a successful offensive against unequal pay for equal work.

When, after 1890, convincing the public that its pay scales were generous became important to the PGC, it could do so by publicizing the stokers' rates alone, even then neglecting to mention the seasonal quality of the pay. Average wages of common hands were less than half of the stokers' in 1889. The comparative data that engineers gathered from neighboring firms showed that the PGC's compensations were in line with the lowest-paying industries—fertilizer, animal-rendering, and glue companies. Engineer Audouin, who led the fact-gathering mission, was surprised to learn that the Lebaudy and Sommier sugar refineries, notorious exploiters of Italian and Belgian labor, paid the unskilled as well as the PGC. Refinery workers were hired at 3.75 francs a day and could earn 4.50 to 5.50 francs with experience.[91] A clearer understanding of market wages came as something of a revelation to the PGC's managers. Up to this point they had hoped to be able to ignore the market. Whether the new awareness undermined their self-righteousness about labor policies is doubtful.

The low pay that the gas company offered inevitably generated a rapid

---

88. Ibid., no. 163, "Assimilation des ouvriers (4 février 1903)."
89. On the efforts to create an internal labor market, see chapter 4.
90. AP, V 8 O¹, no. 148, "Procès-verbaux de la quatrième audience donnée le 3 mars 1892 aux délégués" (remarks of Gabanon).
91. Ibid., "Renseignements sur les salaires journaliers des ouvriers pris chez différents fabricants."

turnover of the labor force. After all, common hands could earn more elsewhere, suffer no less from seasonal layoffs, and often have tasks that were less painful. Even the greasemen, who were commissioned, had a resignation rate of 7 percent in a year of recession, like 1889, and 19 percent in a year of dramatic labor shortages, like 1881.[92] Wage earners, however, were by no means committed to a peripatetic existence by preference or by life-style. Michelle Perrot has correctly identified an "aspiration for rootedness and for security of employment and retirement" among common hands, and it is clear that an appreciable portion of those at the PGC sought those arrangements.[93] They became possible when political pressures and bourgeois reform altered the wage policies of the firm. Average pay rose 16 percent, to 5.63 francs, by 1895, not counting the profit-sharing bonus introduced in 1893 (30–38 centimes a day).[94] Furthermore, the small pensions of 360–600 francs promised by the company in 1893 made employment more attractive.[95] Such remuneration still did not attain the level of largesse the PGC publically proclaimed, but the unskilled nonetheless seized on the improvements to construct an element of stability in their own lives. Twenty-nine percent of the ditchdiggers in the distribution department, 36 percent of the workers in the mechanical shops, and 54 percent of the chemical-products laborers accumulated at least ten years of seniority by the end of the century. Despite the grueling routine in the coke department, 52 percent of the laborers stayed on the job at least ten years.[96] One greaseman aptly expressed the new outlook on the PGC as employer. Admitting to having committed a serious error on the job, he begged the director to inflict no more than a long suspension. "Being fired—that would be death," he lamented.[97] General laborers seemed eager to define themselves as the personnel of one firm and make long-term commitments to it as soon as competitive pay made that situation viable. Like stokers, common hands came to depend on the PGC for steady employment.

The intervention of the city of Paris in the labor affairs of the gas com-

92. Ibid., no. 148, report of Perrin to director, December 24, 1881; no. 90, report of Arson to director, January 11, 1889. Up to 1890 the PGC seemed to hire roughly fifteen hundred new workers a year.
93. Michelle Perrot, "Une Naissance difficile: la formation de la classe ouvrière lyonnaise," *Annales: Economies, sociétés, civilisations* 33 (1978): 834–835.
94. AP, V 8 O¹, no. 148, "Etat comparatif des salaires."
95. So eager were wage earners for the benefits of a pension that they offered to contribute to the pension fund through a withholding of pay. See ibid., no. 155, "Règlement relatif aux versements à effectuer par le personnel ouvrier (1892)."
96. Ibid., no. 151, "Personnel des ouvriers"; "Ouvriers des travaux chimiques"; no. 156, "Augmentation des salaires depuis 1 mai 1890."
97. Ibid., no. 162, letter of Le Blais to director, n.d.

pany ended a prolonged period of helplessness. The unskilled may have admired the ability of the stokers to force wage concessions on management, but they had rarely been able to duplicate the success. Hence the earnings gap between the two sorts of laborers widened continuously. When the company was founded, general laborers received two-thirds of the stokers' daily pay; by 1890 the former received less than half.[98] Only in the very few years of exceptional labor shortages in the capital did the unskilled acquire the bargaining power that the company could not easily resist. Common hands found such power only in 1867, 1876, and 1881. Otherwise, the few job actions that occurred ended in repression.[99]

The lamplighters were the most aggressive of the general laborers. The second jobs that they held gave them some independence; furthermore, they knew that the disruption of public lighting even for a brief time would create public ire against their parsimonious employer. These advantages, real though they were, profited lamplighters not at all in 1865. Inspired by a successful strike among coach drivers, lighters demanded a raise from 65 francs to 90 francs a month and threatened to desert their rounds if it was not conceded. This threat made managers organize one of their acts of "salutary intimidation." They created a substitute corps of lighters, composed of inspectors, greasers, and auxiliary lighters (those still in the midst of their probationary periods). On the day before the threatened strike the director sent the substitutes to meet the regular workers with letters of dismissal. Eventually the company took back most of them, excluding only the perceived agitators. The rehired lighters had to accept a loss of their seniority in step pay and of their annual bonuses. If the potential strikers of the 1860s expected the municipal council to plead for leniency on their behalf, they received no support whatsoever from that quarter.[100] The exquisite stagecraft choreographed by the company in response to the strike threat told unskilled laborers that they could expect neither success nor clemency.

Even the modest wage gains that laborers were able to win during the boom of 1876–1882 came at a price. The PGC soon compensated for the raise by hiring foreign workers in large numbers. The result was new ten-

98. Ibid., no. 149, "Augmentations des dépenses annuelles résultant des améliorations depuis 1889."

99. For examples of wage demands by common laborers, see ibid., no. 771, report of April 12, 1865 (fol. 46); no. 768, "Usine de la Villette," report of March 20, 1861; no. 752, report of May 6, 1864; Préfecture, B/a 176, report of March 6, 1880.

100. AP, V 8 O¹, no. 148, "Etude relative à une augmentation du salaire des allumeurs (15 juillet 1865)"; "Rapport de la commission nommée à l'occasion de la grève des allumeurs (28 juin 1865)."

sions and divisions among the common hands.[101] The PGC clearly knew how to dominate this underprivileged personnel—and intended to do so. Given the sour state of the gas industry during the 1890s, it seems unlikely that common hands would have received meaningful improvements had the city not transformed the balance of power by intervening in their behalf.

• • •

Until the last decade of the nineteenth century the PGC employed thousands of workmen but had not truly formed a manual personnel of its own. Almost in spite of managerial policies, the labor force became tied to the firm, and an identifiable proletariat of gas workers came into existence. By no means was this process of labor-force formation unique. Analogous developments occurred at mine pits, railroad lines, steel mills, and machine-building plants all over France at roughly the same time.[102] What was distinctive about the gas workers was that they came by the means to make management listen to their grievances. Only part of the labor force responded pragmatically and flexibly to the opportunities opened by the crisis of the liberal order. Defining what the workers wanted, not to mention achieving the goals, proved to be a difficult task. Still, there is no reason to suppose that other sorts of industrial workers would have used the opportunity differently.

101. Ibid., no. 157, report of Gravier to Audouin, November 29, 1897; Préfecture, B/a 176, report of March 8, 1880.
102. Joan Scott, "The Glassworkers of Carmaux, 1850–1900," in *Nineteenth-Century Cities*, ed. Stephen Thernstrom and Richard Sennett (New Haven, 1969), pp. 3–48; Lequin, *Ouvriers de la région lyonnaise*, pp. 123–156; Trempé, *Mineurs de Carmaux*, 1:189–253; Jean-Paul Brunet, *Saint-Denis, la ville rouge* (Paris, 1980); Noiriel, *Ouvriers dans la société française*, chap. 3; Hanagan, *Nascent Proletarians*, chap. 3.

EIGHT

Labor Protest in an Era of Social Reform

The outstanding concerns of fin-de-siècle labor history—a general crisis of industrial discipline, achievements in building working-class institutions, and harsh repression of protest—were all visible at the Parisian gas plants. Studying the gas workers permits us to explore the dynamics of the larger trends in microcosm. The *gaziers* even traversed the long path of the French labor movement from direct, informally organized action to indirect participation within national, bureaucratic unions.[1] How and why they did so clarifies many important points about the construction and collapse of peaceable industrial relations in France.

Reformist Syndicalism in Action

The logic of labor protest might seem to dictate that artisans would use their skills to defend their interests through direct action at the workplace but that industrial workers, especially recent rural immigrants, would have to rely on a centralized political party to advance their cause.[2] Unrest at the gas plants belies such a tidy generalization. The PGC's manual per-

---

1. Charles Tilly, *The Contentious French: Four Centuries of Popular Struggle* (Cambridge, Mass., 1986), chap. 10; Michael Hanagan, *The Logic of Solidarity: Artisans and Industrial Workers in Three French Towns, 1871–1914* (Urbana, Ill., 1980), pp. 214–217; Val Lorwin, *The French Labor Movement* (Cambridge, Mass., 1966), chaps. 1–5.
2. Bernard Moss, *The Origins of the French Labor Movement, 1830–1914* (Berkeley and Los Angeles, 1976), pp. 25–26. The textile operatives of the Nord often form the basis for such a generalization. See Robert Baker, "Socialism in the Nord, 1880–1914," *International Review of Social History* 12 (1967): 357–389, and Claude Willard, *Les Guesdistes: Le Mouvement socialiste en France (1893–1905)* (Paris, 1965).

sonnel engaged in collective protest centered at the workplace. The choice was not between syndicalism and socialism but rather between a syndicalism centered on strike action and one based on solid, carefully constructed organization. The *gaziers* tolerated patient organization building and an incremental approach to resolving their grievances in inverse proportion to their bargaining power with their employer.

The strategy of forming trade unions to pursue collective interests does not appear to have originated with the workers themselves. The law of 1884, which legalized unions, produced no spontaneous movement among the gas personnel. Formal organization began with the opening of negotiations between the PGC and the prolabor municipal council of the 1890s. The initiative probably came from outsiders and politicians. Their motives were to improve the condition of the workers and to develop a clientele. The first union of PGC workers, a fleeting one, was the project of one Jules Roques. A shadowy figure today, Roques was a journalist who edited the Socialist *L'Egalité*.[3] Roques chose to organize stokers exclusively. He presided over their union and penned their demands. On May 1, 1890, he led a strike. Even though the stokers won a raise, they were disillusioned by the outcome of the action (for reasons we shall explore later). They apparently quarreled with Roques, and the union fell apart.[4]

A second union, having nothing to do with the first and even rejecting its legacy, was formed June 1891. Its membership was entirely different. Stokers were not involved in its formation, nor did they seek to join it. To the second—and more permanent—union belonged common laborers from the courtyards, the lighting service, and the coke department. Initiators of the new movement were Socialist municipal councilmen, who assured gas workers of their support and protection. Jean Allemane, a Socialist who subordinated politics to trade union activity, was quite active among the organizers.[5] This time the fruits of outside intervention took root. An indigenous leadership appeared to exploit the favorable political circumstances that make unionization possible. The common laborers employed by the PGC joined the union in large numbers. By the mid-1890s the Chambre syndicale des travailleurs du gaz was one of the largest, if

3. Claude Bellanger et al., *Histoire générale de la presse française*, 5 vols. (Paris, 1969–1976), 3:372. The police appeared to have no file on Roques even though he was prosecuted for publishing pornographic illustrations. See AP, V 8 O¹, no. 1063, "Grèves de 1890 et de 1899," clipping from *L'Egalité*, May 4, 1890.
4. AP, V 8 O¹, no. 151, "Grève des chauffeurs (1 mai 1890)."
5. Ibid., no. 148, "Rapport sur la réunion du mercredi le 11 novembre 1891 à la Bourse du Travail"; "Rapport sur la réunion du 19 juillet 1891"; Préfecture, B/a, 1424, reports of June 27, November 12, 1891, January 16, and November 22, 1892. The editor of *Le Rappel*, Charles Bos, was also active in encouraging the union.

not the largest, union in Paris. It was also wealthy and had influence with local politicians and the press. As such, it was rather an exception in French labor history, but one whose evolution is nonetheless instructive.

The origins of this union were inseparable from the foundering of the liberal order at the end of the nineteenth century and the development of a political will to attempt the integration of wage earners into the republic. The municipal council announced its intention of helping workers win their rights, defined largely in terms of better pay. The situation has important implications for the question of relations between French workers and the nineteenth-century state. Scholars have debated whether the state functioned as an arm of capital at moments of labor unrest or whether it pursued a conciliatory role in the interest of public order.[6] Whatever the intentions of the authorities, the comportment of gas workers points to a vast chasm of distrust between wage earners and the state. Workers did not act spontaneously to gain the state's support. They had taken no steps to importune officials during the numerous confrontations prior to 1890. Even when the company had behaved in a heavily repressive manner, neither stokers nor common hands (with the exception of lamplighters, who were paid in part by the government) had tried to draw the authorities to their side. In truth, the gas workers did not reach out to the state until the state—in the form of the municipal council—reached out to *them*. That happened as the left majority committed itself to a new round of republicanization. Such an extended hand was necessary to make workers active contenders for power within the existing political order. Even with the hand outstretched from above, a large number of gas laborers, as we shall see, turned their backs on the state. This segment of the labor force was not able to explain its behavior in terms of theoretical principles, but it was acting on the syndicalist assumption that the liberation of workers was the task of workers alone.[7]

The indigenous leaders who directed the second union never fully renounced their distrust of the state, but they soon developed policies firmly

6. Arguing for the repressive nature of the state, at least until the end of the century, is Michelle Perrot, *Workers on Strike: France, 1871–1890,* trans. Chris Turner (New Haven, 1987), pp. 280–303. Describing a more flexible policy are Charles Tilly and Edward Shorter, *Strikes in France, 1830–1968* (Cambridge, 1974). The economist Gerald Friedman finds that the American government was more repressive than the French and that French strikes were more likely to be successful as a result. See "Strike Success and Union Ideology: The U.S. and France, 1880–1914," *Journal of Economic History* 48 (1988): 1–25.

7. See Peter Stearns, *Revolutionary Syndicalism and French Labor: A Cause without Rebels* (New Brunswick, N.J., 1971). His assertions that militant syndicalism had the shallowest of roots among the mass of workers and that the vast majority sought only moderate reforms are not fully borne out by this study.

aimed at grasping the extended hand. They were also eager to listen to the paternalistic rhetoric of management set on bourgeois reform. They staked the success of their leadership and of the union on the viability of piecemeal reforms in the seemingly favorable climate of the 1890s. The same nine or ten men guided the union from its origins through the strike of 1899. Their backgrounds were humble and rooted in the milieu of the rank and file. Four had been team heads in the coke yards. The other members of the union's governing board had been commissioned workers in the lighting service, lamplighters, greasemen, and waxers.[8] These leaders quickly escaped from the influence of Socialist politicians and stamped their own strategies and theoretical positions on the union. Manifesting varying degrees of ideological awareness, they all became reformist syndicalists. That stance by no means isolated them in prewar Paris. Indeed, revolutionaries like Victor Griffuelhes frequently lamented that the capital had no major unions of the ideological coloration of which they approved. The programs of the reformists have largely been forgotten by historians but deserve to be far better known.[9]

The strongest influence over the Chambre syndicale des travailleurs du gaz in its early years came from Alfred Brard, a former team head from the coke yards. He was the general secretary of the union until 1893, when he won a seat on the municipal council from the district that contained the La Villette plant. Brard's views on labor movements had many affinities with those of Maurice Claverie, his counterpart at the employees' union. Brard was just as much a reformist syndicalist and just as flexible. His electoral platform proclaimed that he "had always thought that theories do not suffice; that fine words do not provide bread; that actions are better than words; that realities are better than hopes, which often cannot be realized anyway."[10] Though Brard ran successfully as an "independent Socialist" in two municipal elections, he was a stranger to the Socialist group at City Hall. He was too committed to the role of councilman in service of the unions to support the policies of the Socialists on the gas question. Eventually, he changed his political label to a more appropriate

---

8. AP, V 8 O¹, no. 148, "Renseignements sur les principaux ouvriers dits délégués des Travailleurs du gaz"; report of September 17, 1892.
9. It is interesting to compare the French leaders to the head of the British gas workers' union, Will Thorne. See his autobiography, *My Life's Battles* (London, n.d.), and his biography, Giles Radice and Lisanne Radice, *Will Thorne: Constructive Militant* (London, 1974). Thorne was clearly more energetic and imaginative than the people who led the French gas unions.
10. Préfecture, B/a 195, "Election de 1900, XIXe Arrondissement"; AP, V 8 O¹, no. 148, "Procès-verbaux des audiences données aux délégués du syndicat"; report of July 25, 1891.

"syndicalist." Several Socialist candidates challenged Brard in his last campaign in 1900, and by vying for votes on their right, he not only retained his seat but also won a reputation for being a Nationalist in some circles. The visibility of Brard's rightward drift was reinforced by his qualified support for the Chamon project of 1901, which he viewed as giving workers as much as they could expect. In reality, Brard had not joined the anti-Dreyfusard right; he was simply a reformist syndicalist who avoided large ideological issues and lacked an abiding animosity for capitalism. This position did not make him an anomaly among the union's activists.

After Brard departed from the board to serve the gas workers at city hall, the leadership passed to Jean Darène, who was still more naive about the use of power than Brard and more opportunistic in his quest for immediate gains. His understanding of the workers' position in French society transcended classic divisions between the left and the right. The union newspaper, which Darène edited, expressed his anti-Semitic views. Somehow Jewish stockholders of the PGC were especially guilty of exploitation, and Darène saw the possibility of cooperating with the gentile ones. He was also xenophobic and blamed foreign workers for intensifying the problems that French laborers faced. The antipathy for foreign wage earners that Darène expressed was probably widespread in this union, which may at times have excluded them.[11]

Darène's hopefulness about reform in this era of liberal crisis was coupled with gullibility and perhaps even an overweening respect for hierarchy. Darène was completely duped by Director Godot's ploy of agreeing to enforce labor rules only to have lower managers violate them. He retained his faith in the director's word long after it was reasonable to do so. The union leader explained the many abuses of authority that his own newspaper reported as a matter of ignorance on the part of top management, which, he insisted, sought to be just in the face of intransigent supervisors.[12] Darène's guiding vision was some sort of permanent cooperation between well-intentioned management and the moderate union. He perceived in the politics surrounding the gas concession the occasion for a corporatist accord with the PGC.[13] Ultimately, Darène's lack of critical insight led to inept strategies at moments of crisis.

11. *Le Journal du gaz. Organe officiel de la chambre syndicale des travailleurs du gaz*, no. 81 (April 20, 1896): 3; no. 90 (September 5, 1896): 3; no. 21 (October 30, 1893): 3.
12. Ibid., no. 83 (May 20, 1896): 1.
13. AP, V 8 O¹, no. 150, letter of the executive commission of the Syndicat des travailleurs to director, September 1892. The union leaders reminded Godot of "the work the union has done to realize a renewal of the monopoly."

The corporatist implications of Darène's approach to union affairs merits further investigation, for they were not at all unique. We have already observed the strain of thought in Claverie and Brard. Scholars usually associate corporatism with social thought inspired by Catholicism, preindustrial tradition, and hostility to class analysis. Yet reformist syndicalism and corporatism shared several key assumptions and could readily dovetail. Both outlooks focused on the interests shared by capital and labor. Both assumed that the employer had the capacity to make major improvements in the lives of his workers. Corporatists and nonrevolutionary syndicalists agreed that the enterprise, not the political arena, was where reform had to occur. Corporatists were intent on combatting "state socialism," and the union leaders thought of political influence mainly as a source of leverage to negotiate with the employer.[14] The boundaries between the two outlooks were likely to be especially blurred in this era of nascent corporate capitalism. The separation of ownership and control confused reform-minded syndicalists; it allowed them to represent managers as simply a part of the personnel.[15] The bureaucratic structure of management at the PGC led Claverie, Brard, and Darène to envision engineers and workers in an easy cooperation—one as the brains, the other as the muscle. Furthermore, the freedom that large enterprises enjoyed from market constraints opened the possibility of the company's sharing its monopolistic profits with the personnel. Reformist syndicalists inevitably found attractions in corporatist solutions to labor unrest, particularly at a moment when managers advocated measures of social peace.

Other union leaders were somewhat less optimistic or naive than Darène. They were sometimes openly skeptical about his roseate assessments of management's intentions. Nonetheless, they were just as committed to reformist syndicalism. The policy of delivering ultimatums to the PGC or of striking was not one they advocated. They differed from Darène in having more faith in the good intentions of the municipal council than in the company. They believed that the city could wring further concessions from an employer who was unresponsive, either out of ill will or lack of thought.

Though reformists too, the Socialists on the municipal council found their relations with the gas union leaders to be highly problematical. The Socialist councilmen strove to improve the lives of the gas personnel, but

14. At the CGT's celebrated Congress of Amiens in 1906, the reformist syndicalists were just as insistent as the revolutionaries on independence from political parties.
15. At a union meeting in July 1891, Brard affirmed that director Camus was not "an enemy of workers" but simply an "employee of the stockholders." See AP, V 8 O¹, no. 148, "Rapport sur la quatrième réunion du syndicat (25 juillet 1891)."

their solution to the gas question, municipalization, required waiting until after 1905 for dramatic ameliorations. Union leaders inevitably found Radicals, and especially the Nationalists, more open to discussing immediate gains for the rank and file. Thus, close ties between Socialists and syndicalists failed to develop despite a shared concern for the plight of the gas workers. Ironically, the leaders of the gas workers might have found more common ground with reformist Socialists had they been less reformist as syndicalists.

The progress achieved by the union was ultimately dependent on the employer's will to grant concessions, and the breakdown of negotiations with the city at the end of 1892 dimmed those prospects. From 1893 to 1898 the union leadership faced frustrations, for the company was not responsive, and the municipal council was not able to impose reforms. There were moments when even Darène lost his optimism. In May 1896 the secretary expressed his disappointment with Director Godot: not that the director had abandoned his concern for the personnel, but he placed too much trust in his subordinates. Darène reluctantly concluded that Godot cared more for the principles of hierarchical authority than for social justice. Reaching the acme of disillusionment in late 1896, Darène broached the possibility of some sort of "demonstration" to shake management out of its routine.[16] The impasse forced the union to reformulate its demands and its strategies. It dropped the long-standing negotiating points of a minimum wage of five francs and equalization of pay and put in their place far-reaching demands, the eight-hour day and tenure for all workers who had been with the firm five years.[17] The boldness of the new projects was more a sign of resignation than one of radicalization. The union leaders realized that little would be accomplished until the larger gas question was resolved one way or another. They were establishing an agenda for the PGC's successor.

In a speech to the assembled members the union president stated that the goal of collective action was assuring "a certain material well-being [*une petite aisance*] for workers."[18] Though there is no conclusive way to survey the views of the rank and file, there is equally no reason to suppose they were fundamentally out of step with the goals and tactics of the indigenous leaders. Gas workers did flock to the union in large numbers;

---

16. *Journal du gaz*, no. 92 (October 5, 1896): 3.
17. The minimum wage was realized as a result of the 600,000-franc grant in 1896. Municipal politicians may have been behind the new demands. The city tenured its own workers in 1895. See AP, V 8 O^1, no. 154, "Mesures prises par le Conseil municipal en vue de l'amélioration de la situation du personnel."
18. Ibid., no. 148, "Rapport sur la réunion du mercredi 11 novembre 1891."

the company, the police, and the municipal council concurred that the majority were members. The figure of 6,783 members that Darène advanced in May 1899 was creditable and implied that nearly every common laborer belonged.[19] The superintendent of the La Villette plant understood the strength of the union's attraction enough to be troubled and insulted by it. Cury noted that until 1892 workmen had come to him to air grievances or ask favors. Once the union era opened, the personnel relied on the delegates.[20] It is clear that the leaders did try to discover the will of the rank and file and act on it. We have already seen the popularity of the five-franc minimum wage, and union officers took up that demand for a long time, often against their better judgment. When the PGC first granted the profit-sharing plan, some leaders were inclined to celebrate it as a major victory and give low priority to the minimum wage. They soon learned, along with management, that workers were attached to the latter goal and would not count their year-end bonuses as part of the wage. Godot insisted that officers convince workers of their good fortune, but the leaders expressed helplessness to do so. The lamplighter Chapelle affirmed that he personally "was in agreement with the company in terms of principles" but that his members "were not mathematicians and did not understand these calculations."[21] Union leaders prudently abandoned the effort to make the rank and file understand. The union ended its meetings in 1893 with the cry "Long live the five-franc minimum wage!" but not necessarily because leaders wanted that to be the rallying point.[22]

The leaders' respect for managerial prerogative and their optimism about the good intentions of upper management also had resonances among the mass of wage earners. Common hands did have trouble with immediate supervisors, and their vocabulary expressed it. They referred to the foreman as *le patron,* with all the resentment and fear that that title implied.[23] Indeed, the alleged injustices perpetrated by the foreman had long been sources of complaint and would soon become major themes of protest. Nonetheless, the rank and file shared their leaders' expectation that the engineers who headed departments would be men of wider vision and of equity. That is to say, Emile Cheysson's view of engineers as disinterested authorities ready to replace the arbitrary foreman had credence on the shop floor. Similarly, Darène's faith in the director's justness had its counterpart below, in the internalization of a paternalistic ethos among

19. *Journal du gaz,* no. 154 (May 5, 1899): 1.
20. AP, V 8 O¹, no. 148, report of Cury, March 24, 1892.
21. Ibid., "Procès-verbaux des audiences données aux délégués du syndicat," p. 3.
22. Ibid., no. 148, clipping from *Le Journal des débats,* May 28, 1893.
23. Ibid., no. 159, Louis Saget to director, n.d.

general laborers. Workers initiated contact with the chief executive to ask for his aid and for his intervention in their personal problems. One coal hauler, who was barely literate, wrote a rambling letter to Godot, full of complaints about his ungrateful and lazy sons. The worker had nothing to request from the director, but he apparently needed to explain his situation to his employer.[24]

One historian of British labor has commented on workers' fractured and indistinct notion of employers as a class, and still more as "the enemy."[25] This vision is clearly relevant for the mass of workers at the PGC as well as for union leaders. The identification of friends and enemies was all the more difficult in the new sort of enterprise that was arising, with its bureaucratic layers of authority and its encumbered face-to-face relations. Thus, the failure of union officials to confront management aggressively and the respect they generally accorded engineers met with comprehension from the rank and file.

The mass membership achieved by the gas union provides insights into the French labor movement because it was so uncharacteristic. The ability to mobilize so many laborers as permanent, dues-paying members casts doubt on the common arguments that French wage earners were too fiercely independent to submit to formal organization or too entranced by a romantic, revolutionary faith in apocalyptic action.[26] French laborers were willing to unionize when there was little danger of revenge from the employer and when that was the best option for obtaining results. The gas workers' union also stands out for having attracted the unskilled rather than the most qualified laborers. The aberrant situation points not only to the exceptional political circumstances but also to the influence of the workplace situation in determining the shape of collective action. At the mercy of their employers, the common hands readily seized the opportunity to gain some control over their fate by grasping the extended hand of the state. Stokers, by contrast, could rely on informal cooperation to redress grievances because of their relative power to disrupt operations at the workplace. Such power encouraged them to pursue goals that Darène's

---

24. Ibid., no. 162, J. Depoix to director, n.d.; no. 150, "Demandes de secours, 1875–1899." Elinor Accampo has argued that paternalism had a strong appeal to the workers she studied. See *Industrialization, Family Life, and Class Relations: Saint Chamond, 1815–1914* (Berkeley and Los Angeles, 1989), chap. 5.
25. Patrick Joyce, "Labor, Capital, and Compromise: A Response to Richard Price," *Social History* 9 (1984): 67–76.
26. Reaffirming these long-standing stereotypes are Gordon Wright, *France in Modern Times*, 3d ed. (New York, 1981), p. 291, and Gérard Noiriel, *Les Ouvriers dans la société française: XIXe–XXe siècle* (Paris, 1986), pp. 263–267.

union dared not countenance.[27] The organization of skilled industrial workers did not proceed along the same lines as that of the unskilled, and reformist syndicalists were not prepared to deal with the skilled workers.

The union officials were ideologically and temperamentally out of their element with the upsurge of labor militancy created by the stokers in 1898. Darène in particular developed tactics that were inept and ultimately unreasonable. The union had always hoped that the stokers would join, but when they finally did, the leaders were alarmed by the spirit of vindictiveness. The "winds of revolution" blowing through the union, against which Darène warned, appeared quite threatening—all the more so in that further concessions from the PGC suddenly appeared possible once again. Another round of talks between the company and the city opened in 1899. Hope of movement on one front and fear that militants could undermine progress pushed Darène to undertake a bold, but futile, experiment. The union secretary was ready to abandon a neutral stance regarding the gas question and use the moral authority of the union to obtain a prolonged charter for the PGC. In return Darène had a list of benefits that management would grant to the workers—larger pensions, the eight-hour day, and tenured positions. In July 1899 he began to establish his stance by writing in the union newspaper that "the most resolute enemy of the worker is not the company but the city. The company would grant our demands, at least in part, if it could be certain of a renewed charter." A few days later (July 20) the union journal openly announced the corporatist policy of working with the PGC to obtain benefits for both it and the personnel but added that the union was "ready to combat our ally if it does not give us complete satisfaction."[28] The tactic was of course infused with Darène's naive optimism regarding the good intentions of management. It was particularly ill timed in that the war of nerves between management and stokers was near an explosion. Indeed, Darène made his plan public just before Godot gave permission to crush the union should any strike occur. Clearly, the union leaders were badly out of touch not only with the engineers' intentions but with the stokers' militancy as well. The stokers were forcing the union to accept a new agenda that reformist syndicalists wanted desperately to eschew.

27. See Alain Cottereau, "The Distinctiveness of Working-Class Cultures in France, 1848–1900," in *Working Class Formation: Nineteenth-Century Patterns in Western Europe and the United States,* ed. Ira Katznelson and Aristide Zolberg (Princeton, 1986), pp. 111–154. Cottereau would find the stokers' tactics and strategies characteristic of a wide segment of the French labor force.
28. *Journal du gaz,* no. 158 (July 5, 1899): 1; no. 159 (July 20, 1899): 1. On the behind-the-scenes cooperation, see AP, V 8 O¹, no. 160, "Août 1899."

The Crisis of Industrial Discipline

That there were major differences in collective behavior and outlook between stokers and general laborers is a revealing finding. After all, the two groups were one in most ways. They had identical social backgrounds. Stokers were recruited among the common laborers and did unskilled work for part of the year.[29] As stokers aged, they reentered the ranks of the general hands. Both types of wage earners became dependent on the PGC at roughly the same time. Despite these shared experiences, there was an undeniable gulf between stokers and general laborers. The stokers failed to provide leadership for their more oppressed comrades, and union formation divided the two still further. The stokers' indifference to permanent organization made them far more representative of the nineteenth-century French labor movement as a whole. Moreover, their periodic, direct challenges to managerial authority after 1890 also reflected wider currents of unrest among skilled laborers in France.

Though the stokers did not join Brard's organization in significant numbers, they were not adverse to unionization in principle. Indeed, they had formed the first trade union in 1890. The police believed that all or nearly all of the stokers had joined it. Its organizer, Jules Roques, had used his newspaper to defend the stokers' cause when agitation surfaced in the spring of 1890. Under Roques's presidency the union strove to be exclusive. Its high monthly fee of five francs (more than a day's wage for the unskilled) opened it only to stokers.[30] From the beginning of the union era stokers were destined to act separately from general laborers.

Stokers did not need a union to win concessions from their employer, as their history before 1880 demonstrated. Yet their concerns shifted, and new interests encouraged new strategies. Stokers eagerly joined a union in 1890 because they were angry, and the threat of a strike emerged at once. The issues mobilizing them now were quite different from the wage concerns that had generated agitation before 1880. As dependent workers, stokers of 1890 were upset by the arbitrary pattern of layoffs the PGC practiced. The stokers understood seniority as the valid basis for according the right to continue to serve in the distillation rooms during the slow season. But factory managers refused to honor the principle, which the director had accepted, in a systematic manner. This grievance first brought the stokers and the Socialist journalist Roques together. He pleaded their cause in L'Egalité, the only journalist to do so other than Henri Rochefort.

29. AP, V 8 O¹, no. 163, "Personnel ouvrier—jours de congé."
30. Ibid., no. 148, report of July 25, 1891.

The stokers were also discontent with the company's administration of their sick-pay fund. Though the stokers contributed 1 percent of their nine-to-ten-franc wages to the fund, the company awarded them only two or three francs as "half pay" when they missed a day of work because of illness. Moreover, there were changes of details in the work routine that stokers found irksome. Managers had recently changed the mix of coals, increasing the portion of a hard, heavy variety (cannel coal). The change made the stokers' task more difficult. The stokers now wanted some checks on the arbitrary power of the company and limits on their exploitation.[31]

The chargers relied on Roques to translate their grievances faithfully into formal demands, but he did not do that well. The statement he penned on April 29 mentioned the augmentation of the "already super-human work load," but he stressed the need for higher pay. The journalist made a raise from three to five francs per metric ton the central demand.[32] A pay increase, however, was no longer the primary matter to stokers, and gaining it did not produce satisfaction. Caught by surprise, the PGC immediately promised a raise, but the stokers struck anyway, on May 1, 1890, France's first Labor Day. Some 350 stokers remained off the job for a week. The timing of the action, coinciding with the new festival of labor power, expressed the complexity of the stokers' challenge better than did Roques's negotiating position.[33] He and the company quickly came to an agreement on a 10 percent raise (3.30 francs per metric ton of coal distilled) and justice on the matter of sick pay. In the meantime, the PGC had come close to reestablishing full production by recruiting seasonal stokers from the provinces. The strikers drifted back to the gas plants to the extent their employer would have them.[34]

In a narrow sense, the strike had been a success: the company had granted a raise, and management was licking its wounds over the defeat. Nonetheless, the stokers did not define the settlement as successful, though they surely would have prior to 1880. A police report noted that workers "would rather have had [concessions] on lighter work loads than on wages."[35] Moreover, the raise by no means ended the grumbling

31. Ibid., no. 1063, "Grèves de 1890 et 1899."
32. Ibid., no. 151, Roques to director, April 29, 1890.
33. On this festival of labor, see Michelle Perrot, "The First of May 1890 in France: The Birth of a Working-Class Ritual," in *The Power of the Past: Essays in Honor of Eric Hobsbawm*, ed. Geoffrey Crossick et al. (London, 1984).
34. AP, V 8 O¹, no. 151, "Grève des chauffeurs (1 mai 1890)."
35. Préfecture, B/a 176, "Grève des chauffeurs gaziers, 1890." See, especially, the report of May 13. There was a similar pattern to the large strike wave that hit the

among the stokers, and managers reported on rumors of new strike actions through June.[36] Far from being bolstered by a recent success, the stokers' union soon fell apart as a result of recriminations and disappointments among the rank and file. Eight years later Darène and his comrades could still cite the 1890 strike as a disillusioning experience that kept stokers from joining the gas workers' union.[37]

The sudden effervescence of 1890 was indeed followed by eight years of somnolence among stokers. Immediately after that strike the company was able to undertake its most aggressive attack to date on the source of the stokers' bargaining power—without meeting any visible resistance whatsoever. Factory managers finally substituted the scoop for the shovel (see chapter 4), thereby reducing the dexterity and, to a lesser extent, the endurance necessary to charge retorts. The threshold of recruitment was lowered without quite bringing stoking to the level of common labor.[38] The stokers' acquiescence made managers crow about their recovered sense of control over the labor force. Cury, the ancient superintendent of the La Villette plant, was so confident of his ascendancy that he even suppressed the fifty-centime bonus that chargers had long received. That move earned him a slight rebuke from his superior, who was not eager to press his luck, on the grounds that the change had been done "not to save money but rather to reassert control over the workers."[39]

Disillusionment with the recent strike may have been one reason for the stokers' passivity in view of the fundamental threat to their bargaining power. It was also the case that the chargers conspired in their own deskilling. The company had imposed the scoop during the height of the slow season. Not only were the workers aware of their good fortune to have jobs, but also their opposition to the tool was weakened by the thought that it could prolong their days in the distillation room. By rendering charging somewhat less taxing, the scoop favored a longer career at high pay. Apparently disillusionment, coupled with the caution imposed by dependency, undermined protest over a serious attack on the stokers' status as skilled workers.

---

textile industry of the Nord on May Day, 1890. See William Reddy, *The Rise of Market Culture* (Cambridge, 1984), pp. 305–309.

36. AP, V 8 O^1, no. 151, report of Cury to Euchène, June 13, 1890.

37. *Journal du gaz*, no. 134 (July 5, 1898): 3.

38. AP, V 8 O^1, no. 148, "Résumé des avis donnés par les chefs de service sur les demandes formulées par la chambre syndicale (décembre 1891)."

39. Ibid., report of Gigot, October 21, 1890. The bonus had been given for many years to the stokers who worked the shovels; Gigot insisted that superintendents give the bonus to the stokers who took the handle of the scoop.

The birth of a new gas workers' union in mid-1891 left the vast majority of stokers indifferent. Managers continually congratulated themselves that stokers were staying away from the Chambre syndicale des travailleurs du gaz.[40] Even the union newspaper revealed (in 1898) that although eight-ninths of the common hands had joined, only a quarter of the stokers, at most, were members.[41] The aloofness of the stokers, reflecting the very different perspective on protest separating them from workers with whom they otherwise had much in common, entailed divergent strategies and goals. The skilled workers now disdained the wage-centered concerns of the reformist union. Moreover, they distrusted the patient organization building and negotiations with public authorities. The stokers' power on the shop floor, weakened but not eliminated by the scoop, allowed them to remain faithful to a direct-action strategy even though the public authorities were willing to help them procure material gains. The stokers intended to use their bargaining power to extract concessions directly from their employer. Their passivity regarding the union was not at all a matter of contentment. In fact, the stokers were seething with resentment, but the union was unable to tap it. That anger finally exploded in the second half of 1898.

During the summer and autumn of that year—a moment of general labor unrest in Paris—the stokers began to flock to the union. Eventually as many as a thousand may have joined within the space of just a few months.[42] The union leaders, at once pleased and apprehensive about the new recruits, organized plant-by-plant meetings for the purpose of hearing complaints and channeling the resentment into acceptable directions.[43] Yet stokers were not interested in listening to the reformists; they had their own reasons for entering the union en masse. They were intent on forcing the union to confront their central grievance—the arbitrary power of superintendents and foremen to insult, punish, lay off, fire, and reward. The sudden unionization of the stokers announced that they were willing to abide such authority no longer.

The source of the stokers' vexations in 1898 was not a recent problem, nor was the grievance felt by chargers alone. Darène's organ, the *Journal du gaz*, had from its initial issues reported on supervisors' unjust or vindictive treatment. Long before the stokers provoked collective protest over the matter, the union sheet had lamented the freedom of foremen to ter-

40. Ibid., report of Gigot, April 15, 1892.
41. "Usine d'Ivry," *Journal du gaz*, no. 134 (July 5, 1898).
42. *Journal du gaz*, no. 137 (August 20, 1898): 1; no. 142 (November 5, 1898): 1.
43. Ibid., no. 135 (July 20, 1898): 1. Every issue thereafter (up to the strike of August 1899) had lengthy reports on these rallies.

rorize workers by threatening to fire them, deprive them of a bonus, or demote them to poorly paid work. The supervisors' arrogance, bribe taking, utter lack of civility, and pleasure in seeing workers cower were common themes in the union press.[44] Louis Sagot, a barely literate courtyard worker, complained to Director Godot that his *patron*, the team head, had laid him off while retaining a man who had far less than Sagot's seven years of seniority. Sagot felt the sting of the injustice all the more in that he had followed the team head's orders to frequent a particular café. "Besides," Sagot wondered, "weren't layoffs supposed to be by seniority [*par numéros*]?"[45] The *Journal du gaz* may well have expressed a common sentiment among the native workers in linking this sort of complaint to immigrants. The charge was that foreign workers were especially supine, and their subservience brought them favors from supervisors while proud French workers suffered. The union press found young French stokers, newly arrived from the provinces, almost as culpable of forgetting their dignity and buying favors from foremen. The *Journal du gaz* fumed against spineless Auvergnats, "whose approach to the foreman is distinguished by heavy servile steps, and breath redolent of sauerkraut and sausage."[46] Quite possibly, the union paper was projecting on a clearly identifiable minority the self-hatred *gaziers* felt as a result of their own subservience. In any case, the authority of supervisors was clearly a painful dilemma for all the PGC's workers. Unlike common laborers, stokers committed themselves to resisting it as the century drew to a close.

In truth, resentment of the power of immediate superiors was an international problem that inflamed industrial relations in all advanced countries of the late nineteenth century.[47] Only in France, though, did the grievance precipitate a widespread industrial crisis, and the stokers were full participants in it. The stokers' resentment arose from a corporate power structure that retained strong face-to-face elements despite the firm's large size and bureaucratic division of labor. Within the PGC, at least, the distribution of authority was the result of management's conscious designs. We have seen that the director sought to distance himself

---

44. See, for example, ibid., no. 11 (May 20, 1893): 3; no. 20 (October 5, 1893): 2; no. 29 (February 20, 1894): 2. The police were well aware of the grievance too. See Préfecture, B/a 1424, report of June 13, 1893.
45. AP, V 8 O¹, no. 159, Louis Sagot to director, n.d.
46. *Journal du gaz*, no. 68 (October 5, 1895): 3.
47. See, for example, Walter Licht, *Working for the Railroad: The Organization of Work in the Nineteenth Century* (Princeton, 1983), pp. 171, 254; Tamara Hareven, *Family Time and Industrial Time: The Relationship between the Family and Work in a New England Industrial Community* (Cambridge, 1982), p. 304; Will Thorne, *My Life's Battles* (London, n.d.), p. 74.

from the management of individual factories. Responsibility for daily operations resided with the division head and plant superintendents. They, however, were preoccupied with a multitude of matters and in practice left personnel matters to immediate supervisors, foremen, team heads, and paymasters (*pointeurs*). The rules of the corporation formally denied foremen the right to hire, lay off, or fire, but these powers came to be part of their duties. So much was this the case that both the engineers and the workers casually spoke of foremen doing the hiring and firing.[48] Even when an engineer may have regretted his foreman's decision in a particular instance, he dared not reverse it for fear of calling authority into question. Before the union era the informal power of immediate supervisors had been a matter of convenience for busy engineers, but once workers began to organize, it became part of a managerial strategy to combat the union. The "good intentions" Darène attributed to Director Godot quickly disappeared down the hierarchical chain of command. Commitments made at the top were never enforced, and the director could defend himself by proclaiming his powerlessness. Engineers eagerly harnessed the foremen's venom for the unions in their struggles to preserve what they could of authoritarian paternalism. Delegating authority in that way often meant losing control over supervisors and permitting them to use their command for personal gain.[49] Yet the engineers accepted the abuses as a lesser evil.

Whether the corruption and oppression that the stokers denounced were as pervasive as they contended is impossible to say. There is no doubt, though, that their grievances had a basis in reality. The PGC disciplined a foreman and a paymaster for running cafés in 1888 and tried to prevent supervisors from operating shops near the gas factories.[50] Yet as long as the engineers relied on foremen to intimidate workers, they could not easily control the supervisors' lives off the job. An incident that occurred in 1899 involving a union delegate substantiates the charges of venality. The delegate was about to be laid off as a delayed punishment for his participation in the March strike, and he offered his foreman ten francs to retain his post. The factory engineers learned about the bribe and sought to use it to cast opprobrium on the union. Management ostentatiously challenged workers, "all too ready to accuse foremen and team

48. AP, V 8 O¹, no. 763, "Rappel du règlement, 20 avril 1869"; no. 150, Darène to Lecoeur, February 16, 1893; no. 148, report of Cury, October 22, 1891; no. 151, "Revendications générales—personnel ouvrier."
49. Workers often complained about foremen who exploited them for their personal interest, but the company never followed up on the charges. See *Journal du gaz*, no. 37 (June 20, 1894): 3; no. 148 (February 5, 1899): 2.
50. AP, V 8 O¹, no. 685, deliberations of January 25, 1888.

heads of venality," to stop tempting supervisors.[51] The company may have been successful at embarrassing the union, but it also admitted, in an oblique manner, that payoffs were a problem. There is no reason to suppose that the practice was of recent origin, but the stokers' unwillingness to abide the abuses any longer was new. Their militancy in 1898 was in effect a revolt against both the abuses and the very nature of face-to-face authority.

When the union began its round of mass meetings in response to the influx of stokers, the leaders' hope was to convince the new members that an eight-hour day was what they needed. The proposal entailed handling two four-hour charges a day instead of three. A serious drawback for the proposal was that stokers would have to accept a large pay cut for doing a third less work. Darène never tired of explaining to skeptical chargers that they were better off earning 7.50 francs for eight hours than 11.50 for twelve. He insisted that they would have to purchase only one restaurant meal a day. More important, cutting the workday would raise the number of posts the company needed to fill by a third. Thus, the stokers' jobs would be secure, and the chargers could easily get year-round work if they wished. Moreover, Darène reasoned that with the cruel physical toll of three charges a day reduced, stokers might expect to prolong their years in the distillation room.[52] Such arguments might have been influential in 1890, when stokers had refrained from protesting the scoop, but the logic no longer convinced them. The urge to put supervisors in their place overwhelmed practical arguments this time.

The stokers barely disguised their impatience with the eight-hour proposal. Instead, they took over the rallies and focused the discussions on their own issue—the discriminatory authority of supervisors. Stokers complained about their humiliation at the hands of vindictive foremen. They lamented the unjust fines and arbitrary job assignments and bitterly recalled the many times supervisors had abused rules on layoffs. The stokers used the meetings to represent themselves as victims of venality, vanity, and vengence. Foremen, they asserted, rewarded the most subservient of workers and persecuted those who stood up for their rights. They argued forcefully that bribery permeated power relations on the shop floor. Supervisors required them to patronize the stores their wives ran, drink in cafés with which they had a financial connection, and lodge in boarding houses that made payments to the foreman. Avoiding a seasonal layoff, the stokers affirmed, required a bribe. The chargers made it clear in the

51. Ibid., no. 159, report of Hadamar to Euchène, March 9, 1899.
52. *Journal du gaz*, no. 133 (June 20, 1898): 2; no. 135 (July 20, 1898): 2.

fall of 1898 that the eight-hour day, even with its practical promise of steady work, was not what they cared about most deeply. Instead, they manifested a powerful drive to gain control over the work experience— not in the sense of enforcing a "craft control" over production, which they had never enjoyed, but rather by compelling superiors to govern by fixed, uniform, and equitable rules to which workers had given their consent.[53] Their surge of militancy was a gesture of rebellion against managerial authority.

So forceful was the stokers' expression of victimization that they compelled union leaders to abandon their own agenda. The leaders had to admit that the eight-hour day was not winning a commitment from the chargers. Already in June 1898 Darène announced his intention of using the union newspaper to expose the acts of arbitrariness committed by supervisors.[54] Having been impressed by the urgency of the issue, Darène took it upon himself to raise it with Godot. By the end of the summer the union was claiming a victory: the director had promised to order superintendents to follow general rules and administer punishments uniformly.[55] Yet Darène was not able to stem the rising tide of militancy because the new order brought no better results than had previous ones. Throughout the fall and winter the *Journal du gaz* lamented that vicious supervisors were destroying trust between the company and the union and forcing the latter to become confrontational. Finally Darène capitulated entirely to the stokers and adopted as the union's primary goal the implementation of fixed and uniform rules (*règlement unique*) governing all aspects of work.[56] The militant stokers had come to dominate the union after having ignored it for so long.

As we have seen, the stokers had always been practitioners of direct-action syndicalism *avant la lettre*, and true to their habits, they did not wait for reformist union leaders to guide, channel, or propose peaceful means of negotiating over authority. Instead, they began an incipient insurrection within the gas plants during the fall of 1898. It was this offensive that made Darène warn of "a revolutionary wind, the reign of dangerous agitation." He was not the only union official to lament the members' sudden will to "crush everything . . . to forment a revolution."[57] Another

53. Ibid., nos. 137–160. Licht, *Working for the Railroad*, pp. 260–271, makes the important distinction between control over the work *process* and control over the work *experience*.
54. *Journal du gaz*, no. 133 (June 20, 1898): 2.
55. Ibid., no. 137 (August 20, 1898): 2.
56. Ibid., no. 150 (March 5, 1899): 1.
57. Ibid., no. 148 (February 5, 1899): 1; no. 150 (March 5, 1899): 2.

reformist retrospectively described the situation prior to the strike of 1899 in precisely the terms that management might have used: "Workers burned with a desire to start a struggle. . . . In the factories, managers were no longer masters. . . . The acceptance of discipline had disappeared."[58] The Socialist councilman Blondeau might have agreed with that account of a crisis of authority too. When he attended a mass meeting of stokers in March 1899, he was frightened by the soaring spirit of vengence and the cries of "Vive la grève générale!" Blondeau's calls for caution brought expressions of disdain from the assembled stokers.[59]

Production engineers, for their part, were painfully aware that stokers had suddenly turned the tables on them and were administering some "salutary intimidation" of their own. The so-called Laurent affair of October 1898 was the opening round of the showdown that the engineers had long predicted. On the advice of a hated foreman, Laurent, the superintendent of the La Villette plant fired a stoker. His comrades viewed the firing as an act of injustice and put down their tools. The superintendent, now alarmed by the gravity and solidarity of the stokers, backed down and admitted that a mistake had been made.[60] This incident, occurring at a moment of intense labor unrest in Paris, set a precedent for future confrontations in gas factories.

A repetition of the general features of the Laurent affair next March pushed tensions to the breaking point as far as management was concerned. This outburst occurred at the Clichy plant, which was run by the most severe superintendent, Hadamar, and by the most vindictive foremen. Correspondingly, the spirit of revolt was strongest among the stokers of that factory, according to Darène.[61] Under these circumstances the aggressive behavior of Hadamar was exceedingly provocative—probably intentionally so. The superintendent had planned for some time to fire two general laborers for poor work and insolence. Instead of taking the step at the moment of their offense, Hadamar waited for the slow season to commence and laid them off in spite of six and twelve years of seniority. Stokers, highly sensitive to the principle under attack and in no mood to compromise, immediately issued an ultimatum to rehire the workers or face a strike. The next day, 200 of the 230 stokers left their posts. At least half of their comrades at the La Villette and Landy (Saint-Denis) plants joined them. Hadamar was more than eager to pursue the fight, but the director could not allow the conflict to continue because of negotiations

58. Ibid., no. 164 (October 5, 1899): 2.
59. AP, V 8 O¹, no. 159, "Rapport sur la réunion du 21 mars 1899."
60. *Journal du gaz*, no. 141 (October 20, 1898): 2–3.
61. Ibid., no. 148 (February 5, 1899): 2.

with the city. He ordered the rehiring of the two workers and allowed all the strikers to return to their jobs. The superintendent and foremen had to overcome their sense of humiliation in the face of the reported "insolence" as the workers triumphantly reentered the plant.[62] At this point the engineers concluded bitterly that the stokers had become their masters. Though the stokers had previously called foremen their *patrons,* they now seemed resolved to escape such subordination.

These victories gave stokers not only a heightened sense of power—the "insolence" to which the engineers referred—but also a sense of elation and even generosity. The latter sentiments emerged when they tested authority one more time before the disastrous strike of August. In the wake of the strike at Clichy, superintendents prepared for more agitation by substituting a smaller and lighter scoop, which could be handled by workers of average strength. Stokers were quite aware of the strategic implications of the new tool and, in addition, found that it prolonged their work routine.[63] Thus, delegations at each plant asked superintendents to return to the large scoop. Significantly, the delegations bypassed normal union channels and went directly to the plant managers. Once again the superintendents backed down (though perhaps only because they now had a more sinister trap in mind).[64] The manager of the Passy plant could not help noticing how congenial his stokers became the moment their request was granted: the stokers treated the large scoops with great care and worked with renewed energy. He reported that the workers lost the "scowling air" they had had for the past weeks. Now, the superintendent noted, the stokers had become "good-natured; they banter with the foremen—something they had not done for a long time."[65] Evidently, the stokers were basking in their newly discovered power. It did not take much to make these physical giants satisfied—even submissive. Unfortunately for all concerned, managers were not the least bit inclined to compromise even when they recognized that the stokers were easily appeased by token gestures and quick to obey those who accorded them a modicum of respect.

That the eight-hour day was the subject of the last and fateful test of authority shows how little power the stokers had, in the end, to shape issues. Yet that was hardly the only peculiar feature of the strike of August 1899. "What a bizarre strike it was," asserted Darène when it was

62. AP, V 8 O[1], no. 159, "Grève, mars 1899."
63. It took two fillings of the large scoop to load a retort and three fillings of the small scoop.
64. AP, V 8 O[1], no. 160, "Renseignements sur le service."
65. Ibid., report of Bodin to Gigot, July 1, 1899.

over. "Its cause was a demand for lower pay!"[66] In a superficial sense the strike broke out over a trivial pay demand; but that demand ultimately stood for the issue of authority at the workplace. It will be recalled that the engineers, probably following a plan to manipulate the stokers into striking, initiated a companywide trial of the eight-hour day with two charges.[67] Management did this in mid-July even though the union was no longer pressing the issue. The company decreed a pay formula for the trial that was bound to be confusing and inflammatory. Workers would receive four francs per metric ton of coal distilled for the first 1,750 kilograms and then only 3.30 francs for each additional ton. It was inevitably troubling that the base pay was higher than the incentive rate. Stokers understandably believed rumors that the company was prepared to pay four francs for each ton.[68] To the extent that the seventy-centime difference directly contributed to the strike, it was because the higher pay cushioned a bit the one-third reduction in earnings that would result from the eight-hour day.

The pay issue became confused with larger matters when the union hastily sanctioned a strike over the demand for four francs. That action in itself was a sign of events spinning tragically out of control, for the union leaders were not at all favorable to aggressive action. At a poorly attended general meeting at the Bourse du Travail on the night of August 7, the demand for four francs was made, and Darène solemnly warned against it. The eight-hour day was part of the accord he wished to make with the company, in return for which he would put the union behind a renewed charter for the PGC. Moreover, he had been urging management for some time to bolster the prestige of the moderates and calm the "winds of revolution" in the union. Darène apparently believed that the eight-hour trial was the answer to his pleas. When that very concession produced further agitation, he became paralyzed. Late in the night he allowed the handful of workers present to take a strike vote, and it passed, 40 to 15. Then Darène fatefully committed the union to the action he had just opposed, a move that would later be the basis for charges that he was cooperating with the company to rid the PGC of its militants. About 750 out of 1,100 stokers answered the union's strike call.[69]

<hr>

66. *Journal du gaz*, no. 161 (August 20, 1899): 2.
67. On the likelihood that managers plotted to foment the strike, see chapter 4.
68. There are some suggestions that the union leaders themselves spread the notion that the PGC would pay workers four francs, perhaps to promote enthusiasm for the eight-hour trial. See AP, V 8 O¹, no. 151, report of Euchène to Hadamar, July 24, 1899.
69. Ibid., no. 159, "Pièces adressées à Monsieur le juge de paix du XVe Arrondisse-

There can be no doubt that authority, not pay, was the real issue in the strike. The action was entirely out of proportion to the demand. With four francs stokers would have earned fifteen to thirty centimes more a day, a pittance considering they were already taking a huge pay cut. The strike was a gesture of insubordination. Stokers disliked the way the company had suddenly disrupted their work routines. They resented the peculiar pay scale, about which the company had been absolutely inflexible, and they were indignant about having to face such a deep pay reduction. With the union having committed itself to the strike, the stokers felt they had its authority to uphold. Above all, the stokers were attempting to maintain the momentum of the Laurent affair and the March strike. They were unwilling to allow a return to the company's authoritarian paternalism. Management understood the strike in precisely that manner. The engineers explained it as being rooted in a "spirit of indiscipline," which was raging out of control. Granting four francs would have trivial financial consequences, the chief of production admitted, but "the loss of authority would be incalculable." In his view, the strikers were truly "rebels" who physically threatened foremen and were "a danger for the company, for Paris, for society."[70]

The engineers' inveterate pessimism about workers' character at last yielded genuine insight. Though the strike was not about wages, neither was it simply about regular, uniform work rules. There is a case to be made that stokers looked past the matters of security and equity to engage in a gesture of rebellion for its own sake. For several years they had disregarded the blandishments of politicians intent on being generous to laborers. They had given no support to the campaign for an eight-hour day, despite its practical promises. And their alarming militancy, which terrorized normally self-confident managers in 1898–1899, signaled an anger that transcended reasoned calculation of interests. The stokers surely wanted an application of the *règlement unique*, but they were also groping to declare their utter opposition to managerial authority.

The strike of August 8 had little chance of success. Stokers were divided and perplexed by the eight-hour issue with such a steep reduction in pay. Those at the Passy plant chose not even to participate in the trial.[71] The demand for four francs addressed no basic issue whatsoever. The company,

ment"; "Réunion extraordinaire du 7 août,"*Journal du gaz*, no. 161 (August 20, 1899): 1.

70. AP, V 8 O¹, no. 159, "Grèves de mars et août 1899," report of Euchène, September 14, 1899.

71. Ibid., "Instructions à Messieurs les régisseurs (7 août 1899)."

for its part, had made excellent preparations. It quickly rounded up seasonal stokers from the provinces and promised them year-round jobs. During the especially steamy weeks of August 1899, demand for gas was minimal anyway. Moreover, the union treasurer absconding with the strike funds devastated morale. It is little wonder that superintendents found the atmosphere in the distillation rooms entirely transformed after the strike was over. Workers were "respectful" of the foremen and happy to have jobs.[72]

Management was adamant about excluding many strikers from the gas plants, not only in the immediate aftermath of the strike but also permanently.[73] The municipal council passed one resolution after another over the next decade in favor of the unemployed strikers and even appropriated funds to aid their families, but the engineers could not be moved. They held to their view of the strikers as dangerous rebels who attacked legitimate authority. Indeed, the managers were ultimately ready to pay the price of career security to defend the principle of authoritarian paternalism. The PGC came to an end in 1907 without having rehired all the strikers of 1899.

• • •

The militancy of 1898–1899 was at once complex, puzzling, and revealing. It is time to proceed from narrative to analysis in order to explore the implications of the gas workers' protests. Examining the strike from the perspective of the gas firm alone is inadequate. By no means were the stokers unique in challenging managerial authority as the nineteenth century drew to a close. We have seen that gas clerks and other white-collar employees had already been protesting discretionary power when the stokers' militancy surfaced. Manual workers were also turbulent. The Laurent affair occurred just as Paris was in the grips of an upsurge in labor unrest. Navvies had declared a strike; railroad and construction workers had followed them in the fall of 1898. This was the first nationwide attempt at a general strike. Stokers first forced gas management to back down in a city filled with more than forty thousand strikers.[74] Challenges to the authority of foremen had already been a major theme in Parisian strikes for several years, and workers' aggressiveness on the issue climaxed as stokers were rallying to Darène's union. The machine-building

---

72. Ibid., "Grèves de 1899—articles de journaux."

73. Ibid., report of Gigot to director, November 10, 1899. The company considered 147 stokers too "dangerous" to rehire.

74. France, Office du travail, *Statistique des grèves et des recours à la conciliation et à l'arbitrage survenus pendant l'année 1898* (Paris, 1899), pp. 108–109, 112, 252–270.

industry of Paris and the suburbs erupted just before the PGC did. At the beginning of 1899 automobile workers at one firm walked out because a foreman fired a worker for being five minutes late. Only a few weeks before the stokers initiated their ill-fated strike, mechanics at the imposing Dion-Bouton Automobile Company just outside Paris insisted on the firing of a foreman whom they despised. The haughty marquis de Dion could not crush their revolt and in the end yielded. The militancy against industrial authority persisted for several more years in the automobile plants.[75] Gas managers were quite correct to view the Laurent affair and the March strike in Clichy as part of a generalized movement against foremen.[76] The engineers clearly saw that their right to dominate skilled industrial workers would have to be defended with force.

The challenge to managerial authority was especially strong in Paris, but it was not confined to the capital. The stokers' offensive coincided with a decisive takeoff in union membership throughout France as a whole. The unions they entered were increasingly radical; revolutionaries were pushing aside the proponents of cooperation with a reform-minded government.[77] What that radicalization meant on a local level is well illustrated by the revolutionary tide in Limoges. John Merriman has found that between 1895 and 1905 "economic, social, and political conflict seemed to merge with everyday life" in that provincial city.[78] The tumultuous decade contained not only angry confrontations between workers and the bourgeois state but also a series of violent strikes led by skilled porcelain workers. "The most explosive strike issue," Merriman notes, "was that of industrial discipline, particularly the role of the foreman, who emerged as the most visible and vexing representation of the boss."[79] Part of the same general confrontation were the angry and highly publicized strikes of Le Creusot and Monceau-les-Mines in 1899. As at the PGC, workers in the company towns were resisting the heavy hand of managerial paternalism. The steel workers of Le Creusot insisted on union recognition, respectful treatment from their superiors, and suppression of the employer's private

75. Lenard R. Berlanstein, *The Working People of Paris, 1871–1914* (Baltimore, 1984), pp. 173–188.
76. AP, V 8 O¹, no. 160, report of Masse to Gigot, September 5, 1899; report of Maubert to Lévy, July 22, 1899.
77. Yves Lequin, *Les Ouvriers de la région lyonnaise*, 2 vols. (Lyon, 1977), 2:304–307. The entry of the Socialist Alexandre Millerand into the government in 1899 set off a struggle between syndicalists eager to cooperate and those who feared entanglement.
78. John Merriman, *The Red City: Limoges and the French Nineteenth Century* (New York, 1985), p. 183.
79. Ibid., p. 219.

police force during their vigorous September strike. The confrontation ended with the creation of a workers' council to advise management on disciplinary measures. Premier René Waldeck-Rousseau, who arbitrated that dispute, was well aware that the job actions at this moment had more than immediate gains at their roots. He sensed that they engaged the wage-earning population emotionally. Daily demonstrations by workers monopolized the streets of Saint-Etienne, Le Havre, Carmaux, Vienne, and Marseille for times in late 1899. Strikes in the Nord, the Loire, the Saône-et-Loire, and the Doubs provoked repeated rallies and fund-raising activities of exceptional magnitude. The manifestations of class solidarity persisted until 1901.[80] Clearly, the last years of the nineteenth century— known mainly for the dramas of the Dreyfus Affair—also contained a crisis of skilled factory workers, who rebelled against their subordination at the workplace.

To the limited extent historians have discussed the crisis of industrial discipline, they have portrayed it essentially as resistance to proletarianization.[81] Skilled laborers were presumably protesting their employers' efforts to rationalize manufacturing, tighten discipline, and curtail their mastery of the production process. The crisis, in this view, was a stage in the inevitable evolution of capitalism, with industry progressing to the point of intensive mechanization, international competition, and excessive capacity. Foremen were caught between employers, who tried to assert greater control over production, and workers, who were unaccustomed to tight discipline and unwilling to accept it. As the most accessible symbols of managerial authority, they bore the brunt of workers' resistance.

The labor disturbances at the turn-of-the-century gas plants do not sustain this interpretation and instead advance a very different one. The intensification of work and the interference of supervisors were not closely connected to the stokers' attack on managerial authority. Both developments had long histories prior to 1890. Proletarianization did not impinge on stokers in 1898; they had experienced a deterioration in their work situation long before. Indeed, the most thoroughgoing act of deskilling undertaken by the company, the introduction of the scoop, passed without

80. Léon de Seilhac, *Les Grèves* (Paris, 1903), pp. 152–229; Pierre Sorlin, *Waldeck-Rousseau* (Paris, 1966), pp. 467–469; Reddy, *Market Culture*, pp. 309–323.
81. Michelle Perrot, "The Three Ages of Industrial Discipline in Nineteenth-Century France," in *Consciousness and Class Experience in Nineteenth-Century Europe*, ed. John Merriman (New York, 1980), pp. 149–168; Merriman, *Red City*, chap. 7; Berlanstein, *Working People*, chap. 5.

incident. Far from being the result of the rationalization of production, the stokers' militancy was the direct cause of a new round of it, with the precipitous introduction of the stoking machines. In short, the crisis of industrial discipline at the PGC was not the outcome of a particular moment in capitalistic development.[82]

The crisis, rather, was an emotional manifestation of rising aspirations on the part of the stokers. The arbitrary power of supervisors had always been a fundamental feature of their work experience. They had to put up with foremen who insulted them, discriminated against them, and made crucial decisions about their lives. The stokers, along with many other sorts of wage earners and employees across France, were now willing to take steps to end or reduce their subordination. Vengeance against the supervisors was on their minds. Whether spontaneously or not, they came to accept the goal of fixed bureaucratic rules to which they had consented as the proper solution to their oppression. In 1899 the stokers believed—and their superiors feared—that a new form of managerial authority, promising predictability and equity, was within their grasp.

The problem of industrial discipline flared into a general conflagration in turn-of-the-century France because of exceptional political circumstances. It was a moment of hope, restlessness, and tension on the part of republicans. For several years the Republic had sympathetically considered ways to make the industrial order more acceptable to the masses, and the rise of Nationalist agitation before and during the Dreyfus Affair tilted the regime still more to the left. Wage-earners, along with other working people, had long hoped for a further round of republicanization of the social order, extending even to the workplace. Sensitive to the emerging possibilities as the liberal order foundered, wage earners and employees were quick to force their agenda to the fore.[83] It was certainly not a coincidence that stokers exploded over their subordination to foremen just as the Chamber of Deputies was considering a bill to regulate finings and firings. Indeed, Maurice Claverie saw in the legislation the solution to the antiauthoritarian grievances that were stirring the gas workers.[84] The

82. See chapter 4 for a discussion of technological change within the PGC. The crisis of discipline of 1899 was not simply a matter of a sudden revival of the business cycle. If it had been, the stokers' militancy would have surfaced in 1896. See appendix, fig. A3.
83. Michelle Perrot, *Workers on Strike*, p. 314, points out that strike waves often coincided with left-leaning governments. She concludes that the strikes "though rarely political in their objective . . . frequently had political origins." The finding is relevant to the gas workers at the turn of the century.
84. AP, V 8 O[1], no. 149, Claverie to president of Conseil d'administration, July 20, 1899.

turn of the century was a moment when *le peuple* came to expect much from their Republic—more than republican politicians were ultimately prepared to deliver.

Hatred of the kind of power that foremen wielded was not simply learned on the shop floor from experience. There is the *visceral* nature of the workers' emotions to consider. The stokers' outburst expressed a political culture that was profoundly antiauthoritarian and antihierarchical. The skilled workmen contested not just abuses of authority but also the principle of discretionary authority itself. Their categorical rejection of the legitimacy of face-to-face authority differentiated them from labor aristocrats in Britain or from the members of the Freie Gewerkschaften. At the same time, stokers shared their aversions with French white-collar employees, with whom they did not otherwise identify. For all their differences, the two groups accepted a binary vision of authority: there could be either equality or arbitrariness. This political culture found expression even in the highest circles of power as the twentieth century dawned. Only in France did prominent members of the governing party, now the Radicals, denounce personal authority as an unacceptable privilege. In this sense the crisis of 1899 was the outcome not only of shop-floor strife but also of a distinctive political culture that had deep roots in popular politics and flourished temporarily under the Radical Republic.

There is an irony in the stokers sharing an ideology of legitimate authority with office clerks and with petit bourgeois politicians while failing to join with their unskilled comrades at the gas plant in united action. An account of protest at the PGC testifies to the palpable weakness of factory labor as an experience that could forge a cohesive working class. However much the stokers and common hands shared on and off the job, they could not find a basis for agreeing on interests, strategies, and goals. The cleavages were largely the result of differences in their situation at the workplace. The stokers' bargaining power allowed them to contest grievances when the laborers were helpless and to formulate goals that the unskilled could not hope to redress even under the best of circumstances. Factory labor produced compartmentalization, not a melding of differences among the exploited.

Political realities after 1890 reinforced the cleavages created by the work situation. General laborers surmounted their suspicion of the state because they had no other options. Powerless before their employer, the only form of collective action open to them was the sort the authorities sanctioned. Hence they consented to patient organization building and sent their reformist leaders to negotiate for them. The skilled workers, by contrast, had the option of using their own proficiencies to extract concessions from the company. Hopes for small improvements in pay or even for pensions did not entice them to abandon direct action. The stokers set their own agenda, and at its core was control over the work experience. Different political options and uneven workplace power operated in tandem to keep the gas workers divided.

Not only did the *gaziers* fail to unite as a class; they also failed to grow progressively in class consciousness. The convention of taking the linear development of the working class as normative, so common in labor studies, does not receive support from the case of the stokers.[85] These workers simply did not evolve from a preindustrial stage to a class-conscious one. The stokers of the 1860s, even as peasant-workers, were fully capable of frustrating the designs of their stern superiors. Their status as independent workers made them interested in wages, and they pursued the agenda with sophistication and success. The stokers of the 1890s had nothing to teach the earlier generation in terms of tactics and consciousness. The later generation had not become notably more interested in organization nor more likely to identify their concerns with those of other sorts of laborers. The stokers of the 1890s had a different agenda because they were now dependent workers, and they pursued their interests as best they could. Common hands, for their part, were no less responsive to immediate circumstances when they rallied to their union in the 1890s. Alain Cottereau proposes that historians put aside the preoccupation with degrees of consciousness and focus on "how the practices of workers proceed from the logics and strategies adapted to the situation they confront."[86] His situational approach to class formation accurately characterizes social conflict at the Parisian gas plants.

A final irony of 1899 is that it completely misrepresented the stokers' future. The tensions and antipathies expressed during the strike linked stokers to many sorts of working people throughout France. The stokers' action reflected the principal contours of the French labor movement as a whole—its local autonomy, its ephemeral commitment to trade unions,

---

85. Older and current works in labor history reflect the expectation of linear development, but the questioning of that convention has recently become intense. Indeed, class analysis itself has been subjected to serious scrutiny, with the assertion that class is an externally imposed category, not a lived experienced. See William Sewell, "Uneven Development, Autonomy of Politics, and the Dockworkers of Nineteenth-Century Marseille," *American Historical Review* 93 (1988): 604–637; William Reddy, *Money and Liberty in Modern Europe* (Cambridge, 1987); Gareth Stedman Jones, *Languages of Class* (Cambridge, 1983); Joan Wallach Scott, "On Language, Gender, and Working-Class History," in *Gender and the Politics of History* (New York, 1988), pp. 53–67.
86. Cottereau, "Working-Class Cultures," p. 113.

and its direct action. Yet the strike of 1899 was their last outburst with such features. As the twentieth century began, the stokers would no longer exemplify the labor movement as it currently stood. Instead, they would point to its future by rallying to a bureaucratized union that operated within the parameters set by the bourgeois state. This change, too, was a legacy of the pursuit of social peace by a Radical Republic at its height of social experimentation.

Advancements in Political Integration

The engineers should have realized that their victory over the union would inevitably be Pyrrhic. The rank and file wanted a union, and since political realities deprived the company of the weapon of intimidation, the workers would have one again. The principal question was what kind it would be. Darène's organization had fallen apart after the August strike, and two options existed after that disaster and after the Nationalists' municipal victory in May 1900. Some of Darène's associates formed a union that sought close ties to the corporation. Whether this was a bona fide company (or "yellow") union remains unclear since its official relations with the PGC were tenuous at best. Nonetheless, the leaders did not hesitate to proclaim, "We are 'yellow' and we don't get 'red' about it." [87] They argued, as management did, that the fatal strike had been the fault of dangerously rebellious laborers. The company unionists believed that the municipal revolution of 1900 presented a golden opportunity for workers to support the PGC in its negotiations with the city and be rewarded for doing so. They imagined that the company would accept all the workers' legitimate demands and that the engineers would learn to cooperate with the personnel. Only a few general laborers rallied to the company union. The firm's failure to rehire the strikers of 1899 may have discouraged membership. Moreover, the option lacked warm support from management and from the Nationalist councilmen. The disintegration of the Nationalist movement in Paris after 1902 undermined its raison d'être entirely. [88]

Far and away the more successful option was the revival of reformist syndicalism under the leadership of Louis Lajarrigue. This former mechanic for the PGC had joined the strike of 1899 without enthusiasm but out of a sense of duty. The yellows subsequently attacked him as a radical, but he was nothing of the sort. In fact, he became a worthy successor to

---

87. *Journal du gaz*, no. 186 (November 5, 1901): 2. On the yellow unions, see Zeev Sternhell, *La Droite révolutionnaire: Les Origines françaises du Fascisme* (Paris, 1978), chap. 4.
88. Préfecture, B/a 1424, report of April 12, 1903.

Brard and a supportive colleague to Claverie, of the clerks' union. Lajarrigue's proposed solution to the gas question was close to Claverie's call to give "the gas works to the gas workers." He accepted much of the class collaboration Claverie envisioned without duplicating Darène's naive trust in the engineers' goodwill.[89] Lajarrigue would never attempt to initiate deals with the company that could alienate the councilmen. The former mechanic took over Brard's seat on the municipal council when the latter died (in 1903) and continued his pragmatic defense of organized workers' interests. Lajarrigue was no closer to the Socialist aldermen than Brard had been, but his syndicalism scrupulously respected political realities.[90]

The new union secretary's success derived from his judicious assessment of the political situation. He foresaw that Parisian councilmen would bestow on gas workers benefits that were well beyond realistic expectations for wage earners in other industries. With the strike of 1899 having served to reinforce public sympathy for the PGC's personnel, *gaziers* would receive decent pay, civil-servant status, job tenure, bureaucratic rules regulating work conditions, and retirement benefits. These advantages would be guaranteed in the charter of whatever firm carried on gas production, and the engineers would have to accept them as final. Lajarrigue correctly envisioned that the gas company would become a quasi-public service that used some profits to support a privileged personnel. By the time the PGC's old charter had expired, Lajarrigue's expectations had been entirely realized.[91]

Not surprisingly, common laborers rallied to a union that operated within that framework, as they had before 1900. This time, however, so did most of the stokers. Perhaps the PGC's intransigence on rehiring had eliminated or intimidated the most militant of them, but the positive reasons for accepting the path of moderation were surely dominant. The striking stokers of 1899 had belatedly achieved their goals by other means. The ones who labored in the distillation rooms in 1906 no longer had to face supervisors who held arbitrary power over them. Wage earners at the PGC had fixed careers, clear and uniform rules governing the work experience, and a review board to resolve disputes when irregularities arose. The *gaziers* had gained far more security, better pay, and more control over their work conditions than impoverished immigrants to the capital had

89. AP, V 8 O¹, no. 1632, "Personnel, 1906–1920"; no. 150, "Rapport sur la manifestation en faveur de la paix, accompagné des renseignements sur l'industrie du gaz à Londres."
90. See *Conseil municipal*, July 3, 1903, for votes on which Lajarrigue and the Socialist group of aldermen parted company.
91. AP, V 8 O¹, nos. 162–163.

any right to expect. Even the stokers seemed to recognize their good fortune and now protected it within the context of a bureaucratic and reformist union.

The impulse for direct action and the anarchic rage characteristic of 1899 had not disappeared entirely among the stokers. A small group remained outside Lajarrigue's organization. Some established contacts with the revolutionary wing of the Confédération générale du travail and tried to win their comrades to class conformation. Their militancy was not simply a legacy of the recent past; it was also the response to a new problem that younger stokers confronted—technological displacement. The PGC and its successor firm speeded the introduction of stoking machines in the decade prior to World War I. Even in the face of the new threat, most stokers no longer supported taking matters into their own hands and spiting a regime that offered valuable benefits. The militants proved to be no more than a minor annoyance to the reformists.[92]

Lajarrigue held to an ambitious and idealistic vision for his union that was not altogether compatible with the consummate pragmatism of his policies. He wanted Parisian gas workers to help *gaziers* all over France obtain similar benefits. To this end he participated in the formation of, and presided over, a national federation.[93] Furthermore, he strove to make his privileged *corporation* into a model and an inspiration for the syndicalist world. He set about using the growing wealth of the gas union to build workers' institutions. Under his direction the union established a vacation home by the sea and a retirement colony for aged *gaziers*. During Aristide Briand's ministry Lajarrigue read the premier's Socialist tracts and claimed inspiration from them when he proposed that workers serve on the board of directors of the new gas company.[94] Of course, Lajarrigue was never able to explain how other sorts of workers could obtain the advantages his followers enjoyed while operating within legal and pacific channels. There were also clear limits to his idealistic endeavors. He never asked members to make sacrifices to the larger working-class movement,

92. *Les Travailleurs du gaz: Organe officiel de la chambre syndicale des travailleurs de la Compagnie du gaz*, no. 147 (April–May 1906): 1; no. 153, (September 5, 1906): 1.

93. Actually, the impetus for a national federation appears to have come from the provinces following a protracted strike among gas workers in Bordeaux, but Lajarrigue was happy to lead the movement. See *Journal du gaz*, no. 125 (February 20, 1898): 1.

94. AP, V 8 O¹, no. 1257, "Project de maisons ouvrières"; *Travailleurs du gaz*, no. 253 (April 20, 1910): 1; Préfecture, B/a 1425, report of February 24, 1911. On Briand's project, see M. Dezès, "Participation et démocratie sociale: L'Expérience Briand de 1909," *Le Mouvement social*, no. 87 (1974): 109–136.

nor did he take steps to come to the aid of oppressed wage earners outside the gas company. Most stokers willingly followed his lead.

Though Lajarrigue hesitated to admit it, his aspirations and strategies virtually precluded the use of the strike as an instrument of class action. He intended to rely on reasonable demands, impressive displays of solidarity, and, above all, on political pressure. Of course, he had to be careful to distance his union from any public demonstration of "revolutionary" intent. Thus, he kept his followers out of the massive May Day strike movement of 1906, the denouement of the crisis of industrial discipline.[95] When the electrical workers struck the next year, Emile Pataud, the head of their union, pleaded with *gaziers* to support the action, but without success. Relaying orders from his vacation house in Brittany, Lajarrigue made sure that gas workers remained aloof.[96] He even conspired in the exploitation of other wage earners to maintain the advantages of his privileged following. The tenure system under which the gas personnel operated soon became bloated with laborers who had the requisite one year of seniority. Lajarrigue protected his membership by arranging with the Parisian Gas Society (the successor to the PGC) to penalize newly hired laborers. They would be fired on their 364th day of work so that the pool of workers with "permanent" status would shrink. Some laborers were to be fired at once to hasten the process.[97] There seemed to be little discontent within the tenured rank and file over these pragmatic—even egocentric—decisions.

As a national figure who claimed to represent the future of syndicalism, the leader of the gas union came to have prominent enemies. Revolutionary syndicalists like Victor Griffuelhes saw in Lajarrigue all that was wrong with reformism. Lajarrigue became the particular bête noire of Pataud, the "prince of darkness" who had led the electricity strike. This revolutionary believed that the *gaziers* had become "incapable of any energetic action. . . . All their activity consisted of appeals to the authorities." He concluded that Lajarrigue's respect for legality and gradualism had "mummified [the workers] in attitudes of submission." The only hope Pataud saw for the *gaziers* resided in a handful of militant stokers.[98]

95. Préfecture, B/a 1424, report of April 23, 1906. The police reports (as well as the union newspaper) make it clear that Lajarrigue had to overcome some internal opposition to his decision not to participate in the strike. For a good description of May Day 1906 and its context, see Tilly, *Contentious French*, pp. 315–321.
96. Préfecture, B/a 1424, report of October 5, 1907.
97. AP, V 8 O¹, no. 1632, Rouland to prefect, June 14, 1910; report of Keck to prefect, January 17, 1910; report of Rouland to prefect, June 30, 1910.
98. Emile Pataud and Emile Pouget, *Comment nous ferons la révolution* (Paris, 1909), pp. 37, 42.

Thus, the gas workers' union survived the PGC. It became large, influential, and rich. Admirers of British unionism regularly cited it as an example of what French workers could achieve. Radical critics saw in it a model of how easily wage earners could succumb to bourgeois egoism if leaders did not pursue the tactics of class confrontation. The stokers had eventually followed the lead of the common hands. So recently the practitioners of unmediated conflict in disregard of the political consequences, the stokers now settled for sending leaders of a formal organization with national affiliations to negotiate for them. They became indirect contenders for power within a capitalistic and parliamentary regime. The stokers may have extracted an exceptional price for such behavior, but their choice was in step with many other skilled industrial workers in France.[99]

Conclusion

The case of the *gaziers* demonstrates that French factory proletarians did not readily entrust their fate to a centralized political party. Nor were the more qualified industrial workers quick to renounce localized, direct action as their principal means of resolving grievances. Even the common hands looked to indigenous leaders who were resolutely syndicalist, not Socialist. So little respect did the leaders have for Socialists that they cooperated more easily with Radicals and with Nationalists on the municipal council. The widespread commitment to workplace-centered action (whether direct or not) probably owed much to workers' long-standing sense of internal exile within the republic and also to the revolutionary inheritance within French political culture.[100]

Two contradictory features marked the gas workers and many other French laborers around the turn of the century. On the one hand, some wage earners tried to attack managerial authority, a cause that brought stiff resistance from employers and public charges of outright "rebellion." On the other hand, many workers relaxed their fundamental distrust of the state and committed themselves to large, organized interest groups working within channels established by the state. The synthesis of syndicalism and socialism toward which the leftist parliamentary leader, Jean Jaurès, had been building became increasingly relevant under the circumstances.[101] The second trend did not simply reflect underlying structural

99. Merriman, *Red City,* pp. 245–250.
100. Tony Judt develops this explanation for the weakness of socialism in "The Labor Movement in the Nineteenth Century," in *Marxism and the French Left* (Oxford, 1986), pp. 24–114.
101. Michelle Perrot, "On the Formation of the French Working Class," in *Work-*

shifts from a nineteenth-century artisanal economy to a twentieth-century industrial economy. The gas workers, quintessential nineteenth-century factory proletarians, passed through each phase of the transition from direct action to a nationally organized labor movement.

Both of these turn-of-the-century features had their source in the intensified involvement of the state in pacifying industrial society. Even the rather modest reforms of the Radical republicans had important repercussions. A serious problem for the reformers was the failure of factory work to generate a unified working class and, still less, one that was uniformly attracted by practical gains. Depending on whether laborers had much or little bargaining power at the workplace, they took the favor of the state as a signal either to challenge their employers' mastery or to build bridges to politicians of whatever stripe who promised benefits. To the extent that the public authorities appeared to be encouraging "rebellion" against industrial discipline, they had to draw back from efforts to encourage moderation. This paradox plagued the Radical Republic.[102]

By no means was the insurrectionary impulse put aside once and for all, even though political integration achieved decisive gains around the turn of the century. The events of the 1890s at the Parisian gas plants illustrated the waves of action and disengagement that characterized the protest of industrial workers.[103] Later, the shocks of World War I and of the world depression would spark new bouts of unrest. The gas workers' experience showed that only exceptional benefits from the state could permanently reconcile industrial workers to their subordination at the workplace. Rarely was the liberal order in France so thoroughly shaken that it would generalize such concessions.

---

ing Class Formation: Nineteenth-Century Patterns in Western Europe and the United States, ed. Ira Katznelson and Aristide Zolberg (Princeton, 1986), pp. 108–110.

102. For Clemenceau's experience, see David Watson, *Georges Clemenceau: A Political Biography* (London, 1974), pp. 169–206.

103. See Noiriel, *Ouvriers dans la société française,* pp. 263–267, on the cycles of militancy and quiescence among workers.

Conclusion

Parisians would have acknowledged thankfully that few enterprises were as evil as the Parisian Gas Company. Yet it would be facile to dismiss the firm as too peculiar to provide general lessons. In fact, the history of the PGC encompassed some of the fundamental experiences of French people as their country industrialized, and even its unique features were revealing. Having made gas and its by-products "luxury" commodities intended for customers who did not care much about price, the PGC quickly assumed characteristics that placed it among the general run of French enterprises despite its exceptional size. Methods of production were slightly antiquated by international standards. The company long depended on expensive, skilled labor that had to be cajoled and coerced into higher productivity. It was not the structural weaknesses of the French economy nor the backwardness of French consumers that imposed these features on the PGC. They arose from entrepreneurial decisions that were conservative, risk-avoiding, and unresponsive to the lucrative opportunities of mass marketing.

The evolution of the PGC illuminates why industrial development was more of a seamless web in France than in other nations. The rise of big business did not spawn the traumas that the proverbial transition from the familial to the bureaucratic was supposed to induce. Even in the PGC, which announced its centralizing principles from the first, bureaucratization was not the basis for most aspects of industrial relations. For better or, in this case, for worse, face-to-face authority prevailed. To escape it, to impose bureaucratic rules, became the moving force behind much collective protest. Even more significant for explaining the continuities in modern French social history was the developmental pattern of the social groups thrown up by economic change. These groups appropriated the models and norms of preindustrial categories. The decision makers in the firm accepted the careers of state engineers as an inspiration. Employees, responding to the differentiation that management made between them and manual workers, insisted on their affinities to civil servants. Skilled industrial workers lived the theoretical trajectory of adjustment to industrialization in reverse. As long as they were not dependent on one industry for a livelihood, they voluntarily traded hard work and subjugation for higher pay. Becoming proletarians of one firm brought them to revert, as it were, to the model of artisanal protest—alternating between apathy and radicalism, scornful of bread-and-butter issues, and intent on attacking the liberal industrial order at its roots. A final reason for continuity was the failure of economic development to reshape the French labor movement. The factory proved to be a weak instrument for forging a unified proletariat, which fragmented on its own and under pressure from the outside. It is no wonder the rise of big business in this country reinforced rather than upset older patterns of French culture.[1]

The ostensibly unique features of the PGC derived mainly from the firm's intense entanglement in the national crisis of the liberal economic order as the nineteenth century entered its last decade. Aspirations for social harmony conflicted with the grim reality of explosive tensions within the gas company and without. There was nothing preordained about labor conflict in the PGC; in fact, few firms had so many potential bases on which to build cooperation. The company could easily have provided a model of harmonious industrial relations well before the quest for social peace arose as a broad and diversified movement. Managers, however, refused to invest their labor policies with generosity. They took as their guiding principles the austere dictates of duty and the rejection of material progress as a legitimate goal for the masses. Still more forcefully did they deny that labor had any protection against the decisions of superiors. In the last decade of the nineteenth century the balance of political forces temporarily came to weigh against managers' authority. Engineers then tried to preserve their authoritarian paternalism through reform but ultimately fell back on repression. In the France of the Radical Republic, repressing the rights of working people exacted a price.

It is ironic that the national government fretfully anticipated a "clerico-military" coup during the summer of 1899. The labor unrest in the gas plants that August, just as Dreyfus's second court-martial at Rennes was convening, might have warned the authorities that there would be a very

1. See Michael Miller, *The Bon Marché: Bourgeois Culture and the Department Store, 1896–1920* (Princeton, 1981), pp. 239–240. Miller argues that the French bourgeoisie was committed to change because it had learned how to pursue change without undermining its own traditions. A study of the PGC shows how industrialization could fit within those traditions.

different source of trouble. Whatever right-wing plots there were fizzled dismally. The government of republican defense, however, soon found it had more problems contending with agitation among its presumed friends, the working people. Although the widespread industrial disorders did not threaten the regime, they did place severe pressure on the government by taking its promises too seriously. To describe the Dreyfus Affair as a civil war within the bourgeoisie, a battle into which workers entered only reluctantly and belatedly, is a commonplace.[2] What scholars have generally overlooked is that the emotional climax of the Affair coincided with a distinctive wave of unrest among the common people. The two outbursts of republican righteousness were connected in complex and elusive ways that will require further exploration. The bourgeoisie and the working people shared some common enemies as well as some common advocates, but there were also fundamental antagonisms. The bourgeois movement sought to consolidate the gains of the Opportunist Republic, whereas the popular movement provided the impetus to move beyond that regime of compromise. There can be no doubt that Dreyfusard liberalism prevailed in the long run, but not before the popular, antiauthoritarian forces had an impact on national political life.

Historians have long stressed the superficial changes in spirit and legislation entailed in the advent of the Radical Republic.[3] The fate of the PGC after 1890 shows that the assessment needs qualification. The will to reform may not have been invincible within the Radical Republic, but nonsocialist politicians did commit themselves to a new political economy, and they were supported by a mass awakening to the possibility of change at the workplace. The power of the state to order and stabilize industrial relations expanded by choice. Indeed, these forces launched the most serious effort to reformulate the social responsibilities of the state between the Second Republic and the Popular Front. Arguably, the accomplishments of the fin-de-siècle left produced a more decisive turning point in industrial relations than either the Second Republic or the Popular Front. Charles Tilly has focused attention on the first decade of the twentieth century as a crucial moment of transformation in modes of protest: local contention shifted to a wider, often national, arena; formal organizations

2. Madeleine Rebérioux, *La République radicale? 1898–1914* (Paris, 1975), chap. 1, provides a recent analysis of the divisions created by the Affair.
3. The leading textbook on modern French history states that "the transition from Moderate to Radical rule . . . brought no sharp change in the republic's structure or spirit." Gordon Wright, *France in Modern Times*, 3d ed. (New York, 1981), p. 263.

became the agents of expression; workers sought to compete for the favors of the state rather than undermine it.[4] Such was the experience of the gas personnel. The history of the PGC illustrates why these broad changes in the contours of French political life may have taken hold in the decade before the Great War even if the Radical Republic ended by changing less than its leaders intended or its enemies feared.

The annals of the gas firm expose not the superficiality of the efforts to republicanize the workplace but rather the fatal weaknesses of those efforts. Reformers of both the left and the right offered their hands to working people with the expectation that doing so would bring appeasement. They did not fully appreciate that they were treading on passionate issues. The struggle for control over the work experience engaged the militancy of the new proletariat of skilled factory workers. They and clerical employees were quite sensitive to opportunities to throw off discretionary authority. Such were the origins of the crisis of industrial discipline in fin-de-siècle France. The general outpouring of emotions ultimately frightened moderates and discouraged the attempts to extend republican rights. The crisis also provided grounding for the social defense that was central to the national revival sweeping bourgeois France just before the war.

Integral to the sociopolitical history of the PGC and, indeed, of modern French industry was the incendiary potential inherent in the exercise of private authority. On the one hand, industrial elites insisted on an absolute domination of the company's personnel while advancing claims to authority on liberal grounds.[5] The elite based its legitimacy on state-certified expertise and professed to make irrevocable decisions from impartial evaluations of individual performance. The managers demanded even greater discretion over compensations than impersonal market forces would allow. On the other hand, subordinates were profoundly suspicious of such claims. In the name of democracy and republican rights they refused to acknowledge the legitimacy of discretionary authority. These stances validate William Reddy's characterization of the Third Republic as

4. Charles Tilly, *The Contentious French: Four Centuries of Popular Struggle* (Cambridge, Mass., 1986), p. 389.
5. Alain Cottereau's current work on the *conseils de prud'hommes* suggest that such a managerial ideology may not have been timeless. He finds a certain cyclical movement in manager's demands for a free hand on the shop floor. The early years of the Second Empire—the moment the PGC was founded—marked an intensification of managerial authority. Cottereau also finds the opposition to discretionary authority strengthening in the last decade of the century, as I have. See "Justice et injustice ordinaire sur les lieux de travail d'après les audiences prud'homales," *Le Mouvement social*, no. 141 (1987): 25–59.

an "illiberal society stuffed into a liberal box."[6] The potential for conflict over industrial discipline increased in France as an ever-larger portion of the laboring poor became dependent servants of one firm.

The broad vision of modern France that this microanalysis supports may leave capitalism as the principal source of structuring and tensions, but it also emphasizes the grievances that arose around the question of authority. The popular unrest of the turn of the century was really of a piece with the quasi-permanent civil war that constitutes modern French history. Attempts to understand the dramatic conflicts that recurred from 1848 to 1968 in terms of clear-cut class confrontation have been no more successful than similar efforts regarding the Great Revolution. Strife between labor and capital was part of the unrest, to be sure, but it was usually mediated through struggles over rights, authority, and dominant ideologies.[7] Whereas piecemeal reforms or appeals to nationalism frequently blunted direct class conflict (as they did among the gas personnel), hostility to discretionary authority prevailed over these diversions. Alexis de Tocqueville noted long ago that the French Revolution unleashed a passion for "equality," and much of the nation's political life has entailed efforts to define and realize this principle. The measures that pacified the gas personnel on that score were not available to the general public. Thus, the patterns of domination and subordination that so troubled the PGC contributed in major ways to the chronic unrest that has marked French industrialization down to the present.

6. William Reddy, *The Rise of Market Culture: The Textile Trade and French Society, 1750–1900* (Cambridge, 1984), p. 323.
7. Michel Winock, *La Fièvre hexagonale: Les Grandes crises politiques de 1871 à 1969* (Paris, 1986). On recent trends in the historiography of the Great Revolution, see Jack R. Censer, "Commencing the Third Century of Debate," *American Historical Review* 94 (1989): 1309–1325.

Appendix

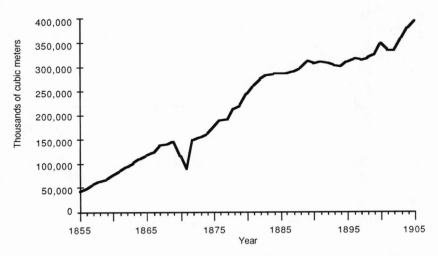

Fig. A1.   Annual Gas Consumption (in thousands of cubic meters). From AP, V
8 O¹, no. 907, *Rapports présentés par le Conseil d'administration à l'Assemblée
générale, 1856–1905.*

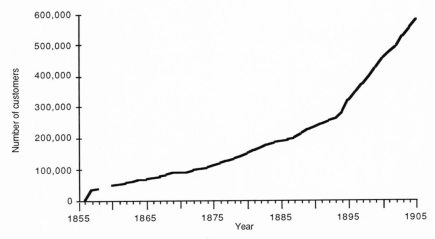

Fig. A2.   Number of Gas Customers. From AP, V 8 O¹, no. 907, *Rapports présentés par le Conseil d'administration à l'Assemblée générale, 1856–1905.*

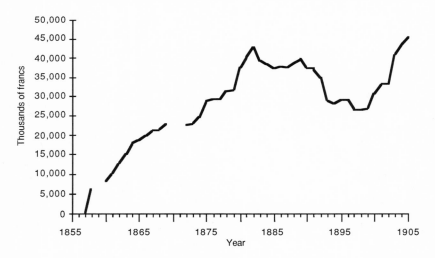

Fig. A3.   Gross Profits (in thousands of francs). From AP, V 8 O¹, no. 907, *Rapports présentés par le Conseil d'administration à l'Assemblée générale, 1856–1905.*

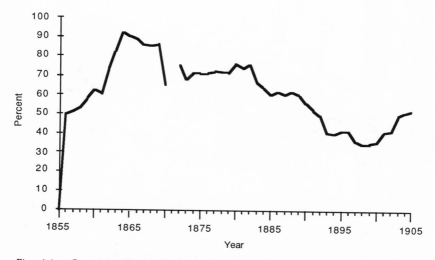

Fig. A4. Operating Ratios (gross profits as percentage of expenditures). Profits to city not deducted. From AP, V 8 O¹, no. 907, *Rapports présentés par le Conseil d'administration à l'Assemblée générale, 1856–1905.*

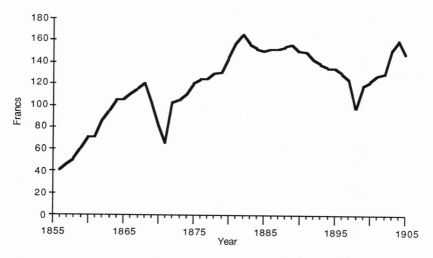

Fig. A5. Dividends Distributed per Share (in francs). From AP, V 8 O¹, no. 907, *Rapports présentés par le Conseil d'administration à l'Assemblée générale, 1856–1905.*

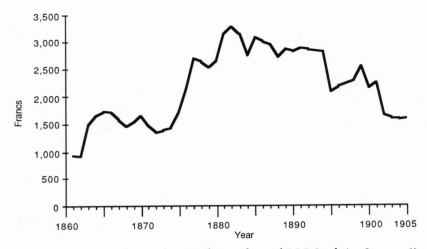

Fig. A6. Market Value (in francs) of One Share of PGC Stock (on January 1).
(Note: The stock split two-for-one in 1870. Subsequent figures have been doubled
to make them comparable to the earlier values.) From *Le Temps*, 1860–1905.

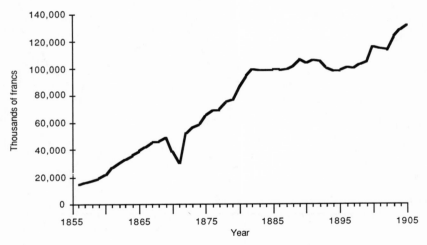

Fig. A7. Corporate Revenues (in thousands of francs). From AP, V 8 O¹, no.
907, *Rapports présentés par le Conseil d'administration à l'Assemblée générale,
1856–1905.*

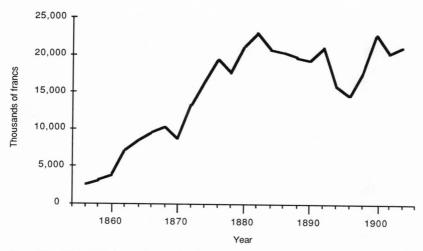

Fig. A8.   Revenue from By-products and Coke (in thousands of francs). (Note: Values calculated for even-numbered years only.) From AP, V 8 O¹, no. 907, *Rapports présentés par le Conseil d'administration à l'Assemblée générale, 1856–1905.*

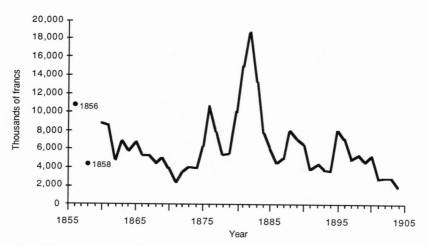

Fig. A9.   Annual Capital Investment (in thousands of francs). From AP, V 8 O¹, no. 907, *Rapports présentés par le Conseil d'administration à l'Assemblée générale, 1856–1905.*

Index

Compositor: Graphic Composition, Inc.
Text: 10/13 Aldus
Display: Aldus